Selling China

Foreign Direct Investment during the Reform Era

China is one of the most popular investment destinations in the world. For a number of years in the 1990s, China was the second largest recipient of foreign direct investment (FDI) worldwide. Many hail China's large FDI absorption as a celebrated achievement of its reforms. In this book Yasheng Huang makes a provocative counterclaim: the large absorption of FDI by China is a sign of some substantial weaknesses in the Chinese economy.

Huang's premise is that FDI is, fundamentally, a microeconomic phenomenon rather than a macroeconomic phenomenon. Under certain macroeconomic conditions, such as expanding markets or low labor costs, whether a country gets more or less FDI relative to domestic investments depends on the relative competitiveness of foreign versus domestic firms. FDI inflows into China surged in the 1990s because domestic firms were uncompetitive and failed to capitalize on new business opportunities. Foreign firms responded by investing in China.

Huang identifies two sources of uncompetitiveness. One is a political pecking order of firms that allocates China's broad economic resources to the least efficient firms – state-owned enterprises – while denying the same resources to China's most efficient firms, that is, private firms. The result is an across-the-board uncompetitiveness of Chinese firms. The other is a substantial fragmentation – itself caused by state ownership – that constrains the growth and investment options of domestic firms more than it does foreign firms.

The primary benefits associated with China's FDI inflows are concerned with the privatization functions supplied by foreign firms, venture capital provisions to credit-constrained private entrepreneurs, and promotion of interregional capital mobility. Huang argues that, while these are important and laudable benefits, one should ask why domestic firms cannot supply the same functions. This broader question requires an evaluation of China's reform strategy. China's partial reforms, while successful in increasing the scope of the market, have so far failed to address many allocative inefficiencies in the Chinese economy.

Yasheng Huang is Associate Professor at Harvard Business School and author of *Inflation and Investment Controls in China* (1996). He is a recipient of the Social Science Research Council–MacArthur Foundation Fellowship.

Cambridge Modern China Series

Edited by
William Kirby, Harvard University

Other books in the series:

Selling China

Foreign Direct Investment during the Reform Era

YASHENG HUANG

Harvard Business School

CAMBRIDGE UNIVERSITY PRESS

PUBLISHED BY THE PRESS SYNDICATE OF THE UNIVERSITY OF CAMBRIDGE
The Pitt Building, Trumpington Street, Cambridge, United Kingdom

CAMBRIDGE UNIVERSITY PRESS
The Edinburgh Building, Cambridge CB2 2RU, UK
40 West 20th Street, New York, NY 10011-4211, USA
477 Williamstown Road, Port Melbourne, VIC 3207, Australia
Ruiz de Alarcón 13, 28014 Madrid, Spain
Dock House, The Waterfront, Cape Town 8001, South Africa

http://www.cambridge.org

First published 2003

Printed in the United States of America

Typeface Times New Roman 10/13 pt.   *System* LATEX 2$_\varepsilon$ [TB]

A catalog record for this book is available from the British Library.

Library of Congress Cataloging in Publication Data

Huang, Yasheng.
Selling China : foreign direct investment during the reform era / Yasheng Huang.
    p.   cm. – (Cambridge modern China series)
Includes bibliographical references and index.
ISBN 0-521-81428-6 (hb)
1. Investment, Foreign – China.   2. China – Economic conditions – 1976–2000.
I. Title.   II. Series.
HG5782 .H8355   2002
332.67′314′0951–dc21   2002024674

ISBN 0 521 81428 6 hardback

Dedicated to the memory
of my parents, Huang Kang and Tan Jiakun

Contents

List of Tables and Figures

List of Abbreviations

AAPA	Average asset per affiliate
BAIC	Beijing Automotive Industry Corporation
BGF	Beijing Gear Factory
CHF	Central holding firm
CJV	Cooperative joint venture
CMA	Chinese Manufacturers' Association
CSI	China Strategic Investment
ECE	Ethnically Chinese economy
EJV	Equity joint venture
FAW	First Automotive Works
FDI	Foreign direct investment
FDIPA	FDI per affiliate
FER	Foreign equity ratio
FIE	Foreign-invested enterprise
FMC	Foreign marketing control
GDP	Gross domestic product
GKG	Guangdong Kelon (Rongsheng) Group
GNP	Gross national product
IFC	International Finance Corporation
IMF	International Monetary Fund
JV	Joint venture
LDC	Less developed country
M&A	Merger and acquisition
MES	Minimum efficiency scale
MNC	Multinational corporation
MTBF	Miles traveled between failures
NCIC	Nanchang Chemical Industrial Corporation
NPL	Nonperforming loan

OECD	Organisation for Economic Co-operation and Development
OP	Outward processing
PBC	People's Bank of China
PLA	Proportion of the largest affiliates
PPG	Pittsburgh Plate and Glass Industries
PPP	Purchasing power parity
R&D	Research and development
R&DE	Research and development expenditure
RCC	Rural Credit Cooperative
RMB	Renminbi
SAIC	Shanghai Automotive Industry Corporation
SER	State equity ratio
SLR	Social liability ratio
SME	Small and medium enterprise
SOE	State-owned enterprise
SPC	State Planning Commission
SVW	Shanghai Volkswagen
TFP	Total factor productivity
TVE	Township and village enterprise
UCC	Urban Credit Cooperative
UNCTAD	United Nations Conference on Trade and Development
WFIE	Wholly owned foreign-invested enterprise
WTO	World Trade Organization

Synopsis of the Book

China is one of the most popular investment destinations in the world. For a number of years in the 1990s China accounted for 50 percent of foreign direct investment (FDI) going into developing countries, and China was the second largest recipient of FDI in the world. Government officials, business practitioners, and economists hail China's large FDI absorption as a celebrated achievement of the reform era.

The central claim of this book is that the large absorption of FDI by China may be a sign of some substantial weaknesses in its economy. The book starts from the premise that FDI is, fundamentally, a microeconomic phenomenon rather than a macroeconomic phenomenon. At a given level of macroeconomic fundamentals, such as an expanding market or low labor costs, whether a country gets more or less FDI – relative to domestic investments and relative to contractual arrangements between foreign and domestic firms – depends on the relative competitiveness of foreign versus domestic firms. FDI inflows into China surged in the 1990s because of the combination of some substantial problems in China's corporate sector and China's promising macro fundamentals.

Three sources of problems in China's corporate sector are identified in this book. One is a political pecking order of firms that allocates China's financial and broad economic resources to the least efficient firms – SOEs – while denying the same resources to China's most efficient firms, that is, private firms. The second problem is that China's political and legal institutions have marginalized the economically most efficient firms – China's truly private enterprises. The cumulative effect of the economic and legal discrimination against private firms was an across-the-board uncompetitiveness of China's corporate sector in the 1980s and much of the 1990s: SOEs were beset with internal inefficiencies, while private firms lacked resources and property rights security to grow and to develop. The third factor is a substantial market fragmentation – itself in part caused by state ownership – that constrains the growth and investment options of domestic firms more than it does foreign firms.

This book argues that the primary benefits of China's FDI inflows have less to do with the provision of marketing access and know-how transfers, technology diffusion, or access to export channels, the kind of firm-level benefits often touted in the literature. Instead, the primary benefits associated with China's FDI inflows have to do with the privatization functions supplied by foreign firms in a context of political opposition to an explicit privatization program, venture capital provisions to private entrepreneurs in a system that enforces stringent credit constraints on the private sector, and promotion of interregional capital mobility in a fragmented economy. These are important and laudable benefits, but one should ask why domestic firms cannot supply the same functions and benefits.

This broader question requires an evaluation of China's reform strategy. This book poses a conjecture that China's reform strategy, so far, has been motivated to save, not to dismantle, socialism. Partial reforms, while having successfully increased the scope of the market, have so far failed – and are unlikely to be able in the future – to tackle some of the fundamental inefficiencies in the Chinese economy. To deal with these inefficiencies requires effecting the security of and a deep commitment to private property rights. This is a profoundly political choice that the Chinese state, sooner or later, will have to confront directly.

Preface

Field research on this book began in the fall of 1998, after I joined the faculty of Harvard Business School. The project represented a steep learning curve. My previous work had dealt with general political economy issues and with public policy institutions in China. Foreign direct investment (FDI) as an economic phenomenon and many detailed aspects of the Chinese economy were a substantial departure from both the empirical focus and the methodological approach of my earlier research.

Harvard Business School provided a rich and stimulating environment as I delved into this new topic. I became acquainted with and, gradually, engaged in many business and FDI issues by learning from my colleagues and by teaching and developing course materials for one of the most successful courses at Harvard Business School: Business, Government and International Economy, popularly known among our students as "BGIE." As readers will discover, the thrust of the argument I develop in this book is strongly institutional, an area of political economy I have always been interested in, but my institutional argument is anchored in a firm understanding of the business dynamics and economic logic of FDI issues. In this respect, I have benefited greatly from my affiliation with Harvard Business School.

In addition to a helpful learning environment as I embarked upon a different intellectual trajectory, I benefited specifically from the advice and guidance of my colleagues. My thanks first go to Professors Pankaj Ghemawat, Tom McCraw, Debora Spar, and Lou Wells, who patiently read several drafts of this book, closely followed the progress – as well as the setbacks – of the project, and provided detailed and valuable comments on the argument, tone, and organizational structure of the book. Professors Tarun Khanna, George Lodge, Huw Pill, Julio Rotemberg, Bruce Scott, Richard Vietor, and David Yoffie kindly read a finished draft, and their comments helped me sharpen the argument and avoid some of the errors that might have gone undetected.

Professors Dorothy A. Leonard and Michael Yoshino commented on early chapters during a formative stage of the project. I owe special thanks to Professor Warren McFarlan, whose encouragement and guidance helped me navigate many of the challenges not only during this book project but also as I was adapting to a new teaching and research environment. The Division of Research at Harvard Business School, under its successive directors, Professors Kenneth Froot and Paul Gompers, provided generous funding that made this research possible.

I also have received a lot of help from colleagues outside Harvard Business School. At Harvard, I have benefited from discussions with Professors Bill Alford, Richard Cooper, Marshall Goldman, Merle Goldman, William Kirby, Roderick MacFarquhar, Dwight Perkins, Elizabeth Perry, Tony Saich, Ezra Vogel, and, before his passing, Ray Vernon. Over the years, I have held many discussions on economic and FDI issues related to China with Professors Jun Fu at Tsinghua University, David Li at Hong Kong University of Science and Technology, Minghong Lu at Nanjing University, Albert Park at the University of Michigan, Minxin Pei at Carnegie Endowment of International Peace, Yingyi Qian at the University of California at Berkeley, Ed Steinfeld at MIT, and Shang-jin Wei at Brookings Institution. Although these discussions may not be explicitly manifested, I have gained many insights from them and I have used them as a backdrop for the argument developed in the book.

I owe special gratitude to Professor Barry Naughton at the University of California at San Diego for an extremely thoughtful, thorough, and detailed commentary on the book manuscript when it was submitted for review at Cambridge University Press. Professor Naughton and I may still disagree on a number of issues, but there is no question that his critique has prodded me to rethink some of my positions and arguments in a rather fundamental fashion. My thanks also go to Professors Paul Beamish at the University of Western Ontario, Pieter Bottelier at Johns Hopkins University, Athar Hussain at the London School of Economics, Robert Lawrence at the Kennedy School of Harvard, Linda Lim at the University of Michigan, Charles Wolf at the Rand Corporation, Christine Wong at University of Washington, Chenggang Xu at the London School of Economics, and Bernard Yeung at the Stern School of New York University for their comments on individual chapters of the book.

Over the years, I have presented portions of the research at many conferences, seminars, and symposia at American Enterprise Institute, Brookings Institution, Cato Institute, Council on Foreign Relations, Harvard University, *Institutional Investor* magazine, International Monetary Fund, the Organisation for Economic Co-operation and Development, Pacific Forum, Sloan School at MIT, William Davidson Institute at Michigan Business School, World Bank, and the World Economic Forum. I cannot acknowledge the contributions of all the participants individually. Let me acknowledge them here collectively.

A number of people outside academia have also been extremely helpful to me. In particular, I acknowledge Drs. Xinghai Fang and Ruiyan Hu at the Shanghai Stock Exchange; Dr. Fred Hu at Goldman Sachs; Shiyi Pan and Xin Zhang at Redstone Industrie Corporation; Brewer Stone at Prudential Insurance; Pam Yatsko, formerly at *Far Eastern Economic Review*; Suzher Yan, previously at Schroders; and Dr. Yujun Zhang at the Shenzhen Stock Exchange for many informative discussions on financial and private sector development issues in China. Dr. Chunbin Zhang at Dow Chemical kindly supplied an explanation of silica production processes, and Jane Liang of Fidelity provided help on statistical methods. I also express my profound thanks to many Chinese and foreign managers who agreed to be interviewed for this project.

During research and writing, I have benefited from having several capable research assistants. They are Nicholas Bartlett, Jason Mann, Sarah Matthews, Kirsten O'Neil, and Virginia Wilmerding. Jennifer Gui, now at the World Bank, and Xiaoping Chen, now at Harvard Law School, helped research in Chinese at various stages of the project. Camille Yeh and Fred Young at the Asia-Pacific Research Center of Harvard Business School in Hong Kong provided contacts, conducted interviews, and arranged for critical logistical support. Mary Child, Scott Parris, and Stephanie Sakson at Cambridge University Press were always supportive and helpful. Last, but not least, my thanks go to Nancy Hearst at Harvard's Fairbank Center for providing me with excellent editorial assistance, as she has done for my other research projects so many times before. Although I might wish otherwise, none of the people I have acknowledged so far can be held responsible for any of the errors or misjudgments that may still be present in this book.

During the past five years while I was working on this project, members of my family helped me deal with many of the stresses, intellectual or otherwise, that arose during this phase of my research and professional career. My brother, Jingsheng Huang, a businessman with many years of experience in China, gave me a practitioner's perspective on FDI issues. My wife, Jean Yang, had to endure my many long absences away from home while coping with her own professional challenges. During many dinner conversations, Jean, a product of Harvard Business School and now a business consultant, questioned my analyses of firm strategies, sometimes over the screaming protests of our three-year-old daughter. This book could not have been written without her unfailing support and encouragement. Our daughter, Kunkun, was born just when this book project started. More than once I wondered why my project did not make as much progress as she did.

Finally, as a parent myself now, I will never forget the teachings and guidance of my own parents. My father, Huang Kang, passed away in 1993, and my mother, Tan Jiakun, left us when this field research began in 1998. During the chaotic period of the 1970s, when schools were closed in China and the formal educational system virtually collapsed, it was my parents who taught me the value of learning and knowledge. I am forever indebted to them. This book is dedicated to their memory.

Boston, Massachusetts   Yasheng Huang
April 2002

Selling China

Foreign Direct Investment during the Reform Era

1

Introduction

In a *New York Times* article entitled, "Funny, I Moved to Beijing and Wound Up in Pleasantville," Elisabeth Rosenthal, *Times* reporter in China, provides a humorous account of a typical weekend outing in Beijing. She describes driving her kids to a soccer game in a sports-utility vehicle (most probably made by Beijing Jeep, a joint venture, or JV, with DaimlerChrysler), loading up on toilet paper supplies at Price Smart, stopping by one of the over forty McDonald's in Beijing for a Big Mac, and Dairy Queen or Baskin-Robbins for a sundae. She writes, "So this is what the Communist Party means by 'socialism with Chinese characteristics'! But isn't this what it's like in Des Moines?"[1]

To elevate – or, depending on one's view, to denigrate – Beijing all the way to Des Moines is arguably a sign of one of the hallmark events in modern times: China's integration into the world economy. Foreign firms, either singly or as JVs with Chinese firms, have established a ubiquitous presence in China. Rosenthal could also have mentioned that on China's congested streets, the indisputable king of the road is the Santana, a sedan with a 1970s' look and a 1980s' engine design. The Santana is assembled in Shanghai by a JV with Volkswagen. In 1998, for every 100 passenger cars sold in China, forty-eight were Santanas.[2] Coca-Cola and Pepsi-Cola account for a growing share of China's soft drink market; the top three brands of cellular phones are all foreign: Nokia, Ericsson, and Motorola. Motorola's 100 percent subsidiary in Tianjin alone accounted for 50 percent of cellular phone sales and 70 percent of the pager market in the mid-1990s (Wang 1997).

The dominance of these large Western multinational corporations (MNCs) in technologically sophisticated and capital-intensive industries, and in consumer product markets characterized by substantial advertising expenditures,

---

[1] This is from Rosenthal (1998).
[2] Reported in China Automotive Technology Research Center (1999).

is relatively easy to explain. Typically, MNCs have dominant positions in these areas, not only in China but also in many other countries, because of their deep technological and capital advantages. Such "Des Moinesization" garners more press attention and, during the rounds of negotiations leading to China's entry into the World Trade Organization (WTO), invited close political and policy scrutiny from both the Chinese and Western governments. But investments by large Western and Japanese MNCs in fact constituted only a small portion of total foreign direct investment (FDI) flows into China during much of the 1990s. A significant portion of FDI flows into China originated from investors of a very different stripe. They are small and medium enterprises (SMEs), and they operate simple and labor-intensive production and assembly processes. They are typically from China's neighboring regions, such as Hong Kong, Macao, and Taiwan, which I refer to as ethnically Chinese economies (ECEs) in this book, but also from other countries as well. The foreign SMEs have built up huge capital positions in a number of Chinese industries and have acquired more substantial control over China's export marketing channels to the world market compared with their presence in a number of other Asian countries.

Another issue that often gets lost in policy discussions on market access and regulatory and legal treatments of foreign firms operating in China is that China was already one of the most FDI-dependent economies in the world, even before its accession to the WTO in 2001. Beginning in the early 1990s, FDI rose rapidly, not only relative to FDI inflows into other countries but, more important, relative to investments undertaken by domestic firms, especially investments by domestic nonstate firms. The pervasive presence of FDI is sometimes found in rather surprising quarters. For example, in 1995 there were 432 foreign-invested enterprises (FIEs) engaged in ivory and jade carving and sculpturing.[3] (FIEs refer to firms in China with a foreign equity stake of at least 25 percent.) In an industry in which the Chinese have had hundreds of years of practice and at which they are expected to excel, foreign firms held 88 percent of the equity ownership of these FIEs. Another little-noticed fact is that as FDI rose rapidly in the 1990s, contractual alliances with foreign firms – such as subcontracting operations run and operated by Chinese entrepreneurs on behalf of foreign firms – declined substantially in absolute terms.

This book sets out to explain these and other seemingly distinct patterns of FDI in China. In doing so, I make two claims. First, I take what can be termed a "demand perspective" on FDI. My argument is that a perspective that stresses the role of motivations and constraints of Chinese firms as driving forces behind FDI patterns yields rich insights. This contrasts with what can be termed as a

---

[3] This refers to industry level no. 4311 in the Chinese Industry Classification Standard.

"supply perspective" on FDI, which stresses the motivations and capabilities of foreign firms. The presumption is not that a supply perspective is unimportant; in a study on FDI, the importance of a supply perspective is assumed. However, two considerations warrant some special attention to a demand perspective. First, a demand perspective may be less obvious in certain FDI questions than a supply perspective. Second, as is evidenced later in this chapter, an important research question in this book is to explain the preponderance of an ownership arrangement – that is, FDI – over contractual arrangements in China's labor-intensive, export-oriented, and perfectly competitive industries. From a supply perspective, this can be puzzling. A supply perspective would not predict the dominance of FDI over contractual arrangements (such as export processing and assembly operations). A demand perspective can resolve this puzzle.

My second claim follows from the first. Two institutional features of the Chinese economy shape the demand perspective on FDI: the political pecking order of Chinese firms and the fragmentation of the Chinese economy. I explain this claim more fully and explore its implications for FDI in the next chapter. Suffice it to mention here that the political pecking order favors, legally and financially, inefficient state-owned enterprises (SOEs) at the expense of efficient nonstate firms, especially truly private firms, and the economic fragmentation reduces domestic capital mobility across regions. The cumulative result is that domestic firms are less competitive than they would be otherwise. In this context, when the country opened up to FDI (but maintained restrictions on foreign debt and imports) in the early 1990s, FDI rose substantially. This is the gist of the argument in this book.

Such a line of research entails significant analytical and policy implications. Chinese officials and foreign business practitioners laud China's large FDI inflows as one of the most celebrated achievements of the reform era. Institutions such as the World Bank have credited FDI as a main driving force behind China's economic success.[4] International rating agencies routinely use FDI flows as an important macroeconomic indicator to assess China's creditworthiness. Academic researchers are equally enthusiastic about FDI flows into China. They tout the enormous benefits of FDI for China, such as technology transfer, the introduction of marketing know-how, and capital infusion.[5] Much of the received wisdom is correct, but what has been missed is that FDI has brought about these benefits in China in a specific context: China's financial and economic institutions have worked to reduce the ability of domestic firms, especially domestic private firms, to provide some of the same benefits brought about

[4] See, e.g., World Bank (1997b).
[5] Some of the writings are reviewed in the appendix to Chapter 2.

by FDI. The central claim of the book is that FDI has come to play a substantial role in the Chinese economy because of systemic and pervasive discrimination against efficient and entrepreneurial domestic firms. This discrimination was not purposely instituted to benefit foreign firms; at least this was not a dominant consideration. It was instituted mainly to benefit the inefficient SOEs. As such, China's large absorption of FDI is not necessarily a sign of the strengths of its economy; instead, it may be a sign of some rather substantial distortions.

I develop and substantiate this claim step by step in later chapters. The primary aim of this chapter is to lay out a number of empirical patterns of FDI in China. As much as possible, I place the Chinese patterns in a comparative perspective. Viewed in isolation, these patterns may not strike the analyst as unusual, but taken as a whole, they suggest that FDI in China may have been driven by different dynamics as compared with FDI developments in other countries.

The depiction of China's FDI patterns below is fairly detailed because, simply put, the devil is in the details. In part because of the perception that the reasons for FDI inflows are obvious – such as a large and growing market, cheap labor, and so on – many of these patterns have not been presented or analyzed elsewhere in detail. Laying out these details here is the only way to convince the reader of the need for a new perspective. As will become evident, demonstrating the unusual FDI patterns in China is a central building block of my argument: If FDI patterns in China are unusual, it must be true that the underlying causes of FDI are unusual as well.

This chapter begins with a description of China's FDI patterns. I then devote considerable space to a discussion of a number of data issues on China's FDI, including what is known as "round-trip" FDI. This is followed by a presentation of some of the common explanations that may shed light on various aspects of China's FDI patterns. The chapter ends with definitions of terms and an outline of the organizational structure of the remainder of the book.

FDI PATTERNS IN CHINA

Foreign investment is defined as "direct" when the investment gives rise to "foreign control" of domestic assets. Thus, according to the International Monetary Fund (IMF), FDI "is made to acquire a lasting interest in an enterprise operating in an economy, other than that of the investor, the investor's purpose being to have an effective voice in the management of the enterprise." In the United States, the Department of Commerce defines inward FDI when a foreign investor's stake exceeds 10 percent. A 10 percent threshold is quite common among countries in the Organisation for Economic Co-operation and Development (OECD). Under this definition, if a foreign firm acquires more than 10 percent of a stake in a U.S. concern on the New York Stock Exchange, this capital inflow is credited to the FDI account in the balance of payments statistics, not to the portfolio account.[6] In China, foreign equity capital inflows are classified as FDI only if they lead to a foreign equity stake at or above 25 percent. Thus, the Chinese set a more stringent threshold for FDI and for corporate controls.

The different statistical thresholds for FDI may impose some problems to compare the specific dollar amount of FDI between China and other countries, because the Chinese definition precludes those foreign investments that establish an equity stake of between 10 and 25 percent in a Chinese firm. Thus, the Chinese classification scheme understates China's inward FDI.[7] But conceptually, the higher FDI threshold in China in fact helps the analyst get to the heart of the FDI concept – that FDI is about foreign *control* of a domestic firm, not about the specific dollar amount of foreign capital. As Graham and Wada (2001) have noted, much of the inward FDI in the United States has financed acquisition of existing enterprises listed on the stock market, while the majority of China's inward FDI has financed the establishment of new enterprises.[8] Because these Chinese firms are not publicly traded corporations, foreigners need to acquire a greater equity stake to establish "an effective voice in the management of the enterprise." In the following paragraphs, to the extent possible, I compare Chinese FDI patterns with those in other countries. Readers should bear in mind that my claim that Chinese FDI patterns appear to be distinct from those observed in other countries is based on cumulative and collective evidence on a host of dimensions, not just on one single dimension.

Five notable FDI patterns are substantially distinct from patterns observed in other countries. First, China's reliance on FDI – relative to domestic investments, especially domestic investments made by nonstate firms – is very high. Second, the sharp rise in China's reliance on FDI has been accompanied by a precipitous drop over time in contractual alliances, such as export processing and assembly, between foreign and domestic firms. Third, FIEs – firms funded by FDI – have achieved an important position in the Chinese economy. Their dominance in

---

[6] A more detailed discussion of problems associated with the standard definition of FDI can be found in Graham and Krugman (1994).

[7] Under the Chinese classification system, for example, most foreign purchases of China's B shares are not counted as FDI because they usually amount to about 10 percent of the issuing firms' equity. Ford purchased 20 percent of the B shares of Jiangling Motors, which would not count toward FDI by the Chinese definition (Ma 1995). (B shares are company shares on China's two stock exchanges that are available to foreign investors.)

[8] Graham and Wada (2001) equate the establishment of new enterprises in China with green-field investments. As I show in Chapter 5, many of the new enterprises in fact result from acquisitions, not green-field investments.

China's labor-intensive and export-oriented industries is far more substantial than their presence in a number of other Asian economies. Fourth, while FIEs are present in many industries in China, empirical evidence from other countries shows a high industry concentration. FIEs are also present in many regions of China, including interior and land-locked provinces that are far away from Hong Kong. Fifth, FDI projects in China are very small, and there is evidence that the parent firms making these investments are also very small, compared with other firms in the same home economy that did not make investments in China. Again, this is different from patterns observed in other countries, where it is the large firms that tend to invest abroad.

Taking these five patterns together suggests that FDI has played a more important role in the Chinese economy than many analysts have realized. The unique patterns indicate that the underlying dynamics of FDI in China may be different from those in other countries. In the following paragraphs I first present the empirical patterns of FDI in China and then show that some of these patterns cannot be fully accounted for by the existing explanations.

A Substantial Reliance on FDI

From 1979 to 2000, on a cumulative basis, China absorbed a total of $346.2 billion in FDI, as shown in Table 1.1.[9] Most of the FDI occurred since 1992. Between 1992 and 2000, the cumulative FDI inflow amounted to $282.6 billion, or about 93 percent of the total FDI amount between 1979 and 2000. By any measure, China's record of attracting FDI is impressive. During many years in the 1990s, China claimed to be the world's second largest recipient of FDI, after only the United States. Between 1992 and 1999, FDI flows into China accounted for 8.2 percent of worldwide FDI and 26.3 percent of FDI going to developing countries.[10]

The absolute size of FDI, however, does not tell the whole story. The size of FDI flows should be gauged relative to the size of the host economy. The absolute size of FDI flows to the United States in 1996 was roughly twice as large as FDI flows to China, but the U.S. economy was seven times as large (on the basis of the official foreign exchange conversion) as that of China. In this sense, the United States was less "dependent" on FDI than China even though flows into the United States were much larger. A more useful measure is FDI

---

[9] Unless otherwise noted, all the dollar figures in this book refer to U.S. dollar.

[10] Data on global FDI flows and on FDI going to developing countries are from United Nations Conference on Trade and Development (2000).

normalized by the economic size of the host country. This is a relative measure of FDI. By this measure, it is clear that China's dependency on FDI is substantial.

A common measure of the relative size of FDI is the "FDI/capital formation ratio," given by the amount of FDI inflows in one year divided by the total fixed asset investments made by foreign and domestic firms in the same year.[11] (In the paragraphs below, I use the term *FDI dependency* to refer to this ratio.) Column 3 of Table 1.1 presents three different measures of the relative FDI size during four periods in the 1980s and 1990s. The four periods represent different phases of continuous FDI liberalization, as briefly summarized in the table. Column 3a uses the fixed asset investments undertaken by all firms, including foreign firms, as the denominator. Column 3b includes only the fixed asset investments by nonstate firms, that is, collective firms, FIEs, and domestic private firms. Column 3c includes the fixed asset investments made by private firms and FIEs. One noticeable trend is the sharp rise in the FDI/capital formation ratio beginning in 1992. When we use the fixed asset investments undertaken by all firms, including FIEs, the ratio rose from 4.2 percent in 1991 to 7.5 percent in 1992. In 1994, the ratio reached 17.1 percent. Column 3b shows a more rapid increase in the FDI/capital formation ratio when FDI is normalized by investments made by nonstate firms.

SOEs account for a large portion of fixed asset investments. Since the investment activities of SOEs are heavily influenced by the government, it is more appropriate to compare the level of investment activities of foreign firms with that of nonstate domestic firms. Nonstate firms, including FIEs, are more market-driven and are subject to harder budget constraints compared with the SOEs. As the Hungarian economist Janos Kornai points out, SOEs are afflicted with an "investment hunger" and are prone to overinvesting regardless of the market demand for their products (Kornai 1980). Thus, it is more meaningful analytically to compare the investment behavior of FIEs with other nonstate firms. Between 1993 and 1997, FDI accounted for over 30 percent of the fixed asset investments made by nonstate firms in each year, and during the same

---

[11] This measure, while commonly used in academic studies, is not without problems. Not all FDI goes to finance new equipment and plant investments. Some FDI flows finance the acquisition of existing assets. Thus, a portion of both the numerator and the denominator may measure different economic activities. (I thank Professor Huw Pill for pointing out this problem.) An additional problem is that this measure may systematically understate FDI dependency in some economies, while overstating FDI dependency in others. For example, the capital market is less active in Asia than it is in the United States. This may exaggerate FDI dependency in the United States where much of the FDI finances the acquisition of existing assets. For example, in the late 1990s, the FDI/capital formation ratio rose sharply in the United States. This must have been a result of the sharp rise in merger and acquisition activities, which may warrant using total stock market capitalization as the denominator.

Table 1.1 *Various Measures of Foreign Capital Inflows to China, 1979–2000*

	(1) Amount ($ billion)			(2) Shares of total foreign capital inflows[a] (%)		(3) Actual FDI inflows as % shares of fixed asset investments by different types of firms, all including FIEs (%)[d]		
	(1a) Total foreign capital[a]	(1b) Actual FDI inflows[b]	(1c) Contractual alliances[c]	(2a) Actual FDI inflows	(2b) Contractual alliances[c]	(3a) All firms	(3b) Nonstate firms	(3c) Private firms
(1) FDI regime: Permitting FDI								
1979–1982	12.5	1.17	–[e]	9.36	–	–	–	–
1983	1.98	0.64	0.28	32.1	14.1	0.9	2.6	–
1984	2.71	1.26	0.16	46.5	6.0	1.6	4.5	–
1985	4.65	1.66	0.30	35.8	6.4	1.9	5.7	–
(2) FDI regime: Selectively encouraging FDI								
1986	7.26	1.87	0.37	25.8	5.1	2.1	6.2	–
1987	8.45	2.31	0.33	27.4	3.9	2.3	6.4	–
1988	10.2	3.19	0.55	31.2	5.3	2.5	6.9	–
1989	10.1	3.39	0.38	33.7	3.8	2.9	8.0	–
1990	10.3	3.49	0.27	33.9	2.6	3.7	10.9	–
1991	11.6	4.37	0.30	37.8	2.6	4.2	12.4	–

			(3) FDI regime: Substantial FDI liberalization					
1992	19.2	11.0	0.29	57.3	1.5	7.5	23.5	–
1993	38.9	27.5	0.26	70.6	0.7	12.1	30.8	56.0
1994	43.2	33.8	0.18	78.1	0.4	17.1	39.2	62.3
1995	48.1	37.5	0.29	78.0	0.6	15.7	34.4	53.7
1996	54.8	41.7	0.41	76.1	0.7	15.1	31.8	47.8
			(4) FDI regime: Streamlining FDI approvals and WTO agreement					
1997	64.4	45.3	1.47	70.3	2.3	15.0	31.7	46.9
1998	58.6	45.5	1.47	77.6	2.5	13.3	28.9	42.6
1999	52.7	40.3	1.52	76.6	2.9	11.2	24.0	34.9
2000	59.4	40.7	1.71	68.6	2.9	10.2	20.5	29.0

[a] Total includes foreign loans.

[b] Actual FDI inflows refer to FDI inflows on a materialized basis.

[c] Contractual alliances refer to activities such as asset leasing, compensation trade, and product processing and assembly between foreign and domestic firms. They correspond to "other investments" in Chinese statistical reporting before 1997. Since 1997 Chinese statistical authorities have included Chinese company share issues abroad in the "other investments" category. The data reported in this table exclude the company share issues abroad. Product processing and assembly account for almost all of this category of investments, 97.4 percent in 2000.

[d] Fixed asset investments refer to purchases of new plants, property, and equipment by both domestic and foreign firms in a given year. All the ratios include investments by FIEs in the denominator. (3b): Nonstate fixed asset investments refer to total investments minus investments by SOEs. (3c): Private fixed asset investments refer to total investments minus investments by SOEs and collective firms.

[e] – : Data not available.

Sources: State Statistical Bureau, *Zhongguo tongji nianjian* (China Statistical Yearbook), various years, and State Statistical Bureau, *Zhongguo duiwai jingji tongji nianjian* (China Foreign Economic Statistical Yearbook), various years.

period, on average, FDI accounted for about 53 percent of the fixed asset investments made by domestic private firms and FIEs. There is no question that FDI is a significant source of investment financing in China.

Table 1.2 presents data on FDI/capital formation ratios in China and a number of other countries to provide a comparative perspective. The data are broken down by three periods: 1986–91, 1992–98, and 1999–2000. China's FDI dependency varied during these three periods. Compared with other countries in the table, it was initially low in the first period; it rose to a very high level in the second period; and it began to decline to a moderately high level in the third period.

Between 1992 and 1998, on average, FDI flows into China accounted for about 13 percent of the gross capital formation of all firms annually. This ratio is one of the highest among the countries in the table, even compared with countries traditionally considered to be very FDI-dependent, such as countries in Southeast Asia. As pointed out earlier, even though the United States attracted a greater amount of FDI, the relative importance of FDI in the United States, at 6.9 percent during the 1992–98 period, was far smaller than it was in China. Compared with other Asian economies, China was less dependent on FDI in the 1980s, but its FDI dependency was among the highest in the region in the 1990s. China's FDI/capital formation ratio during the 1992–98 period was lower than that in Singapore and Malaysia, but much higher than that in Indonesia, Thailand, and the Philippines. The standard wisdom is that China is more similar to the Southeast Asian countries than it is to Korea, Taiwan, and Japan in terms of FDI dependency.[12] That is true, but in fact China was among the most highly FDI-dependent economies in Asia during much of the 1990s. This is also the case if one uses gross domestic product (GDP), not fixed asset investment, to normalize FDI inflows.[13] (China's FDI/GDP ratio is high whether one uses the

---

[12] This "standard wisdom" was represented to me by one of the anonymous readers for Cambridge University Press.

[13] Urata (2001) presents the FDI inflow/GDP ratios for nine Asian economies (China, Hong Kong, Korea, Taiwan, Indonesia, Malaysia, the Philippines, Singapore, and Thailand) between 1986 and 1997. From 1986 to 1991, China ranked between number four and number seven among these nine economies. From 1992 to 1997, China consistently ranked either as number two or number three most dependent on FDI, behind Singapore and, sometimes, Malaysia. Take 1995 as an example. In that year, China's FDI/GDP ratio was 5.1 percent, compared with 2.2 percent for Indonesia, 2.0 percent for the Philippines, and 1.2 percent for Thailand. (It was 4.8 percent for Malaysia and 8.5 percent for Singapore.) The choice of 1995 was not arbitrary. Because FDI flows can fluctuate more than GDP, I chose a medium ratio for China rather than either the highest or the lowest ratio. In 1993 and 1994, China's FDI/GDP ratio was high, at 6.4 percent and 6.2 percent, respectively, compared with 4.9 percent in 1997. The year 1997 probably should not be used either, because the Asian financial crisis might have adversely affected FDI flows into the Southeast Asian countries. The FDI/GDP ratios are from Urata (2001).

official exchange rate or the purchasing power parity rate.[14]) The claim that China is highly dependent on FDI does not at all hinge on benchmarking China against traditionally small recipients of FDI, such as Japan and Korea.[15]

China's FDI dependency, in a comparative perspective, is all the more striking if one takes into account the substantial investment roles of SOEs in China. As already pointed out, SOEs – subject to softer budget constraints compared with nonstate firms – are prone to overinvest. It is reasonable to expect a country with substantial public sector investments to have a lower FDI/capital formation ratio. For this reason, China's high FDI/capital formation ratio – inclusive of investments by SOEs – compared with other countries with a far smaller public sector is powerful evidence of the substantial role of FDI in the Chinese economy. Another way to illustrate the same point is to derive a FDI/capital formation ratio net of investments by public sector entities. This is indicated by the bracketed numbers in column 1b of Table 1.2. By this measure, China's FDI dependency was the second highest among all the countries represented in the table. During the 1992–98 period, China's FDI/capital formation ratio net of public sector investments was 27.9 percent, after Singapore (30.3 percent) but higher than Malaysia (24.3 percent). (That Singapore, Malaysia, and China have a very high FDI dependency ratio is not accidental. I return to this issue in Chapter 7.)

In the 1999–2000 period, shown in column (1c) of Table 1.2, China's FDI dependency declined compared with many countries in the table. A major factor was the rapid and sudden surge in FDI dependency among the advanced

[14] As is well known, purchasing power parity (PPP) exchange rates can vary from official exchange rates by a wide margin and, depending on which exchange rates are adopted, the FDI dependency ratios will differ dramatically. An additional source of complications is that extremely different purchasing power parity exchange rates exist. Even when a purchasing power parity rate on the high end is used, China is still more dependent on FDI than many other countries, albeit at a smaller magnitude of difference. The FDI/PPP-based GNP ratio in 1994 was 0.78 percent for Asia as a whole and 0.81 percent for the industrial countries. At the same time, it was 1.13 percent for China, thus making China about as dependent on FDI as Canada (1.25 percent), France (1.46 percent), Australia (1.46 percent), and Portugal (1.07 percent). It was more dependent on FDI than the United States (0.69 percent), Japan (0.03 percent), Italy (0.21 percent), and the United Kingdom (0.98 percent). These data are reported in Li and Lian (1999).

[15] Other researchers have also noted China's high FDI dependency. Françoise Lemoine (2000), in a detailed descriptive analysis of China's FDI, makes the following remark: "FDI capital stock represented 25 percent of China's GDP in 1998, a ratio almost comparable to that existing in smaller economies which were opened to international capital flows long before China. . . ." Lemoine points out that on a per capita basis, China's FDI inflows appear to be low, compared with other Asian countries. In 1998, FDI stock per capita in China was only $160. This measure is highly questionable. On a per capita basis, China is low on many other fronts. To illustrate this point, by this measure war-torn Angola would be considered more attractive than China as an FDI host. In 1999, FDI stock per capita in that country was $537.

Table 1.2 Relative FDI Size, Macroeconomic Developments, and Business Environment, Various Years

Countries	(1) Annual average FDI flows/gross fixed capital formation, all firms' ratios (nonstate fixed asset investments only), %			(2) Gross domestic savings rate, 1994–97 (%)	(3) Current account balance/GDP, 1994–97 (%)	(4) Business environment for foreign investors		
	(1a) 1986–91	(1b) 1992–98	(1c) 1999–2000			Rank in terms of ease of foreign acquisitions, 1996 (out of 46 countries)	Business environment rank, 1996–2000 (out of 60 countries)	Corruption perception rank, 1997 (out of 52 countries)
China	2.9 (8.6)	13.1 (27.9)	10.6 (21.5)	41.8	2.7	41	44	41
Philippines	6.6 (8.1)	8.3 (10.2)	7.6 (9.4)	15.5	−8.5	40	35	40
Indonesia	2.3 (3.4)	5.4 (8.9)	−13.7 (−22.7)	33.5	0.0	37	46	46
Thailand	5.5 (6.5)	5.6 (7.2)	11.9 (17.6)	38.0	−6.3	42	30	39
Malaysia	14.7 (22.8)	16.9 (24.3)	22.1 (30.3)	40.0	−0.8	43	24	32
Taiwan	3.6 (4.3)	2.2 (2.7)	11.8 (14.2)	25.6[a]	−2.7[a]	39	21	31
Korea	1.3 (1.6)	1.2 (2.0)	8.1 (10.7)	35.7	−1.8	46	29	34
Singapore	37.6 (49.7)	22.9 (30.3)	24.2 (32)	50.9	16.4	30	6	9
Brazil	1.6 (2.1)	7.7 (9.0)	27.6 (33.9)	20.1	−0.8	29	38	36
Mexico	8.3 (10.9)	13.5 (17.1)	10.7 (15.6)	21.4	0.5	28	34	47

India	0.3 (0.5)	2.2 (3.4)	2.1 (2.5)	21.2	−2.6	35	45	45
United States	6.5 (7.7)	6.9 (8.1)	15.8 (18.3)	15.6	−1.6	19	1	16
Canada	5.3 (6.1)	9.3 (10.6)	33.6 (38.6)	20.4	1.7	32	5	5
United Kingdom	13.6 (16.3)	13.5 (15.6)	41.9 (54.7)	14.7	−0.9	10	4	14
Russia	– (–)	2.0 (2.2)	9.1 (10.5)	27.7	4.3	45	53	49
Poland	0.01 (0.6)	13.1 (16.0)	20.6 (23.7)	16.7	−1.7	31	31	29

Note: Tables 1.1 and 1.2 are compiled from different sources and it is possible that the data for China may not match perfectly in the two tables.

a: 1994 only.

Sources: FDI data are from United Nations Conference on Trade and Development (1998, 1999, 2000, 2001). Private investment, savings, and resource balance data are from the World Bank, *World Development Report*, various years, and World Bank (1995a). For Taiwan, the source is Asian Development Bank (1995). The measure of ease of foreign acquisitions is based on a survey conducted by the International Institute for Management Development in Switzerland. Respondents were asked to rate countries according to a 11-point scale. A perfect score, 10, is given to countries that do not impose any restrictions on foreign acquisitions and 0 is given to countries where foreigners may not acquire control. The data are reported in International Institute for Management Development (1996). The business environment rank is a broader measure devised by the Economist Intelligence Unit. The country ranks for the 1996–2000 period are reported in "Business Environment Scores and Ranks" (2001). The corruption perception rank is devised by Transparency International; the 1997 data are reported on http://www.gwdg.de/~uwvw, accessed on October 23, 2001.

developed countries, such as the United States, the United Kingdom, and Canada, and developing countries, such as Brazil, Korea, and Thailand. It should be stressed that this sudden rise in FDI dependency constituted a substantial deviation from earlier dependency levels in these countries, suggesting that a number of country- and period-specific developments may have contributed to this outcome.[16] Those developments are outside the scope of this book, but what needs to be explained is that China's FDI dependency also declined relative to its earlier level during the 1992–98 period.[17] This development is directly relevant to our analysis. A convincing explanation ought to be able to account for the initial rise of China's FDI dependency ratio as well as its later decline.

Demise of Contractual Alliances

China's heavy dependency on FDI forms a sharp contrast with the small and declining role of contractual alliances with foreign firms as a source of financing. As shown in Table 1.1, the amount of contractual alliances declined substantially both relatively – that is, compared with FDI – and *absolutely*. In 1988, contractual alliances amounted to $550 million, but by 1994, they had declined to $180 million. A fundamental contention in this book is that China's FDI absorption ought to be examined *in conjunction with* this simultaneous sharp decline in contractual capital inflows. The research question does not simply ask why China received so much FDI, but why FDI inflows increased seemingly *at the expense of* contractual capital inflows.

A contractual alliance here refers to an arrangement between a foreign firm and a domestic firm, whereby the domestic firm performs processing and assembly work for the foreign firm, often according to product specifications and/or on the basis of raw materials and other inputs provided by the foreign firm. The most popular form of contractual alliance in China is export processing, where the Chinese firm processes or assembles inputs supplied by the foreign firm and turns over the finished products to the foreign firm. The

---

[16] It is likely that the huge mergers and acquisitions in the "new economy" sector of the advanced countries contributed to this rise in FDI dependency and that the financial crises in Korea, Brazil, and Thailand induced an increase in the type of FDI-seeking opportunities related to financial distress in those economies. In Korea, for example, much of the FDI since 1998 went into the troubled financial industry. See Huang and O'Neil-Massaro (2002). Of course, the financial crisis did not induce FDI in those countries where the crisis impaired political stability and economic growth prospects, as witnessed by the net outflow in Indonesia.

[17] The Asian financial crisis did affect China's FDI inflows on the supply side. In 1999, the FDI inflows on the materialized basis declined to $40.3 billion from $45.5 billion in 1998. However, it should be noted that the relative FDI level began to decline before the Asian financial crisis, in 1996.

finished products, by definition, are exported, although the foreign firm may do additional work – such as labeling and packaging – before selling them to its customers. Depending on the specific arrangements, the Chinese firm may or may not own the inputs or the finished outputs. The prevailing practice in China is that the foreign firm extends what amounts to a buyer credit line to the Chinese firm and the Chinese firm pays for it in the form of the finished outputs. If the Chinese firm does not own the output, it receives a processing fee for its services, factoring in the interest costs. If the Chinese firm owns the output, their prices will reflect both the interest charges on the buyer credit and the processing fees due to the Chinese firm. The contractual capital inflows, recorded and reported by Chinese statistical authorities, are the monetary value of the inputs, equipment, and/or raw materials extended by foreign buyer-firms to the domestic firms as loans. (In fact, before 1988, the Chinese government reported contractual capital inflows as a form of "commercial credit.")[18]

The distinction between FDI and a contractual alliance is that under an FDI arrangement, the foreign firm has legal control over the enterprise – the FIE – whereas the foreign firm does not have legal control over the production facility under a contractual alliance. In reality, as Sung, Liu, Wong, and Lau (1995) have pointed out, the de facto operating control by the foreign firm is substantial in an export-processing operation even though it is Chinese-owned. As the senior partner, production is carried out according to the orders and specifications of the foreign partner. The foreign firm also dispatches its own employees to inspect the quality of the output and to conduct quality controls on site. Another similarity between an export-processing operation and an FDI facility established by a firm based in an ECE is that both are export-oriented. In fact, at least in the early 1990s, export-processing operations carried a greater weight in Chinese exports than FIEs. In 1992, exports from assembly and processing operations accounted for 18 percent of China's exports, compared with 12 percent from FIEs in the same year.[19]

---

[18] For a detailed description of contractual capital inflows, see Wu and Zhang (1995). Sung, Liu, Wong, and Lau (1995) believe that export-processing operations in Guangdong province were underreported by the Chinese statistical authorities because the reported figures do not include what they call "nonpriced" equipment, equipment supplied by the foreign partner that is not explicitly paid for by the Chinese firm. They show that the true export-processing figure is much greater if the full value of nonpriced equipment is included. However, they also show that even the adjusted figures on export processing declined over time, and they were still much smaller than the FDI figures.

[19] Export share data of export-processing operations are from Sung, Liu, Wong, and Lau (1995), p. 63. The share of FIE exports is calculated from data in State Statistical Bureau (1995), pp. 339 and 553.

To the extent that there is any difference at an operating level, the difference actually favors export-processing and assembly operations over FIEs. Based on research on Guangdong province and data from the early 1990s, Sung, Liu, Wong, and Lau (1995) find no evidence of significant differences in technology and labor intensity between FIEs and export-processing operations. FIEs, in the opinion of the authors of this study, were "no better than processing operations in the transfer of management skills." In fact, processing operations might command an edge in efficiency because they operate in an extremely competitive environment and are more export-oriented (Sung, Liu, Wong, and Lau 1995).

Precisely because the operating differences between FIEs and contractual alliances are not substantial, it is all the more interesting to explore why equity capital inflows have risen while contractual capital inflows have experienced a dramatic decline. It is equally interesting to explore the reasons why since 1997 contractual capital inflows have risen sharply, as indicated in Table 1.1. As I explain in greater detail later in this chapter, an examination of equity and contractual capital flows is not just an empirical matter; it is an analytical matter as well because most of the FDI studies begin with the question, "Why does a firm not rely on a contractual exchange when doing business abroad?"

Economic Weight of FIEs

It follows naturally that the large FDI inflows would have led to a substantial role of FIEs in the Chinese economy. This is demonstrated in Table 1.4 (p. 24). As of 1995, FIEs controlled over half of China's manufactured exports, or 51.2 percent, as shown in the bottom row of column B. Because FIEs are restricted in the primary industries and FIEs are not allowed to be pure trading corporations, their export share of total exports is smaller; in 1995, it was 31.5 percent.[20] In Guangdong province, FIEs have established a more dominant export position. FIEs accounted for 45.5 percent of Guangdong's exports in 1995, 49.4 percent in 1997, 51.8 percent in 1998, and 50.7 percent in 1999 (Guangdong Statistical Bureau 2000). Nationwide, FIEs dominate the export channels in a number of industries, such as electronics and telecommunications, garments and footwear, leather products, printing and record pressing, cultural products, and plastics. In 1995, they accounted for over 60 percent of Chinese exports in these industries.[21] Nor are sales shares insignificant either. In four

---

[20] Export data for 1995 are from State Statistical Bureau (1996b). For some unknown reason, the Chinese government no longer released disaggregated FIE export data, broken down by economic sector or industry, after 1995.

[21] The source of data is Office of Third Industrial Census (1997). The firms covered by the *Third Industrial Census* are firms with an "independent accounting system." This raises a number of

industries, the sales shares of industrial FIEs exceeded 50 percent of industry sales and accounted for 21 percent of all manufactured sales in 1995. This share grew to 32.1 percent by 2000.[22]

Again, it is easier to illustrate the substantial role of FIEs in the Chinese economy by benchmarking China against other economies. FIEs in China have established a far more dominant position in export production than their counterparts in Taiwan. As of the mid-1970s, FIEs in Taiwan accounted for only 20 percent of Taiwan's manufactured exports.[23] The share of FIEs in China's exports exceeds that of not only Taiwan but other Asian countries as well during comparable stages of development. Data on the export production of foreign firms are scarce, but two authors, Seiji Naya and Eric Ramstetter, provide some of the most complete statistics. Their paper shows that, except for Singapore, where MNCs have traditionally dominated domestic firms, no other Southeast Asian country came close to the 51 percent share of manufactured exports claimed by Chinese FIEs.[24] In Korea, between 1974 and 1978, foreign firms accounted for 24.9 percent of manufactured exports. In Thailand, in the 1970s, the share ranged from 11 to 18 percent, and in 1984 it was 5.8 percent.

Table 1.5 (p. 32) presents FIE shares of total exports in three economies: China (1995), Taiwan (1980), and Indonesia (1995). The table breaks down export data by labor-intensive and capital- (or technology-) intensive industries. Two patterns emerge. One is that the FIE shares of exports in labor-intensive industries are much higher in China than in Taiwan or Indonesia.[25] For example, garment and footwear FIEs accounted for 60.5 percent of exports in China, but only 5.7 percent in Taiwan and 33 percent in Indonesia. FIEs similarly dominated exports in leather and furniture in China to a far greater extent than they did in Taiwan and Indonesia. The second pattern is that in capital- (or technology-) intensive industries, FIEs in China and Indonesia dominated exports to a far greater extent than they did in Taiwan. This is a more common pattern in developing countries, not only because the local capabilities in modern industries are low but because the goods being produced are intermediate inputs, such as electronic components. Japanese firms, for example, have invested heavily in Southeast Asia to produce electronic components, which are

data issues. See the appendix to this chapter for a detailed explanation of a number of data issues involved in using the *Third Industrial Census*.

[22] Calculated from data provided in State Statistical Bureau (2001).

[23] The export share data for Taiwan come from Ranis and Schive (1985).

[24] All the data on Korea and the Southeast Asian countries are from Naya and Ramstetter (1988). Data for later years are more difficult to find, except for the export production data by FIEs in Indonesia cited in the text.

[25] Professor Lou Wells has kindly provided help in obtaining Indonesian data as well as suggesting Indonesia as an appropriate benchmark comparison.

reexported to the parent firms.[26] Ownership arrangements are more common for this type of goods, because often the only way for local producers to gain access to the supply chain of the MNCs is to be part of the MNC system. (In contrast, garments, footwear, and furniture are final goods or near-final goods.)

These two patterns together suggest that China is unique mainly in that it seems to have received a lot of labor-intensive and export-oriented FDI. Overall, FIEs accounted for a far greater share of manufactured exports in China (51.2 percent) than in Taiwan (20.6 percent) or in Indonesia (29 percent). A related observation is that Taiwan and Korea are unique in that they were less dependent on FDI in capital- and technology-intensive industries. But they are not unique when it comes to FDI in labor-intensive industries. Other developing economies have developed successful export capabilities in labor-intensive products through contract production, just as indigenous firms did in Taiwan and Korea in the 1960s and 1970s.

In her detailed study, Lemoine (2000) draws the conclusion that "[d]espite the size of China's economy, the part taken by foreign affiliates in its manufacturing industry and exports is comparable with that they play in other developing Asian economies." She presents data that show, however, a lower share of value-added and employment by FIEs in the Chinese manufacturing industries compared with Indonesia, Malaysia, and Taiwan. The low employment share, at 11 percent in China, compared with 23 percent in Taiwan, 38 percent in Malaysia, and 14 percent in Indonesia, is easily explained by the excess employment among state-owned enterprises in China. Chinese economists estimate that about one-third of SOE workers are redundant; that is, laying off these workers would have zero impact on the output of SOEs. The low share of value-added is entirely consistent with our observation here that a large portion of FDI in China finances labor-intensive industries, and therefore on this measure we would expect FIEs in China to account for a lower share. This reinforces the point about the unusualness of China's FDI patterns. In other economies, including those that have achieved export successes, FDI does not go into labor-intensive industries; FDI mainly goes to high value-added industries.

The export dominance of Chinese FIEs is not because they are more export-oriented than Taiwanese FIEs *at the firm level*. In fact, they are less export-oriented. On average, FIEs in Chinese manufacturing industries in 1995 exported 38.6 percent of their output, as shown in column D of Table 1.4, but FIEs in Taiwan in 1976 exported a much higher share, at 46 percent (Ranis and Schive 1985). Thus, at least compared with Taiwan, that FIEs in China

---

[26] A good discussion on this topic is found in United Nations Conference on Trade and Development (1998), esp. pp. 209–21.

export so much output abroad results from their sheer dominance of Chinese export production, not from export-orientedness at the firm level. This distinction is critical. The export dominance of FIEs in China is the result of their substantial overall role in the Chinese economy, rather than export efficiency at the firm level.

While FIEs have played an instrumental role in China's successful export drive, it should be noted that they both have created exports and may have replaced exports previously produced by Chinese-owned firms. As noted above, export-processing operations declined in absolute terms between 1988 and 1997, and while export-processing firms accounted for a larger share of Chinese exports than FIEs in 1992, by 1996, within only four years, exports by processing and assembly operations fell to 16 percent of Chinese exports, while FIEs' share of exports increased to 33.8 percent.[27] This was mainly due to a massive conversion of contractual alliances between domestic and foreign firms into FIEs during this period, as noted in two economic studies.[28]

The significant position of FIEs in the Chinese economy raises a natural question about control. Corporate control is a complicated concept, but the simplest measure is the investor's share of the equity ownership. The higher the share, the more control the investor is said to have, since equity ownership is usually an indicator of how decision-making power is apportioned among investors, through, for example, the number of board seats one can appoint. Since many FIEs in China are JVs, decision making is shared among Chinese and foreign investors. The allocation of decision-making power is determined on the basis of their respective shares of equity ownership.

Foreign firms have established majority controls over FIEs in most industries. Only in seven out of twenty-eight manufacturing industries are foreign firms found to have an average aggregate minority equity position; that is, the total equity value owned by the foreign firms is less than 50 percent of the industry sum of FIE equity.[29] State-owned monopolies or oligopolies are typically found in those industries where foreign firms have minority stakes. The tobacco

---

[27] Data on export processing are from General Administration of Customs of the People's Republic of China (1996), p. 11, and the FIEs' export data are from State Statistical Bureau (1997b), pp. 589 and 604.

[28] Sung, Liu, Wong, and Lau (1995) comment that "the conversion of processing operations into JVs may not indicate any upgrading of hard technology or soft technology." Wu and Zhang (1995) believe that the processing operations were converted into JVs to produce higher value-added products. But it is difficult to reconcile the latter explanation with the surge of contractual alliances in recent years.

[29] Most of the industries, including the more capital-intensive industries, have a large number of enterprises. For example, there were 1,409 FIEs in the transport equipment sector in 1995. The high foreign equity share is not the result of large equity positions of a few foreign firms.

industry is probably the most illustrative example. It is run by a single government agency, the China Monopoly Bureau of Tobacco Industry, which operates integrated production from tobacco procurement to cigarette making. But even in this heavily monopolistic industry, the combined equity stake of foreign firms already reached 46.9 percent by 1995. While foreign firms have been able to make inroads into industries explicitly reserved for the most powerful government corporations, nonstate indigenous firms have been largely excluded.

Another characteristic is that foreign majority equity controls seem unrelated to some of the well-known features of these industries. Foreign majority controls span both labor-intensive industries, such as garments, footwear, and leather products, and capital-intensive industries, such as chemicals, machinery, and instrument manufacturing. This across-the-board foreign equity control contrasts with the Taiwanese pattern. In Taiwan foreign firms have dominant equity positions in certain industries, such as garments and footwear (71.8 percent), lumber and bamboo products (75.7 percent), and leather and fur products (79.6 percent). But in quite a number of industries, they are mere minority investors (such as nonmetallic minerals, chemicals, and the machinery industry).[30] Thus, in China not only do foreign firms have larger equity positions and thus putatively greater corporate control over FIEs, their controls are uniform across industries.

The Pervasive Presence of FIEs

Our third illustration of the substantial role of FDI in the Chinese economy is the ubiquitous presence of FIEs; that is, firms established through FDI can be found in many industries and in many regions of the country. This is surprising on two counts. One is that in other countries FDI tends to congregate toward certain industries rather than being dispersed evenly across many industries. The other is that the wide geographic dispersion of FDI contrasts sharply with the substantial and increasing immobility of domestic capital.

FDI theory suggests that FDI is usually concentrated in industries characterized by an oligopolistic dynamic. Summarizing the theoretical work on FDI, Theodore Moran writes, "barriers to entry and imperfect competition are the sine qua non for the FDI process to be possible" (Moran 1998). Behind this statement lies a set of postulates about the high costs of overseas investments, market failures associated with trading intangible assets via arm's-length transactions, and the distribution of advantages and disadvantages between host and foreign firms. I revisit some of these claims in the next chapter in greater detail.

---

[30] The Taiwanese data are reported in Ranis and Schive (1985).

Empirical research on FDI has found strong evidence to support this theoretical expectation. For example, in a survey article Newfarmer and March find that over 80 percent of foreign subsidiaries in Mexico and Brazil were in industries with four-firm concentration ratios exceeding 50 percent. Similar concentration patterns of foreign firms were found in Peru, Chile, Colombia, and Malaysia.[31] According to Bruce Kogut, FDI in Central European countries exhibited a similar pattern. Foreign firms were found in only a few industries, such as autos, consumer products, and telecommunications. And the investing firms were familiar ones, such as ABB, Coca-Cola, and Proctor & Gamble.[32]

The same conclusion can be reached by looking at the distribution of FDI outflow from the perspective of the investing countries. According to a study by the U.S. Conference Board, the sectors of U.S. firms with the most international activities are transportation equipment, instruments and related products, electric and electronic equipment, machinery, and chemicals. An interesting and revealing finding in this study is that the sectoral distribution of investment abroad is driven primarily by industry characteristics rather than by the level of economic development of the host countries. For example, despite the wide gap between Canada and Mexico in terms of income levels, labor skills, and technological sophistication, the sector distribution of the presence of U.S. firms in these two countries is remarkably similar; that is, industries that tend to set up operations in Canada are also industries with substantial operations in Mexico. Only in two industries, chemicals and electronics, does one find significant differences (Taylor and Henisz 1994, pp. 17–18).

One may argue that Latin American and Central European countries provide an inappropriate benchmark for China since they are hosts mainly to Western MNCs, whereas much of the FDI materializing in China originates from Asian firms. According to this view, Western firms tend to congregate in oligopolistic industries, while Asian firms operate in conditions closer to perfect competition. Another objection is that Western investments are typically oriented to the domestic markets of the host economies, whereas investments originating from Asian countries are more export-oriented. It is possible, then, that some of the differences between China and Latin America stem from differences in the suppliers of FDI capital.

While these objections seemingly focus on a purely factual distinction among capital suppliers, they are based on an underlying idea – often unstated–that FDI

---

[31] This research is summarized in Moran (1998).

[32] Central Europe exhibits a familiar pattern of oligopolistic rivalry among foreign investors. FDI may disturb national oligopolies, although, as Kogut points out, multinational corporations prevail in industries characterized by oligopoly. See Kogut (1996).

activities undertaken by Asian firms require a separate analytical paradigm. On a priori grounds, it is difficult to see why an entirely different analytical framework has to be invented for Asian MNCs. Just as their Western counterparts, Asian MNCs incur extra costs from investing abroad as compared with investing at home, and thus the logic that firms must possess special advantages to be able to succeed abroad should equally apply. But empirically, Chinese FDI patterns also differ significantly from those observed in other Asian economies.

To avoid attributing a particular pattern of industry distribution of FDI to investor characteristics – such as those associated with Western MNCs versus those associated with Asian MNCs – I use Hong Kong investments in four Asian economies – China, Taiwan, Malaysia, and Indonesia – to control for a supply perspective focusing on differences among investors. Table 1.3 shows the percentage shares of Hong Kong direct investments in three manufacturing industries in these four Asian economies. Except for in China, Hong Kong investments exhibit a similar degree of high industry concentration. In Indonesia,

Table 1.3 *Manufacturing Industries with the Largest FDI Values from Hong Kong in Indonesia, Malaysia, Taiwan, and China (%)*

	Indonesia (1976)	Malaysia (1977)	Taiwan (1974–79)	China (1993)
Industry with the largest Hong Kong FDI	Textiles (55.3%)	Textiles (57.9%)	Chemicals (52.9%)	Electronics (23.4%)
Industry with the second largest Hong Kong FDI	Chemicals (14.6%)	Food manufacturing (9.1%)	Electronics and electrical appliances (28.8%)	Plastic products (12.1%)
Industry with the third largest Hong Kong FDI	Metal products (9.2%)	Chemicals (8.3%) Electrical and electronic appliances (8.3%)	Garments and footwear (4.7%)	Textiles (11.2%)
Percentage shares of total Hong Kong FDI	79.1%	75.3%	86.4%	46.7%

Note: Most of the data on ECE FDI in the Chinese sources lump together FDI from Hong Kong, Macao, and Taiwan. For this reason, I instead use the data from the Federation of Hong Kong Industries.

Sources: Data on Indonesia, Malaysia, and Taiwan are from Chen (1981). Data on Hong Kong investments in China are from Federation of Hong Kong Industries (1995).

the top three manufacturing industries with the most Hong Kong investments accounted for 79.1 percent of total Hong Kong investments; in Malaysia, it was 75.3 percent; and in Taiwan, it was 86.4 percent. (While these data are from the 1970s, data from the 1990s show a similar pattern of sector concentration of Hong Kong FDI.)[33] In China, the top three industries, electronics, plastic products, and textiles, only accounted for 46.7 percent of total Hong Kong FDI as of 1993. Table 1.4 provides further evidence of the fragmentation of industry distribution of FDI in China. Among the twenty-eight manufacturing industries, none received more than 10 percent of total FDI. In column A, the highest share was 9.6 percent in the electronics and telecommunications industry. The textile industry followed, at 8.9 percent.[34] (Interestingly, industry distribution of FDI in Singapore is relatively dispersed, although not to the same extent as in China. In 1980, the top three manufacturing industries with the largest shares of FDI accounted for 54 percent of the total.[35] I argue in Chapter 7 that the similarities between China and Singapore stemmed from similar policy factors.)

Taiwan provides a suitable benchmark for China because it provides controls for a number of factors on the FDI supply side. Taiwan attracted export-oriented FDI in the 1960s and 1970s, due to rising labor costs in Japan. This is similar to the relocation of industrial assets from Hong Kong to China in the 1980s and 1990s.[36] Comparing China with Taiwan thus controls for the market orientation of the FDI suppliers (i.e., investors in Taiwan and in China both sought to establish production platforms for export). We can also impose controls on investor characteristics by comparing the industry distribution of FDI from Hong Kong in Taiwan with the industry distribution of FDI from Hong Kong in China. In this way, if there is still a difference in the industry distribution between China and Taiwan, we cannot attribute it to the fact that Hong Kong

---

[33] For example, in Malaysia, the top three industries with the most Hong Kong FDI accounted for 58.9 percent of the total materialized Hong Kong FDI in 1994. In the same year, on an approval basis, the top three industries in Indonesia with the most Hong Kong FDI accounted for 77.6 percent of the total Hong Kong FDI. These data are calculated on the basis of Tables 4.2 and 4.3 in Yeung (1998).) In the text, I use data from the 1970s because the industrial groupings are most similar to those in China, thus facilitating a direct comparison. The materialized amount may differ from the approval amount if an investor fails to invest the pledged amount of capital.

[34] All the data are the materialized basis.

[35] Data are based on Lim and Fong (1991).

[36] In the 1960s and 1970s, as wage costs in Japan rose rapidly, Japanese firms began to move some of their labor-intensive activities overseas, either via direct investments or subcontracting, mainly to Taiwan and Korea. Westphal, Rhee, and Pursell (1985) document this phenomenon in Korea. Japanese investors were responsible for 39 percent of FDI flows into Korea between 1967 and 1971 and 71 percent between 1972 and 1976. Similar to Hong Kong investments into China in the 1980s and 1990s, much of the Japanese investment took the form of second-hand machinery, which Japanese firms could no longer operate profitably at home.

Table 1.4 Industry Characteristics of FIEs in Chinese Manufacturing Industries, 1995 (%)

Manufacturing industries	(A) Distribution of materialized FDI	(B) Shares of FIE exports of all exports	(C) Shares of FIE sales of all sales	(D) Shares of FIE exports of FIE sales	(E) Average foreign equity stakes in FIEs
Food processing	1.5	57.5	21.2	24.5	57.5
Food manufacturing	4.6	38.7	30.5	16.6	64.0
Beverage manufacturing	4.4	37.8	26.2	4.5	56.4
Tobacco processing	0.1	2.5	0.6	17.3	46.9
Textile industry	8.9	28.6	17.9	48.6	52.0
Garments and footwear	6.0	60.5	50.8	71.7	63.3
Leather and related products	3.6	73.2	54.1	73.6	63.9
Timber processing and related products	1.4	57.7	27.3	31.5	54.2
Furniture manufacturing	0.8	75.1	30.7	45.8	53.9
Papermaking and paper products	3.1	53.4	17.0	20.8	61.8
Printing and record pressing	1.6	79.4	18.3	19.8	51.7
Cultural, educational, and sports articles	1.9	69.0	50.7	81.3	73.6
Petroleum processing and products	0.2	8.5	1.4	21.8	48.1
Chemical materials and products	5.8	31.6	12.6	22.7	57.5
Medical and pharmaceutical products	2.0	21.9	18.3	16.9	46.2
Chemical fibers	1.4	41.5	12.7	26.3	48.9
Rubber products	1.8	53.3	25.0	39.7	59.1
Plastic products	5.1	77.2	33.1	42.6	54.4
Nonmetal mineral products	7.7	38.9	11.4	21.4	51.5
Smelting and pressing of ferrous metals	1.7	6.3	6.2	9.3	42.7

Smelting and pressing of nonferrous metals	1.2	24.4	12.5	18.0	40.4
Metal products	5.5	61.1	26.6	47.2	59.5
Ordinary machinery manufacturing	4.0	30.6	14.5	21.9	52.6
Special purpose equipment	1.9	35.5	9.0	27.9	51.0
Transportation equipment	5.9	30.4	25.2	7.6	46.5
Electric equipment and machinery	6.6	58.3	21.8	34.3	57.7
Electronics and telecommunications	9.6	94.5	60.8	59.1	61.0
Instruments	1.8	71.8	38.8	51.2	65.8
All manufacturing	100.0	51.2	21.0	38.6	55.1[a]

Note: The data are based on enterprises with independent accounting systems. These firms account for 85 percent of the industrial output value. For some of the FDI issues involved in these data, see the appendix to this chapter.

[a] Calculated as simple average of foreign equity stakes in twenty-eight industries. Weighted average (aggregate foreign equity value/aggregate FIE equity) equals 55.6%.

Source: Office of Third Industrial Census (1997).

investors dominate China's FDI inflows. Finally, the FDI regimes in China and Taiwan were broadly similar in the area of export-oriented FDI. Like China, Taiwan aggressively sought out export-oriented FDI, although it maintained various controls on FDI aimed at the domestic market.[37]

First, there are a number of data issues. All the data reported below refer to manufacturing industries only. This is by design. Taiwan is poor in natural resources and it would bias the comparison if all industries were included. Service industries are excluded because in both economies a number of service industries were closed to FDI. Second, the Chinese data are for 1995, whereas the Taiwanese patterns are based on data for 1976. In part, this is a function of data availability, but there are substantive considerations involved as well. To compare China with Taiwan in the 1970s helps to control for the different levels of economic development. By the mid-1970s, Taiwan had already experienced fifteen years of export promotion and encouragement of export-oriented FDI, exactly the same stage as China by 1995. Another substantive reason is that in the mid-1970s, FIEs in Taiwan accounted for a higher share of Taiwan's manufactured exports than they did in the 1980s, according to data provided in the study by Naya and Ramstetter (1988). Because FIEs in China had already established a solid position in China's export production, it is more analytically sound to compare China with Taiwan when FIEs also accounted for a high share of Taiwan's exports.

Despite some common factors that might drive FDI toward similar patterns in these two economies, the Chinese FDI distribution differs dramatically from that of Taiwan. According to detailed data reported in a study by Ranis and Schive (1985), in 1976 almost half (41 percent) of Taiwan's inward FDI in the manufacturing industries went to electronics and electrical appliances; on the other hand, pulp paper and related products received almost no FDI (0.8 percent). In contrast, in China at a similar industry aggregation (i.e., a two-digit level), FDI inflows were far more evenly distributed across industries. In 1995, similar to Taiwan in 1976, electronics and electrical appliances claimed the largest share, at 18 percent, but this is less than half of the Taiwanese figure

---

[37] In 1960, the government in Taiwan enacted the Statute for the Encouragement of Investment to provide incentives to foreign investors, such as tax holidays and the redesignation of agricultural land as factory sites. In 1966, the government established export-processing zones to encourage foreign firms to relocate their production sites. In the 1960s and 1970s, Taiwan's FDI regime was considerably more liberal than that in the Latin American countries or Korea. In principle, Taiwan allowed 100 percent foreign ownership, lower tax rates, generous tax holiday treatments, and accelerated depreciation schedules. In reality, the policy heavily courted export-oriented FDI rather than FDI that would result in competition with domestic firms. For discussion, see Wade (1990), esp. pp. 148–57.

in the same industry. The lowest industry share for China is found in lumber and bamboo products, at 2.2 percent, which is still about three times the lowest industry share figure for Taiwan (0.8 percent). The three industries with most of the FDI accounted for 69.4 percent of total FDI flows in Taiwan, compared with 40.3 percent in China.[38] Data on later years and on investments from Hong Kong also show a concentration pattern. In 1987, the three manufacturing industries in Taiwan with the highest values of FDI from Hong Kong accounted for 63.9 percent of the total FDI from Hong Kong, compared with 46.7 percent in China.[39]

A more straightforward measure is the standard deviation value of the industry distribution of FDI. The standard deviation value calculated on the basis of the percentage share of FDI across eleven two-digit manufacturing industries – as reported in the Ranis and Schive study – in Taiwan is 11.3. In China, for the same eleven two-digit industries, the figure is only 4.1. Investments by firms based in ECEs are not a significant contributing factor to the FDI concentration in Taiwan or to the FDI dispersion in China. In 1987, the standard deviation values for the industry percentage distribution of Hong Kong FDI and overseas Chinese FDI in Taiwan were, respectively, 7.4 and 8.7, about twice the levels for China.[40]

One may argue that the FDI regime in China is more liberal than that in Taiwan. Thus, the difference in the industry distribution of FDI between China and Taiwan may result from different degrees of FDI restrictions in the two economies. As an empirical matter, it should be pointed out that China's FDI regime in the 1990s was by no means laissez-faire. There were numerous sector and ownership restrictions imposed on foreign investors. But to show cleanly that the FDI regulations are not responsible for the dispersion of FDI in China, let us compare China with Hong Kong, an economy widely known for its completely neutral treatment of domestic and foreign firms and for its lack of any sector-specific capital controls. Hong Kong's inward FDI flows, consistent with other countries, exhibit a concentration rather than a dispersion across different sectors. The three industries with the largest amounts of FDI in 1970 accounted for 76.6 percent of total FDI inflows. In 1979, this share declined to 52 percent, but it is still substantially higher than the Chinese figure.[41]

[38] Chinese industry data are reported in Office of Third Industrial Census (1997).

[39] Calculated on the basis of data in Investment Commission of Ministry of Economic Affairs (1995).

[40] Calculated on the basis of data in Investment Commission of Ministry of Economic Affairs (1995).

[41] Hong Kong data are given by Haggard (1990), Table 8.3, p. 204.

The second indicator of the pervasive presence of FIEs is their geographic dispersion. Many Chinese officials and Western researchers believe that FDI is highly concentrated in the coastal provinces to the neglect of China's hinterland provinces. For example, in a presentation at a National Bureau of Economic Research conference in 1997, Zhang Shengman, a Chinese Ministry of Finance official and a managing director at the World Bank, argued that China "must strive for a more desirable distribution of capital flows, both geographically (more to the interior) and sectorally (more to some service sectors, retailing, banking, insurance, etc.)."[42] Two researchers, Edward Graham and Erika Wada, in a study on FDI in China make the following observation: "[V]ast areas of China, including ones where much state-owned industry is located, have not been touched by FDI" (Graham and Wada 2001, p. 5). In recent years, the Chinese government has made FDI promotion a prominent component of its development strategy for the central and western provinces.

The data that are often cited to support the geographic concentration hypothesis is that Eastern China accounted for 84.5 percent of cumulative FDI between 1985 and 1991 and 87.3 percent between 1992 and 1998 (Gipouloux 2000). The problem with this view is that it relies on statistics on the percentage shares of FDI distributed among Chinese provinces. Recall, however, that during the 1990s China attracted an enormous amount of FDI, and thus a small portion of FDI going to the interior provinces is still a significant number. According to statistics provided in Gipouloux's study, the interior regions of China accounted for about 13 percent of cumulative FDI inflows between 1992 and 1998. During this period, cumulative FDI flows into China as a whole amounted to $242.3 billion. This means that the interior regions of China received $31.5 billion in FDI. To put this number in perspective, India's entire FDI inward stock, as of 1997, was only $11.2 billion. In addition, the poor, hinterland provinces of China absorbed either more than or about the same level of FDI as some of the star economies in Latin America in the 1990s. As of 1997, the FDI inward stock for Argentina was $36 billion and for Chile was $25.1 billion.[43]

The true puzzle is not why the poor, land-locked provinces do not receive much FDI; the puzzle is why they get any at all. These areas of China are not expected to be competitive on the FDI front. Linguistic and cultural ties with the ECEs are not strong, and, to the extent that FDI is a "neighborhood affair," these regions of China are far away from all the major FDI suppliers. But the fact is that even in some of the most remote provinces in China, FDI

---

[42] See Zhang (1999), p. 181.

[43] The data on India, Chile, and Argentina are provided in United Nations Conference on Trade and Development (1998), Annex Table B.3.

accounts for a surprisingly high proportion of fixed asset investments. And, unlike those for Guangdong province, the FDI figures for these provinces are unlikely to be contaminated by a statistical distortion known as "round-trip FDI" – the fake FDI recycled back to China from Hong Kong. (Data issues related to round-trip FDI are discussed in detail in the next section of this chapter.) In 1995, the average FDI/capital formation ratio for fourteen interior and western provinces was 4.9 percent; if investments by SOEs are excluded, the ratio was 14.9 percent.[44] The 4.9 percent figure puts these provinces above Taiwan (2.2 percent), Korea (1.2 percent), India (2.2 percent), and Russia (2.0 percent). (All the numbers refer to the 1992–98 period.) The 14.9 percent figure, that is, FDI normalized by investments of nonstate firms, would make China's interior and land-locked provinces number six out of the fifteen economies represented in Table 1.2 (excluding China). While Lemoine argues that the FDI distribution pattern in China is uneven, in her own paper (2000, p. 30) she shows that the FDI stock/GDP ratio for interior provinces was 10.9 percent in 1998. To put this number in perspective, in 1998, the FDI stock/GDP ratio for North America was 10.5 percent, for Central and Eastern Europe, 12.9 percent, and for South, East, and Southeast Asia, 10.5 percent.[45]

The geographic dispersion of FDI is even more intriguing in light of the substantial barriers to interprovincial domestic investments. As foreign firms are able to establish operations in many parts of the country, domestic firms tend to stay in their own localities and build facilities within their own jurisdictions. This is not because foreign firms are big and domestic firms are small. In Chapter 6, I describe a situation in which a small Hong Kong firm, China Strategic Investment, was able to acquire 200 firms across nine provinces, whereas, as of 1998, all the facilities of the largest automotive firm in China, Shanghai Automotive Industrial Corporation, were located in Shanghai.

There is solid evidence that during the period when FDI rose rapidly, the mobility of domestic capital declined. The World Bank reports in a 1994 study that profitability variations across different regions in China, taking into account the tax rate differentials, increased during the reform era (World Bank 1994, p. 54).[46] Trade protectionism is one reason; the outward capital

---

[44] There are sixteen provinces that are classified as interior or western provinces. No FDI data are available for two of these provinces – Inner Mongolia and Tibet. The remaining fourteen provinces are Shanxi, Anhui, Jiangxi, Henan, Hubei, Hunan, Sichuan, Guizhou, Yunnan, Shaanxi, Gansu, Qinghai, Ningxia, and Xinjiang. The figures are calculated on the basis of data provided in State Statistical Bureau (1996a).

[45] These figures are from United Nations Conference on Trade and Development (2000), Annex Table B.5.

[46] While it is possible that interbank lending can substitute for some of the cross-regional investment activities, it is doubtful that it has done so completely. The World Bank report points out that

controls – imposed on firms under the local governments to prevent them from investing in other provinces – are a likely contributing factor as well. More direct evidence is that some Chinese provinces depend on FDI more heavily than they depend on investments from other provinces. Take Guangdong province as an example. In 1992, Guangdong invested about 2.5 percent of its total investments in other provinces, while other provinces' investments in Guangdong amounted to 1.7 percent of Guangdong's total investments. In the same year, FDI accounted for 31.7 percent of Guangdong's investments, far surpassing both Guangdong's export of capital to other regions and its import of capital from other regions.[47] In dollar terms, the 1.7 percent of investments in Guangdong from other provinces amounted to $260 million. To put this number in perspective, in 1992, firms based in tiny Macao, known more for its casinos than its computers and more for its gangs than for its garment making, invested $202 million in China and $169.6 million in Guangdong. This is a startling fact: Macao's investments in Guangdong amounted to 65 percent of what the rest of China invested in Guangdong.[48]

This outsized investment position held by foreign firms is by no means limited to Guangdong, a province that has wooed foreign investments particularly aggressively. Sichuan, an interior province traditionally isolated from the outside world, also depended more heavily on FDI than on investments from other provinces. In 1992, investments from other provinces represented 0.2 percent of Sichuan's total investments, and Sichuan's investments in other provinces amounted to 4.5 percent of its total investments. Foreign investments, however, represented 5.4 percent of its total investments. Figure 1.1, based on data compiled by the World Bank, shows that in four out of six provinces, FDI exceeded inward investments from and outward investments to other provinces by a substantial margin. The lone exception was Shanghai, which received far more inward investments from other provinces than it received foreign investments.

FDI in Perfectly Competitive Industries and the Preponderance of Small Investors

In a widely used textbook on FDI, Richard Caves writes (Caves 1996, p. 25), "MNEs [multinational enterprises] are logically incompatible with

---

most of the interbank lending was to satisfy short-term liquidity requirements, not long-term investment needs. See World Bank (1994).

[47] Guangdong's investment figure is calculated from World Bank (1994), Table 2.6.

[48] To clarify, China bans FDI in casinos and thus Macao's large investment position cannot be attributed to this source of its competitive advantage.

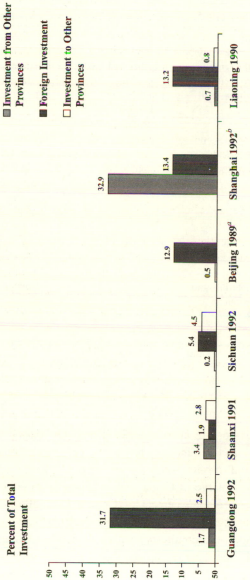

Figure 1.1 FDI and interprovincial domestic investments, for selected provinces (%). [a] Investment from other provinces unavailable. [b] Investment to other provinces unavailable. *Source:* Based on World Bank (1994).

Table 1.5 *Export Shares of FIEs in Total Exports of Three Economies: China, Taiwan, and Indonesia (%)*

	China (1995)	Taiwan (1980)	Indonesia (1995)
Labor-intensive industries	Garments and footwear: 60.5 Leather and fur products: 73.2 Furniture: 75.1	Garments and footwear: 5.7 Leather and fur products: 9.6 Lumber and bamboo products: 2.7	Garments and footwear: 33.0 Leather and related products: 19.7 Furniture: 14.0
Capital- or technology-intensive industries	Electronics and electrical appliances: 83.4	Electronics and electrical appliances: 50.5	Electric, measuring, and photographic apparatus: 78.8 Computers and parts: 91.8 Machinery and vehicle parts: 86.1
	Paper and paper products: 53.4 Chemical materials and products: 31.6	Pulp paper and paper products: 4.5 Chemicals: 34.9	Paper and paper products: 29.8 Chemical materials: 42.3
Manufacturing industries	51.2	20.6	29.0

Sources: Chinese data are from Office of Third Industrial Census (1997) and Taiwanese data are from Ranis and Schive (1985), Table 2.12, p. 109. Indonesian data are unpublished and were provided to the author by the Indonesian government through the kind assistance of Timothy S. Buehrer and Lou Wells. Professor Lou Wells generously provided English translations of the Indonesian text.

the purely competitive organization of an industry." The reason is, as Caves observes, "purely competitive industry has ample new local entrants to compete down the windfall profits in the foreign market" (Caves 1996, p. 25). Yet FDI has been very large in China's labor-intensive industries. According to one estimate, about 50 percent of China's FDI inflows in the late 1990s went into labor-intensive manufacturing industries (Tseng and Zebregs 2002). Table 1.5 shows the dominant position of FIEs in China in the export of labor-intensive products, compared with FIEs in Taiwan and Indonesia. While one can argue that the export dominance of FIEs is due to their control of access to Western markets, it should be noted that in a number of labor-intensive industries, the FIE shares of industry sales seem to be substantial as well, although one should interpret the domestic sales data with some caution.[49] In 1995, FIEs accounted for 30.7 percent of sales in furniture manufacturing, 50.8 percent in garments, and 54.1 percent in leather and related products.

One of the reasons why FDI is so substantial in labor-intensive industries is the presence of many foreign SMEs among foreign investors in China. The active role of foreign SMEs in China is revealed in a number of ways. One is the small size of the FDI projects. The other is that FDI projects tend to be small across the board; that is, the small size, at least in the mid-1990s, is not a function of the investors' ethnicity.

The best way to illustrate the small size of FDI projects is to compare the size of FDI projects in China with those in other countries funded by investors from the same economy. In this way, we control for the characteristics of the investors. According to Yang (1997), the average capitalization of Taiwanese investments in China ranged between $735,000 and $1 million during the 1991–94 period. In contrast, Taiwanese investments in Southeast Asia averaged between $3 million and $6 million during the same period. But, as noted by Yang (1997), Taiwanese authorities restricted investments in China by limiting the size of individual FDI projects. This restriction, no doubt, led to the smaller FDI projects in China by Taiwanese investors. However, it is important to point out that the average actual investment size was far below the limit imposed by the Taiwanese authorities ($1.5 million). Also FDI projects funded by firms from countries without investment restrictions are similarly small. Affiliates of Singaporean firms in China are much smaller than affiliates of Singaporean firms in other countries. According to the Singapore Department of Statistics, in 1995, the average equity capital per overseas affiliate of Singaporean firms was $4.8 million. A similar measure would put the size of Chinese affiliates of Singaporean firms at $1.9 million.[50]

A common measure of the size of firms is their employment. By this measure, the FIEs in China are substantially smaller than the FIEs in Taiwan. The detailed employment data of FIEs in Taiwan, broken down by manufacturing industries, come from Ranis and Schive (1985, p. 123). They show that the average number of employees per manufacturing FIE in Taiwan in 1975 was 362. This compares with 152 employees per manufacturing FIE in China in 1995.[51] To control for

---

[49] The data are based on Office of Third Industrial Census (1997). See the appendix to this chapter for some data issues.

[50] The data on the average equity investment size of Singaporean overseas affiliates are from Singapore Department of Statistics (1998). Data on Chinese affiliates of Singaporean firms are from State Statistical Bureau (1997a).

[51] The employment data for Chinese FIEs come from Office of Third Industrial Census (1997).

the possible difference arising from different industrial distributions of FDI – for example, there could be more FDI in labor-intensive industries in China – we can look at the average employment size per FIE on an industry-by-industry basis. There is no question that average employment is much smaller in China than in Taiwan in the same industry. A garment/footwear FIE in Taiwan hired on average 381 persons in 1975, compared with 166 persons in a garment/footwear FIE in China in 1995. In leather and fur products, the average FIE employed 363 persons in Taiwan but only 248 persons in China. In electronics, 789 persons worked for a Taiwanese FIE on average, but only 192 worked for a Chinese FIE on average.

Is the small size of FDI projects in China the result of investments from ECEs? Not really. As measured by the average dollar value of foreign capital per FDI project (on an approval basis), investment projects funded by some of the non-ECE investors are either smaller or about the same size as investment projects funded by investors from ECEs.[52] In 1995, the average value of pledged foreign capital per FDI project funded by investors from Hong Kong, Taiwan, and Macao was, respectively, $2.4 million, $1.2 million, and $2.1 million. The same figures for projects funded by investors from Japan, Korea, Thailand, Canada, and the United States were, respectively, $2.6 million, $1.5 million, $2.1 million, $1.8 million, and $2.2 million.[53]

Theoretically, although not plausibly, a large MNC can invest in numerous small, independent FDI projects, and thus the project size may not be an accurate gauge of the size of the parent firm. Thus, a more revealing indicator is the size of the parent firm making investments in China, not the size of its investment projects in China. According to a 1997 survey carried out by the Hong Kong–based Chinese Manufacturers' Association (CMA), firms without any investments in China were larger than firms with investments in China.[54] Noninvesting firms employed on average 109 persons, compared with 81 employees at investing firms. Firms with 109 employees are classified as large firms by CMA standards (firms under 100 persons as SMEs). Another corroborating piece of evidence is that industries with a smaller average firm size – measured by employment per establishment – have a slightly higher proportion of firms

---

[52] All the figures reported here on the average dollar value of foreign capital per FDI project are on an "approval" basis, that is, the amount of foreign capital pledged by foreign investors. Often the materialized foreign capital is much smaller than the pledged amount but the Chinese authorities do not disclose the number of FDI projects on an actual basis, which makes it difficult to calculate the average dollar value per FDI project on a materialized basis.

[53] Calculated on the basis of data provided in State Statistical Bureau (1999a).

[54] The findings are reported in "Survey Report on CMA Members' Investments in the Mainland" (1998).

with investment positions in China than industries populated by larger firms. This is shown by the negative correlation between the average employment size of a firm and the proportion of firms with actual or planned investment projects in China (based on 1993 data). The bivariate correlation is –0.07. Large firms based in Hong Kong are slightly less likely to invest in China than smaller firms based in Hong Kong.[55]

Here, again, China's patterns differ from those observed in other countries. FDI research shows that large firms are more likely than small firms to invest abroad. This is true of both developing and developed countries. Lall (1986) has found that larger firms in India are more likely to invest abroad. The same dynamic works in the United States. According to a study by the U.S. Conference Board, very large American manufacturing firms – defined as firms with annual sales exceeding $5 billion – average thirty-six plants in fourteen countries.[56] The number of overseas plants drops precipitously to around thirteen for firms with annual sales between $1 billion and $5 billion. As the size of the firm decreases from medium to small, the number of overseas plants drops further. A firm with annual sales revenue of between $100 million and $500 million on average operates two plants abroad, whereas a firm with below $100 million in sales operates one plant abroad. One of the interesting findings is that the share of foreign sales does not decrease nearly as linearly as the number of overseas plants. For example, very large firms sell about 35 percent of their products abroad; very small firms sell about 20 percent of their production abroad. This confirms the prediction by theorists such as Richard Caves that overseas investments are a high-cost affair. Smaller firms thus prefer to service overseas markets via an arm's-length mechanism in order to avoid incurring the high costs of making investments abroad.

FDI DATA ISSUES

The simplest explanation for some of the patterns of China's FDI described above is that China's FDI statistics are wrong. Two types of statistical distortions are possible. One concerns how FDI activities are classified. Because a large portion of China's FDI comes from ECEs, it can be questioned whether it is appropriate to classify direct investments from ECEs as FDI. The second issue has to do with round-trip FDI – direct investments made in China by overseas subsidiaries or affiliates of companies headquartered in China. Neither of these

---

[55] The correlation analysis is performed on data from a survey of the members of the Hong Kong Federation of Industries. See Federation of Hong Kong Industries (1995).

[56] This section is based on Taylor and Henisz (1994).

data issues materially affects the characterization of China's FDI patterns presented in the previous section.

FDI Classification

Much of the Chinese FDI inflow consists of capital from three ethnically Chinese economies: Hong Kong, Taiwan, and Macao. FDI from these three sources accounted for 59.3 percent of China's total FDI inflows between 1978 and 1999.[57] Because these three ECEs are tied to mainland China politically, albeit to varying degrees and in complicated ways, the question arises as to how "foreign" their capital actually is. If the FDI originating from these three ECEs is reclassified as intracountry capital flows, then China would be an underachiever in terms of FDI relative to its economic potential, not an overachiever, as claimed here.[58]

Classifying direct investments from ECEs as FDI is not wrong. Note that the IMF defines FDI as an investment activity across two different economies, not across two different countries. In some cases different economies may nevertheless belong to the same political sovereign entity (country). That Hong Kong and Macao are now sovereign territories of China does not change the fact that their firms are subject to completely different economic and regulatory regimes from firms based in mainland China. Hong Kong and Macao maintain their own currencies, economic institutions, and court systems. In addition, they are separate members of the WTO. Their governments pursue autonomous monetary, taxation, and tariff policies. All of the above is even more true of Taiwan. (Taiwan became a separate member of the WTO after China's accession.) It should also be noted that the height of FDI inflows – defined as a proportion of China's total FDI inflows – from Hong Kong and Macao was during the 1992–95 period, which preceded the political unifications of Hong Kong (1997) and Macao (1999) with China.

China's FDI classification is entirely consistent with the IMF definition and with reporting norms in other countries. To illustrate this point, take the British classification of FDI as an example. Before British rule ended in 1997, the

---

[57] http://www.moftec.gov.cn/moftec_cn/tjsj/wztj/wztj_menu.html, accessed October 2001.

[58] Wei (1995) argues that China is an underachiever if only FDI from the OECD countries is included. He excludes FDI from the ECEs not on the grounds that the ECEs and China are politically integrated but on the grounds that FDI from the ECEs is not a traditional form of FDI. Although the point is valid that FDI from the ECEs is not traditional, it is still necessary to explain its incidence and magnitude. As I discuss in greater detail in the concluding chapter of this book, international business scholars have paid a great deal of attention to the rise of what are known as "third-world" MNCs.

British government classified direct investments originating from Hong Kong as FDI in exactly the same way it classified investments in Britain from China, India, or the United States.[59] The reason is that the Hong Kong economy was considered to be a separate *economic* entity from Britain before 1997, just as Hong Kong is now considered to be a separate *economic* entity from China. Another example is that of the Netherlands Antilles, a Dutch territory that is a part of the Kingdom of the Netherlands. All the investments originating from the Netherlands Antilles into the Netherlands are classified as FDI by the Dutch authorities.[60] The reason is that the Netherlands Antilles enjoys a substantial degree of political, economic, and regulatory autonomy, a status granted by the Dutch to the islands in 1954.[61]

As will become clear in the next chapter, the central argument of this book focuses on the organization of China's economic and financial institutions as an explanation for the country's FDI patterns. Ultimately, the core substantive research question in the book has little to do with semantics – whether Hong Kong or Macao is classified as a "foreign" territory. The real issue is: How have fundamentally different economic, legal, and regulatory institutions, such as those that exist between China on the one hand and the ECEs on the other, affected investment patterns in China? As long as it is an incontrovertible fact that there are profound institutional differences between China and the ECEs (just as there are between China and the United States), it is irrelevant how the direct investments from the ECEs are labeled.[62]

Round-Trip FDI

The round-trip FDI is far more troublesome and complicated on substantive grounds. Round-trip FDI refers to direct investment capital that is first exported by Chinese firms and then imported back into the country. As such, round-trip FDI has no effect on China's total capital inflows as the capital that is imported

---

[59] In 1992, the British government recorded $280 million in FDI from Hong Kong. In 1993, $459 million in FDI went from Britain to Hong Kong. See Organisation for Economic Co-operation and Development (2000).

[60] For example, in 1990, $1.8 billion in FDI was recorded as FDI originating in the Netherlands Antilles to the Netherlands and $795 million as FDI originating in the Netherlands to the Netherlands Antilles. See ibid.

[61] For example, the Netherlands Antilles has its own central bank and its own currency; despite its name, the guilder is in fact tied to the U.S. dollar rather than to the Dutch currency.

[62] It may be tempting to draw a parallel between outward investments from New York City in its adjacent regions and Hong Kong's investments in China. The parallel is correct as a factual statement that investment activities have originated from two cities, but not for much else. The institutional gulf that separates China from Hong Kong cannot be overstated.

is canceled out by the capital that is first exported. The size of round-trip FDI is not known and is extremely difficult to calculate. The World Bank, without revealing its methodology, estimated round-trip FDI to be around 25 percent of total FDI inflows in 1992.[63] There are lower estimates as well. One study estimates that 15 percent of foreign investments in Shanghai between 1980 and 1992 originated from Chinese subsidiaries in Hong Kong (Naughton 1996b, p. 316). Tseng and Zebregs (2002) report an estimate that puts round-trip FDI in 1996 at 7 percent of China's FDI inflows.

There are two ways that round-trip FDI may have contributed to China's FDI patterns. First, round-trip FDI would inflate the FDI/capital formation ratio by making the numerator artificially large and the denominator artificially small. Second, the small average FDI project size may be a function of the round-trip FDI. The observation that only large firms invest abroad is based on the idea that investments abroad are costly and such costs are fixed and up front. But if the investors are the home-grown type, presumably such costs are less of a deterrent, even if the investing firm is small.[64] Similarly, since they do not need the usual firm-specific advantages – such as high research and development (R&D) content and other intangible assets – to succeed in China, they can be found in many industries, not just those industries in which these firm-specific advantages are important.

There are two approaches to tackle the round-trip FDI problem. One is an empirical approach, where we ask, "Does the presence of round-trip FDI fundamentally alter the FDI patterns that we observe in China?" We can answer this question by making some plausible assumptions about the magnitude and nature of round-trip FDI activities. The other approach is conceptual, where we ask, "Does the presence of round-trip FDI validate or refute the central argument of this book?" If the round-trip FDI validates our argument, this would add more power to our explanatory framework. A good explanation of China's FDI should be able to account for both the real and the fake FDI.

We make three assumptions about the round-trip FDI in China. First, the highest estimate of the round-trip FDI is close to its true magnitude. Second, FDI from Hong Kong, more than from other areas, is most afflicted by the round-trip FDI problem. Third, Guangdong province, more than other provinces, is most affected by round-trip FDI, both as a supplier and a recipient, because of its

---

[63] See World Bank (1996) and also Tseng and Zebregs (2002). In an earlier study, I arrive at a similar estimate by correlating China's capital outflows with its FDI inflows, using data from the 1980s to the mid-1990s. According to this methodology, round-trip FDI accounted for about 23 percent of China's FDI inflows. See Huang (1998), especially ch. 3.

[64] It is likely that relatively large firms engage in round-trip FDI. This is because it is an expensive proposition to establish a legal domicile and to maintain an affiliate in Hong Kong.

close economic, ethnic, and geographic ties with Hong Kong. In applying these three assumptions to the FDI data, I rely on the most conservative approach; that is, the data will be adjusted in such a way that is certain to overstate round-trip FDI and understate true FDI. In this way, if the FDI patterns depicted earlier in this chapter still hold, we have confidence that these patterns are not caused exclusively by round-trip FDI.

Does the presence of round-trip FDI fundamentally alter the conclusion that China is heavily dependent on FDI? Not at all. The FDI/capital formation ratio is most sensitive to the presence and magnitude of round-trip FDI, and netting out 25 percent of China's FDI inflows between 1992 and 1998 (25 percent as the highest estimate of round-trip FDI) will yield a FDI/capital formation ratio of 9.9 percent for the 1992–98 period. At 9.9 percent, China has the sixth highest FDI/capital formation ratio in Table 1.2. If one is to use the FDI/capital formation ratio net of SOEs' investments, this would yield a ratio of 21 percent.[65] At 21 percent, China has the third highest ratio in the table, after Singapore and Malaysia.

The second adjustment to the FDI/capital formation ratio is to assume that all of Hong Kong's direct investment in Guangdong province is round-trip FDI and to net it out from China's FDI data. For the 1992–98 period, this results in a FDI/capital formation ratio of 10.3 percent (inclusive of SOE investments) and 22 percent (exclusive of SOE investments). Both ratios will still rank China as one of the most FDI-dependent countries in Table 1.2. It should be stressed here that these two adjustments definitely overstate the magnitude of round-trip FDI. The 25 percent estimate refers to China's FDI situation in 1992, when round-trip FDI was known to be the most serious. In 1996, in contrast, round-trip FDI was estimated to be only 7 percent.[66] Yet in my adjustment, the 25 percent estimate is applied to the entire period. Second, assuming that all of Hong Kong's direct investments in Guangdong were from round-trip FDI clearly overstates its size. From a Chinese publication, for example, Fu (2000, p. 187) reports an estimate that puts round-trip FDI in Guangdong at 2 percent of the inward FDI in the province. The point of doing this exercise is not to come up with a realistic estimate of the size of China's true FDI but to show that the observation that China is heavily dependent on FDI is robust, even under some of the most unreasonable assumptions about the size of its round-trip FDI.

---

[65] It is important to note that round-trip FDI is not unique to China. Some of the FDI ostensibly from Taiwan can be traced to ethnic Chinese entrepreneurs in Malaysia (Fukushima and Kwan 1995).

[66] Reported in Tseng and Zebregs (2002).

Nor does round-trip FDI seem to have affected other Chinese FDI patterns. One way to demonstrate the patterns of China's true FDI is to compare FDI from non–Hong Kong sources with FDI from Hong Kong – presumably inclusive of round-trip FDI. Several conclusions can be drawn. First, the round-trip FDI does not change the assertion that ECE investors have played a substantial financing role in the Chinese economy. Both Taiwan and Macao, unlikely conduits of round-trip FDI, have supplied an enormous amount of FDI to China. Second, the round-trip FDI is not the only factor that has contributed to the diminution of FDI projects in China. As we have seen, the small average size of individual FDI projects is across the board. Japanese, Korean, American, and Thai FDI projects are not substantially larger than FDI projects funded by Hong Kong firms.

Third, the geographic and industry dispersion of FDI cannot be exclusively attributed to round-trip FDI. This is easily shown by calculating the standard deviation values of the percentage shares of FDI – broken down by supplier sources – across regions and industries. Across thirty provinces of China, during the height of round-trip FDI, FDI originating from Taiwan, Japan, and the United States in 1992 and 1993 was more evenly distributed than FDI from Hong Kong and Macao. The regional distribution of FDI is calculated on the basis of both the percentage shares of the number of FDI projects and the percentage shares of the value of the FDI projects across the thirty provinces.[67] Thus, the kind of FDI least affected by round-trip FDI is in fact slightly more dispersed. There are no substantial differences in the standard deviation values for the percentage share of FDI distribution across twenty-eight industries – measured on the basis of charter capital of FIEs – between FIEs funded by ECEs and FIEs funded by non-ECEs. In 1995, the standard deviation value for ECEs was 2.7; for non-ECEs, it was 3.0.[68]

Fourth, data less contaminated by round-trip problems also demonstrate the export dominance of FIEs and the majority controls of FIEs by foreign firms. Fujian province, which is located directly across the straits from Taiwan, is also a popular destination of export-oriented FDI, mainly from Taiwan. The likelihood that its FDI data are contaminated by massive round-trip FDI is quite low. FIEs accounted for 36.2 percent of Fujian's exports in 1991, 42.4 percent in 1992, and 51.7 percent in 1993. The foreign equity stake in FIEs in Fujian is substantial. In 1993, the equity of foreign firms, as a proportion of the equity

[67] In 1992, the standard deviation value of the percentage distribution of Hong Kong and Macao FDI across thirty Chinese provinces is 5.3 and 7.3, for project number and project value, respectively. These two values for Taiwanese FDI are 4.3 and 5.3; for Japanese FDI, 4.5 and 4.8; and for American FDI, 4.9 and 5.0. Data are provided in State Statistical Bureau (1994a).

[68] Calculated on the basis of data provided in Office of Third Industrial Census (1997).

capital of FIEs in Fujian province, was 71.1 percent (Fujian Commission of Foreign Economy and Trade and Fujian Statistical Bureau 1994, pp. 76–78 and p. 93). Jilin province, located on China's northeast border with North Korea and populated by heavy industry SOEs, is not a magnet to either real or fake FDI. Yet in 1993, exports by FIEs already accounted for 40 percent of the exports from that province.[69] Furthermore, foreign majority controls are prevalent among FIEs that are unlikely to be funded by round-trip FDI. In 1997, the average foreign equity stake of India-funded FIEs in China was 79.9 percent, and of Indonesia-funded FIEs, it was 75 percent.[70]

Last, there is no evidence that round-trip FDI alone is responsible for the large-scale substitution of contractual alliances for export-oriented FIEs in export production. This kind of substitution has occurred in Guangdong province but also on a massive scale in Fujian province. In 1988, Fujian exported $33.7 million via export processing; in 1992, the figure declined to $28.5 million. During the same period, exports by FIEs in Fujian grew from $122.5 million to $1.3 billion (Fujian Statistical Bureau 1994).

Does the presence of round-trip FDI invalidate our argument? This is the conceptual aspect of the issue. I defer this discussion to Chapter 3, after the analytical framework of the book has been presented. But suffice it to mention here that round-trip FDI is fully compatible with – and indeed it is an economic phenomenon that is predicted by – my analytical framework. Round-trip FDI itself is not a mere statistical phenomenon. To the extent that round-trip FDI entails some costs to a firm engaging in it, we want to know what drives a firm to invest in this rather roundabout way. To be sure, the favorable tax and other benefits granted to FIEs are one factor motivating this type of capital flow, but there are also other factors at work, such as the insecurity of private property rights and the entry restrictions on private firms. These institutional factors, which I examine in greater detail in subsequent chapters, drive up round-trip FDI as well as one-way genuine FDI. Round-trip FDI is a symptom of the very institutional dynamics I am examining in this book.

UNUSUAL FDI PATTERNS?

Are the FDI patterns described above unusual? What I have done so far is show that some of the patterns seem to be different from empirical patterns elsewhere

---

[69] Export data of FIEs in Jilin province are from Jilin Bureau of External Economic Cooperation and Jilin Statistical Bureau (1994) and export data of Jilin province as a whole are from State Statistical Bureau (1996a).

[70] Data on equity ratios in this section are available from State Statistical Bureau (1999a).

and, to some extent, different from theoretical expectations. But this does not, in and of itself, establish that these patterns are unusual. One may easily argue that China is distinct from other countries and thus its FDI patterns ought to be different as well. For example, China's market is large and therefore it should be more attractive to foreign investors. China may be distinct but being distinct does not necessarily mean that it is unusual.

The idea that China's FDI patterns are unusual implies that some of the common explanations may not fully account for these patterns. If so, these patterns become "puzzles" that a social scientist should attempt to solve. What I do next is show that some of the prevailing explanations may not be fully compatible with China's FDI patterns. This is not to suggest that these explanations are either adequate or inadequate as general explanations for FDI. Indeed, an important reason to examine these explanations against China's FDI patterns is to show that there are some unusual features in the Chinese economy that may have led to a number of anomalies in its FDI patterns. The analytical task is to understand these anomalies better, not to discard the existing theories. There is also no presumption that the explanations explored below are universally accepted. The purpose is to consider all the alternative explanations first before reaching the conclusion that China's FDI patterns are unusual. For this reason, not all of the explanations examined below have been linked to China's FDI inflows or its patterns by previous researchers. Last, as will become evident during the course of the discussion, one of the reasons why a prevailing explanation may not apply well is not necessarily because it is wrong, but because it may be wrong for a research question that is formulated in a specific fashion. Whenever possible, I define the research issues as specifically as possible.

Macro Fundamentals

Researchers and business analysts have suggested that China's macro fundamentals are an important determinant of its FDI inflows. These macro fundamentals include political stability, rapid market expansion, a cheap but disciplined labor force, and its financing requirements. In part due to the perception that the reasons for China's large FDI inflows are obvious, the statements that link these factors to China's FDI inflows are rather general and often are made in an off-hand fashion.[71] What I do below is specify more clearly how these macro

---

[71] For example, Louis Kraar of *Fortune* writes, "Drawn by China's capable pool of low-cost labor and its growing potential as a market that contains one-fifth of the world's population, foreign investors continue to pour money into the PRC." See Kraar (1994). Luo writes, "China's attractiveness to foreigners, however, remains bright. First, China's growth performance is

fundamentals may have affected China's FDI inflows and determine whether their postulated effects on China's FDI are consistent with our portrayal of China's FDI patterns. I focus on political stability, market size, and financing needs here and defer the discussion on labor costs to the section on rationales for FDI arrangements.

FDI explanations centering on political stability and market size are most useful when the aim is to understand changes in the *absolute* level of FDI or the FDI attractiveness of one country relative to other countries. As shown in Table 1.1, the level of FDI in China increased dramatically in the early 1990s. In 1989, inward FDI amounted to $3.4 billion, but in 1992, it shot up to $11 billion and in 1994 to $33.8 billion. Several things occurred during this period. First, the bloody crackdown on student demonstrators in 1989 obviously caused foreign investors to be concerned about China's political stability. This concern was alleviated substantially in 1992, when Deng Xiaoping made a dramatic trip to South China and called for further opening to the outside world. Second, after emerging from an austerity program instituted in 1989 to cool inflation, China's economic performance began to pick up in 1991 and 1992. This changed the sentiment of foreign investors about the future of the economy. It was around this time that Lawrence Summers, then the chief economist at the World Bank, made his famous prediction – on the basis of a purchasing power parity estimate of China's GNP – that China could surpass the United States in total output by 2014 (Summers 1992). Against this background, the level of FDI inflows increased dramatically, and during the 1990s, China became far more attractive to foreign investors than, say, India. Studies that show an empirical correlation between market size and FDI rely on some measures of the absolute level of FDI.[72]

Political stability and market expansions, however, are unable to fully explain the sharp rise in the *relative* level of China's FDI inflows. (The relative level refers to FDI as a share of total fixed asset investments.) These two positive macro fundamentals should appeal to *both foreign and domestic investors*. This point can be illustrated by looking at the United States in Table 1.2. During the 1990s, the United States experienced rapid economic growth, which presumably would have increased the interest of foreign investors. Indeed, the absolute level of FDI increased, from $49 billion annually during the 1986–91 period to $77.5 billion annually during the 1992–98 period, but the relative ratio hardly changed. It was 6.5 percent during the 1986–91 period and 6.9 percent during

---

outstanding. With an average annual GDP growth of 12 percent in 1991–96, China is one of the fastest growing economies in the world" (Luo 1998).

[72] For a study on FDI locational issues in China, see Cheng and Kwan (2000).

the 1992–98 period. This is because domestic firms, attracted by the same expanding market, increased their investments as well.

Contrast this situation with China. As shown in column 3 of Table 1.1, the FDI/fixed asset investment ratio rose from 2.9 percent in 1989 to 7.5 percent in 1992 and 17.1 percent in 1994. The FDI/nonstate fixed asset investment ratio increased even more dramatically, from 8.0 percent in 1989 to 23.5 percent in 1992 and 39.2 percent in 1994. As shown in Table 1.2, China's FDI/capital formation ratio increased from an average of 2.9 percent during the 1986–91 period to 13.1 percent during the 1992–98 period.

Why would expanding opportunities created by China's rapid economic growth and political stability appeal to foreign investors more than to domestic firms? There is no compelling reason why domestic firms in China, attracted by the same propitious macro fundamentals, should not have been strongly motivated to increase their investments. To be sure, the relationship between the growth of FDI and the growth of domestic investments does not have to be one-to-one, but it is important to stress that the change in the relative level of FDI between 1989 and 1994 was dramatic. In 1994, the FDI/nonstate fixed asset investment ratio (39.2 percent) was almost five times that in 1989 (8.0 percent). Clearly, something else was at work to drive up the relative level of FDI so quickly in the 1990s. A simple invocation of China's expanding market size as a driver of FDI inflows – defined in this book as the relative level of FDI – is not an adequate explanation. Other explanations such as FDI liberalization – to be explored next – and the inability of efficient domestic firms to secure financing – to be analyzed throughout the book – have to be considered.

One reason for a high FDI/capital formation ratio can be a low savings rate, which creates difficulties for domestic firms to finance investment activities. In a number of African countries, the savings rate is low or even negative, necessitating imports of capital from abroad. FDI is a form of capital and the FDI/capital formation ratio can be very high if FDI makes up for a savings-investment shortfall. Chad and Uganda, for example, had a high FDI/capital formation ratio in the 1990s; at the same time their savings rate was negative (Chad) or low (Uganda).[73]

The need for FDI as a source of financing is definitely not present in China.[74] Economists have noted that – but few have studied why – China has consistently

---

[73] FDI and macroeconomic data can be found in standard sources. See, e.g., United Nations Conference on Trade and Development (1999) and World Bank (2000).

[74] This discussion does not assume that it is correct to view FDI as purely a source of financing. Most FDI researchers tend to view FDI as a source of know-how and technology. My discussion here is designed to illustrate that FDI in China, for sure, should not be viewed as merely a financing source.

generated surpluses on its current *and* its capital accounts, leading to a large accumulation of foreign exchange reserves and suggesting that it is a net capital *exporter*. Paul Krugman has noted that this combination of surpluses on both its current and capital accounts is "a curious development policy" (Krugman 1999). An important reason behind China's capital account surplus was its huge FDI inflows when the country was not short of capital.

The rapid increase in the FDI/capital formation ratio in the 1990s coincided closely with a rise in China's savings rate. China has one of the highest savings rates in the world. Between 1986 and 1992, the Chinese savings rate was around 36 percent, and between 1994 and 1997 it rose to 42 percent.[75] The puzzle is that China's reliance on FDI deepened at the very time when the capital shortage was apparently being alleviated. In the 1990s, China was not only one of the world's largest recipients of FDI, but it was also one of the largest capital exporters. Its current account surplus, as a percentage share of its GDP, came to 2.7 percent, as shown in Table 1.2. This dynamic means that FDI has not contributed to an increase in China's capital formation. This is quite different from patterns in Thailand and Malaysia, as noted by Lardy (2002, p. 120). As of October 2001, China's official foreign exchange reserves exceeded $200 billion. A large portion of China's official foreign exchange reserves, according to an article in the *Wall Street Journal*, was invested in treasury bonds issued by the U.S. government (Smith 1998). If the high and rising FDI/capital formation ratio was due to a lack of financing of domestic firms, a shortage of funds was not the reason. The reason, as I detail in the next chapter, has to do with how the Chinese financial institutions choose to *allocate* China's vast pool of capital.

FDI Liberalization

A more plausible explanation for the rapid increase in the FDI/capital formation ratio in the 1990s is a policy decision: In 1992, the Chinese government decided to significantly liberalize its FDI regime. The government removed a number of sectoral and regional restrictions on FDI: It decentralized approval authority from the central government to local governments, and it signed a number of agreements with the United States that committed the Chinese government to increase market access and strengthen intellectual property rights protection.[76]

---

[75] The savings rate is defined as the difference between GDP and final consumption divided by GDP. The data are reported in State Statistical Bureau (1998a).

[76] For more details, see Lardy (1994).

The FDI liberalization hypothesis is convincing to explain the general direction of the change in the relative level of FDI; that is, all else being equal, a more liberal FDI regime should be accompanied by a rising FDI/capital formation ratio. The enormous magnitude of the change, that is, a fourfold increase in the FDI/nonstate fixed asset investment ratio within five years between 1989 and 1994, suggests that FDI liberalization could not be the only factor at work. For one thing, even before the 1992 liberalization, China was already very dependent on FDI as measured by the FDI/nonstate fixed asset ratio.

Research on FDI in Japan suggests that the FDI regime is only one of many factors affecting FDI inflows. The Japanese government repealed its 1950 Foreign Investment Law in 1980, which removed all formal restrictions on inward FDI, but FDI inflows did not increase significantly until ten years later, and even today Japan remains one of the smallest recipients of inward FDI among the industrialized countries. There are many structural barriers in the Japanese economy that constrain FDI, regardless of the characteristics of the FDI regime. These structural barriers range from cross shareholdings among Japanese firms, low-cost financing to member firms in the Keiretsu system, legally permissible collusion among Japanese firms, the design of the patent system, and idiosyncrasies in the Japanese labor market.[77]

Unlike in Japan, the effect of the FDI liberalization in 1992 in China was not only immediate but also enormous. The rapidity of the growth of this ratio suggests that there may have been structural "facilitators" of FDI in the Chinese economy, which lay latent during the period of FDI controls in the 1980s but which were unleashed quickly once the FDI controls were attenuated. The FDI liberalization, in and of itself, did not give rise to these structural forces in the Chinese economy. As an analyst, one needs to go beyond FDI liberalization to understand these underlying structural forces.

The fact that an economy is open to FDI does not mean that it will be inundated with FDI. A liberal FDI regime permits FDI to come in, but the actual materialization of FDI depends on many other factors. Taiwan provides an example. Beginning in the mid-1980s, the government began to deregulate FDI controls by abolishing local content requirements, removing caps on profit remittances, relaxing foreign exchange regulations, and streamlining the FDI approval process.[78] However, during the 1986–91 period, the annual average FDI/capital formation ratio in Taiwan was 3.6 percent, and it declined to 2.2 percent during the 1992–98 period.

---

[77] See Encarnation and Mason (1990), Lawrence (1993), Dunning (1996), Weinstein (1996), and McDaniel (1999).

[78] For a review of the FDI regime in Taiwan, see United States Department of Commerce (1995) and Economist Intelligence Unit (1995).

Similarly, the United States is completely open to FDI, but its FDI dependency is far smaller than that of China. An international comparison here is revealing because China's FDI regime was not particularly liberal in the 1990s despite its substantial liberalization in 1992. Table 1.2 shows that in terms of ease of foreign acquisitions, China ranked fifth from the bottom among countries included in the table. In terms of business environment, it ranked forty-fourth among sixty countries surveyed by the Economist Intelligence Unit during the 1996–2000 period. China was more dependent on FDI than some countries with more liberal FDI policies. This is not to suggest that FDI liberalization does not matter, but that FDI liberalization is not the only determinant of FDI.

Apart from FDI-specific policies and regulations, the quality of a country's institutions also affects its FDI. Corruption is generally thought to deter FDI. Wei (1996b), based on a statistical analysis of bilateral investment from fourteen source countries to forty-five countries during the 1990–91 period, reports that corruption deters inward FDI in the same way as income taxes on MNCs, and the corruption effect is large.[79] From this point of view, China's substantial reliance on FDI is surprising. Table 1.2 reports the corruption perception index devised by Transparency International in 1997. China is ranked forty-first among fifty-two countries. According to a survey by the Political and Economic Risk Consultancy conducted in the mid-1990s, China was rated by foreign managers as the most corrupt on a list of eleven Asian countries that included some of the most notoriously corrupt countries in the world, such as India and Indonesia.[80]

---

[79] It should be mentioned that Wei (1996b) finds no East Asian or Chinese exceptionalism; that is, he finds that the deterrent effect of corruption holds both for the East Asian region as a whole and for China. One problem with this finding is that Wei excludes non-OECD countries as suppliers of FDI in his regression analysis. This means that 50 percent of China's FDI inflows are not included in his study. There is a more substantive problem as well. The East Asia regional dummy and China dummy in his regression analysis can incorporate effects that have nothing to do with corruption. For example, if Hong Kong firms possess genuine competitive advantages to invest in China over American firms, then the China dummy variable would incorporate this effect and would be negatively related to FDI investments from the United States. The reason is that American firms would "cede" China to other Asian firms because they would rationally decide that they cannot compete with Asian firms in certain product lines. Thus, the negative East Asia and China dummies can capture this market-ceding effect on OECD firms, that is, East Asia and China deter OECD investments because OECD firms do not think that they can win there. This would have nothing to do with sensitivity to corruption in the region. One observes similar dynamics in Latin America. For example, American telecommunications firms are not nearly as active as Telefonica, a Spanish telecommunications firm, in acquiring assets in the region because they may believe that Telefonica is better positioned to deal with many of the associated macroeconomic and political risks in Latin America.

[80] The survey results are reported in Li and Lian (1999).

A Cultural Perspective

Researchers attribute the preponderance of SME investors in China to the large FDI inflows from the ECEs. The idea is that the ECE investors possess cultural and relationship advantages when investing in China; in a poor legal system, cultural and ethnic proximity helps reduce the normally high transaction costs of doing business (Wei 1995). This reasoning provides a good starting point to analyze the specific effects of cultural affinity on FDI.

The cultural perspective – as well as a perspective stressing the influence of geographic proximity – is most convincing when explaining the country composition of China's FDI inflows, that is, why China gets more FDI from the ECEs, as opposed to, say, FDI from the United Kingdom (after controlling appropriately for a number of relevant factors).[81] One caveat, however, is that FDI from the ECEs has accounted for a far higher share of China's total FDI inflows than it did in Taiwan at a comparable stage, even though overseas Chinese investors should possess the same cultural and ethnic advantages when investing in Taiwan. Between 1952 and 1995, Hong Kong investments accounted for only 8 percent of total FDI inflows into Taiwan and overseas Chinese investors accounted for about 13 percent (Investment Commission of Ministry of Economic Affairs 1995). (The 13 percent figure includes a portion of FDI from Hong Kong that was credited to overseas Chinese companies based in Hong Kong.) In contrast, during the 1979–99 period, FDI from Hong Kong alone accounted for almost 50 percent of China's total FDI inflows.

To be sure, Hong Kong FDI data may incorporate investments of firms headquartered in other countries, including those based in China, and thus they may not accurately track the FDI of "overseas" Chinese. If we assume that half of Hong Kong's FDI originated from indigenous firms in Hong Kong, Hong Kong's share of China's FDI inflows would still be several multiples of Hong Kong's share of its FDI in Taiwan. In addition, FDI inflows from economies less afflicted with statistical problems – such as Taiwan and Macao – have also been similarly large in China. Between 1988 and 1999, FDI from Taiwan amounted to 9.3 percent of China's total FDI inflows and for a number of years in the 1990s, FDI from Macao – population 400,000 with a GDP of only $6.7 billion – was equivalent to 2 percent of China's FDI inflows. Despite its size, in 1994

---

[81] Many causes may lead to greater investment flows among culturally similar countries. Cultural familiarity may reduce transaction costs associated with cross-country investments. Another mechanism is that some of the investments may be motivated on altruistic grounds. For example, after 1992, ECE entrepreneurs not only invested in China but also donated schools and hospitals to their ancestral homes and villages. I owe this observation to Pieter Bottelier, the former chief of resident mission of the World Bank in China.

firms based in Macao invested $509 million in China. This was about 70 per-cent of Korean investments, 197 percent of German investments, 74 percent of British investments, or 236 percent of Canadian investments.[82] That said, the general claim that China should receive more FDI from the ECEs than from other sources because of the cultural and geographic proximity is correct; the question concerns the magnitude of the FDI from the ECEs.

One could extend the cultural perspective to explain the size of individual FDI projects in China. A logical implication of the idea that shared culture can reduce transaction costs – which are fixed and large – is that on average the ECE investors should be smaller than the non-ECE investors. This is because both small and large ECE investors can overcome China's legal imperfections, while only large non-ECE investors can do so. Thus, one would find both small and large investors from the ECEs but only large non-ECE investors in China. This is not borne out by the data. On average, FDI projects funded by investors from Japan, the United States, and Korea were not substantially larger – and in some cases they were smaller – than projects funded by investors from Hong Kong and Macao, as noted previously. While ECE investors for sure command a cultural advantage compared with non-ECE investors, it does not appear to be the case that the ability of SME investors to invest in China is due exclusively to this cultural advantage. Firms from outside the ECEs seem to be able to operate small projects in China as well, and the preponderance of SME investors is not at all limited to ECE investors.

The cultural perspective also produces some anomalies. For example, as noted previously, there is some evidence that smaller firms in Hong Kong tended to have a higher propensity to invest in China than larger firms in Hong Kong. The cultural perspective would not predict this outcome. A small firm based in Hong Kong possesses just as much cultural advantage as a large firm based in Hong Kong, and on the cultural dimension both firms should be equally predisposed to invest in China. Conceptually, the cultural and ethnic advantages should help both large and small firms based in the ECEs. Empirical evidence from other countries suggests that cultural and ethnic affinities between home and host countries do not increase the investment propensity of smaller firms. For example, by looking at FDI flows from the United States to Britain and Canada, two Anglo-Saxon countries with common linguistic and cultural ties with the United States, FDI researchers report that large U.S. firms dominate the

---

[82] Calculated from data provided in Ministry of Foreign Trade and Economic Cooperation (1995). Unlike the Cayman Islands and Bermuda, small islands that also have an outsized capital position abroad, Macao is not known as a tax haven. As evidence, Macao holds no investment position anywhere in the world outside of China.

population of American firms investing in these two countries. American firms with multiplant operations and firms with a preponderant sales position in an industry are most likely to be investors in Canada and the United Kingdom.[83]

The cultural perspective seems to have a limited explanatory power when it is applied to other aspects of China's FDI patterns. For example, the cultural perspective is not particularly useful to explain the high FDI/capital formation ratios and the dispersion of FDI across different industries and regions. The reason is that a convincing explanation of these patterns would delve into issues related to the relative advantages foreign firms hold over domestic firms. On this question, the cultural perspective is irrelevant. The cultural affinity of ECE investors gives them an advantage compared with an investor from the United States, but it does not give them a cultural advantage compared with an investor from Guangdong province. An indigenous entrepreneur, by definition, possesses more cultural advantage on his own home turf compared with an investor from an ECE.

A cultural perspective is potentially relevant when it explains a choice between a contractual arrangement and an ownership arrangement for a firm from an ECE. However, the prediction would go in the opposite direction from what is observed in the data. Here, the reasoning offered by Wei (1996a) that cultural affinity reduces transaction costs applies: Because a Hong Kong entrepreneur is familiar with the situation in China in general and in Guangdong province in particular she is in a better position to assess the proclivities of her Chinese partner and she faces fewer contractual hazards. Evidence uncovered by Professor Ezra Vogel in his research on Guangdong province shows that many of the Hong Kong firms return to do business in their ancestral home regions. Half of the export-processing contracts in the Dongguan region of Guangdong were with former Dongguan residents now living in Hong Kong (Vogel 1989, p. 176). Trust was easily established. Cultural familiarity and detailed knowledge of the region, not to mention strong family ties, should promote contracting as a business practice. This is true elsewhere. Research on Italy shows that social capital – trust established by ethnic and regional ties – facilitates the more frequent use of longer-term contracts such as checks rather than cash (Guiso, Sapienza, and Zingales 2001).

This discussion is relevant to an issue that has surfaced many times in this chapter: Do investor characteristics affect FDI patterns in China? If they do, then a supply perspective makes more sense. If they do not, a demand perspective may be called for. One may wish to point out that many of the investors from Hong Kong are agency firms on behalf of Western retailers, such as Gap or

---

[83] See Caves (1974) and Meredith (1984).

Nike. Could this explain the predominance of ownership arrangements in labor-intensive industries in China in the 1990s and that of contractual arrangements in Taiwan in the 1960s?

The answer is no. As has been pointed out, cultural affinity would favor contracting (or at least it would not be averse to contracting), while cultural distance would favor ownership arrangements. This logic would predict more FDI arrangements in Taiwan and more contractual arrangements in China, precisely the opposite from the observed patterns. As an empirical point, in the 1960s, the firms that sourced from Taiwan were Japanese trading corporations, which controlled marketing access to Western retailers, just like many of the Hong Kong firms today. Mitsubishi, for example, actively sponsored Taiwanese entrepreneurs wishing to enter into footwear production, similar to the functions provided by Hong Kong firms to export-processing firms in Guangdong province. There is no evidence that either a cultural affinity between buyer and supplier or an agency function itself is fundamentally incompatible with contractual arrangements. Thus, it is analytically more meaningful to examine those conditions that affect the feasibility of contract production, not who is doing the direct investments.

Rationales for FDI Arrangements

As FDI rose in the 1990s, contractual capital inflows declined substantially. One possibility is that in the 1990s many foreign investors took over export production facilities previously owned and independently run by Chinese entrepreneurs. To understand the rise of export-oriented FDI in labor-intensive industries, it is important to examine the dynamics behind this large-scale substitution between equity and contractual arrangements. Below I review a number of explanations – all based on straightforward economic and business rationales – to see whether they may account for this substitution. But first let me explain why the demise of contractual capital inflows is puzzling.

The Puzzling Development of Contractual Alliances. FDI researchers typically begin their inquiries by assuming that a FDI decision is not a forgone conclusion. They ask, "Why not contract with another firm?" In a study on FDI in labor-intensive industries, Lou Wells observes, "Two concepts are rather widely held among researchers concerned with foreign direct investment: (1) to survive abroad, a firm needs some kind of advantage over local competitors, and (2) a firm must have some reason to internalize that advantage through ownership rather than contracting with another firm" (Wells 1993, p. 182). FDI is widely viewed as embodying technology and know-how, and under certain conditions an FDI ownership arrangement may be thought to be a more efficient way to transfer technology and know-how from the parent firm located in the home country to its affiliate located in a host country. In his classic formulation, Stephen Hymer – widely regarded as one of the first theorists on FDI – argues that FDI is "an *instrument* which allows business firms to *transfer* capital, technology, and organizational skills from one country to another" (emphasis added to illustrate the key premises in the conceptualization of FDI as an economic phenomenon) (Hymer 1970, p. 443).

Analyzing FDI thus requires specifying both the kind of "technology and organizational skills" in question and the conditions under which this transfer cannot be effected contractually. In this section, I show that a perspective narrowly based on know-how transfer cannot explain the preponderance of ownership arrangements in China. The kind of technology and know-how involved in many of the labor-intensive and low-tech FDI projects in China can theoretically be transferred through a contractual mechanism, and there is ample empirical evidence that the contractual mechanism has been used successfully to transfer this type of technology and know-how in other countries.

Let me stress that the absolute decline of contractual alliances, from $546 million in 1988 to $179 million in 1994, presents a pattern sharply different from that observed in other developing countries. In other developing countries, such as Mauritius, foreign investors initially dominated the production and exporting of labor-intensive products, but local entrepreneurs gradually learned the crafts and mastered the skills, and over time they displaced the foreign producers.[84] One can also see this "displacement" effect in Asia in the 1970s and 1980s. Naya and Ramstetter (1988, p. 62) present time-series data of shares of manufactured exports by foreign firms in three economies, Singapore, Taiwan, and Thailand, in the 1970s and 1980s. In all these economies, the shares of foreign firm exports declined over time. Data from Taiwan show the same trend (Ranis and Schive 1985, p. 109).

To be sure, China started out in the early 1980s with an initially low level of entrepreneurship because of the systematic suppression of the private sector during the Cultural Revolution. But it should be stressed that FDI inflows only became significant in 1992, some fourteen years after the economic reform. Also, it is the direction of the change, not just the level, in the FDI inflows that is puzzling. From a know-how point of view and based on the experience of other economies, one would expect an initial dominance of FDI arrangements in China, when Chinese entrepreneurs were just beginning to produce for the world market, but a rise in contractual alliances over time. In China, the sequence

---

[84] The experience of Mauritius is covered in Wells (1993).

was reversed. Are Chinese entrepreneurs losing know-how and skills over time as the economy develops and as China's export capacity expands rapidly? This scenario would seem highly implausible. The timing of the demise of contractual alliances suggests that it cannot be explained by FDI liberalization; the decline began in 1989 before the large-scale FDI liberalization in 1992. Furthermore, as shown in Table 1.1, beginning in 1997 contractual alliances began to rise again, very sharply, even though during this period FDI policies became more liberal.

If the direction of the change in the Chinese command of know-how is puzzling, the preponderance of FDI arrangements, which would imply a low level of Chinese know-how, is also not easy to explain, as evidenced by the fact that FDI can be found in industries in which indigenous entrepreneurs should be, ex ante, quite strong. As pointed out before, FDI in China is distributed quite evenly across Chinese industries. FDI is found not only in modern industries (such as automobiles or electronics), but also in traditional industries at which Chinese entrepreneurs have excelled for hundreds of years. Domestic entrepreneurs should possess adequate or even superior know-how in these industries compared with foreign firms.

An example here is the Chinese arts and crafts industry, which produces ivory and jade sculptures, carpets, personal ornaments, silk handicrafts, porcelain, cloisonné, and so on.[85] This is an indigenous industry par excellence. Even in this industry, foreign firms have established a sizable presence, with some 1,504 manufacturing FIEs operating in 1995. It is also interesting that one-third of the foreign investors (518) came from outside the ECEs. Both ECE and non-ECE investors were able to establish majority equity controls over these FIEs (73.7 percent and 63.5 percent, respectively).[86] While one might conceive of scenarios in which ECE investors also excelled in the traditional arts and crafts, it is not obvious why domestic entrepreneurs would be inferior to non-ECE investors.

Putative Benefits of FDI Arrangements (1): Host Firm. The prevalence of equity arrangements *at the expense* of contractual arrangements in China suggests that there are putative benefits associated with FDI in excess of contract export production. Let me postulate what these benefits might be, from the perspective of both the recipient of FDI and the investor. For the purpose of this discussion, I focus on export-oriented labor-intensive production. The FDI literature is fairly clear about the benefits associated with equity arrangements when production

---

[85] These are industry level nos. 4311 to 4319 in the Chinese Industry Classification Standard.
[86] The data are from All China Marketing Research Co. Ltd. (1999).

involves substantial use of proprietary know-how and intangible assets. Since FDI arrangements in China are pervasive in the manufacturing and export of products such as garments, furniture, and leather and fur products, on the surface, the prevalence of FDI arrangements must be due to benefits other than transferring R&D content and proprietary and intangible assets.

The following benefits are among those often associated with equity arrangements in the production and export of labor-intensive products. To the Chinese firms, they are access to overseas markets, superior quality controls provided by foreign producers, and capital. Two questions arise regarding these benefits. The first is whether or not FDI arrangements have provided these benefits – in excess of the costs of entering into the arrangements. The second question is whether or not these benefits are *uniquely* provided by FDI arrangements, that is, whether the same benefits could have been provided by a contractual alliance with a foreign firm if such an alliance had been viable. To put it another way, on straightforward economic and business grounds, are there reasons to believe that contractual alliances are intrinsically and massively inferior to FDI arrangements in providing the aforementioned benefits?

The answer to the first question is yes. The fact that export production in China has grown rapidly and that goods manufactured in China are now readily available in the West is prima facie evidence that FDI arrangements have indeed brought about these benefits. The second question is difficult to answer because it asks for a counterfactual scenario. We have to rely on analytical reasoning and empirical evidence from other economies to make an evaluation. The question is simple: Can straightforward economic and business rationales account for the demise of contractual alliances between 1988 and 1997 in labor-intensive industries and for the substantial substitution of contractual alliances with FDI arrangements? The answer is no. The reason is that in these industries the functions of a foreign firm making the investment and those of a foreign buyer do not differ fundamentally. Here, a description of the role of a foreign contractual buyer in Taiwan's bicycle industry is illuminating (Chu 1997, p. 60):

> The role of foreign buyers here resembled very much that of the multinational corporation (MNC) making direct investment in the LDCs [less developed countries], except that the foreign buyers did not commit their capital directly. For they both initiated the process, helped the local producers to set up production, monitored progress, checked the product, offered financing via issuing letters of credit, and marketed the products in developed countries, etc. The local producers were responsible only for the production stage of the whole operation in both cases.

As this quote shows, many of the benefits associated with labor-intensive FDI are not unique to FDI. A contractual alliance, by definition, provides a Chinese producer with access to overseas markets. Under such an alliance, a foreign firm places an export order with a Chinese producer, specifies the product characteristics and delivery schedules, and, under certain arrangements, extends buyer credits to the Chinese producer in the form of inputs or machinery. In a pure processing operation, a Chinese producer receives a processing fee but does not take ownership of the outputs: The outputs still belong to the foreign firm. After the finished outputs are shipped to the foreign firm, the foreign firm sells them to its customers. What I have just described is an export event. It is true that FDI arrangements provide access to overseas markets, but contractual alliances do so as well.

A foreign firm can impose direct quality control and supervision via a contractual alliance. In many developing countries, including China, the foreign firm and the domestic producer coordinate closely on quality controls. Ezra Vogel describes export-processing operations in Guangdong province as follows (Vogel 1989):

> The contracts themselves were relatively simple in the late 1980s. The Hong Kong side supplied the *lai liao* or *san lai* – the materials, the model of what was to be done, and the equipment that must be imported into China. Hong Kong managers remained on site or commuted daily or weekly to train the workers and ensure close attention to management. When necessary, personnel were sent from Hong Kong to repair the machinery or redesign the product to fit changing market conditions.

Another potential benefit associated with FDI is capital. But why does a domestic producer have to obtain capital through equity financing (FDI) and not through other mechanisms? It is important to stress that most FDI researchers would not view FDI as a pure financing mechanism but rather as an arrangement that transfers resources more efficiently than a contractual mechanism. If the only benefit is capital, then we need to ask why other sources of capital are unavailable. It is easy to understand that buyer credits from a foreign firm might be insufficient for a domestic firm wishing to expand its businesses. One reason is that buyer credits typically comprise raw materials or other inputs rather than capital equipment. Second, an indigenous entrepreneur may need more working capital and cash to hire more workers and to pay their wages in order to expand production further.

In theory, an indigenous firm can turn to a local bank to obtain financing. (We already established that there was no shortage of capital, and in fact China exported capital in the amount of 3 percent of GDP every year in the 1990s.)

Indeed, this is how indigenous entrepreneurs in Taiwan financed their export production. As shown in Table 1.5, Taiwan, widely regarded as one of the most successful export economies, did not rely heavily on FDI to produce and export labor-intensive products. According to a study on Taiwan's footwear industry by Brian Levy, a World Bank economist, many of these Taiwanese producers were doing contract work for Japanese trading corporations, which controlled access to Western markets in the same way Hong Kong and Taiwanese firms do today. Japanese firms did not provide any capital, as Levy explains (1991, p. 156, n10):

> There was little need for the Japanese to provide technical or financial support: the technology of footwear production is simple; the initial investment requirements are small; and . . . working capital was made available automatically in both Taiwan and Korea to exporters.

The ability of a domestic entrepreneur to obtain financing is a key factor in making a contractual arrangement feasible. In Chapters 3 and 4, I show that the allocation of capital by China's financial institutions has a substantial impact on the choice between FDI or a contractual arrangement for China's export-oriented private entrepreneurs. A major difference with Korea and Taiwan is that working capital in China is not automatically available to an exporter, if the exporter is a private entrepreneur. In this context, FDI is superior, especially for those private firms that are expanding their production.

Putative Benefits of FDI Arrangements (2): Foreign Investor. Let me turn to the potential benefits of FDI arrangements for a foreign investor. The key point here is not whether the foreign investor should invest in China or in another country; the decision is, given China's attractive fundamentals, whether he should source from a facility in China or invest in and run his own facility in China. This question addresses the advantages and disadvantages of an ownership arrangement versus a contractual arrangement. I borrow insights from institutional economics to illustrate this issue.

Institutional economists explain the superiority of an ownership arrangement in terms of its ability to solve some of the well-known problems besetting contractual arrangements. Many FDI theorists rely on a version of institutional economics to explain the incidence of FDI.[87] The rationale is a familiar one, and the most famous example in the institutional economics literature is the takeover of Fisher Body by General Motors in 1926 to solve a potential

---

[87] See Buckley and Casson (1976). See Caves (1996) for a recent summary of this large literature.

"hold-up" problem.[88] Fisher Body, an automobile supply firm, refused to build a new automobile body plant adjacent to a GM assembly plant, which GM claimed as necessary for production efficiency. Fisher Body feared that because the proposed plant specifically was to serve GM, GM could behave opportunistically toward Fisher Body once the plant was built. GM solved the problem by acquiring Fisher Body.

The Fisher Body takeover case raises a number of issues about how to analyze developments in FDI and contractual capital inflows in China. The case identifies a conceptual imprecision with the often-repeated statement that Hong Kong firms invest in China because labor costs are low. This claim amounts to saying that GM took over Fisher Body because Fisher Body's production costs were low. Clearly, this is not right. The low production costs at Fisher Body explain why GM wanted to do business with Fisher Body, rather than with another firm, but not why GM had to take over Fisher Body. China's low labor – and land – costs do not automatically motivate a Hong Kong firm to *invest* in China; instead, they motivate a Hong Kong firm (or any other firm) *to do more business* with China, as opposed to doing more business with, say, Mexico. China's low labor costs tell us something about the location of a labor-intensive production facility, but not about who owns it. The locational decision is a part of an FDI decision, but it is not all.[89]

To economize on labor costs, a Hong Kong firm has a theoretical choice between sourcing contractually from a facility in China or investing in and directly running a facility in China. Both methods will save labor costs. China's low labor costs, in and of themselves, do not determine the mechanism whereby the Hong Kong firm chooses to save labor costs. An FDI argument based on geographic proximity between the home and host economies has the same shortcoming. A Hong Kong firm is motivated to do more business with China, rather than with Mexico, because China is close by and is culturally familiar. But whether or not it chooses to invest in China or to source contractually from China is a function of other considerations. By the same logic, the idea that import quotas on garments from developing countries motivate investment decisions is also weak. The key decision is a choice between sourcing contractually or owning and operating directly. The quota observation tells us something about the location of a production facility, but it does not tell us anything about who should own the facility.

The second issue illuminated by the Fisher Body example is that those factors that normally hinder contractual arrangements do not arise in labor-intensive

---

[88] The tale of Fisher Body is recounted in Klein, Crawford, and Alchian (1978).

[89] This idea originates from Dunning (1977), as I explain in the next chapter.

industries. Many of the labor-intensive industries are perfectly competitive. In a perfectly competitive industry, switching costs are low or nonexistent; production assets, such as sewing machines or needles, are of a general-purpose kind; and the industry know-how is nonproprietary. In labor-intensive industries, the normally postulated attributes as important for FDI are absent, such as technological intensity, scale economies, entry barriers, and tacit organizational know-how. Indeed, for this reason, general FDI theorists would not normally predict a high incidence of FDI in labor-intensive industries.

The reasoning by institutional economists should not be taken to imply that FDI arrangements in labor-intensive industries are completely absent, but it does imply that an ownership arrangement should not dominate other forms of business alliances established among distinct firms and that a contractual arrangement should be viable in labor-intensive and low-tech industries. From this point of view, the *preponderance,* not the existence, of ownership arrangements in China's labor-intensive and export-oriented industries *in conjunction with* a dramatic demise of contract production is an anomaly that should be explained.

It is often suggested that an ownership arrangement in which production is internalized helps a firm reduce uncertainty and transaction costs. Is it possible that an FDI arrangement confers this benefit on a foreign investor? For example, there are operating risks in China. A local supplier can breach a contract by delivering lower-quality products, making late deliveries, or churning out products with the wrong specifications.

Such operating risks exist, but in a labor-intensive and perfectly competitive industry such risks are unlikely to be so severe as to derail the entire contractual arrangement. One reason is that substitutability in a perfectly competitive industry is very high, which may reduce the incidence of contractual breaches or limit their damage should they occur. The other is that trading firms in Hong Kong have developed many business practices to keep such risks at a minimum level. I have already mentioned direct supervision as a way to ensure quality. In Chapter 4, I present more details about purchasing arrangements in the garment industry that are designed to protect both buyers and suppliers in the case of a contractual breach or a sudden market change. A long-standing sourcing practice is to divide an order among many suppliers and to rely on a stable network of suppliers over a long period of time. If one supplier breaches the contract, the supply is not too seriously disrupted. Also, relying on a network of stable suppliers helps to develop reputational considerations that will constrain opportunistic behavior. Another practice, in the garment industry, is to mix staples with fashion fare when contracting with a supplier. In that way, if the fashion changes unpredictably, the supplier is protected from the vicissitudes of the market.

The other risk is at a legal level. Economists have argued that FDI, as an equity arrangement, provides a safeguard against contractual hazards – that is, those hazards that arise when a foreign firm is subject to unexpected adverse changes in a host nation. For example, a local contractual partner can renegotiate the terms of the contract after the fact or inappropriately capture the profits of past R&D undertaken by the foreign firm. Such problems are likely to be more prevalent in countries that offer poor property rights protection and where the rule of law is underdeveloped. Foreign firms thus favor equity arrangements and majority controls because they have more operating control.[90]

While this is a plausible explanation for the prevalence of ownership arrangements in capital- and technologically intensive industries, it is less plausible when it comes to labor-intensive industries. Contractual sanctity is most important in situations where switching costs are very high, but in a perfectly competitive industry, by definition, switching costs are low. Thus, there is less need to rely on an ownership arrangement to safeguard against a contractual breach. It should be stressed that most of the subcontracting in the export-oriented industries is between ECE firms and Chinese firms. The level of trust is high. In a poor legal system, ethnic and familial ties can serve to solidify contractual arrangements. Finally, as an empirical point, contract production in labor-intensive industries is perfectly compatible with a poor legal system. Korea and Taiwan developed successfully and perfected contract production and exporting in the 1960s and 1970s at a time when their legal systems left much to be desired.

It is important to note that like a production contract between a foreign and domestic firm, FDI is a contract as well. If anything, a foreign firm may prefer a production contract because it is short-term, while an FDI contract is long-term. Under a poor legal regime, economic agents may operate on a short-term horizon as they are not confident about committing to a long-term arrangement. FDI is a safeguard against a specific form of contractual hazard, mainly those that arise when substantial intangible assets are involved in production. For example, a local firm may free ride on the brand name, reputation, and R&D of the foreign firm in situations in which the foreign firm maintains an arm's-length relationship with the local firm. This is the reason why FDI, instead of technological licensing, is found to be prevalent in countries that have a poor intellectual property rights regime (Oxley 1997). However, FDI is not a safeguard against all the contractual hazards that result from a general

---

[90] I thank Professors Pankaj Ghemawat, Tarun Khanna, Dwight Perkins, and Lou Wells for raising this issue.

underdevelopment of the rule of law. Bad laws and ineffective legal enforcement are detrimental to both FDI contracts and production contracts.

So far, I have raised more questions than I have provided answers. My purpose has been to make the case that we need to look at the causes of China's FDI dynamics more closely. Starting in the next chapter, I explain the patterns presented in this chapter. To do so effectively, let me first define certain terms and explain the empirical sources of my information. I then outline the organizational structure of the book.

Throughout this book, I use a number of terms that refer to corporate organizations established by foreign investors in China. A foreign-invested enterprise (FIE) refers to any enterprise domiciled in China, with foreign equity capital at or above 25 percent of the total equity capital of the firm. An FIE can refer either to a wholly owned subsidiary of a foreign firm or to a firm jointly owned by a foreign and a Chinese firm. In this book, a joint venture (JV) refers to any enterprise in China with joint equity interests from foreign and Chinese investors. This conventional Chinese usage is more encompassing than that in Western business studies. JV, in standard business studies, refers to an enterprise (or a project) over which two independent firms have joint and shared controls. Under Chinese usage, a foreign investor can own 99 percent of the equity interest in the firm and the firm will still be classified as a JV. Clearly, in such a JV arrangement, control is no longer shared between the foreign and domestic firms. In the business studies literature, such a firm is typically known as a majority-owned plant, in which the majority shareholder exercises operating control.

An alliance is a broad concept referring to a governance structure in which separate firms enter into agreements of joint decision making. There are myriad forms of alliances among firms, including "jointly owned ventures, licensing relationships, joint R&D programs, co-marketing programs, and partial equity investments" (Gomes-Casseres 1996, p. 35). In our context, the main distinctions fall between ownership alliances such as JVs, on the one hand, and contractual alliances such as technological licensing, leasing, and product processing, on the other. Under an ownership alliance, two or more firms have an equity stake and jointly make decisions about all aspects of operations. Under a contractual alliance, the separate firms have a nonequity relationship with each other, but that relationship can involve intense and close interactions over a long period of time. Also joint decision making may be limited to certain areas, such as product designs, quality controls, and technological developments, rather than encompassing the entire spectrum of decision making.

The term multinational corporation (MNC), as used in this book, is indistinguishable from a foreign firm. Usually, MNCs conjure up the image of corporate giants operating in many nations. One of the distinct characteristics of FDI flows into China is that firms based in ethnically Chinese economies (ECEs) have supplied a large portion of the FDI. Many of these firms are quite small, and China may be the only overseas location in which they operate. For the sake of economy of words, such investing firms are also referred to as MNCs in this book.

Empirical materials for this book come from two main sources. First, my research assistant and I conducted some thirty interviews between 1998 and 2001 in Beijing, Hong Kong, Shunde (in Guangdong province), Shanghai, and Suzhou (in Jiangsu province). To arrive at the demand perspective of FDI, I interviewed Chinese managers in JVs or managers in Chinese firms that have invested in JVs with foreign firms. Some of these interviews formed the basis for a number of the case studies in this book. One difficulty of conducting extremely detailed case studies in China is the paucity of company-level data. All my case studies are supplemented by data – on financial performance, the structure of shareholdings, and so on – from other sources.

The other source consists mainly of data from a variety of channels. FDI flow and stock data are from familiar sources, such as the *Chinese Statistical Yearbook* for various years. Statistics on the details of FIE operations are drawn from the *Third Industrial Census*, conducted in 1995 (the previous two industrial censuses were conducted in 1975 and 1985). By far, this is the most comprehensive compilation of financial, employment, and product data on Chinese firms. Prior to publication of the *Third Industrial Census*, information on FIE operations was scattered and incomplete, preventing systematic analyses. Another important source of data on FIEs is a database (hitherto referred to as the FIE database), as part of the 1995 census, compiled by the All China Marketing Research Corporation, a consulting arm of the Chinese State Statistical Bureau.[91] However, unlike the *Third Industrial Census*, the data here are at the firm level. The FIE database contains a number of performance and balance sheet indicators of *all industrial* FIEs operating in China as of December 31, 1995. Thus, it presents the most detailed and most disaggregated depiction of FIEs to date.

---

[91] According to the company brochure, it boasts the most up-to-date commercial information and a nationwide data collection and analysis network. The FIE database was purchased from this consulting firm. There is no discernible bias in the data despite the commercial nature of its provenance. The data are unprocessed. I have aggregated some of the data to an industry level to confirm that they are consistent with the data in the *Third Industrial Census*.

To the best of my knowledge, it has never been analyzed, either in China or in the West. The drawback, however, is that more recent data are not available in the same detail. This hampers an analysis of more recent trends. The other drawback is that it only includes firms with an independent accounting status. I address issues related to this drawback in the appendix to this chapter.

I have also relied on a large sample survey to present evidence of the attitudes of Chinese local officials toward FDI. With cooperation from the Research Center for Contemporary China at Peking University, in 1999 I designed a questionnaire survey – called the Local Leadership Survey in this book – that examines the attitudes of Chinese local officials toward various aspects of FDI. The FDI survey was a part of a larger survey on environmental issues, but officials targeted for the survey were from a wide cross-section of local governments, not just officials from the environmental agencies. For each city, 200 officials were selected. The sample included 1,444 local government officials in eight cities.[92] Most of the officials (85.9 percent) represented in the survey are middle-level officials, that is, at the division level of the city governments. The survey was implemented between January and July 1999. The response rate was 90 percent. To ensure honesty, accuracy, and a high response rate, researchers from the Research Center for Contemporary China closely supervised the entire survey process.

This book comprises seven chapters, including the current chapter. Chapter 2 lays out an analytical framework to interpret various FDI patterns in China. I call this framework an institutional foundation argument. Such a coinage is meant to convey the idea that China's FDI patterns are heavily influenced by characteristics of its financial and economic institutions. Chapter 3 describes various problems in China's corporate sector. Chapters 4 through 6 apply the institutional foundation argument to analyses of FDI inflows. Chapter 4 examines the impact of the political pecking order on FDI involving mainly nonstate firms. Chapter 5 looks at FDI flows involving SOEs in China. Chapter 6 explores China's notorious economic fragmentation and the effects of economic fragmentation on FDI. Chapter 7 concludes the study by offering a number of broad analytical and policy implications from our analysis of FDI.

---

[92] These cities are Shanghai, Guangzhou, Shenyang, Chengdu, Lanzhou, Zibo, Wenzhou, and Zhangjiagang. This is a good mix of cities, ranging from very big (Shanghai) to relatively small cities such as Zibo and Wenzhou. Also, the range of private sector development is wide among these eight cities. Shenyang is a bastion of SOEs while Wenzhou has a very advanced private sector.

Appendix to Chapter 1: Data Issues *in the* Third Industrial Census

The data reported in Table 1.4 are based on the *Third Industrial Census* conducted in 1995. It is the most complete data source available. One drawback is that it is based on data reported by firms with an "independent accounting system." Firms in this category maintain their own financial accounts, and these firms account for 85 percent of the industrial output value. My main concern is whether the census includes all the export data. If those firms lacking an independent accounting status were to produce a large portion of China's export products, then there would be an upward bias in the data on the FIEs' export shares. This is unlikely to happen for two reasons. One is that direct exporting is done only by large firms, and all the large firms have an independent accounting status. One way to show this is to examine the plausibility of an estimate of FIEs' export shares in China's total manufactured exports, which assumes that the omitted firms from the *Third Industrial Census* directly export the same proportion of their output as those firms included in the census. Lemoine (2000, p. 21) supplies such an estimate and shows that FIEs' exports as a percentage share of China's manufactured exports were 41 percent in 1997. This is lower than the 51.2 percent as reported in the *Third Industrial Census* for 1995. If we rule out the possibility that FIEs' export share declined between 1995 and 1997, then the difference should be attributed to different statistical reporting procedures.

It is almost certain that Lemoine's estimate is too low (and it is likely that the 51.2 percent figure is too high, as explained below). One clue is the figure she cites from the Chinese sources that FIEs' share of China's total exports was 55 percent. It is impossible that FIEs' share of China's manufactured exports should exceed their share of China's manufactured exports. During the 1980s and much of the 1990s, the government did not allow the exporting of natural resources and major agricultural products by nonstate firms, including FIEs. FIEs were also not allowed to set up dedicated trading concerns. FIEs were allowed and indeed encouraged to export their own output. For this reason, at least the direction of the data as reported in the *Third Industrial Census* is more accurate than Lemoine's estimate. While FIEs accounted for 51.2 percent of China's manufactured exports, they accounted for only 31.5 percent of China's total exports. For the same reason, the estimates on the sectoral share of FIEs' exports produced by Lemoine all have a downward bias.

That said, it is still possible that the figure reported in the *Third Industrial Census* has an upward bias. The more likely bias comes from not including indirect exporting engaged in by smaller – and, more likely, private – firms. For example, if a private firm without such an independent accounting status sells its products to a foreign trade corporation, the *Third Industrial Census* will not be able to record this transaction because the census includes data only on industrial enterprises. To check whether this omission is serious, I have examined other Chinese publications that report FIE exports. One, based on customs data, reports that FIEs in 1995 accounted for 52.6 percent of Chinese exports of garments and footwear (Wang 1997, p. 353). This is lower than the 60.5 percent reported in Table 1.4 but does not alter any of the substantive conclusions reached in this chapter.

The magnitude of the reduction of FIEs' export share in garments and footwear is also consistent with information from an interview. According to Jimmy Chen, the vice president of Jiangsu Garment Import and Export Corporation, in the early 1990s, his firm purchased about 1 to 2 percent of garments from private firms and this share rose to 20 percent in the mid-1990s.[93] The private sector is more developed in Jiangsu, and thus it is likely that the share of the private sector is higher than the national average. If we use the 52.6 percent figure, this would imply that private firms supplied about 8 percent of China's garment exports through foreign trade corporations. It is possible, however, that the upward bias in the FIEs' production share in the domestic sales data is more serious and thus one should interpret those data with caution.

[93] Interview, October 2001.

2

An Analytical Framework

This chapter presents an analytical framework to interpret the many facets of FDI described in the previous chapter. I call this framework an institutional foundation argument. The institutional foundation argument differs from many of the standard perspectives on FDI in two aspects. First, it focuses on the motivations of and constraints on Chinese firms to account for some of the FDI patterns. Second, it makes the claim that institutional features of the Chinese economy powerfully create and shape these motivations and constraints.

Some of the ideas in the institutional foundation argument are built on a number of prominent themes in the economic literature on FDI. In this chapter, I briefly review these themes. The summary is not meant to be comprehensive but to highlight those insights that will become the critical building blocks in my own explanation of many of the seemingly unusual FDI patterns in China. In the concluding section of this chapter, I raise some potential implications about this way of analyzing FDI in China. Foremost among these implications are the benefits and costs of China's method of attracting FDI. While China's huge FDI inflows are beneficial both to promote growth and to facilitate economic restructuring, it is important to recognize that FDI's disproportionate role is predicated on a number of institutional distortions in the Chinese economy.

The chapter begins with a description of research motivations, questions, and strategy. This is followed by a presentation of the analytical framework. I then consider two rival hypotheses that approach the issue from different angles. The last section presents the conclusions.

RESEARCH MOTIVATIONS, QUESTIONS, AND STRATEGY

Many existing accounts of FDI in China do not examine FDI patterns in as detailed a manner as presented in Chapter 1. Such an examination serves to illustrate many interesting aspects of China's FDI but, more important, to make a case of the need for a new perspective. In this section, I discuss the research motivations for this book, and then pose and define the research questions and describe the research strategy.

Motivations

Existing accounts of China's FDI too readily take FDI as a given and obvious choice for foreign and domestic firms, and they often implicitly conceptualize FDI as the only feasible option to realize many of the alleged benefits – such as labor cost savings and access to overseas market channels. (I summarize a number of existing studies on China's FDI in the appendix to this chapter.) One of my motivations to write this book is that the existing accounts cannot adequately explain for many of the patterns described in Chapter 1. On the issue of choosing an FDI option, for example, I have shown that the systematic and pervasive preference for FDI over the contractual alternative is not preordained. Such a preference requires an explanation.

Most FDI studies on China explore the economic effects of FDI, government policies toward FDI, and performance or corporate characteristics of FIEs, in part because of the perception that the causes of China's high FDI inflows are obvious. Relatively little attention has been paid to understanding why China's FDI inflows, relative to domestic investments or contractual alternatives, have been so enormous in the first place. My claim is that these causes are not at all obvious.

As interesting as the FDI questions are, my deeper motivation is to use China's unusual FDI patterns to shed light on a number of institutional characteristics of the Chinese economy. As I detail in a later section, three prominent institutional characteristics of the Chinese economy shape FDI patterns in China. First, China's financial system allocates resources according to a political rather than an economic pecking order of firms. At the top are the inefficient state-owned enterprises (SOEs) and at the bottom are the most efficient private firms. Second, China's legal system offers poor protection to private firms. And third, there is substantial fragmentation in the Chinese economy. Local governments restrict trade of goods and flows of capital to other regions. Domestic capital mobility across regions is especially low. These three characteristics have affected China's FDI patterns profoundly.

The claim that a set of institutional distortions has induced FDI inflows provides a new perspective on China's FDI. The prevailing view argues that economic growth and cheap labor have fueled much of China's FDI inflows. *Selling China* does not dispute this view; instead, it seeks to provide an additional perspective that views China's FDI inflows as an *institutional* phenomenon. As such, some of China's FDI patterns may reflect institutional inefficiencies and weaknesses. Because many have touted China's ability to attract a large inflow of FDI as an unblemished success, my third motivation is to make the case that it is necessary first to gain a fuller picture of exactly why China is so attractive as an FDI destination.

China has done many things right by putting its macro fundamentals on a solid footing, which is an enormous achievement. There is no question that a portion of FDI into China is the result of its impressive economic achievements. The issue is whether there is another side to China's "attractiveness" to foreign investors. Until the late 1990s, an apparently large share of the market growth opportunities accrued to the foreign firms and a small share to the efficient domestic private firms. As will become evident in the rest of this chapter, this outcome did not happen by design. Instead, the original intention was to channel resources and growth opportunities to SOEs, but SOEs failed to benefit from these opportunities due to their operating inefficiencies. Foreign firms spotted an opportunity and invested heavily in response. Thus, part of China's attractiveness to foreign investors may have stemmed from the distortions and rigidities of a half-reformed socialist economy. This is a cautionary tale when we reflect on the successes of and lessons from China's reform strategy.

Questions

Selling China focuses on FDI, rather than on foreign debt or other forms of cross-border transactions, for both empirical and conceptual reasons. As an empirical issue, the central government has strictly regulated large-scale borrowing from foreign banks and foreign bond markets while it has liberalized FDI controls. (Small-scale buyer credits from foreign manufacturers, as pointed out in Chapter 1, were allowed.) The "equilibrium" balance between foreign debt and FDI is a complicated issue and beyond the scope of my inquiry. Suffice it to say that this combination of a restrictive debt policy and a permissive FDI policy is not unusual among developing countries. The conceptual side of the issue is more relevant. As pointed out in the last chapter, China is a net capital exporter. Thus, in aggregate, the huge FDI inflows into China have not been driven by a shortage of capital. Even in the absence of regulatory constraints on foreign loans, it is unlikely that many of the small-scale producers in garment or footwear production – an important part of our FDI story – would have had unfettered access to foreign bank loans. Also, there is an ownership angle to the theme developed in this book. As I illustrate in Chapter 5, some of the FDI financed acquisitions of the assets of SOEs, many of which had borrowed heavily from the banks themselves. This veritable privatization story necessarily entailed an ownership change. Debt capital was less relevant.

The central research question in this book concerns the causes of China's FDI inflows, not the effects of China's FDI inflows. The distinction between causes and effects of FDI is fairly straightforward, but it can get lost in policy and academic discussions on the benefits and costs of FDI. There are both policy and analytical implications from drawing this distinction. I take up the policy implications in the conclusion to this chapter and in Chapter 7. The analytical importance of drawing this distinction is to avoid mistakenly attributing the causes of FDI inflows only to their economic and business benefits. Under certain conditions and in certain industries, a contractual alternative can be equally beneficial to a foreign or domestic firm on straightforward business or economic grounds. (Or the difference in the benefit levels may not be as large as the gap between FDI inflows and contractual capital inflows suggests.) In this situation, an analyst should look for other causes of FDI arrangements beyond the normal business and economic benefits associated with an FDI arrangement.

It is very important to define, as clearly and as specifically as possible, what our dependent variable – and therefore what our research question – is. This matters enormously for the choice of independent variables. I am seeking to explain China's FDI dependency. FDI dependency can be conceptualized along two dimensions. One is the FDI inflows relative to the investment activities undertaken by domestic firms. The other is the level of FDI activities relative to contractual alternatives. There are several specific manifestations of this dependent variable. One would be FDI relative to total fixed asset investments. The other would be the industry or regional distribution of FDI. This is an implicit measure of FDI relative to domestic investment activities because there may be some a priori reasons to believe that domestic firms should be strong in certain industries or in certain regions. If FDI is observed in these industries or these regions, we can conclude that FDI is high relative to domestic investment. The FDI dependency relative to contractual capital inflows can be measured by directly comparing the amount of the two kinds of capital inflows and/or by examining the composition of China's exports broken down between FIEs and domestic firms. The presumption is that in labor-intensive industries contractual mechanisms ought to be feasible, if not dominant.

It is important to stress that I am not attempting to explain questions related to an absolute level of FDI inflows, for example, why China gets more FDI than, say, Mexico, or why China received $40 billion in 2000 but only $4 billion in 1991. (The international and historical comparisons in Chapter 1 are about the relative ratios between foreign and domestic investment activities.) By definition, factors such as labor costs, market size, culture, and geographic proximity between FDI suppliers and recipients do not feature prominently in my explanation of China's FDI dependency as defined above. This is not because these factors do not matter for FDI; they matter enormously, but they are less relevant to this particular formulation of my research question.

For example, labor costs, culture, and geographic proximity, in and of themselves, do not explain a high or rising FDI/capital formation ratio. The reason is simple: Domestic firms enjoy these advantages even more than foreign firms. (While an ethnic entrepreneur from Hong Kong is Chinese, she is no more Chinese than a Chinese entrepreneur in Guangdong. The same reasoning applies to geographic proximity.) It is not clear why labor costs and cultural and geographic considerations would automatically favor an FDI arrangement over a contractual alternative. If anything, the cultural argument may favor a contractual arrangement. Market size may advantage a foreign firm if the foreign firm is better endowed than a Chinese firm to respond to future market growth opportunities. Whether such an advantage is important is decided on an industry-by-industry basis, and in this book I have deliberately chosen industries where foreign firms do not necessarily hold a decisive advantage over domestic Chinese firms (such as the home appliance industry or low-tech, labor-intensive, or traditional industries).

For this and other reasons, the empirical scope of this book focuses on manufacturing industries and, within manufacturing industries, on those product segments in which domestic firms ought to be, a priori, somewhat capable versus certain foreign firms. This focus precludes FDI in natural resource prospecting, drilling, high-tech manufacturing industries, and service sectors such as banking.[1] It is taken for granted that FDI in those industries should occur; the analytical task is to explain the portion of FDI that may not have to occur on straightforward economic grounds and to explain its incidence based on the institutional dynamics identified in this book.

Strategy

My primary interest is to analyze and examine FDI as an aggregate phenomenon – that is, a collection of many facets of China's FDI that comprises the patterns portrayed in the last chapter. Through such a study, I seek to gain a better understanding of the operations of the Chinese economy in the 1990s as well as its FDI patterns. The unit of analysis is at the country level, not at

---

[1] Other reasons to focus on the manufacturing industries include better data availability and relatively liberal entry policies for foreign firms. Natural resources and the banking sector are substantially more restricted than the manufacturing industries.

the firm level. But macro patterns are formed by micro mechanisms – that is, individual FDI decisions made by many firms. This requires a research strategy that combines an analysis of aggregate data, on the one hand, with in-depth case studies, on the other. The case studies in this book are designed not to probe into the detailed histories and operations of the firms in question but to illustrate the larger institutional contexts in which they operate and which motivate or constrain their decisions. They provide a rich and intuitive understanding of the aggregate patterns of China's FDI.

The extensive data presentation and analysis are also an integral component given that my research objective is to understand and interpret FDI as a reflection of how the Chinese economy operates. To the extent possible, I try to illustrate the actual mechanisms of the institutional dynamics directly, but limitations on data or case materials do not always permit a straightforward demonstration of the underlying causal mechanisms. In these situations, I suggest plausible linkages by identifying areas of consistency between my hypotheses and FDI patterns.

AN ANALYTICAL FRAMEWORK

This book takes as a given the analytical focus of studying FDI, as defined by Richard Caves (1998, p. 6): "why some allocation decisions are made through spot transactions or arm's-length contracts, while others are internalized within business organizations." As FDI theorists argue, an FDI decision is the result of obstacles to transferring know-how or other resources via a contractual method. This line of inquiry has been used not only to analyze FDI from advanced industrial economies, but also to study "mobile exporters" in Asia and FDI in labor-intensive industries originating from less developed countries (Wells 1993). To explain why China gets so much FDI, one first has to demonstrate why contractual means of know-how transfer are not feasible. We can also raise a related issue: If we observe a foreign firm investing heavily in industry A, we should want to know why a domestic firm has not invested heavily in the same industry. Domestic firms operating on their home turf, in standard economic accounts of FDI, are assumed to command certain advantages over foreign firms.

I have borrowed these two ideas – that FDI results from contractual failures and that domestic firms command certain advantages – from a number of economic theories of FDI. In particular, the theory of industrial organization and the theory of transaction costs in institutional economics are extremely useful in devising an analytical framework to approach the FDI question in China. My own explanation focuses on the motivations and capabilities of domestic firms to explain many of the FDI patterns described in the last chapter, but the underlying analytical framework is similar to that commonly found in a number of economic theories of FDI. In this section, I first present several themes in these FDI theories and then I present and build my own argument on the basis of these themes and extend the framework to the Chinese setting.

Economic Theories of FDI

The economic literature on FDI is voluminous. This section is not meant to review the entire economic literature on FDI but to present those themes that are directly pertinent to my research questions.[2] My summary of these topics is abbreviated and does not capture all the nuances that many of the writings on FDI contain. The purpose is to show the similarities and differences between my argument and some of the themes in the economic literature on FDI.

FDI theorists note two kinds of market imperfections that may impede a contractual arrangement. One has to do with the structural imperfections of the market. These structural imperfections can be a function of a number of industry characteristics, such as scale economies, R&D intensity, and a high degree of product differentiation, or they may be due to firm-level attributes, such as the kind of know-how and capabilities that are difficult to codify and transfer across different organizations. Firms derive market power from possessing these characteristics, and they exercise their market power more efficiently by internalizing production across different locations under the same ownership roof. When these firms expand into multinational territories on account of their market power, they become MNCs. This reasoning is known as an industrial organization perspective of FDI.

Central to the industrial organization perspective is the view that when operating abroad foreign firms incur large, up-front costs, which rival host firms on their own turf happily do not incur. These costs range from the intrinsic difficulties of managing cross-border operations to the costs of gathering information and developing expertise about foreign markets and about foreign political, social, and legal environments. To be successful, a foreign firm must possess

---

[2] Because of the emphasis on contractual failures as a cause of FDI, my brief summary here leans more heavily toward those works that base their postulates about FDI on some aspects of imperfect markets, while generally omitting works assuming efficient markets as drivers of FDI. Theories assuming perfect markets can be divided into several categories. One is based on the idea that firms in countries with low rates of returns seek higher returns by investing abroad. Another models FDI as attempts by firms to diversify their portfolios to minimize risks. A third emphasizes market size as a driver – on the pulling side – of FDI. For a useful summary, see Lizondo (1995).

internal, ownership-specific advantages over rival domestic firms in the host economies to offset these extra costs. One source of these advantages is their market power, as identified above.[3]

The second kind of market imperfections has to do with transaction costs.[4] As noted by some theorists, the market power argument of the industrial organization perspective predicts certain firms will go abroad, but it does not predict why MNCs necessarily need to internalize operations and production sites scattered across different countries. FDI is an ownership arrangement under which firms place geographically dispersed activities under the same ownership. But there are other mechanisms MNCs can resort to in order to reap the benefits from the advantages they hold. They can, for example, sell or lease their assets to another firm. This is where the transaction cost perspective comes in. For one reason or another, these arm's-length transactions are not viable because of the significant transaction costs involved.

The list of potential market failures is daunting. Many of the firm-specific advantages involve intangible assets such as specialized and tacit knowledge about products, production processes, and organizational arrangements. This presents a problem in pricing, because such intangible assets assume typical "public goods" characteristics. The fixed costs of their production are very high, but their marginal costs are low or near zero. While from a society's point of view, their pricing ought to reflect their marginal costs, as Caves (1996) points out, nobody gets rich by selling things at a zero price. Another handicap has to do with the "tacitness" of the involved assets. A firm may derive its advantage from some sort of know-how shared but dispersed among its employees or from its "repertory of routines." These do not lend themselves easily to exact specifications and therefore are extremely difficult to be transferred contractually between two independent and separately owned firms. An additional difficulty has to do with specifying the ownership rights over intangible assets precisely. Suppose firm A rents out some knowledge about production processes to firm B but firm B makes a subsequent improvement upon this knowledge. How should the added revenue benefits be divided between firm A and firm B? Problems such as these (but not limited to these) deter market transactions.

British scholar John Dunning integrated the structural imperfection and transaction cost perspectives and added a third perspective, locational advantages. This is the so-called eclectic approach to FDI.[5] The eclectic approach addresses

---

[3] Pioneering work in this field is done by Hymer (1976). For a good summary of this large body of literature, see Lizondo (1995) and Caves (1996).

[4] Buckley and Casson (1976) is the classic work incorporating a transaction cost perspective into an analysis of FDI.

[5] The eclectic approach is most frequently associated with Dunning (1977, 1988).

three central questions related to FDI. The first is the type of firms most likely to invest abroad. Here, the industrial organization theory supplies an answer: These firms are likely to be in industries that have a number of distinct structural characteristics that constitute ownership-specific advantages. The second concerns where these firms choose to exploit their ownership-specific advantages. Dunning focuses on comparative factor costs, transport costs, market size, and government policies as factors determining the location of investment activities. The third question is why firms choose to internalize, rather than exploit contractually, their ownership-specific advantages. This is the transaction cost perspective. These three perspectives together are known as the ownership-location-internalization framework of FDI.

The economic perspectives on FDI – those rooted in reasoning about the structural imperfections of certain industries and transaction costs – offer a number of specific empirical predictions, one of which is that FDI tends to be concentrated in oligopolistic industries. In general, this prediction has received strong empirical confirmation. A significant exception, however, concerns investments by the so-called third-world MNCs. Not all FDI originates in large, oligopolistic MNCs and not all FDI is found in technologically intensive industries. In the 1970s FDI began to come from what are known as "third-world MNCs." Such FDI financed export-oriented, labor-intensive production and simple assembly operations in the host economies. Our discussion of FDI in China originating from the ECEs involves this type of FDI.

The most prominent example of labor-intensive and export-oriented FDI comes not from a third-world country but from Japan. (Third-world MNCs can be used to denote the characteristics of the invested industries, rather than simply the level of the income of the investing country.) Japanese scholar Kiyoshi Kojima first noticed the difference in FDI between Western and Japanese MNCs. He points out that Japanese FDI tended to congregate toward export-oriented and labor-intensive industries in developing economies that had a comparative advantage in these industries (Kojima 1978). (This is known as the "Kojima hypothesis.") As interesting as this observation is, the issue is to explain why Japanese firms had to reap the benefits of following the host countries' comparative advantage via FDI rather than via other cross-border firm alliances such as contract production or licensing.

A number of scholars have provided a theoretical grounding to explain export-oriented FDI. They have used a similar market imperfection framework as a conventional economic approach, but have identified a source of market imperfections different from that identified by economic theorists. There are two issues involved in an effort to understand why the third-world MNCs can be active investors. One is to specify the kind of advantage a third-world MNC holds over a first-world MNC. Another is to specify the kind of advantage a third-world MNC holds over a rival domestic firm in the host economy. On the first issue, a third-world MNC may supply equipment and machinery that are more flexible and are designed for smaller volume production runs more suited for developing countries. On the second issue, a foreign firm may have broad entrepreneurial capabilities over firms in host economies, and it may be more able to spot business opportunities and to design and market products better than local firms. Hong Kong firms, for example, are often said to hold an advantage over domestic firms in product design and marketing capabilities.[6]

However, the putative entrepreneurial advantages of Hong Kong firms may still be insufficient, at least from the point of the view of the traditional economic perspective. Foreign advantage is a necessary condition leading to FDI, but not a sufficient condition. Before concluding that foreign advantage leads to FDI, an analyst has to consider why a contractual mechanism has failed to utilize this advantage across different locations. FDI, as the economic logic indicates, must rest on some version of market failures. There may be two scenarios in which contractual mechanisms may fail, and an FDI arrangement may be required to organize production in a labor-intensive industry. One is that the market for second-hand machinery is inefficient, and it is often difficult to match the right human capital with the right physical capital. For an indigenous entrepreneur to start from scratch, the high search costs to find the right machinery and to develop the necessary skills within a short period of time are formidable obstacles. FDI, in this particular circumstance, may be superior to a contractual arrangement. Another potential risk associated with a contractual arrangement is that local contractees may fail to enforce the production contracts, and should such failures occur, it is difficult to penalize the local producers. Foreign buyers must bear all the risks of failures by contractees, adversely affecting their reputation and therefore future sales. Internalization is a safer approach.[7]

The Relative Competitiveness of Foreign Firms

For the purpose of this book, an extremely useful idea from the economic theories of FDI – as presented above – is that FDI is a function of the competitiveness of firms in a home economy over firms in a host economy. FDI theorists may focus on different dimensions of "competitiveness" of foreign firms, that is, whether foreign firms are competitive because of their proprietary and intangible

---

[6] On these two issues, see Lecraw (1977), Wells (1978), and Chen (1983).
[7] See Wells (1993).

assets or because of their entrepreneurship. But the underlying framework is clear: To succeed abroad, a foreign firm has to be more "competitive" than firms in the host economy on certain dimensions. In writing about FDI in third-world countries, Caves puts forward the following hypothesis: "[I]f entrepreneurial capability is a resource in inelastic supply (as in LDCs), foreign investment can occur simply because a nonnative entrepreneur can excel marginal native entrepreneurs" (1996, p. 239).

The insight of this statement is that FDI activities occur because of *relative*, not absolute, advantages on the part of "nonnative entrepreneurs." That is to say, in order to succeed, a foreign entrepreneur has to be better than a local entrepreneur, but she does not have to be the best in the world. While this logic applies everywhere, it may apply in particular to developing countries because local entrepreneurs there can be assumed to be less capable. The relative competitiveness between nonnative and native entrepreneurs can be stylized in the following simple expression:

$$\text{Relative foreign competitiveness} = \frac{\text{Competitiveness of foreign firms}}{\text{Competitiveness of domestic firms}}$$

This shorthand expression is not meant to be a mechanical device to calculate the ratios of foreign to domestic competitiveness; rather, it is used as a heuristic illustration of the circumstances in which FDI may occur. Relative foreign competitiveness can be affected by one or a combination of two circumstances.[8] First, a nonnative entrepreneur can be very good. She may possess patents that give her an unrivaled advantage in a product area; she may possess deep organizational and managerial capabilities that cannot be codified and transferred efficiently via a contractual arrangement. Or she may have developed sophisticated R&D capabilities. Note that this is the standard economic perspective on FDI as summarized in the previous section. Another and equivalent way that a foreign entrepreneur may have an edge is that the native entrepreneur is, in the words of Caves above, "marginal." He is not innovative or market savvy and fails to adjust to changing market conditions or respond to new market opportunities. Or he may be ignorant and organize his business activities inefficiently.

This idea is illustrated in Figure 2.1. Either high foreign competitiveness or low domestic competitiveness (or some combination of both) may contribute to

---

[8] Given the wide-ranging views – from R&D content to entrepreneurship – in the economic literature on what constitutes the necessary advantages for a foreign firm to succeed in a host economy, I have not defined "competitiveness" precisely. Indeed, the gist of the analytical framework proposed here is that relative foreign competitiveness cannot be a fixed and precise concept. Relative foreign competitiveness depends on the level and composition of the competitiveness of domestic firms that are heavily affected by institutional factors.

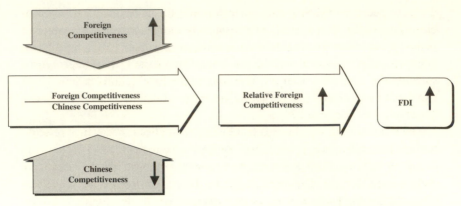

Figure 2.1 Two sources of relative foreign competitiveness.

high FDI inflows by raising relative foreign competitiveness, other things being equal. A logical inference from this way of conceptualizing FDI is that FDI can increase either because foreign entrepreneurship is strong or because domestic entrepreneurship is weak (or some combination thereof). To take this statement to its next logical step, the analytical payoff from examining the sources of the strong capabilities of foreign firms is as high as the analytical payoff from examining the sources of the weak capabilities of domestic firms. After all, at a given level of the numerator, a low value of the denominator results in a high value of our stylized equation of relative foreign competitiveness, as does a high value of the numerator at a given level of the denominator.

For some reason, almost the entire analytical apparatus in FDI studies is devoted to studying how strong foreign entrepreneurship and capabilities lead to high FDI. Since FDI incidence depends on the relative competitiveness of foreign versus domestic firms, the standard analysis of FDI does not involve an in-depth analysis of why indigenous entrepreneurs are weak. As long as foreign entrepreneurs hold an advantage relative to domestic entrepreneurs, FDI is likely to occur. Whether the competitive differentials are the result of a high numerator (foreign competitiveness) or the result of a low denominator (domestic competitiveness) leads to an observationally equivalent outcome, that is, a rise of relative foreign competitiveness (and possibly more FDI). For the substantive claim of the traditional economic perspective, it does not matter which is the source of the high relative foreign competitiveness.

But which factor is driving up FDI inflows entails important implications for assessing policies and the underlying causes of FDI flows. All else being equal, one would prefer a situation in which FDI inflows are driven by a high value of the numerator to one driven by a low value of the denominator. This is true especially if the low denominator is a result of regulatory and policy distortions rather than a result of more exogenous factors such as levels of economic development. The distinction between these two sources of relative foreign competitiveness is also analytically interesting. As I elaborate in greater detail in the concluding chapter, this way of thinking about FDI may shed additional light on why the so-called third-world MNCs have been prominent direct investors in certain economies.

China is a developing country and its firms do not have capabilities in many modern industries such as consumer durables, automobiles, aircraft, or other technologically sophisticated products. In addition, in those product segments characterized as "global industries," Chinese firms are similarly uncompetitive versus incumbent firms in developed economies that already enjoy unsurpassable edges in scale economies, market reach, and technological leadership. This is an exogenous source of China's weak capabilities. But China's FDI patterns, documented in Chapter 1, suggest that the weak local capabilities are not completely exogenous. FDI flows, equity, and export dominance on the part of foreign firms, unlike in other countries, cut across *all industries* in China, including traditional industries. Surely, one can argue, Chinese firms ought to be competitive in *some* industries – at least in those traditional industries in which Chinese entrepreneurs have excelled for hundreds of years. An across-the-board presence or dominance of FDI would imply that Chinese entrepreneurs lack capabilities across the board, including in traditional industries.

Furthermore, it is difficult to reconcile the absolute decline of contractual alliances over time with the view that FDI inflows are driven purely by the lack of capabilities of domestic Chinese entrepreneurs. While Chinese entrepreneurs might have started with a low initial level of capabilities in the early 1980s, it would be implausible to argue they could have lost capabilities over time as the Chinese economy and exports greatly expanded. Also, it should be stressed that my empirical comparisons with Taiwan in Chapter 1 are based on data on Taiwanese FDI patterns in the 1970s. While Chinese firms may be less entrepreneurial and less efficient compared with Taiwanese firms today, it is possible that the capabilities of Chinese entrepreneurs in the 1990s were roughly comparable to those in Taiwan in the 1970s. Yet Taiwan did not import FDI – presumably embodying know-how – in labor-intensive industries near the level at which China did in the 1990s.

Many of the questions raised above suggest that a more productive way to think about China's high FDI dependency is not to assume, as an exogenous factor, a low level of capabilities on the part of Chinese firms in all industries. Rather, a more useful approach is to focus on the ability of Chinese entrepreneurs to use whatever capabilities they have to create profit-making business entities.

The ability to do so depends on their access to financing, legal protection, and market opportunities, all of which are strongly affected by the design and operation of China's economic institutions. This is the topic I turn to next.

Institutional Foundation Argument

As quoted in Chapter 1, the reason Caves rules out FDI in perfectly competitive industries is because local firms can easily "compete down the windfall profits." The massive presence of FDI in China's perfectly competitive industries, industries in which either the know-how requirement is not substantial or the Chinese may command superior know-how, suggests that there are barriers to the ability of Chinese firms "to compete down the windfall profits." These barriers, artifacts of the Chinese economic system, are rooted in the way China's legal, economic, and financial institutions operate. Determining what these barriers are and linking them logically to China's FDI patterns are a central aim of my hypothesis.

The institutional foundation argument is a specific formulation of the demand perspective on FDI. I focus on three prominent institutional characteristics of the Chinese economy during much of the reform era: a political pecking order of firms that favors the least efficient firms, the SOEs, at the expense of the most efficient firms, the domestic private firms; substantial insecurity of property rights for private entrepreneurs; and economic fragmentation. Below I first describe these three institutional characteristics and their consequences. I then link them to China's FDI patterns.

Institutional Characteristics of the Chinese Economy. In Chapter 3, I illustrate the specific manifestations of these institutional characteristics; for now, let me briefly introduce them and comment on their effects. This presentation is meant to capture the broad contours of these characteristics, not all the fine details. As I show in the next chapter, these institutional characteristics have not remained fixed over time; the political and financial treatment of private firms has improved in the 1990s and rather dramatically since 1997 when the government, for the first time since the reform era, endorsed a limited privatization program.

The first prominent institutional characteristic refers to the allocation of precious financial resources and business opportunities according to a political rather than an economic pecking order of firms. A political pecking order is inefficient in that at the top of the order are the inefficient state-owned enterprises and at the bottom are the more efficient private firms. In the appendix to this chapter, I describe the ownership taxonomy of firms in the Chinese economy and present evidence that the efficiency levels of Chinese firms – here

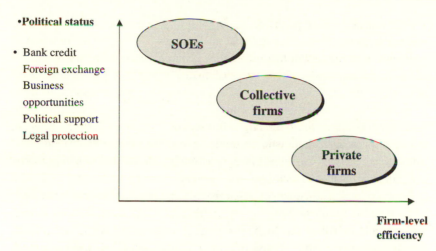

Figure 2.2 Political pecking order of domestic firms in China.

defined as total factor productivity – correlate inversely with their political status. Figure 2.2 presents a graphic and simple representation of the political pecking order of firms, with SOEs at the top, collective firms in the middle, and private firms at the bottom.[9] Closely related to the political pecking order of firms is the insecurity of property rights and the lack of full political legitimacy conferred on private enterprises, the second institutional characteristic in our story.

The third institutional characteristic is China's economic fragmentation. Fragmentation means that China's factor and product markets are poorly integrated across different regions of the country. Capital market segmentation is especially severe. Like the political pecking order of firms, economic fragmentation did not occur by happenstance. It is a direct – although largely unintended – result of deliberate political and policy choices. Most important, there is political control of capital, that is, both capital stock and flows are controlled not only by the government but, more important for our purposes, by different regional authorities.[10] The political control leads to a situation whereby assets

---

[9] I include domestic firms in the political pecking order only because the political pecking order is my independent variable. As will become clear in the remainder of this chapter, China's high FDI dependency is a result of this political pecking order. Thus, FIEs are a phenomenon to be explained and should not be confused with the explanatory variables themselves.

[10] Ultimately, there is political fragmentation as well. Despite political authoritarianism, the political integration among the regional authorities is in fact very shallow. This political fragmentation, in the context of the political control of capital, has a specific economic effect: Because capital

are not transferable across different political jurisdictions and domestic firms are unable to engage in cross-regional investments.

It should be noted that to some extent economic fragmentation is a direct result of the political pecking order of firms. The political control of firms is in place fundamentally because of a reluctance to transfer control of firms to private entities. Local political control of SOEs is viewed as an efficiency-improving measure within the larger framework of state ownership. Thus, all three institutional characteristics examined in this book are internally consistent with one another and can all be traced to a deeply political decision to preserve, if not expand, state ownership.

Four economic consequences ensue from the political pecking order of firms and economic fragmentation.[11] First, inefficient SOEs have built up a large and valuable asset base due to the generous infusion of subsidized credit from the banking system. But because of poorly aligned incentives and weak profit motivations, they have accumulated massive financial losses and huge unfunded explicit and implicit liabilities on their balance sheets. The entire state sector throughout the 1990s operated on the verge of insolvency. Second, the political pecking order inflicts severe credit constraints on Chinese private firms. These credit constraints arise not because private firms are inefficient but because they are private. Until 1998, the largest Chinese banks were instructed not to lend to private firms. It should be noted here that unlike in other countries where the formal financial system often discriminates against firms on the basis of size, in China small collective firms in fact are not credit-constrained.[12] The discrimination is on the basis of the *ownership* of firms.

Third, the lack of full political and legal legitimacy has had a great impact on the character of private firms in China. In the 1980s, private firms simply did not become a significant force on China's economic landscape. In the 1990s, the entry of private firms was massive, but few matured or developed a sophisticated corporate structure or a national reach. To be sure, during the reform era, the Chinese economic system has been sufficiently flexible to allow ad hoc solutions to deal with property rights problems, but these solutions often inflict high transaction costs on private entrepreneurs, thus hampering the growth and quality of private sector development.

Fourth, a direct effect of China's economic fragmentation is that domestic firms located in one region find it costly to respond to business opportunities

---

assets are controlled by mutually independent and disparate political entities, capital market segmentation is substantial. On political fragmentation, see Lieberthal and Oksenberg (1988).

[11] I am laying out the logic of my argument here. Evidence is presented in later chapters.

[12] Park and Shen (2000) make this argument.

in other regions. A less direct effect is that domestic firms may end up less competitive than they could be. In many ways, market fragmentation reduces the value of an enormous advantage that is unique to China as compared with many developing countries: a large internal market with heterogeneous characteristics. An integrated market might have been a good training ground for fostering truly competitive domestic firms. Firms can be forced to innovate to satisfy exacting and varying market conditions, and they can achieve size more easily when the internal market is large. Economic fragmentation essentially carves up a large and varied market into small and homogenous segments. The quality of competition is low and firms strive for regionalized monopoly rent rather than true competitiveness.[13]

Implications for FDI. The poor profitability of the state sector, the credit constraints on the part of Chinese private firms, the insecurity of private property rights, and the weaknesses of domestic firms have all driven up China's demand for FDI. First, discrimination against private firms may increase China's appetite for FDI *at the expense* of contract production. Under the political pecking order of firms, private entrepreneurs are credit-constrained. They therefore find it difficult to enter into contract production with foreign firms even if they possess the requisite know-how and capabilities. This is especially true when a firm expands its production and needs more cash – to pay workers, and so on – rather than just material inputs that can be provided via a pure export-processing operation. An export contract – offered by a garment firm in Hong Kong, for example – provides a business opportunity but not funds. Export-oriented FDI brings both.

As pointed out in Chapter 1, export-processing operations often involve a form of buyer credit from manufacturing and agency firms in Hong Kong to a Chinese producer. Thus, a buyer credit line may alleviate the credit constraints imposed by domestic banks. However, two scenarios prevent a full alleviation of domestic credit constraints through this mechanism. One is that the size of the buyer credit, especially from Hong Kong manufacturing firms, which themselves are very small, may not be large. More often than not, the buyer credit consists of production inputs, raw materials, or some old capital equipment. For a private firm wishing to expand its business, cash is necessary to hire more workers and to procure materials not provided by the buyer. A small buyer credit line may enable a private firm to start up a business, but it may not be sufficient for further business expansions. The other scenario is that the legal

---

[13] This way of conceptualizing home market conditions is derived from works by Michael Porter. See Porter (1990) for details of his framework.

and political status of private firms is not fully secure. If the buyer credit is large and the purchase contract is large, a foreign firm may not wish to enter into a contractual arrangement with a legally disadvantaged private firm, even if the private firm is fully capable.

FDI provides a solution to some of these problems. For example, a private entrepreneur may convert his business into a foreign-owned firm. The benefits are twofold: (1) some guarantee of long-term financing and (2) enjoyment of better protection under the legal framework that the Chinese government has developed for FIEs. This motivation may be especially strong among export-oriented private firms, and particularly when there is a need to expand business. FDI would rise on this count.

The uncompetitiveness of private firms may also boost FDI inflows. In the 1980s, even though FDI was restricted, private firms failed to establish a substantial presence on China's economic landscape because of the financial and legal discrimination against them. As China opened its doors to foreign investors in the early 1990s, foreign firms invested heavily in anticipation of seizing more market opportunities. Two reasons may explain the optimism of foreign investors. One is that the Chinese economy grew very rapidly in the early 1990s. The other is that the foreign investors may have calculated that the domestic competition was not strong because private firms were very small and, as is elaborated on below, SOEs were on the verge of insolvency.

Government support for SOEs has also boosted China's demand for FDI. Generous credit and other backing have allowed SOEs to build up valuable asset bases, but they still have been unprofitable because of operating inefficiencies. A valuable asset base combined with poor profitability means that SOEs are potential acquisition targets. Some of the FDI in the 1990s has gone toward financing the acquisition of SOEs' operating assets, an indication of a de facto privatization drive. The ownership dimension of FDI is relevant here: Privatization, by definition, is an ownership change. The reason that FDI seemingly has played a prominent role in China's de facto privatization drive is that the government, while encouraging FDI, has not endorsed an explicit privatization policy. Thus, the assets of SOEs that are available to foreign firms are unavailable to domestic private firms.

Third, economic fragmentation also increases China's demand for FDI. This is because domestic firms may be less competitive when they are restricted to operating in smaller regional markets created by local protectionism. All else being equal, the uncompetitiveness of domestic firms may create more business opportunities for foreign firms. Because they are unable to take over firms in other regions, even when there is substantial excess capacity in those regions, domestic firms resort to investing in new plants and equipment to build up the local industrial base. This can be costly, and the increased capital requirements may translate into a greater demand for FDI.

Last, because domestic firms are constrained from investing outside their own jurisdictions, there may be more investment opportunities for foreign firms. There are no similar constraints on the mobility of foreign capital, and, thus, compared with constrained local firms, foreign firms are freer to fund operations wherever there is a capital shortage. This means that, in effect, foreign firms as a whole have more projects to choose from than domestic firms. For any given fundable project, foreign firms may be competing more among themselves than with domestic firms as suppliers of capital. The overall effect is that foreign companies have acquired a greater financing role in the Chinese economy than they would have in the absence of capital market segmentation.

Explaining the FDI Patterns. In Chapter 1, I speculate that there may be "structural facilitators" for FDI in the Chinese economy. The dynamics outlined above constitute such structural facilitators. These dynamics are perfectly consistent with the five FDI patterns that I describe in the last chapter. To recapitulate, these five patterns are: (1) the high FDI/capital formation ratio, (2) the demise of contractual alliances, (3) the dominance of FIEs in export-oriented industries, (4) the pervasive presence of FIEs, and (5) the small size of foreign investors.

The FDI/capital formation ratio would be high in this system, especially the FDI/private capital formation ratio, which exceeded 50 percent in 1993, 1994, and 1995 (Table 1.1 in Chapter 1). Nonstate firms, especially private firms, faced with the same propitious business opportunities as foreign firms, were too credit-constrained to increase their investments at the rate foreign firms increased theirs. The FDI dependency relative to a contractual alternative would also be very high, because contract production, while being perfectly viable as a business practice, was rendered less viable in China because of the financial and legal discrimination against private firms.

The presence of FDI and FIEs in many industries and regions is also consistent with our framework. FDI flows into capital- and technologically intensive industries partly because of the dynamics postulated by theorists of industrial organization – such as R&D, product differentiation, and scale economies – but there are other reasons as well. One is that these industries are populated by SOEs, which are performing badly. SOEs, as I show in the next chapter, have the best capital equipment and human capital compared with all other firms in China (even including FIEs). Some of the FDI flows have financed their acquisition.

In labor-intensive industries, the exact opposite scenario plays itself out. Efficient private entrepreneurs, often restricted to operating in low-profit-margin, labor-intensive industries, have the business acumen and capabilities to expand production, but they are unable to do so because of financial and legal constraints. Foreign firms provide the capital, the most expensive kind – equity financing. Equity financing brings in more than capital; it also brings a superior legal status to a marginalized private firm and therefore is valued very highly by Chinese entrepreneurs. This is partially indicated by the prevalence and high costs – measured in terms of the amount of business control a Chinese entrepreneur has to give up to obtain the equity capital – of equity financing. In mature industries devoid of any technological risks, foreign firms have established a substantial equity position. In the garment industry, the foreign equity stake was about 63.3 percent in 1995; 64 percent in leather and related products; and 54 percent in furniture manufacturing.

Because equity financing from foreign firms is so valuable, the size of foreign firms need not be large and they need not hold the ownership-specific advantages postulated by FDI theorists as necessary for FDI. To a credit-constrained and legally disadvantaged private firm, the single greatest advantage of a foreign firm is that it is foreign. This is why the size of the foreign investors in China, across the board, is so small and why one can find ECE firms broadly distributed in many industries, including industries in which domestic firms hold a well-documented technological edge. This is also why Chinese firms are willing to incur the substantial costs of establishing an affiliate in Hong Kong in order to acquire FIE status when they make investments. This is the institutional root of the round-trip FDI.

Finally, our institutional foundation argument can explain very well the recent decline of FDI dependency and the rise of contractual capital inflows. Contractual capital inflows began to rise substantially in 1997, the year the Chinese government openly endorsed a limited privatization program and thus conferred some political legitimacy on private firms. The fall of the FDI/private fixed asset investment ratio, from 47.8 percent in 1996 to 29.0 percent in 2000, provides further evidence of how a moderation of the political pecking order can have a dramatic impact on China's relative FDI dependency (Table 1.1 in Chapter 1). As evidence of the growing competitiveness of domestic private firms, the decline in FDI dependency was mainly driven by a huge increase in investments by domestic private firms rather than by an absolute decline of FDI inflows. Our explanation is also consistent with the observation that round-trip FDI has sharply declined during the course of the 1990s. In Chapter 4, I provide more evidence on the "normalization" of Chinese FDI patterns, including a greater industry concentration and a contraction of FDI going into labor-intensive industries. All of these indicate that the Chinese economy is becoming healthier, with less, not more, FDI.

Explanatory Scope. It is important to stress that our argument should not over-reach. FDI consists of heterogeneous types of economic activities, and not all of these types are equally influenced by institutional factors. In this section, I spell out the scope of our explanation.

Our institutional foundation argument is predicated on an uncontroversial premise: There should be some industries in which Chinese entrepreneurs and firms possess advantages over foreign firms, and there should be other industries in which they possess decisive disadvantages versus foreign firms. The set of institutional factors identified in this book, such as the inefficient political pecking order and substantial economic fragmentation, affects FDI incidence most strongly in those industries in which indigenous Chinese firms should have an a priori, viable chance to succeed. (Success here is defined as a capability to defend local market shares from foreign competition or as an ability to supply goods and services to foreign buyers as independent business entities.)

One can easily think of industries in which MNCs possess unambiguous advantages over Chinese firms and in which the prevalence of FDI is entirely consistent with the predictions of the standard perspectives on FDI. Institutional factors exert relatively few influences on this type of FDI. The most obvious examples are FDI originating from what Raymond Vernon describes as "the giants of modern industry, commerce and banking," such as Mobil, Shell, Gulf, BASF, DuPont, AEG, General Electric, Pfizer, and Hoffmann-LaRoche (Vernon 1977). This type of FDI is relatively unencumbered by the influence of institutional factors, and this type of investment has probably increased substantially in recent years. Investments by these firms constitute conventional FDI, which this book does not examine in great detail. It is possible that as China's economic and financial institutions improve, China will become more attractive to conventional FDI.

As an example, one category of FDI concerns the operations of MNCs seeking to sell "global products," to prospect natural resources, or to locate production facilities of highly technologically intensive products close to their customers. Coca-Cola and a Boeing 747 are global products whose characteristics do not vary across different countries. Coca-Cola needs to invest in China to sell to its Chinese customers because of the prohibitively high transport costs of moving bottled liquids from the United States to China. The Chinese preference for bottling investments by Coca-Cola is largely equivalent to their preference for the Coca-Cola drink itself. Resource-prospecting FDI is largely determined by the location of the natural resources being prospected. China either has petroleum or does not have petroleum, and investments in petroleum prospecting and drilling are relatively independent of many of the institutional factors in our analysis.

Our institutional foundation argument should not be interpreted as a substitute explanation for other economic and industry drivers of FDI that have been widely acknowledged as important determinants. Investments in hightech products, such as Nokia's mobile phone units, can be quite successfully accounted for by the economic conceptualization of FDI as a function of R&D intensity, industry concentration, and other firm-specific advantages on the part of MNCs. FDI of this type is relatively unencumbered by institutional influences.[14] It is not the intention of the institutional foundation argument to say that industry characteristics such as R&D intensity and proprietary assets do not explain FDI into China. They clearly do, but they do not explain all of the FDI going into China.

ALTERNATIVE HYPOTHESES

The institutional foundation argument portrays China's FDI patterns as a function of policy and regulatory treatments accorded to different types of domestic firms. A simpler story might focus on a different dynamic: the relative treatments of foreign and domestic firms. According to this story, China gets a lot of FDI because the government, for whatever reasons, treats foreign firms better than domestic firms. Thus, the various patterns of Chinese FDI fundamentally reflect the basic orientation of the FDI regime. An advantage of this explanation is its parsimony and simplicity.[15] A related hypothesis has to do with the direction of causality. An explanation centering on China's FDI regime portrays the low competitiveness of Chinese firms as an *effect* of FDI. A liberal FDI regime lets in competitive foreign firms, which crowd out domestic firms. This is the opposite from the causal direction postulated by our institutional foundation argument, which views the low competitiveness of domestic firms as "inducing" FDI inflows. Let me take up these issues below.

Relative Treatment of Foreign and Domestic Firms

Our framework on the relative competitiveness of foreign firms, ultimately and explicitly, is based on a paired comparison of foreign and domestic firms in terms

---

[14] One can, however, construct an institutional argument to explain the phenomenal success of the Nokia mobile phone units in China. For many years, telephone services in China were monopolized by China Telecom, which charged predatory prices for its services. The extremely high costs of fixed line services essentially raised the demand for wireless communications, which then raised the demand for the provision of wireless technology monopolized by MNCs such as Nokia, Motorola, and Ericsson.

[15] An extended discussion with Professor Julio Rotemberg clarified my thinking on this issue.

of their competitiveness. The question is: Has the high relative competitiveness of foreign over domestic firms resulted from government policy and regulatory treatments that specifically advantage foreign firms? Or has the high relative foreign competitiveness resulted from other factors that have very little to do with FDI per se but nevertheless affect FDI through their effect on the overall competitiveness of domestic firms? This distinction is critical. If China's FDI patterns are driven by relative treatments of foreign and domestic firms, this study tells us a lot about China's FDI policies and regulations. If China's FDI patterns are driven by those factors that make domestic firms uncompetitive (and thereby raise relative foreign competitiveness), then this study is about the deeper dynamics of the Chinese economic and political systems. For a study on FDI, it is not surprising to claim that the characteristics of the FDI regime matter for FDI patterns. Of course, the FDI regime matters. The issue is whether the FDI regime is all there is or whether the broad characteristics of China's economic institutions matter as well or whether they may matter even more.

My claim is that the broad characteristics of China's economic and financial institutions matter for FDI through a lowering of the competitiveness of Chinese firms irrespective of the specific designs and features of China's FDI regime. The clearest illustration of the effect of China's economic institutions on FDI is the economic fragmentation. Economic fragmentation has little to do with China's FDI regime. As I detail in Chapter 6, China's economic fragmentation can be traced to the policy decisions made in the 1950s and to the desire to improve the informational, allocative, and operating efficiencies of SOEs within the framework of state ownership.

There is no convincing evidence that China's FDI regime has favored FIEs over SOEs, and thus the low competitiveness of SOEs cannot be attributed to the designs and features of China's FDI regime. The real complication involves the relative treatment between FIEs and private firms. Because private firms receive the worst treatment, that is, relative to both SOEs and FIEs, then the issue is how to disentangle the effect on private firms of China's FDI regime from the effect of China's political pecking order. Let me deal with these issues below.

SOEs vs. FIEs. Researchers have argued that Chinese government tax policies have favored foreign firms over SOEs.[16] Until the 1994 Unified Tax Law, the statutory income tax rate on SOEs was 55 percent, whereas the rate on FIEs ranged from 15 to 33 percent, with many tax breaks and exemptions.[17] This

[16] Fu (2000) advocates this view. I propose this view in my earlier writing. See Huang (1998).
[17] The discussion on SOE taxation issues is drawn mainly from Wong, Heady, and Woo (1995).

view is quite prevalent in China, but it is seldom closely scrutinized. There are two angles to evaluate it. One is conceptual: Why should a higher tax rate on SOEs affect the performance of SOEs? The other angle is empirical: Even if there are tax benefits conferred on FIEs, can one make a blanket statement that the *aggregate* policy and regulatory benefits conferred on FIEs exceed those enjoyed by SOEs?[18]

Conceptually, it is not straightforward that a high tax rate should affect the performance of SOEs in one way or the other. It should be stressed that the government is both the owner and the tax collector of the SOEs. All else being equal, a high tax rate reduces the residual profits; a low tax rate increases the residual profits. The total amount of resources available to the government, as the tax collector and the shareholder, is not affected. It follows that the economic incentive of the government should not be affected by whether the government derives more revenue as the owner of the firm or more revenue as the tax collector of the firm. This is different from the situation facing a private firm: The government collects the taxes at the expense of the profit distributions to the private investors. For SOEs, a more relevant issue is the manner in which the government uses revenues – whether from taxes or from profit distributions – rather than the tax rates per se. If the government uses the money unproductively, for example, by investing in wasteful projects, rather than in improvements in productivity, this would affect the performance of the SOEs. But in this case it is the behavior of the government, not the tax rate, that matters.[19] As evidence, in 1994, the government cut the statutory income tax rate on SOEs to 33 percent, which equalized their tax treatment with some FIEs. By all indications, the performance of SOEs only became worse.

Aside from the conceptual issue about whether or not differences in income tax rates have affected the performance of SOEs, there is an empirical question about whether the overall tax treatment really favors FIEs. The answer is not clear at all. SOEs are subject to softer budget constraints. While there may be no explicit statutory provisions, in effect, tax exemptions and breaks have been granted to SOEs on an ad hoc basis. The tax code had also benefited SOEs. Until 1994, SOEs could deduct their payment of loan principals against their tax liabilities, whereas all other firms could deduct only their interest payments.

---

[18] Another issue concerns the motivations of local governments and firms in China to seek FDI in order to access the allegedly superior tax and other regulatory benefits accorded to FIEs. In Chapter 5, I deal with FDI motivations in detail to show that benefits such as low tax rates on FIEs are logically incompatible with the apparent strong motivations of local governments for FDI. The poor profitability of SOEs is a better explanation of why local governments desire FDI.

[19] As I show in Chapter 5, most analysts focus on the operating inefficiencies of SOEs, not on the tax rates, as the central problem in the state sector.

SOEs are favored – over FIEs and other firms – in many other respects, such as market access, subsidies, bank credits, and general political and legal protection. In a comprehensive study of FDI, a group of economists from the Chinese Academy of Social Sciences show that FIEs in China enjoy preferential treatments in taxation, tariff exemptions, and pricing flexibility. The report, however, is careful to point out that these preferential treatments are mainly designed to offset the inherent biases in the planned economy that naturally favor the SOEs (Wang 1997). The most notable advantage SOEs have enjoyed is their access to high-growth and high-margin business opportunities. Many industries, such as telecommunication services, automobile manufacturing, banking, and wholesale, impose ownership and performance restrictions on foreign firms. These restrictions are designed to protect the incumbent SOEs.

If FIEs do not enjoy a clear *aggregate* advantage over SOEs, how do we reconcile this fact with the prevalent view that FIEs are favored? It turns out that an important reason concerns the operating inefficiencies of the SOEs. They are not doing well financially, so in this context the tax differences are perceived to have a substantial impact on their financial situation. The Local Leadership Survey provides some pertinent information about this dynamic. When asked to list the most important reason why FDI posed a threat to the medium and large SOEs, 68.8 percent of the respondents chose "FIEs enjoy more favorable government policies than SOEs" as the most important reason. However, 74.4 percent of the same respondents chose "SOEs have many problems on their own" as the second most important reason.[20] Interestingly, when asked to elaborate on the favorable policies for FIEs, the top item cited by most respondents had less to do with policy or regulatory treatments but more to do with the institutional differences between SOEs and FIEs. The answer that garnered the top answer from the respondents, at 32.4 percent, was "FIEs' greater freedom to hire and fire workers," compared with 31.4 percent of the respondents who cited "lower tariffs for FIEs" as the top advantage of FIEs.[21] The choice of a response that is more about the managerial rigidity and bureaucratic controls endemic among SOEs is consistent with our analytical

[20] The survey question is: "We have listed a number of reasons why FDI inflows may pose a threat to medium and large SOEs. Please choose two of the most important reasons." The reasons listed are: (1) FIEs enjoy more favorable government policies than SOEs; (2) FIEs are too strong; (3) The state's support of SOEs is insufficient; and (4) SOEs have many problems on their own.

[21] The survey question is: "Relative to SOEs, what do you think is the most important beneficial condition enjoyed by FIEs?" The choices are: (1) ease of raising funds, (2) lower tariffs, (3) greater freedom to hire and fire workers, (4) greater freedom to invest across industries and regions, and (5) tax exemptions and reductions.

framework that focuses on the operating inefficiencies of the SOEs rather than on the characteristics of China's FDI regime. The FDI regime matters, obviously, as indicated by the choice of "lower tariffs for FIEs," but it is not the only factor, and Chinese officials themselves do not perceive it to be the most important factor.

Private Firms vs. FIEs. As I go into some detail in Chapter 3, private firms lack property rights protection, market opportunities, and access to bank credits compared with FIEs. One of the motivations for the private entrepreneurs to seek out FDI is to access the superior regulatory and legal treatments of FIEs. Thus, the FDI regime story is much more plausible when FIEs are benchmarked against domestic private firms. As an empirical matter, the claim that FIEs enjoy better overall treatments than private firms is correct. Because private firms are at the very bottom of the totem pole, the challenge is to explain how they became uncompetitive. Is it because of the preferential policy treatments granted to FIEs? Or is it because of the preferential policy treatment granted to SOEs? The former is the FDI regime story and the latter is our political pecking order story. Given that this book is about FDI, the FDI regime story is easier to tell; the political pecking order story seems to be a few steps removed from our subject matter.

There are two ways that China's FDI regime may have harmed domestic private firms. One is that a liberal FDI regime permitted entry of competitive foreign firms, which crowded out domestic private firms. The empirical implication is that under an illiberal FDI regime, domestic private firms should do better than they do under a liberal FDI regime. Another mechanism is that some features of the FDI regime itself – such as granting FIEs more market access – undermined domestic private firms. If this is true, then we should expect to see the number of failures of domestic private firms to grow during the period when the FDI regime was liberal. There is no evidence to support either of these two hypotheses. The way to test these two hypotheses is to use 1992 as the dividing line between an illiberal FDI regime in the 1980s and early 1990s and a liberal FDI regime since 1992. Since 1992, the FDI regime became progressively more liberal. Thus, we can use data before 1992 to test the first hypothesis and data since 1992 to test the second hypothesis.

The size of the private sector was very small on the eve of China's FDI liberalization in 1992. Chinese statistical sources only record economic activities of one type of private firm – individual businesses. Individual businesses are small self-employed entities that do not hire labor. They were considered more ideologically acceptable than another class of private firms, which is labeled privately operated firms. Privately operated firms hire eight or more employees. In the 1980s, privately operated firms did not exist on a sufficient scale to warrant an entry in the Chinese statistical sources.

In the 1980s, the government permitted, but imposed various restrictions, on the private sector. In 1991, after more than ten years of economic reform, the size of the true private sector was minuscule. Its share of industrial output value was only 5.7 percent. This did not result from competition from FIEs. FIEs in 1985 only accounted for 0.3 percent of industrial output value.[22] The reason was the severe discrimination against private firms by the Chinese government itself, which had two effects. One was that it politically marginalized the private firms and forced many private entrepreneurs to register their firms as collectively owned. This was an unstable arrangement because of the intrinsic murkiness of the property rights associated with such arrangements. Since the mid-1990s, many of these firms have been either failing or "privatized." Second, the private firms were restricted in their access to growth opportunities in order to protect the SOEs. In 1991, the vast majority of private firms were located in rural areas where entry and regulatory restrictions were less onerous because firms there did not directly compete with SOEs. In the cities, private firms were allowed in restaurant businesses and real estate. Very few were found in industry, especially in heavy industries. In 1991, the individual size of industrial private firms, including self-employed individual businesses, was extremely small, about RMB 28,690 as measured by sales revenue, compared with RMB 1.4 million for an average SOE.[23]

In contrast, the private firms grew much more quickly in the 1990s, although from a low base, and especially in the late 1990s, even though China's FDI regime became more liberal. In 1998, their share in industrial output value reached 17 percent.[24] The reason, as I illustrate in the next chapter, is that

---

[22] This is from Institute of Industrial Economics (1998).

[23] Individual businesses in the urban areas, where the SOEs were located, accounted for only 0.46 percent of the total industrial output value in 1991. Remarkably, the 0.46 percent in 1991 was only a modest increase from the 0.34 percent generated by urban individual businesses in 1985. Equally remarkably, the number of these individual businesses in fact fell, from 45,000 in 1988 to 43,000 in 1990; their employment fell from 1.37 million in 1985 to 1 million in 1990. (This was the result of the economic crackdown by the conservative post-Tiananmen leadership.) In high value-added and high margin heavy industries, which SOEs dominated, the presence of individual businesses was very small. Data in this section are from State Statistical Bureau (1993b), p. 409, and (1994b), p. 403.

[24] State Statistical Bureau (1999b) does not provide data on private firms directly; instead, it provides data on "enterprises of other types." Under "enterprises of other types," data are included for shareholding enterprises and FIEs. In the explanatory notes, "enterprises of other types" are defined as encompassing private and jointly owned firms as well as shareholding enterprises and FIEs. Thus, data on private and jointly owned enterprises are derived from the enterprises of other types minus shareholding enterprises and FIEs. Private and jointly owned enterprises

the political pecking order was gradually attenuated first in 1992 and then more significantly in 1997 when the government, for the first time, explicitly endorsed a limited privatization policy. The development history of the private sector in the 1980s and 1990s directly contradicts the idea that an illiberal FDI regime benefits private firms and a liberal FDI regime harms private firms. The fate of private firms correlates closely with the force of the political pecking order of domestic firms, not with the direction of the FDI regime.

Causal Direction

Apart from the different empirical predictions, a fundamental difference between the FDI regime explanation and our political pecking order explanation concerns the direction of causality. The FDI regime story blames the uncompetitiveness of private firms on the entry of foreign firms. The political pecking order postulates the opposite sequence: The weak domestic firms preceded FDI inflows when the FDI regime was liberalized in 1992. Demonstrating precedence is a necessary, although not a sufficient, condition to establish a causal relationship.

Let me start with a simple observation: The poor performance of SOEs long preceded the large-scale entry of foreign firms, commonly dated to 1992. As measured by percentage shares of posttax profits, the industrial SOEs' losses increased from 10.3 percent in 1988 to 24.3 percent in 1989, 89.9 percent in 1990, and 91.3 percent in 1991. The incidence of loss-making industrial SOEs, that is, the percentage share of loss-making SOEs of the entire population of SOEs, increased dramatically from 10.9 percent in 1988 to 27.6 percent in 1989 (Lardy 1998, p. 35). One should also add that the rising losses in the state sector coincided with a massive tax relief program granted to the SOEs.[25] The FDI regime in the 1990s, whether it favored FIEs over SOEs or not, cannot be responsible for this outcome.

The uncompetitiveness of private firms, as I have shown, also long preceded the entry of foreign firms and, during the late 1990s, when the FDI regime became more liberal, private firms grew more quickly. Conceptually, there is no compelling reason to believe that the entry of foreign firms on its own would necessarily crowd out private firms. Foreign firms may spur the development of

are grouped together under private firms. Whether or not to include shareholding enterprises in the calculation of private firms is a tricky decision. Empirical research shows that as of 1997, the publicly traded firms were overwhelmingly controlled either by the government or by SOEs. See Xu and Wang (1997).

[25] I return to this issue in the concluding chapter of the book.

private firms, for example, by creating buyer and supplier linkages with efficient private firms. The ability of a private firm to become a supplier to a foreign firm would critically depend on its access to financing and on its legal status, that is, those dynamics that are dependent on the institutional factors analyzed in this book.

A far more plausible causal direction runs from the low competitiveness of domestic firms, created by China's political pecking order, to high FDI inflows, not the other way around. Let us think of the 1980s as a period during which the Chinese government enacted barriers against imports and FDI to protect Chinese infant firms. Then let us imagine an allocative decision to support inherently sickly infants – SOEs – at the expense of inherently healthy infants, such as private firms. Both types of firms would have failed to mature and develop. In 1992, when China lifted FDI controls, neither SOEs nor private firms were in a position to compete against FIEs in responding to the newly created business opportunities. The dominance of FIEs ensued.

The history of private sector development in the 1980s and in the late 1990s suggests that the true binding constraint was the political pecking order of firms, not the entry of foreign firms or the liberal FDI policies. To appreciate this point, one can point to Guangdong province, a province that is the home to some of the best and most competitive indigenous firms but also a province that has a very liberal FDI policy. As I show later in this book, compared with other provinces, the political pecking order of firms is enforced less rigorously in Guangdong.

It is also necessary to stress that the political and legal discrimination against domestic private firms long preceded the entry of foreign firms in the 1990s. Beginning in 1957, the Chinese government began to systematically eliminate the private sector by nationalizing its productive assets. In the 1970s, private businesses in sectors traditionally dominated by private entrepreneurs – such as restaurants – were closed down.[26] The discrimination against the private sector was instituted to benefit the SOEs, not the foreign firms. For this reason, the title of this book, *Selling China*, by no means implies that it is a deliberate policy choice to sell off Chinese assets to foreigners. Rather, the "selling" of China should be viewed as an unwitting outcome of a policy to support SOEs and as a result of the failure on the part of SOEs to capitalize on their privileged positions and to respond effectively to the new business opportunities and to the propitious economic conditions.

In fact, foreign firms are often viewed suspiciously in China. Our Local Leadership Survey provides some evidence. The survey asked all respondents

---

[26] An excellent account of the history of the Chinese economy is Zhao (1989a, 1989b).

to rank SOEs, collective firms, private firms, and FIEs on an eleven-point scale (0–10) in terms of their contributions to China's economic development. The survey question is: "Please rank the firms' contributions to China's economic development on a 0–10 scale (0 indicates no contribution and 10 indicates the most important contributions)." Interestingly, while the survey results correspond exactly to our political pecking order of domestic firms, FIEs were consistently ranked below all firms, including private firms: 29.2 percent of the respondents gave FIEs a score of 8 or above, compared with 34.1 percent who chose private firms, 47.9 percent who chose collective firms, and 76.4 percent who chose SOEs.

CONCLUSION

In recent years, scholars have paid increasing attention to the effect of institutional inefficiencies on a variety of economic phenomena in emerging markets. One line of research demonstrates the detrimental effect of the underdevelopment of financial institutions on economic growth and on stock market performance.[27] Another line of research examines the effect on the organization of firms. Business groups, according to this research, serve many financial intermediary functions that financial institutions fail to provide.[28] Our research falls into this broad literature but focuses on a different economic phenomenon: FDI inflows.

The gist of the institutional foundation argument is that FDI is driven by high foreign competitiveness relative to domestic competitiveness. In the Chinese context, the high relative foreign competitiveness is mainly the result of domestic competitiveness being suppressed by China's inefficient economic and financial institutions. On the surface, the institutional factors in our book are not designed by the government either to promote or to restrict FDI, but they all bear upon the FDI question because they affect the level and elasticity of the capacity of domestic firms to respond to new market opportunities and to compete with foreign firms. They affect the relative foreign competitiveness. Our argument focuses on those factors that make indigenous firms weak rather than those factors that make foreign firms strong. Although this is a departure from the standard account of FDI, the underlying reasoning, that FDI reflects superior relative foreign competitiveness, is similar to the reasoning used in the economic literature on FDI.

---

[27] See Morck, Yeung, and Yu (2000) and Wurgler (2000).

[28] See Khanna and Palepu (2000) for an example of this type of research.

Our analytical framework does not say that economic factors such as market size or labor costs are irrelevant to the FDI question. It is patently obvious that market size and labor costs directly bear upon an MNC's investment decisions. (GM is not going to invest in Somalia, no matter how disadvantaged domestic firms are in that country.) Economic factors such as market size and labor costs constitute *necessary* but not sufficient causes for large FDI inflows. Large market size is an allure to both foreign and domestic foreign investors. Suppose efficient domestic investors are not handicapped, then they should increase their investments as much as foreign firms in response to the new business opportunities. Two outcomes may ensue. Foreign investors, sensing strong competition from domestic firms, may rationally decide not to invest. After all, what makes an investment attractive is not the growth of market size per se but the ability to grab a large share of that market. Or foreign investors may decide to go ahead with the investments but their share of total investments remains relatively constant. This is not what occurred in China in the 1990s. Both the absolute and relative sizes of FDI increased dramatically.

Low labor costs are similarly indeterminate on choices between an FDI arrangement and a contractual arrangement. To be sure, low-tech, labor-intensive, and export-oriented FDI is found in countries with cheap labor, but the obverse of that statement is not necessarily true. That is, not all countries with cheap labor necessarily attract a lot of export-oriented FDI. The reason is that there are other ways a foreign firm can reap labor-savings benefits. To explain such a large flow of export-oriented FDI into China and the dominance of ECE firms in China's export marketing, one first has to explain why contract production is unviable in China, even though it is a pervasive business practice in many other countries.

The tenor of the institutional foundation argument is that a significant portion of FDI in China is induced by inefficiencies in Chinese financial and economic institutions. This statement in and of itself does not imply that the *effects* of FDI are inefficient. To argue that FDI inflows are caused by the myriad inefficiencies in the system is not anti-FDI, as sometimes construed by those who disagree with this view.[29] An anti-FDI stance depends not on what one views as the causes of FDI but on what one views as its effects. FDI can be caused by inefficiencies, but its main effect can nevertheless be an efficiency improvement. A good analogy is with medicine. For a patient, medicine is something good to

---

[29] The author has presented this research at many academic, business, and policy-advisory conferences. One common refrain in the comments is that the analysis is anti-FDI. This is an incorrect reading of my way of interpreting FDI. As explained in the text, one needs to draw a critical distinction between an analysis of the causes of FDI and an analysis of the effects of FDI.

have even though the cause for taking the medicine – getting ill – is undesirable. There is no contradiction whatsoever between arguing that FDI can be caused by inefficiencies in the Chinese economy and asserting that FDI can be efficiency-improving. (In fact, one can go further and argue that because FDI is caused by inefficiencies, therefore it must be efficiency-improving.)

What I do take issue with is the idea that China's way of attracting FDI, by suppressing efficient domestic firms, is costless. In the final chapter of the book, I present my view in greater detail and draw some broad policy and analytical implications. These implications have not been rigorously tested and empirically examined; they are natural inferences based on the findings in my book. As such, they should be viewed as conjectures that call for future debate and exchange of ideas.

Let me continue with the medicine analogy as a method to think about the costs of China's way of attracting FDI. Medicine costs money; so does FDI. FDI is a form of equity financing, and equity financing is expensive. As a partial indicator of this cost, Chinese balance of payments recorded an investment income debit of $22 billion in 1998 and $28.6 billion in 1999, compared with only $6.7 billion in 1994 (International Monetary Fund 2001). And in a few years, it is quite possible that China's current account balance will turn negative. At the present time, much of the investment income has been reinvested in China, but the trend may not continue indefinitely. A related economic cost is the forgone revenue of Chinese private entrepreneurs, who have to give up their businesses because of the credit constraints inflicted on them.[30] Furthermore, for any type of medical treatment, it is best for the patient to be able to choose from a variety of medicines rather than being constrained to just one medicine. In this connection, a better strategy to restructure SOEs is to allow and encourage both FDI and privatization rather than to restrict the SOE restructuring to one mechanism only, whether it is FDI or privatization.

FDI may have boosted China's economic and export growth and may have led to a restructuring of SOEs. But in evaluating FDI's contributions, we need to note two issues. One concerns the mechanisms with which FDI may have contributed to Chinese economic growth, and the other concerns the larger context in which FDI has made its contributions. While scholars such as Richard Pomfret and Shang-jin Wei stress mechanisms such as know-how transfers and skill spillovers,[31] my argument stresses the larger benefits that are institutional

---

[30] There can be political and psychological costs of giving up assets to foreigners. I discuss these costs briefly in the concluding chapter. I stress economic costs, however, because political and psychological costs are more subjective.

[31] See Pomfret (1991) and Wei (1995, 1996a).

in nature. FDI financed efficient private entrepreneurs and alleviated China's inefficient political pecking order of firms. FDI also supplied a privatization function on a greater scale than otherwise would have been politically feasible. However, it is important to note that FDI has made these contributions in the context of governmental restrictions on indigenous private firms making the same contributions. By the same logic, FDI is not the only option to achieve economic growth and economic reforms. If privatization of SOEs had been politically feasible, or if private entrepreneurs could have obtained financing to fulfill export contracts, many of the benefits currently associated with FDI could have been realized with a lower level of FDI in the Chinese economy. This is not a glowing assessment of FDI, but neither is it a damning one.

A final medical analogy is that curative FDI, just like medicine, is not the first-best course of action. A person is fortunate to have the appropriate medicine when he is sick, but a better situation is not to get sick in the first place. The same analysis goes for the kind of FDI analyzed here. It would be better for China to be free of credit constraints on private firms, inefficient SOEs, and capital market segmentation, rather than to have attracted huge FDI flows due to these institutional imperfections. A better economic strategy is to tackle these institutional inefficiencies directly, by privatization and by removing regulatory and legal constraints on private firms.

Why China did not choose a strategy that promoted economic and export growth through a vibrant domestic private sector is a political story. At its very core, this book is fundamentally about a deeply political decision to organize economic institutions in certain ways.[32] It is hard to think of a decision that can be more political than a conscious decision to use the massive economic resources at the disposal of the state to support certain firms at the expense of other firms. One may argue that the political pecking order of firms described in this book is consistent with the political objective of preserving stability in a rapidly changing economy and society. Relying heavily on FDI, as a financing and restructuring instrument, is thus a second-best strategy.[33] In the concluding chapter of this book, I return to this issue and deal with it in greater depth. I do not question the logic that political stability should be a paramount concern and that if a heavier reliance on FDI is the outcome, so be it. I do question the specific observation that suppressing China's indigenous private sector is still consistent with its political stability objective. The private sector has been effective in

---

[32] This conception of politics is richly rooted in political science and other social science disciplines. See Polanyi (1944) and Lindblom (1977).

[33] I benefited from discussions with Professors Julio Rotemberg, Bruce Scott, Debora Spar, and Richard Vietor on this issue.

creating jobs, while the state sector has systematically destroyed jobs. SOEs have also impaired stability by accumulating massive nonperforming loans, failing to meet tax obligations, and decapitalizing assets. Privatization was hugely destabilizing in Russia, but one can make a plausible argument that the fundamental conditions in China are quite different from those in Russia and that privatization in China today can be a stability-preserving strategy. Indeed, since 1997, the Chinese government has begun to embrace a greater pace and scale of privatization. If the current pace continues and if the scope of the privatization includes large SOEs, the institutional landscape of the Chinese economy may change dramatically in the near future.

Appendix to Chapter 2

Let me summarize the literature on FDI in China, define categories of Chinese firms, and then present evidence about relative inefficiencies of SOEs.

LITERATURE ON FDI IN CHINA

Existing studies on this topic fall into four general categories. First, scholars have written about the incidence of FDI, that is, why FDI occurs in China in the first place. Second, a large body of research has been accumulated on the economic effects of FDI. Third, there is a large body of research on corporate and performance issues related to JVs operating in China. Last, scholars have explored the complex negotiations and bargaining dynamics between the government and MNCs in the process of FDI absorption.

As indicative of the state of the field, the literature on the incidence of FDI remains quite small. Most FDI researchers take for granted the rationale for MNCs to invest in China – either to economize on labor costs or to take advantage of a fast-growing market – and they focus their attention instead on what are thought to be less obvious lines of inquiries. Naughton (1996a) provides probably the best conceptual framework to explain outward FDI from Hong Kong with his analogy to urban growth patterns commonly found in industrializing countries. Rising cost pressures drive out land- and labor-intensive activities to cheaper sites, and when these sites are located across borders, the movement of production facilities becomes FDI. This kind of argument is known as a "push" explanation of FDI.

Other researchers work on the "pull" side of FDI. The usual pull factors are market size, GDP growth, and levels of human capital. Wei (1996a) reports that the usual pull factors in fact overpredict China's FDI incidence, that is, the predicted level generated by China's market size, economic growth, and human capital endowment is greater than the actual level of FDI absorption. This is directly contrary to the claim I make in this book that China is among the highest FDI-dependent countries in the world.

It should be pointed out that Wei's analysis is restricted to FDI originating from OECD source countries, and thus more than 50 percent of China's FDI inflows are excluded. This omission presents a number of problems. One is that his study relies on a version of the gravity model; that is, the model postulates bilateral patterns of FDI flows as a partial function of the geographic distance between FDI source and FDI recipient countries. But the empirical implementation of this model excludes sources of FDI that are closest to China, and thus it is not surprising that the model predicts that China receives less FDI than it should on the basis of its economic fundamentals. The procedure would predict the same thing for Canada if the inward FDI from the United States were to be excluded.

The more serious problem is that the study assumes that investment decisions of MNCs are independent of one another. It is quite possible that firms based in OECD countries choose not to go to China precisely because Hong Kong investors have gone there. They may view Hong Kong firms as being more skilled in operating in China and thus they may rationally decide that they cannot succeed there. This interpretation would be perfectly consistent with the findings in Wei's study.

Several authors look at changes in FDI over time. Some have attributed the changes to improvements in the FDI regime or in the overall legal environment (Lardy 1994; Fu 2000). Others attribute the change to economic growth (Wang and Swain 1995). Many more studies explore the effects of FDI. The general verdict is that FDI has contributed to China's economic growth and export development, although issues about the causality and the apparent lack of evidence on FDI's boosting effect on capital formation and spillovers are raised in some of these studies. (See Kueh (1992), Lardy (1992, 1996), Naughton (1996a), Wei (1996a), Wu Renhong (1997), Lemoine (2000), Demurger (2000), Graham and Wada (2001), and Tseng and Zebregs (2002).)

Studies in international business literature explore the corporate and performance characteristics of FIEs. One of the first systematic research efforts to describe and analyze the equity structures of Chinese FIEs was Beamish and Wang (1989). Studies on the performance of FIEs include Luo (1995), Luo and Chen (1995), Pan (1996a, 1996b), Luo (1997), and Chow and Fung (1997a, 1997b). Many of these studies are densely empirical. Finally, studies on government policies on FDI include Kamath (1990), Pomfret (1991), Pearson (1991), and Roehrig (1994).

100

TAXONOMY OF FIRMS

At the crudest level, Chinese firms can be divided into four broad categories. The first category consists of SOEs, but within this category there are variant types of SOEs. One is the traditional SOE. Typically, the state exercises a full set of ownership rights – rights to revenue, control, and transfer. The prototype of a traditional SOE, Oi and Walder (1999) point out, is a large urban SOE. The other is the reformed SOE. In this type of firm, the three components of ownership rights are separate. For example, the state may have delegated control rights or even revenue rights to managers in cases where managers have entered into a performance contract. The typical design of such a contract is that managers have the right to the residual income after a fixed payment has been made to the state. Theoretically, the manager bears all the risks and claims all the residual income.

The second category of firms is composed of collective firms. Here again, considerable variations exist. Closest to the SOEs are those urban collective firms owned by SOEs. During the reform era, manufacturing SOEs set up their own subsidiaries to branch out into retail and wholesale businesses or simply to divert surplus labor as firing restrictions prevented them from laying off redundant workers. These SOE subsidiaries are labeled as collective firms in part because of the official classification conventions and in part because of some real operating differences with traditional SOEs. The state does not directly appoint their managers, and for the most part the SOE parent firm appropriates all the returns. Thus, the state intervenes less in the operating decisions of a collective firm than it does in a traditional or even a reformed SOE.[34]

Similarly, labeling township and village enterprises (TVEs) as collective firms rather than as SOEs requires a careful look at the specific arrangements for control and revenue rights. The lowest agency of the Chinese state is the township. Villages are similar to community councils. Township government officials are civil servants and their salaries are paid out of the state budget, although their supplemental income can be derived from the firms they operate. Thus,

---

[34] It should be noted that under Western accounting rules, such a distinction is meaningless. The income of the collective firm would have been reported in the consolidated income statement of the SOE parent over which the state had a full claim. Investing in a subsidiary, just as investing in equipment and machinery, does not change the underlying ownership claims of the state over the entire SOE. In China, the distinction may make some sense since the issue is less about an accounting convention than about the status of the firm versus the state. Since much of the reform effort has been directed toward increasing the autonomy of the enterprise and toward acknowledging the firm as an independent entity separate from the state, the distinction between a traditional SOE and its subsidiary as a collective firm is a real issue in terms of allocating decision rights between the state and the firm.

conceptually, township firms are closer to SOEs than village firms. Second, there is a similar operating distinction between an urban collective firm and a TVE. A number of scholars have argued that a township government is better described as a corporation than as a level of government (Oi 1999). As a corporation, the township government would qualify as an SOE, and thus its subsidiaries – the TVEs – would be labeled as collective firms under the same principle governing urban collective firms. Fundamentally, an ownership distinction between an SOE and a collective firm rests on some aspects of ownership rights being somewhat at an arm's length between the state and the firm. The arm's-length nature of control or revenue rights is not based on a legal formulation but has been established by convention and appears to be well entrenched. As such, the distinction is fairly transparent to government officials and firm managers and serves a useful functional purpose when it comes to credit-allocation decisions, income tax rates, and company incorporation requirements.[35] As legal entities, for many years TVEs were subject to a different body of laws and different income tax rates from SOEs.

The third category of firms encompasses purely private firms. In the Chinese context, these are more likely to be partnerships or proprietorships. The Chinese government further divides private firms into two types. One consists of firms that have hired outside labor (eight persons or more, called privately operated firms); the other consists of firms without hired labor (called individual businesses). This is a purely ideological distinction and it has no relevance to the assignment of ownership rights.

The fourth category of firms consists of firms with mixed ownership structures. FIEs fall into this category, as do firms listed on China's stock exchanges and firms with substantial employee stockholdings. The defining characteristic of this type of firm is that there are multiple shareholders. Control, revenue, and transfer rights are apportioned according to the equity stakes of the investors on a pro rata basis. Positioning these firms on a state–nonstate spectrum is particularly difficult without specific information about the equity stakes of the various investors. In Chinese publications, these firms are usually categorized as nonstate, and sometimes even as private. This can be seriously misleading. The Chinese shareholders of many of the FIEs are SOEs, and the government owns more than 50 percent of most of the publicly traded firms.

---

[35] Qian (1994) explains the distinction between SOEs and collective firms, as follows: "The central government reserves the ultimate rights of reallocation of residual cash flow and the assets in state-owned enterprises, even if the control rights have been delegated to and residual income has been assigned to local governments, while it has no such rights as to the assets of collectively-owned enterprises." It should be pointed out this "right" is not explicitly codified but has been formulated on the basis of long-term conventions and business practices.

Another important observation is that the treatment of firms varies both across ownership categories, that is, between an SOE and a private firm, as well as within an ownership category. The latter point is most clear with regard to the nonstate sector. The state weighs in more heavily on the residual claims and decision rights of a certain type of nonstate firm (notably, those owned and operated by township and village governments) than it does for the more purely private firms. The same pecking order applies to firms within the category of nonstate firms; that is, the state favors those nonstate firms that are closest to SOEs and collective firms – such as township enterprises – more than the purely private firms.

EFFICIENCY LEVELS OF CHINESE FIRMS OF DIFFERENT OWNERSHIP TYPES

One measure of the efficiency of firms is their total factor productivity (TFP). TFP is a widely used measure of the efficiency with which labor and capital are used. Two conclusions emerge from the many studies of the TFP of Chinese firms. One is that the findings on the TFP performance of SOEs are very controversial. The other is that in almost all studies on TFP, the performance of nonstate firms is found to be superior to the TFP performance of SOEs. The second conclusion is more relevant to our political pecking order story,

The earliest research, published in 1988, found an improvement in the TFP of SOEs. According to this study, the TFP of SOEs during the prereform period, 1957–78, was stagnant, but their TFP grew at a sizable annual rate of 4.8 percent between 1978 and 1985 (Chen, Wang, Zheng, Jefferson, and Rawski 1988). A later study found continuous TFP improvements after 1985 (Jefferson, Rawski, and Zheng 1992; Jefferson and Rawski 1994). This research was followed by other works that found similar productivity improvements due to the SOE reforms. Groves, Hong, McMillan, and Naughton (1994) found that the TFP growth of the SOEs in their sample averaged 4.5 percent annually between 1980 and 1989. They also linked specific reform measures to some aspects of the operating improvements of SOEs. For example, firms with output autonomy, more workers on fixed employment contracts, greater proportional bonus payments, and larger retained profits were found to be more productive than other firms.

The findings relating the productivity improvements of SOEs to managerial reforms are controversial. At an empirical level, several studies contradict the positive findings on the TFP growth in the state sector and find the TFP growth of SOEs to be either negative or close to zero.[36] In particular, Woo and Fan (1994) find a faulty procedure in previous studies that generated positive TFP findings on SOEs: The implicit deflator used to calculate the real value-added of the SOEs was unreliable. The earlier researchers had used a declining implicit deflator for a period when the consumer price index and the implicit GDP deflator were both rising. A declining implicit deflator led to a higher estimate of the value-added of the SOEs than otherwise would have been the case. The findings of zero or negative TFP growth shed light on a glaring anomaly in the previous studies, that is, why the purported improvements in the operating efficiency of the SOEs were accompanied by a massive deterioration of their financial performance.

A different line of criticism gets to the conceptual basis of relying on TFP improvements to showcase the success of the Chinese SOE reforms. It is not clear what an improvement in the operating efficiency of SOEs means when the fundamental orientation of the SOEs is not market-driven. Bai, Li, and Wang (1996) question the appropriateness of relying on TFP numbers to generalize about the Chinese reform experience. An SOE may be very "efficient" in a technical sense but it still can be inefficient in an economic sense. It may produce the wrong product or it may be controlled by insiders who siphon off profits at the expense of the state. Or it may perform political functions by hiring more workers than it needs. Given these institutional distortions, there may very well be a divergence between technical and economic measures of efficiency.

One area where China economists do agree is the superior TFP performance of nonstate firms compared with that of SOEs. Unfortunately, because purely private firms are a recent phenomenon, most of the TFP studies do not include private firms in their samples and thus do not demonstrate the comparative efficiency levels of the firms at the two opposite ends of China's political pecking order. Only the SOEs and collective firms – that is, firms in the middle of the political pecking order – are contrasted.

Even the studies that show a TFP improvement in SOEs show consistently superior TFP performance by collective firms. For example, Jefferson, Rawski, and Zheng (1996), while demonstrating positive TFP growth rates for SOEs, show the TFP performance for collectively owned firms to be superior. (In their sample, collectively owned firms include TVEs.) For the 1980–92 period, their study records the annual TFP growth rate among SOEs as 2.0 percent, but for the same period, the annual TFP growth rate among collectively owned firms was 3.43 percent. These results hold for the sample period as a whole as well as for each subperiod between 1980 and 1992.

---

[36] See Woo and Fan (1994) and Parker (1997).

The TFP performance of private firms versus TVEs has not been documented, but we know that in the 1990s, TVEs began to experience massive performance problems. The fact that TVEs outperformed SOEs does not mean that TVEs themselves were good firms. TVEs were smaller and nimbler than SOEs and they were allowed to compete with SOEs at a time when the entry of truly private firms was restricted. In the 1990s, however, TVEs themselves were deeply troubled. Researchers have documented sales of TVEs in certain localities beginning in the mid-1990s, and some of these sales appear to be on a substantial scale (Oi 1999; Park and Shen 2000). According to survey data for four years, from 1994 to 1997, township enterprises as a whole registered losses in 1996 and 1997, whereas private firms consistently outperformed township enterprises in all four years, that is, they had a higher profitability ratio. Only the newly privatized private firms were unprofitable, and they were unprofitable only in the first year of privatization. This is most likely a result of the fact that it was the loss-making TVEs that were privatized (Park and Shen 2000, p. 40). Chen and Rozelle (1999) conclude that private firms were not afflicted with incentive problems and the market was sufficiently developed by the mid-1990s to allow them to procure all the inputs they needed. The advantages the TVEs held in the 1980s – privileged access to markets and bank credits, compared with private firms – had disappeared by the late 1990s.

3

Problems in China's Corporate Sector

In 1998, as part of a program to "clarify ownership rights," the Suzhou municipal government in Jiangsu province began to examine and sort through all the asset holdings under its control. One Suzhou firm, Suzhou Sanguang Group (Sanguang), was scrutinized particularly carefully.[1] Sanguang was an urban collective firm; that is, in a formal accounting sense it was a wholly owned subsidiary of an SOE. While it was highly profitable, its parent SOE was deeply troubled and on the verge of bankruptcy. Now the Suzhou municipal government was very eager to claim Sanguang as its own. As the owner of all the SOEs in the city, it demanded every right to the assets of the subsidiaries of its SOEs.

The perspective of Sanguang was drastically different. Yes, Sanguang was a subsidiary of an SOE, but the government's only investment was a few pieces of old equipment in 1966 when Sanguang was founded. Nor did the state-owned banks lend any money to the firm. In the 1980s, Bao Zhishu, president of Sanguang, and his colleagues had borrowed equipment from other firms and personally paid for all travel expenses. Despite its slim profits, Sanguang paid a substantial amount of money to the parent SOE as "management fees."

In the 1990s, Sanguang's businesses rapidly expanded as a result of two JVs that it had formed. In 1989, on the books, the total value of its assets was only RMB 420,000 ($112,000 at the 1989 exchange rate). By 1997, its assets had grown to RMB 163 million. The firm suddenly was attractive. Bao Zhishu reflected on the new-found interest from the municipal government:

> We are a collective firm. The state did not invest one single cent [in us]. Now we are growing big and it [the state] turns around and imposes strict controls on us. It invested a lot of money in other firms, but those firms are doing terribly. In the end, it sold off those assets at a discount (i.e., 3 yuan

---

[1] The information is based on an interview with Mr. Bao Zhishu, September 28, 1998.

106

of assets sold for 2 yuan). We all feel that this is totally incomprehensible. But what can we do? . . .

I do not have a single share in this firm. I work on the basis of my sense of duty and conscience. In the end, where are my gains? Frankly speaking, I do not feel calm in my heart.

I revisit Bao's decisions to form JVs in the next chapter, but here let me focus on this unpleasant situation in which he found himself. One can analyze his predicament in two different ways. One is to focus on the benefit side. It can be argued that at least Mr. Bao was allowed to run and grow his business, and the nominal status of his firm conferred political and legal cover for an otherwise unacceptable private business entity. The other perspective is to focus on the cost side. As Mr. Bao himself clearly expressed, his incentives to work hard and to be innovative were harmed by the lack of clear ownership rights. One could further argue that unless the fundamental property rights issue is addressed first, a talented entrepreneur such as Mr. Bao will not be able to continue to grow a dynamic business.

This chapter portrays China's economic, financial, and legal institutions from the cost perspective outlined above. I choose this perspective not necessarily because I believe that the benefit perspective, as an empirical description for the 1980s and possibly for the early 1990s, is wrong. The reason for my choice is that in some writings on the Chinese economy the benefit perspective is presented without sufficiently incorporating the cost side. Furthermore, even if we accept the benefit perspective, at most we can argue that Mr. Bao was able to make do with a very bad situation. But in some writings advocating China's reform strategy, this optimization strategy is sometimes taken to imply that the arrangement that led to the situation Mr. Bao faced was somewhat economically beneficial. According to a noted formulation, the Chinese reforms have been "Pareto-optimal": Winners are created without creating losers (Lau, Qian, and Roland 2000). This latter perspective needs to be reconsidered. Mr. Bao was one loser. He could lose his own business; what is more, he had to forgo a substantial amount of revenue that would have accrued to him had private property rights been more secure.

This chapter has several empirical objectives. The first is to identify those costs that may be associated with China's incomplete reforms. One of these costs, I show, is that Chinese-owned and -operated firms as a whole seem to be less competitive than one might expect. The second is to review one component of China's reform strategy that has received less analytical attention: the policies and programs to strengthen SOEs. Often, China's reform strategy is characterized as partial, that is, the reforms were intended to change some aspects of the planned economy – such as the scope of the market allocation of resources, pricing, and foreign trade and investment – but not others, such as the state ownership of firms. This characterization is correct, but there is another side of the reforms that is just as important. This has to do with the political pecking order of firms emphasized in this book. During the reform era, there were policies and regulations that systematically discriminated against domestic private firms and at the same time supported SOEs on a substantial scale. Reforming SOEs and deregulation are a part – and a very important part – of China's reform strategy. Supporting SOEs and discrimination against private firms are another dimension of the economic policies and practices of the Chinese state.

An important objective of this chapter is to fully understand a central actor in the institutional foundation argument: the SOEs. SOEs, as the recipients of privileged treatments from the government and as the reason for the marginalization of efficient private firms, affect much of the FDI dynamics, either directly or indirectly. They are asset-rich but inefficient, and, as I show, they have also contributed to China's economic fragmentation. Why do SOEs, despite the overwhelming advantages they hold across the board, still fail to perform? Illustrating this question is an important aspect of my analysis.

Another objective of this chapter is to highlight the inherent complexities of many of the issues here. Two features of the reform era deserve special mention. One is that the political pecking order of firms has not been implemented uniformly across the country. Some regions, such as Zhejiang and Guangdong, have not adhered to the political pecking order as much as other regions. Probably, this is one of the most fortunate aspects of Chinese economic development, although, as I show in the next chapter, the solution entails costs on its own. The second feature is that over time the Chinese government has alleviated the political pecking order of firms; in particular, the progress in privatization and in improving the political and economic status of private firms since 1997 has been particularly noticeable.

This chapter begins with a description of problems in China's corporate sector, starting with problems confronting domestic private firms. The second section of the chapter examines the specific manifestations of China's inefficient political pecking order of firms. Next, I examine the SOE question in some detail. The chapter concludes with a description of the manifestations and origins of China's notorious economic fragmentation.

PROBLEMS IN CHINA'S CORPORATE SECTOR

I focus on those problems affecting firms owned and operated by Chinese and thus I exclude FIEs from the following discussion. This is not to suggest that

FIEs are not Chinese as legal entities or that they are free of problems; my selection of firms is dictated by the argument I am making. Since the argument is that the problems in China's corporate sector have led to a more prominent role of FDI and FIEs in the Chinese economy than otherwise would have been the case, it is only natural that I exclude FIEs from this discussion.

The problems of Chinese indigenous firms are manifested in three aspects: the immaturity of private firms, financial losses of SOEs, and scale diseconomies. As we have seen in Chapter 2, in the 1980s and early 1990s Chinese private firms had only a small presence in the Chinese economy. During the course of the 1990s, and especially after 1997, the private sector grew quite substantially, but today many private firms are still plagued with organizational and governance problems. On the other hand, SOEs have operated on the verge of insolvency since the early 1990s, despite their privileged status. In industries such as the automotive industry, where scale constitutes an important competitive advantage, Chinese firms chronically operate at high average costs and churn out low production volumes.

It should be emphasized that all three of these problems were present in the Chinese economy – and in fact, they were far more severe – in the 1980s and they all long preceded the large-scale entry of foreign firms. In analyzing these problems, one should attribute their causes correctly. The causes are rooted in the financial and legal policies and practices designed to enforce the political pecking order of firms. They have little to do with FDI inflows or the presence of FIEs in the Chinese economy.

Private Firms: Entry without Maturation

Some economists believe that the rapid entry of nonstate firms is proof that well-defined and secure property rights are not a precondition for the emergence of a private sector.[2] The reason, as Barry Naughton points out, is that many of the distortions inherent in a centrally planned economy act as sufficiently powerful incentives to enterprising private entrepreneurs.[3]

There is no question that the entry of nonstate firms has been impressive. In the 1980s, the growth of collective firms, especially TVEs, was dramatic. In a volume entitled *The China Miracle*, economists Justin Lin, Fang Cai, and Zhou Li hail the increase in the proportion of industrial output value of the "nonstate sector" from 22.4 percent in 1978 to 51.7 percent in 1992 as a major achievement of the reform era (Lin, Cai, and Li 1996, p. 176). But in the 1980s,

---

[2] See, e.g., Singh (1991) and McKinnon (1992).
[3] See Naughton (1996b), esp. the concluding chapter.

most of this growth was engineered by the collective firms within the nonstate category. In 1991, after ten years of reforms, the private sector only accounted for 5.7 percent of industrial output value. In the 1990s, private firms began to grow more rapidly. In 1998, the two categories of private firms – individual proprietorships and privately operated firms with hired labor – accounted for 17 percent of industrial output value, although this was still small compared with the SOEs (28.2 percent) and collective firms (38.4 percent) in the same year. Because many private firms are in the service sector, their role in the entire economy is more important than that in industry.

These macro statistics are often cited as evidence of the impressive achievements of Chinese reforms and legitimately so. But if one were to look at Chinese private firms at a micro level, a different picture emerges. The rapidly rising share in the industrial output value was mainly a result of the massive entry of private firms. Here, China economists got the story right: The entry of new firms does not require well-specified property rights. Entry and development, however, are two different things. Just as a successful birth of a child is no guarantee of his or her healthy growth, the massive and rapid entry of private firms does not lead to the creation of competitive firms unless there are supporting financial resources and a nurturing institutional environment.

After more than twenty years of reforms, the individual size of private firms is inordinately small. The size of a firm is not a perfect metric, and I use this measure suggestively rather than conclusively. But the fact is that China has experienced twenty years of continuous and rapid economic growth, and in certain product segments it is one of the world's largest producers or markets. Yet during this propitious period, one has not witnessed the emergence of truly private world-class firms owned and operated by the Chinese themselves. Of all Chinese firms, private firms have the best chance to develop into competitive firms. Thus, their small individual size may suggest the presence in the Chinese economic system of substantial constraints on their ability to grow.

In 1998, an industrial private firm generated, on average, just RMB 340,000 (about $40,000) in output value. This compares with RMB 52 million generated by an SOE and RMB 2.4 million by a collective firm. The vast majority of private firms in China are individual businesses, that is, self-employed businesses with no hired labor. In 1998 there were about 6 million individual businesses in Chinese industry. For the economy as a whole, most of the private firms cluster in small-scale tertiary industries such as food and small retail businesses – the ubiquitous clothing stands and food kiosks in Chinese cities. In terms of number of establishments, in the late 1990s these small service firms accounted for 56 percent of the total number of private firms in China (International Finance

Corporation 2000, p. 19). The presence of private firms in capital-intensive industries was minuscule during much of the reform era.

The Chinese government differentiates between two types of private firms. One is an individual business, owned and operated by the proprietor himself, with up to eight hired workers. Another is a privately operated firm defined as one that hires more than eight workers. Both are private firms, as their control and revenue rights belong to private entrepreneurs. The difference is political. A private capital owner who hires workers is perceived to engage in labor exploitation in accordance with the Marxist theory of labor surplus extraction. (In *Das Kapital*, Karl Marx used a hypothetical example of a private firm employing eight workers to illustrate his labor surplus theory.) Thus, a privately operated firm is viewed more suspiciously. From an economic perspective, a private firm that has the ability to hire outside labor is more capable of expanding capacity and developing capabilities to engage in sophisticated manufacturing operations. But there are not many private firms of this kind. In 1998, privately operated industrial firms numbered only some 12,000, and the average output value was RMB 2.2 million, far smaller than that of industrial SOEs.[4] Collectively, private firms are less important in the industrial sector than in the economy as a whole.

Apart from individual size, other indicators tell the same story. According to a comprehensive study of China's private sector conducted by the International Finance Corporation (IFC), a distinctive characteristic of Chinese private firms is their informality. They are overwhelmingly family-owned and -operated. They keep themselves purposely opaque, often with three sets of accounting books – one for the government, one for the bank, and one for themselves. Their real status differs from their legal status. They shift their business focus frequently and are far more reliant on internal financing than similar firms in other economies. Very few private firms have matured beyond the initial founding stage in the life cycle of a firm (International Finance Corporation 2000).

Many of these traits are either ad hoc solutions to or a result of the lack of well-defined and secure property rights for private firms and, ultimately, the result of a lack of ideological commitment to private property. Private firms keep different accounting books for fear of predation. The discrepancy between their

---

[4] Data are based on State Statistical Bureau (1999b). Many private entrepreneurs registered their firms as collective firms, but the figures presented in the text refer to openly private firms. As the discussion below reveals, registering firms as collective firms entails major costs for private entrepreneurs. Also, publicly listed firms are not included because these firms are not privately controlled. Government agencies and SOEs have controlling shares in them.

real and legal statuses arises because private entrepreneurs often have no choice but to register their firms as collectives (called "red-hat" firms) in order to access markets and financing that are exclusively reserved for state-controlled firms. They have diversified in order to avoid regulatory risks. They are reliant on internal financing because China's vast financial resources are denied to them. Because listing on the stock market is not an option, family ownership is one of the few vehicles to solve principal-agent problems.

These distortions entail huge transaction costs for Chinese private entrepreneurs, at several levels. One is that the property rights become intrinsically murky. Title disputes may occur if the business is well run and profitable and government bureaucrats are motivated to seize control of the firm. The Chinese press is full of horror stories. According to one, a private entrepreneur registered his firm as a collective, and in a side – and most likely under-the-table – agreement, he gave 30 percent of the equity stakes to the local government, even though he provided all the equity capital. After paying out all the agreed dividends and taxes, he used a portion of the residual profits to settle a loan, which led to an embezzlement charge. He was sentenced to death by a lower-level court. The case went all the way to the country's Supreme Court and his life was spared only when the State Administration of Industry and Commerce, the branch of government in charge of registering firms, confirmed that the firm was in fact privately owned.[5]

The problem may cut in the other direction. The private entrepreneur, by purposely establishing an ownership tie to the government, may expect a bailout if the firm is not profitable. Entrepreneurs, instead of devoting time, effort, and financial resources to business development, work hard to cultivate particularistic ties with government officials and engage in bribery. A study by economists at the Chinese Academy of Social Sciences concludes (Institute of Industrial Economics 1998, p. 82):

> Wearing a "false" hat can be harmful to both the firm and the society. It confuses what formerly was a clear ownership relationship; unclear ownership leads to short-term behavior and muddles the lines of firms of different ownership types. It creates problems for the macroeconomic policies of the government.

The adverse business environment hampered the expansion and corporate development of Chinese private firms. Today, the largest private firm in China is the Hope Group, located in Sichuan province. The firm produces feed grain and

---

[5] This is recounted in Zhang and Ming (1999), p. 53.

other agribusiness products. In 1999, it generated $600 million in sales revenue.[6] In comparison, the largest private firm in India, the Tata Group, generated sales of $7.2 billion in 1995. Its division in the tea business alone generated sales of $163 million in the same year.[7]

To be sure, a firm such as the Tata Group has a long operating history, dating its origins to the colonial period, and it may be naturally more mature and more developed in its corporate form than a similar private firm in China. One should note, however, India is home to some new and dynamic firms as well. Infosys, a software firm, was founded in 1981. Furthermore, China enjoys some substantial advantages over India. The Chinese economic growth rate has been faster, and China's GDP is twice India's GDP. On a number of policy fronts, China has moved much further than India, on foreign trade and FDI, for example.

Or one can argue that the Tata Group is a conglomerate and thus is naturally larger than a more focused firm such as the Hope Group. If the conglomeration has a superior economic logic in a developing economy,[8] then one should probe into the reasons why private firms in China have failed to acquire and develop this corporate form. As will become clear later in this chapter, private firms in China encounter severe legal, regulatory, and financing constraints, and many of China's most attractive business opportunities – banking, wholesale, automobiles, and so on – were off-limits to them. The Hope Group is just one illustration of the fact that Chinese firms appear to be individually small even though they operate in a large market. In Chapter 4, we encounter China's largest refrigerator maker, Kelon. The firm is roughly comparable in size to Koc Holding in Turkey, despite the fact that China's refrigerator market is nine times the size of the market in Turkey (on the basis of unit sales).

The Insolvency of SOEs

In terms of technical performance, economists have documented positive productivity gains among the SOEs.[9] Capital, labor, and total factor productivity (TFP) growth have been positive, at least according to some estimates.[10] But the SOEs' financial performance has been poor. The financial losses of industrial

---

[6] See International Finance Corporation (2000), p. 4.

[7] Information on the Tata Group is from Khanna, Palepu, and Wu (1998).

[8] Khanna and Palepu (2000), for example, argue that group affiliation can provide a superior mechanism to allocate resources and that this benefit is large when the overall financial institutions are inefficient.

[9] Unless otherwise noted, all the SOEs are industrial SOEs, and the data refer to firms that constitute independent accounting units.

[10] See Groves, Hong, McMillan, and Naughton (1994) and Jefferson and Rawski (1994). The econometric results are subject to debate. See Woo and Fan (1994) for a discussion.

SOEs began to rise sharply in the late 1980s, as measured by the ratio of losses to after-tax profits, from 24.3 percent in 1989 to 89.9 percent in 1990 absent any changes in the tax rates (Lardy 1998, p. 35). Their performance temporarily improved between 1992 and 1994, in part because of a rapid monetary expansion that lowered their interest costs and because of a booming market demand. Their losses averaged 61 percent between 1992 and 1994. Thereafter, losses began once again to rise sharply. As a percentage share of SOE post-tax profits, SOEs' losses were 96.1 percent in 1995, 192 percent in 1996, and 204 percent in 1997, at a time when the government granted numerous tax breaks to SOEs. In 1999, after three years of debt and tax forgiveness combined with genuine corporate reforms, such as large-scale bankruptcies and some limited and partial privatization, SOE losses declined to 88 percent of posttax profits.[11] In essence, the state, as the shareholder of the SOEs, has not derived any sizable capital benefits from owning these firms.

The deteriorating performance of the SOEs was accompanied by an alarming rise in their debt levels. In 1997, the debt/equity ratio for industrial SOEs was 1.87, as compared with 0.75 in 1993.[12] Financing SOE growth has endangered the entire banking system. There is wide recognition of the problem of non-performing loans (NPLs) in the Chinese banking sector, but estimates vary as to its magnitude. The official estimate of nonperforming loans in the four state banks for 1998 was RMB 1.7 trillion (about $205 billion) against total outstanding loans of RMB 6.8 trillion. The nonperforming loan ratio was 25 percent. Of the RMB 1.7 trillion of NPLs, about 20 percent, or RMB 340 billion, was considered "nonrecoverable," that is, they exceeded the liquidation value of the borrowers' assets after the borrowers went bankrupt. Chinese NPLs amount to more than 30 percent of GDP; in contrast, the costs associated with the savings and loan crisis in the United States amounted to only 2 percent of GDP.[13]

---

[11] The financial performance data for SOEs are given by Institute of Industrial Economics (2000). The 1999 data are given by State Statistical Bureau (2000).

[12] Figures for the 1980s and 1993 are from Sehrt (1998). The 1997 figure is calculated from State Statistical Bureau (1998d).

[13] One difficulty in arriving at a precise estimate of the amount of NPLs has to do with different classification practices. Chinese standards for loan classifications are loose compared with those used in other countries. First, the Chinese classifications are tied to the status of not the borrower but the loan payment. For example, if a borrower defaults on one loan, but not on a second loan, the Chinese bank increases the provisions against only the loan actually defaulted upon rather than the entire loan portfolio of the borrower. Second, the classification of bad loans is tied to repayment of loan principals but not to interest payments. Third, provisions are made not against the riskiness of the loan portfolio but against the actual default actions. Thus, during a real estate crash, Chinese banks do not normally increase their bad debt provisions against their real estate exposure as long as the borrower is in compliance with the terms of the loan. For a detailed discussion, see Lardy (1998).

The Miniaturization of Chinese Firms

Chinese firms tend to be small across the board. While many institutional impediments constrain the growth of private firms, the output size of Chinese SOEs is also inordinately small. (Here, we refer to size as measured in physical units, not in financial terms.) The reason is the severe extent of fragmentation of the Chinese economy, which leads to a miniaturization of Chinese firms, even in those industries where size constitutes a major source of competitive advantage.[14]

Probably the best illustration of the extent of economic fragmentation in China is the country's automotive industry. The automotive industry is among the most scale-intensive industries, where large firms enjoy cost advantages over smaller firms, that is, average costs fall when the volume of production increases. Commonly, economy of scale is measured in terms of the minimum efficiency scale (MES), that is, the minimum absolute scale of production required for efficiency. For vehicle assembly, the MES is commonly given around 250,000 units at the plant level for a single basic model type.[15] The MES for other automotive products is similarly large. For example, estimates range between 250,000 units to 1 million units for engines and transmissions.

Although recent technological and process innovations may have modified the MES requirements, there is no doubt that the Chinese automotive industry is plagued by scale diseconomies. In 1998 China produced 1.63 million motor vehicles. This output volume was spread among many vehicular classifications and models and among some 115 assembly enterprises, with an average volume of about 14,165 units per firm.[16] Production fragmentation exists not only at the plant level but also at the geographic level. In 1998, only five provinces out of thirty-one did not operate an automobile assembly plant. Passenger car assembly is similarly fragmented. As of 1998, there were nineteen passenger car assembly firms, with a total output of 507,861 units, averaging 26,729 units per firm. To drive these numbers home further, the entire output volume of the 115 assembly firms in China is just slightly larger than the output volume of one single Japanese firm in 1969 (Toyota), with 1.47 million units. The entire passenger car output volume of the nineteen passenger car assemblers in 1998 was only one-half that of Toyota in 1969 (964,088 units).

---

[14] For a comprehensive treatment of this topic, see Steinfeld (2002).

[15] Estimates vary among experts but they all fall within the 250,000 to 300,000 range. See Baranson (1969), Pratten (1971), White (1971), and Rhys (1972).

[16] The figure for assembly enterprises does not include hundreds of firms/plants that specialize in outfitting chassis for special purpose vehicles or plants specializing in components production. The 1998 figures are from China Automotive Technology Research Center (1999).

Table 3.1 *Concentration Ratios of the Automotive Industry: A Four-Country Comparison (Percent of Industrial Output)*

	One-firm ratio	Two-firm ratio	Three-firm ratio
Brazil			
1959	24.8	42.7	60.6
1970	56.1	74.3	91.2
Japan			
1960	32.1	56.1	65.1
1975	33.7	63.6	72.8
Korea			
1975	54.6	77.7	96.4
1986	71.3	88.6	97.9
China			
1985	19.2	38.0	43.0
1992	13.1	26.0	32.1
1993	13.7	25.2	34.0
1994	13.5	26.6	35.7
1995	12.6	23.6	33.3
1996	13.9	27.5	37.8
1997	14.6	25.6	35.6
1998	14.7	25.4	34.4

Sources: Data on Brazil, Japan, and Korea are calculated from various issues of *World Motor Vehicle Data*, compiled and published by the Motor Vehicle Manufacturers Association. Data on China are calculated from Ministry of Machinery Industry (1997b, 1998, 1999).

Because the automotive industry is scale-intensive, the miniaturization of automotive production must be due to China-specific factors rather than to industry dynamics. One way to illustrate this point is to compare China with other countries. The idea here is that underlying economic factors tend to drive concentration ratios to similar levels across different countries. Economic studies have found that concentration ratios in market economies are rooted in production technology, scale economies, and the use of the product. To the extent that concentration ratios within the same industry differ, the cause must lie in country-specific factors.[17]

Table 3.1 compares China with Brazil, Japan, and Korea during the 1960s, 1970s, and 1980s. These countries, like China in the 1990s, attempted to develop an automotive industry, which was already dominated by large incumbent players. Two clear contrasts are evident. One is that as measured by one- to three-firm ratios, the Chinese automotive industry was far more fragmented both at the

[17] The classic analysis along this line is Pryor (1972).

beginning and at the end of the period under comparison. In 1985, the one-firm ratio was 19.2 percent in China, as compared with 24.8 percent in Brazil (1959), 32.1 percent in Japan (1960), and 54.6 percent in Korea (1975). The second contrast is the trend in concentration. Among all three benchmark countries, the automotive industry became more concentrated over time; in China, however, over time the automotive industry became less concentrated. In 1985, for example, the three-firm ratio was 43 percent but it declined to 33.3 percent in 1995 and 37.8 percent in 1996. In the 1990s, the concentration ratios stayed at a low level despite government efforts in 1994 to streamline the industry. Only since 1997 have the concentration ratios stopped declining.[18]

POLITICAL PECKING ORDER (1): SUPPORTING SOEs

In our Local Leadership Survey, as reported in Chapter 2, the respondents were asked to rank the contributions of SOEs to China's economic development. The rankings given by Chinese officials correlate exactly with the political pecking order of firms. SOEs were ranked first, followed by collective firms, and private firms at the bottom. The political preferences do have consequences: They are translated into economic policies, regulatory practices, and credit decisions. In this section, I describe a number of policy and regulatory manifestations of the political pecking order of firms, which favors SOEs to the detriment of private firms.

Policies that supported SOEs encompassed three broad areas: (1) heavy investments in SOEs, (2) bank financing of SOE investment activities at subsidized rates, and (3) importing technology to strengthen the SOEs' technical capacities. These policies have been carried out under an institutional infrastructure that is itself fundamentally statist: China's banking system. I start first with a brief description of China's banking system and then proceed to describe SOE-supportive policies.

The Statist Banking System

The Chinese banking system is composed of three tiers. The first tier consists of what are known as policy banks,[19] and the second tier consists of four

---

[18] It should be stressed that the dispersion of China's automotive facilities did not result from the globalization of the industry. In the 1980s, almost all new entrants were domestic firms. In the mid-1990s, foreign firms began to produce in China, but as JVs with existing Chinese firms. Foreign firms thus did not contribute to the fragmentation of the industry.

[19] These are the State Development Bank, the Import and Export Bank, and the Agricultural Development Bank. Created in 1994, policy banks are mandated to provide investment financing to central government projects and to fulfill state grain procurement plans.

117

commercial banks.[20] The third tier consists of much smaller regional and main banks of the SOEs.[21] In the 1990s, the four commercial banks dominated China's financial system. Together, as of 1993, they accounted for about 81 percent of the total loans. Apart from the extent of their ownership ties to the central government (see below) and their size, roughly speaking, the smaller lower-tier banks are more market-oriented than the policy and commercial banks. Their lending decisions are guided more by profitability considerations and their loan rates are more flexible.

The policy banks and all four commercial banks are 100 percent owned by the state. The shareholding arrangements of the smallest banks are fundamentally statist as well. Their shareholders are either local governments or SOEs. Two dramatic examples show the level of the commitment to keep the Chinese banking system state-owned. First, the one bank with the strongest ties to the private sector, the Minsheng Bank, is in fact under the jurisdiction of the All-China Federation of Industry and Commerce, a government organization overseeing private firms. In the other instance, in 1995, the central government compelled the genuinely private Urban Credit Cooperatives (UCCs) to form shareholding ties with municipal governments with the aim of imposing better financial supervision over them. In a single sweep, the municipal governments became the largest shareholders of the UCCs (renamed urban cooperative banks in 1995). The financial performance of the UCCs was far superior to that of the state commercial banks. In addition, improving financial supervision was a regulatory matter and did not necessarily require an ownership change of these banks (Girardin 1997).

Investment Program

In the 1980s and 1990s, China was investing at "a pace of technological transformation," according to a World Bank economist, "that cannot be matched by any other developing country."[22] The SOEs' fixed asset investment grew at a real double-digit rate for five years out of the thirteen-year period between 1985 and 1998. After the Asian financial crisis in 1997, the fixed asset investment rate accelerated once again, although the focus has been on infrastructure rather than on manufacturing industries. SOE ownership of operating assets,

[20] They are the Agricultural Bank of China, the Industrial and Commercial Bank of China, the Construction Bank of China, and the Bank of China.
[21] Examples of third-tier banks include Pudong Development Bank, Shenzhen Development Bank, Huaxia Bank, Bank of Communications, and rural credit cooperatives (RCCs) and urban credit cooperatives (UCCs).
[22] Quoted by Nolan (1996).

although having declined in relative terms, is still dominant. In 1995, industrial SOEs owned 53.7 percent of the stock of assets, as compared with 74.6 percent a decade earlier. But this decline was less than half of the proportionate shrinkage of the output share of the SOEs (Lardy 1998, p. 30).

Preferential Bank Financing

The rapid growth of SOEs' fixed asset investments occurred during a period when the financial performance of SOEs was deteriorating continuously. Poor operating efficiency, coupled with heavy investments in them, led to a huge accumulation of illiquid assets in the state sector. It also means that their investment activities are financed by external funds. A significant portion of the SOEs' fixed asset expenditures is financed by bank loans. In 1993, some 24 percent of fixed asset investment was financed by bank loans and another 10 percent was financed by the government budget.[23] This benefited the SOEs enormously, in several ways. One is that nonstate firms were often unable to obtain loans. During the inflationary period in the late 1980s and mid-1990s, the central bank reduced credit available to nonstate firms while keeping the monetary tap open to SOEs. This greater credit availability allowed the SOEs to build up capacity and expand market positions just when the nonstate firms had to retrench. In addition, in high inflation years the real loan rates were usually negative, subsidizing the state-owned loan recipients. For example, in 1989 and 1993, the prices of producer goods rose by 19 percent and 24 percent, respectively, but the working capital loan rates were held at 11.3 and 11.0 percent, respectively.[24]

Loan subsidies to SOEs also stemmed from the deliberate intention to benefit SOEs. Until 1996, interest rates on working capital loans for nonstate firms were mandated to be 20 percent higher than the same type of loans for SOEs. Since 1996, SOE loan rates have been used as a benchmark from which rates for nonstate firm loans are allowed to fluctuate upward by 20 percent (but not downward). In fact, many of the loans were more like grants. Debt forgiveness and payment deferrals were routinely granted. Loan obligations were not stringent, as indicated by the high percentage of overdue loans. The loan turnover ratios – defined as the ratio of the number of days in a calendar year divided by the average number of days for a loan to complete one turnover – have declined. In 1991 the ratio was 1.25 times; in 1992, 1.32 times; in 1993, 1.19 times; and

---

[23] Calculated from data in State Statistical Bureau (1996b).
[24] See World Bank (1990) and Lardy (1998).

Table 3.2 *Loan-to-Deposit Ratios and SOE Shares in Selected Provinces,*
1988 and 1993

	Loan-to-deposit ratio		SOE percentage shares (1993)	
Provinces	1988	1993	Industrial output value	Industrial employment
Top three[a]				
Jilin	1.9	1.9	75	100
Inner Mongolia	1.5	1.6	82	70
Heilongjiang	1.6	1.5	83	71
Bottom three[a]				
Fujian	1.2	1.0	40	42
Zhejiang	1.2	0.9	31	28
Guangdong	1.3	0.8	34	32

[a] Refer to ranks in loan-to-deposit ratio in 1993.

Sources: Loan-to-deposit ratios are from Lardy (1998). SOE's output and employment shares are calculated from State Statistical Bureau (1994b).

in 1994, 1.08 times.[25] This laxity in loan obligations was due to pressures by local governments on banks to protect the firms under their charge,[26] but it was also a deliberate policy choice made by the central government to support the SOEs. Between 1998 and 2000, to fulfill his pledge to restore SOE profitability within three years, Premier Zhu Rongji implemented a concerted program to reduce the interest burdens on SOEs via a combination of across-the-board loan payment forgiveness and debt-for-equity swaps.

One of the ways the Chinese banking system has been used to support SOEs is through the interbank lending system. In general, the banking system channels resources from provinces with a large nonstate or private sector to provinces with a large state sector. Thus, loan-deposit ratios vary across different provinces. Banks in rich and more reformed provinces are not able to loan more than their deposits, whereas banks in provinces with a large state sector are allowed to do so. This is shown in Table 3.2, which presents the top three and bottom three loan-to-deposit ratios and the respective shares of SOEs in output value and

---

[25] Cited in Sehrt (1998).

[26] This observation is confirmed by a number of enterprise-level studies. In their study of Chongqing Clock and Watch Company, Byrd and Tidrick find that depreciation charges or taxes on fixed assets were diverted to loan repayments, and in the case that these were not sufficient, industrial-commercial taxes were used for the same purpose (Byrd and Tidrick 1992). Another enterprise-level study, of Changchun Bicycle Factory, reveals that the Changchun municipal government bailed out the money-losing factory in 1983 by exempting all of its tax obligations for 1983 and 1984, in addition to granting a subsidy of RMB 3 million in 1983. The factory was able to take out a new loan, from the same bank, for RMB 4.8 million (Zhang 1992).

employment. The top three provinces all have very high SOE shares in output value and employment, whereas the bottom three provinces, Fujian, Zhejiang, and Guangdong, the most reformed provinces, have a small state sector. The Chinese banking system, in effect, acts as a giant redistributive mechanism to transfer savings from the private sector to finance the investment and social obligations of the state sector.

Technological Upgrading

Building up new fixed assets was complemented by a systematic program to upgrade the technological capacity of SOEs. In 1982, the State Council drafted "Concerning Technological Renovations of Existing Enterprises in a Focused, Step-by-Step Manner." In this document and a series of related ones, the State Council outlined the goal of technological leapfrogging by importing foreign capital goods and technology. Under this program, 550 key firms and research institutes were identified as entities in critical sectors needing special and focused assistance from the state. The electronics and machine-building industries, two industries populated by SOEs, were given priority in the government's technological program. In 1985, the government initiated another round of reforms with the intention of commercializing both the funding and application of the R&D programs of governmental institutions. Numerous high technology zones were established throughout the country.

China imported technology and equipment on a large scale in the 1980s and 1990s. Technology acquisitions focused heavily on acquiring turnkey equipment and machinery. China also entered into many technology transfer programs, such as licensing, servicing, and consultations. Between 1981 and 1989, the state allocated $27 billion to support 17,000 technology importation projects (Simon 1991, p. 581). During the 1981–95 period, China spent $53.5 billion on technology imports; of this amount 72 percent was accounted for by the importation of turnkey projects. Technical licensing, which is a direct payment for technology, constituted 10.5 percent of the total contractual value of technology imports during the same period (Whitla and Davies 1998). The primary beneficiaries of these technology importation programs have been the SOEs. As a survey of firms in Jiangsu shows, in the 1980s most of the imported equipment and technology went to the SOEs (He, Gu, and Yan 1996). This policy bias in favor of SOEs persisted into the 1990s. According to a 1995 survey, 25 percent of sampled SOEs relied on imported equipment technology as their principal source of technical innovations, while 18.4 percent of collective firms did so. For private firms, the figure was only 12.5 percent (China Managerial Survey System 1996).

POLITICAL PECKING ORDER (2): DISCRIMINATION AGAINST
PRIVATE FIRMS

The mirror image of the preferential treatment of SOEs is the poor treatment
received by private firms. In 1996, Gao Shangquan and Chi Fulin, two prominent
economists in China, noted the following (Gao and Chi 1996, p. 104):[27]

> At the end of 1992, the average registered capital of China's privately
> owned enterprises was less than RMB 140,000 [about $26,000 at the
> 1992 exchange rate], and their average output value was only about RMB
> 200,000, thus impeding their expansion. The main reason is that privately
> owned enterprises cannot obtain loans from banks on an equal footing
> with enterprises in the public sector.

I begin with a review of the legal and regulatory restrictions on the private
sector and then describe the financial practices that complement these restrictions. I note that the discriminatory policies against the private sector have not
been enforced consistently over time and uniformly across the entire country.
There is considerable flexibility in the Chinese economic system that has alleviated the constraints on the private sector from being fully enforced. This is
one of the most fortunate aspects of Chinese economic development, and this
flexibility has allowed for the massive entry of private firms under otherwise
difficult circumstances.

Legal and Regulatory Biases

A study by the prestigious Institute of Industrial Economics of the Chinese
Academy of Social Sciences concludes the following (Institute of Industrial
Economics 1998, p. 81):

> In many places, the property and trademarks of private firms or even the
> legitimate civil rights of private investors are not effectively protected
> by law. Violations of rights occur frequently. Because the violators are
> usually a government department, a law enforcement agency, or a firm
> with connections, the majority of private enterprises can only keep quiet.
> If they sue and win, they will lose valuable connections and they will have
> endless trouble on their hands.

This stark and frank assessment reveals the fragile position of private entrepreneurs in the Chinese economy. Among all the constraints on the growth

---

[27] The authors here refer to privately operated firms with hired labor. These firms are larger than
self-employed individual businesses.

of private firms, the low political and legal statuses of private firms are most fundamental and most blatant.

Constitutional Status. The foremost bias against nonstate firms, private firms in particular, is legal in nature. Until 1988, there was no constitutional recognition of the property rights of private firms. Article 11 of the 1982 Constitution acknowledges only the property rights of individual enterprises, defined as self-employed businesses. This conspicuous silence on the property rights of private-operated firms stems from an ideological consideration – the specter of exploitation raised by such firms. In 1988, Article 11 was amended to include a clause that permits private firms and promises to protect their "lawful rights and interests." However, the amended article reserves the right of the state to exercise "guidance, supervision, and control over the private sector of the economy." The amendment also carefully subordinates the private sector to "a supplement to the socialist public economy."[28] This wording is important because it justifies the political pecking order firmly on constitutional grounds. Private firms are allowed to grow but only to the point of not attenuating the socialist character of the economy and only to the extent of complementing the SOEs. Not until March 1999 did the Chinese Constitution acknowledge the private sector as an *integral* part of the Chinese economy and assign to private firms an equal footing with other firms. The private economy is now a component of, rather than a supplement to, the Chinese economy.[29]

To put this issue in perspective, one can compare the legal treatment of private firms with that of SOEs. The Chinese Constitution not only upholds state property rights but protects the "sanctity" of such rights. There is no similar recognition that private property rights are sanctimonious. Given the substantial role of the state in the Chinese economy, this presents a problem: How does a court adjudicate a property rights dispute between a government agency and a private company? Until the 1999 amendment, the constitutional treatment of private firms was inferior to that of FIEs. China's current constitution, adopted in 1982, only six years after the end of the Cultural Revolution, clarifies and offers protection to the legal status of foreign enterprises operating in China (Article 18). Foreign enterprises are permitted "to invest in China and to enter into various forms of economic cooperation with Chinese enterprises and other Chinese economic organizations...." Article 18 also vows to protect their "lawful rights and interests." Thus, from the very beginning of the economic

---

[28] The texts of the 1982 Constitution and the 1988 amendment are found in *Constitution of the People's Republic of China* (1994).

[29] See "Amendments to the Constitution of the People's Republic of China" (1999).

reforms, FIEs were accorded a superior legal status as compared with the private firms, despite the fact that FIEs, theoretically at least, could be 99 percent owned by foreign, and private, investors. (However, many of the FIEs in the 1980s were JVs with SOEs, and from an ideological perspective, they were considered less problematic for this reason.)

Regulatory Restrictions. The report by the IFC cites numerous market restrictions on private firms. According to regulations, private firms are to be excluded from the following types of industries: those that use scarce resources; those that are considered vital to the national economy; and those whose products may pose hazards to public health. According to another list, private capital is not permitted in some thirty industries and in seventeen products belonging to other industries, including banking, railways, freeways, telecommunications, and wholesale networks. Yet another list restricts private capital in automobile manufacturing and chemical fibers (International Finance Corporation 2000, p. 37).

The numerous lists cited in the IFC study are not published, but there is evidence that these restrictions are enforced with some vigor. An example is the scarce presence of private firms in the machinery industry, which the government considers as a "pillar industry." The industry has enjoyed targeted and substantial financial support from the state since the early 1980s, and private firms have been systematically excluded from it. The machinery industry consists of eleven major product groups, and, as of 1997, private firms were found in only three (agricultural machinery, electric appliances, and automobiles), while SOEs and collective firms were present in all of them. This is not because private firms were inefficient. Private firms were more profitable than SOEs and collective firms, and, in electric appliances, they were larger, as measured by the size of their equity capital, than the collective firms and comparable in size to FIEs funded by firms from ethnically Chinese economies (ECEs). Remarkably, many of the sectors that are off-limits to private firms have always been open to foreign investors. To be sure, various restrictions on equity holdings and export and local content requirements are imposed on foreign investors, but there are very few categorical bans on foreign investments. In the 1999 WTO agreement with the United States, the Chinese government promised to remove many of the ownership and product restrictions on foreign investors, and thus the discrimination against private firms will become even more severe, unless there is a substantial improvement in the treatment of the private sector. Access to foreign markets was also restricted during the 1980s and much of the 1990s. While export licenses were routinely granted to FIEs, until 1998 they were seldom granted to private firms. Export licensing is economically valuable as it allows a firm to hold foreign currencies and to bypass the state-owned trading companies. (Trading companies can expropriate the value-added of exports as well as hold the tax returns belonging to the export producers.)

Financial Discrimination against Private Firms

A private entrepreneur recounted the following story. He ran an extremely profitable real estate company in Beijing, and was the largest depositor in a local division of a major state bank.[30] In 1997, he sought a meeting with the head of the bank division through an intermediary. In response to this request, the head of the bank division said: "I have a policy of never meeting with private entrepreneurs. Our bank division once lent money to private farmers in 1954 to buy donkeys. They never returned the money."[31]

This story provides a powerful insight into the mentality and practices of Chinese banks. The division chief was apparently oblivious to the fact that this potential customer was his biggest creditor and that his cavalier response might have caused the private entrepreneur to take his business elsewhere. (He did.) Second, this division chief seemed to be much more forgiving toward his SOE borrowers, many of whom defaulted on their loan obligations. In the late 1990s, the state-owned banks had on their balance sheets nonperforming loans amounting to 25 to 40 percent of their total loan assets, largely because of the bad loans in the state sector.[32]

The third revelation is extremely important: Chinese banks in the 1990s did not discriminate against firms on the basis of *size* but on the basis of *ownership*. (The private entrepreneur in question ran a large real estate company.) This is quite different from the kind of financial bias in many developing countries. In the 1980s and 1990s, small and medium TVEs, firms closely allied with rural governments, accounted for a growing share of rural lending from state financial institutions. Park and Shen (2000) show that in 1985 TVEs accounted for 17 percent of the rural lending by state financial institutions; in 1994, they accounted for 32 percent. This is confirmation of the idea that financial discrimination against private firms was instituted for political reasons, not for economic or administrative reasons (such as the inability to monitor the loans or the lack of capabilities to assess the risks).

---

[30] The government imposes fewer restrictions on private firms in the real estate sector.

[31] Interview with Pan Shiyi, general manager of Redstone Industrie Corporation, August 31, 2000.

[32] The bank manager forgot, or chose to ignore, a force majeure that had led to the defaults by the private farmers in 1954: The government had collectivized agriculture and confiscated the private means of production.

The following paragraphs first describe a set of banking practices that reinforced the lending bias against nonstate firms. Then, I illustrate the point that the political pecking order was enforced across ownership categories of firms – i.e., state versus nonstate – but also within the nonstate category as well. For example, TVEs, although also classified as nonstate firms, were substantially favored over private firms.

Banking Policies and Practices. During the 1980s, China's central bank, People's Bank of China (PBC), issued credit plans to the regional branches of the commercial banks.[33] The purpose was to reconcile the lending priorities of the banks with the investment project lists drawn up by the government agencies. The SOEs submitted their investment plans along with funding requests – for fiscal grants and credits – to the government agencies they reported to. These plans and then the funding requests were reconciled at a provincial and eventually at a central government level. Lending quotas were then issued to bank branches, which made loans on the basis of these quotas. Such a mechanism was in place until 1998, but in the 1990s, bank branches were given more autonomy in their loan decisions.[34] (The autonomy was limited, however, as a popular saying among Chinese bankers indicates, "The government orders the dishes; we pay for them.") Because many of the nonstate firms, especially the private firms, operated completely outside this bureaucratic chain of command, they were unable to submit their investment lists in the first place. Thus, the credit plan formulation process itself already excluded a large number of the nonstate firms.

Until 1998, the four commercial banks, which control most of the banking assets, were instructed to lend to SOEs only, while the much smaller credit cooperatives were instructed to serve private firms as their clients (Institute of Industrial Economics 1998, p. 87). But numerous restrictions were put on the credit cooperatives. The deposit base of the Rural Credit Cooperatives (RCCs) and UCCs was restricted to nonstate firms in the regions where their bank branches were located. They were also restricted to lending to firms only in the same regions. These restrictions hampered the ability of RCCs and UCCs to perform a significant financial intermediation function. The shares of the total loans by these two types of institutions were correspondingly small. In 1996, UCCs accounted for 4 percent of total loans, and RCCs, 10 percent (China

---

[33] The phenomenon of a lending bias on the part of the Chinese banking system in favor of SOEs has been widely documented. The most comprehensive study of the Chinese banking system is Lardy (1998).

[34] For a summary description of investment and credit plan formulation, see Huang (1996) and Sehrt (1998).

Finance Association 1997, p. 465). Also, UCCs and RCCs do not have the level of branch networks of the four state-owned commercial banks. In effect, this division of client base between state-owned commercial banks and credit cooperatives constitutes an explicit lending bias against private firms.

Because of the restrictions, lending to nonstate firms by the four commercial banks remained a minuscule portion of their loan portfolio. In 1996, some 3 percent of the newly extended working capital loans went to urban collective firms, and only 0.1 percent went to purely private enterprises. In comparison, FIEs accounted for about 3 percent of the new lending from the commercial banks in the same year (China Finance Association 1997). At the end of 1998, the private sector claimed less than 1 percent of working capital loans outstanding from Chinese banks and nonfinancial institutions (International Finance Corporation 2000, p. 45). Even banks specifically authorized to lend to private firms lent very little. In 1997, only 6.87 percent of the total credits outstanding at the Minsheng Bank went to the private sector (Institute of Industrial Economics 2000, p. 443). The reason is that banks often consider private firms high risks. Private firms have low prestige and their guarantors may be unreliable (Gao and Chi 1996).

The credit constraints force private firms to turn to usurers for loans at very high rates (Gao and Chi 1996). Or they have to finance their activities from internal sources of funds. The IFC study finds that Chinese entrepreneurs rely on insider financing to a far greater extent than entrepreneurs in the United States, the Czech and Slovak republics, Russia, and even Vietnam (International Finance Corporation 2000, pp. 48–50).

Financial Treatement of TVEs and Private Firms. Chapter 4 compares the demand for FDI from two types of firms, TVEs and private firms. It is thus important to distinguish the financial treatment between them. Although both TVEs and private firms are classified as nonstate, some are more nonstate than others. Township governments own and operate township enterprises. Village enterprises, on the other hand, enjoy substantial and numerous ties to the village governments. Although village officials are not formal civil servants in the Chinese nomenclature, village committees perform a multitude of governmental functions, such as enforcing population control policies and grain procurement. Although TVEs as a whole occupy a lower rung on the political pecking order of firms than SOEs, there is a pecking order within the nonstate sector that favors those firms closest to the state, such as township enterprises, at the expense of purely private firms. This is in part because of the notion that TVEs are government firms.

Jean Oi (1999), a political scientist at Stanford, documents instances in which township and village officials derisively referred to private firms as "underground snakes." Political attitudes aside, the standard banking practices also operated against purely private firms. In the 1990s, banks required loan guarantees, and the guarantors were usually township governments or TVEs. In the event that one TVE defaulted, the remaining solvent TVEs would make the payment. However, private firms were generally excluded from this arrangement.[35] Not surprisingly, private firms in rural areas received far fewer bank credits relative to their economic importance as compared with TVEs. In 1995, for example, private firms and jointly owned firms accounted for 54 percent of the net profits in rural industry, but they received only 14.6 percent of the loans. The firms receiving the largest share of loans, at 60.6 percent in 1995, generated the least amount of net profit (17.8 percent). These were firms at the top of the political pecking order within the nonstate category – the township enterprises. The village enterprises, politically tiered in the middle, received 24.9 percent of the loans while generating 28.2 percent of the net profits.[36] Here, the political pecking order and the efficiency performance among rural firms correspond exactly to that among SOEs, collective firms, and private firms.

Lack of Equity Financing. Equity financing is similarly unavailable. While in the 1990s China's two stock exchanges in Shanghai and Shenzhen had developed rapidly since their founding in 1990, they primarily served as fund-raising vehicles for the SOEs. As one expert commented, "The securities market is essentially a state securities market conceived and designed to support corporatized SOEs."[37] According to one estimate, nonstate listed companies accounted for around 3 percent of all domestically listed companies. Of the 976 companies listed on the Shanghai and Shenzhen stock exchanges as of 1999, only eleven were nonstate firms.[38] For many years, prominent economists in China, Wu Jinglian and Dong Fureng, have called for providing greater listing access for private firms. But progress has been slow. After 1997, when the policy toward the private sector is considered to have been liberalized, a total of only four nonstate firm initial public offerings took place (in 1998 and 1999). In the

---

[35] For analysis emphasizing the role of loan guarantees, see Oi (1999), Park and Shen (2000), and Whiting (2001). For a view that stresses the role of political interference and collateral mobilization, see Che and Qian (1998).

[36] This is based on Table 3 in Oi (1999). It should be pointed out, as Oi does, that the status of private firms has improved substantially. In 1985, private firms generated 42.6 percent of net profits but received only 9.7 percent of the loans.

[37] Quoted from Lin (2000).

[38] See So (2000).

mid-1990s, the equity financing of nonstate firms became more difficult. In 1995, the authorities closed down several regional stock markets that served small and medium-sized firms, ending a source of funds to private firms (International Finance Corporation 2000).

Alleviation of the Political Pecking Order of Firms

So far, I have presented a standard perspective on the lending bias and legal and regulatory discrimination against private firms in the Chinese economy. As a general description, the perspective is correct. There are, however, two modifications. The first, and probably the most important, modification is that the political pecking order was not adopted uniformly across the country. This was an important source of the flexibility in the system that enabled dynamic economic growth and the emergence of competitive firms in some regions of the country. In the next chapter, I deal with some of the limitations of this flexibility. The chief limitation is that the regions that enforced more efficient economic policies tended to be poorly endowed with industrial and technical capabilities. Related to this consideration is that the level of the government that tended to be more economically liberal was also administratively lower-tiered and was able to mobilize only a limited amount of resources.

Probably the most prominent example of economic flexibility is Guangdong province. As we will see in the case study on China's largest refrigerator maker, Kelon, in the next chapter, Shunde county in Guangdong actively sponsored and financed entrepreneurs to start up businesses in the 1980s. The government created innovative arrangements to grant entrepreneurs maximum capacity to run and operate businesses, while carefully managing the political aspects of firm development. This is the famous TVE phenomenon. It worked for a long period of time, although in recent years it has run into considerable strains, in part because the arrangement is suited only to small firms. (For an explanation as to why it does not work for large TVEs, see the appendix to this chapter.)

Such a pro-business approach was not limited to Shunde county. In a fascinating study, Professor Qiwen Lu traces the rise and development of successful Chinese high-tech companies, such as Stone, Legend, and Founder (Lu 2000). In each instance, the entrepreneurs successfully created mutually beneficial arrangements with a government agency or with local authorities to mimic, as best as they could, the operating autonomy of a private firm, while retaining the political status of an SOE. The gist of the arrangement was to delegate control rights of the firm to the entrepreneurs, while the government agency retained the nominal ownership rights. But over time, as Professor Lu shows, the entrepreneurs began to demand formal recognition of their de facto ownership rights. Thus, while the approach worked to the extent of allowing the emergence of entrepreneurial firms, further development at these firms will require deeper institutional reforms.

Some local governments also pioneered in the privatization drive. Shunde, for example, began to adopt a large-scale privatization program as early as 1992. Before 1992, not a single SOE was privatized (Qian 1999). There are other examples as well. Zhucheng in Shandong province experimented with shareholding reforms in 1994 long before the rest of the country (Institute of Industrial Economics 1996, p. 78). There are also regions in China that have a long tradition of supporting private enterprises. The most famous example in this regard is Wenzhou city in Zhejiang province. Wenzhou never had a large SOE sector even during the Cultural Revolution. During the reform era, an informal credit market functioned on a large scale to finance private sector activities.[39] A widespread practice to provide private firms access to China's formal financial system is to allow SOEs to act as agents to intermediate between banks and private firms. But obviously, this is not a preferred arrangement. Given its under-the-table nature, the size of individual loans intermediated through this mechanism cannot be very large. In addition, the separation between the de facto and de jure loan obligations creates default incentives on the part of private firms. This is not a viable business practice. There are also political risks. Both SOE managers and entrepreneurs are known to have landed in trouble for creating such arrangements.[40]

The second modification to our portrayal of the Chinese economy is that over time the central government began to relax the political pecking order of firms. As already pointed out, in the 1980s, the nonstate firms that developed the fastest were collective firms; in the 1990s, the private sector developed the fastest. This was in part because of the substantial improvement in the financial treatment of private firms in the 1990s. The first breakthrough occurred in 1992, when Deng Xiaoping called for a greater opening and scope of reforms during his famous southern tour. The number of private firms increased dramatically, but mainly as a rebound from the suppressive policies toward the private sector adopted by the central government between 1989 and 1991. The main changes involved policy changes; the institutions and long-standing policy practices, such as lending quotas, were not fundamentally altered.

The next breakthrough occurred in 1997, when, at the Fifteenth Party Congress, the government announced its policy of "grasping the big and letting go of the small." "Grasping the big" meant restructuring and consolidating

---

[39] See Liu (1992) and Whiting (2001).
[40] See Institute of Industrial Economics (1998) and Zhang and Ming (1999).

China's largest SOEs. "Letting go of the small" meant that the government vowed support for privatization of small SOEs. (According to a government estimate, small SOEs accounted for some 18 percent of the assets in the state sector as of 1997.)[41] These methods include straightforward sales to private investors, managerial restructuring, alliances with other firms, mergers, leasing, managerial contracting, and employee stock options (State Statistical Bureau 1998c). This was a clear signal that the government intended to retreat from the most competitive sectors of the economy. Politically, this was highly significant. While spontaneous privatization in the local areas had already begun to occur in a number of provinces, an explicit policy stance endorsing privatization conferred political legitimacy on such practices. A leading China economist, Yingyi Qian (1999), commented, "It is quite remarkable for China to have overcome ideological and political opposition to embrace the market system and private ownership without a political revolution."

The treatment of the private sector improved substantially after this policy change, and policy measures designed to neutralize some of the inherent biases against private firms were adopted in rapid succession. In 1998, the central bank replaced lending quotas with softer indicative guidance. The quota system had precluded private firms from even competing for a credit line. In 1998, the government began to grant export licenses to private firms. Access to the equity market was made easier for private firms when, in March 2000, the government abolished the listing quotas – reserved exclusively for SOEs – in favor of a system in which underwriters determine the timing and pricing of new issues.

Fundamentally, the lending bias against private firms did not operate in a vacuum. It reflects a well-entrenched and institutionalized ideological hostility toward private firms. It is indicated by the following mentality among Chinese bankers: "It does not matter if SOEs cannot pay back the loans, even if in the amount of millions or tens of millions of yuan. But if a private firm cannot make a payment, even if it is only RMB 100,000 or RMB 80,000, people suspect trickery."[42] Ultimately, it is the political status of the private firms, more than the specific financial policies of the government, that determines their treatment, not just by the government, but also by their customers, suppliers, and banks. In July 2001, in the most dramatic shift to date, President Jiang Zemin announced that the Communist Party would welcome private entrepreneurs to join its ranks. This policy will have substantial implications for the development of the private sector in China.

[41] This is according to State Development and Planning Commission (1998).
[42] Quoted in Institute of Industrial Economics (1998).

THE CAUSES OF THE PROBLEMS IN THE STATE SECTOR

The failure of Chinese private firms to attain competitiveness is easy to understand. Innate entrepreneurial attributes, such as profit incentives, innovativeness, willingness to take risks, and business acumen, and resources (broadly defined to include financial resources as well as business opportunities) are complementary with one another. For a businessperson to excel and for a firm to be competitive and to sustain its competitive edge, entrepreneurial talent needs to be combined with resources in an efficient manner. Property rights need to be secure to motivate her to work hard and to have a stable expectation of future rewards from current investments of time, effort, and money. The myriad financial, legal, and regulatory biases have worked to the huge detriment of entrepreneurial talent in China. Despite many propitious conditions, China's private firms, with firm output value of only $40,000 as of 1998, seem to be far from reaching their full developmental potential.

The uncompetitiveness of SOEs requires a more extended discussion. SOEs occupy a privileged position and yet they still fail. When it comes to improving a firm's performance and competitiveness, Chinese economic officials and SOE managers have a simple formula: A greater quantity and quality of equipment and machinery equals competitiveness. This fixation with fixed assets has heavily influenced Chinese analyses and policy prescriptions for the SOE problem. Massive financial resources have been invested in SOEs and precious foreign exchange has been expended to acquire advanced equipment and technology from abroad.

In the following paragraphs, I show that SOEs have had the best of China's physical and human capital. The problem is not a lack of resources but a poorly designed incentive structure that does not encourage an efficient deployment of the resources at the disposal of the SOEs. This is a consensus view from many studies of the problems of the SOEs.

Advantages of SOEs

In the late 1990s, a visitor to a typical SOE may have seen machinery and equipment in poor working condition. She may have concluded that the problem was that the SOE did not have sufficient modern technology and equipment. In fact, what she saw represented years of neglect and poor usage of initially valuable capital assets. By any measure, for many years, SOEs were the best equipped firms in China.

Human Capital Advantage. Jefferson, Rawski, and Zheng (1999), citing an innovation survey by China's State Statistical Bureau, show that firms of all ownership types identified SOEs as the most advanced in their product lines. Data from 1985 suggest that the number of technicians as a proportion of the SOE work force was about twice the average industry level, while the number in collective firms and TVEs was only 22.5 percent and 23.3 percent of the average industry level, respectively. By 1989, the technical edge of the SOEs had eroded but the SOEs still commanded a huge lead. Their ratio was 19 percent above the average industry level, while the ratios for collective firms and TVEs were 5.5 percent and 21 percent below, respectively (Jefferson, Rawski, and Zheng 1999, Table 4.2).

In the 1990s, the SOEs possessed better or equivalent levels of physical and human capital, compared not only with nonstate domestic firms but even with some of the FIEs widely acknowledged to be the best-performing firms in China. We measure the quality of human capital in two ways. One is the share of "knowledge workers," that is, engineers and managers, in the labor force. The other measure is the educational level of the employees; more specifically, the proportion of employees with college degrees. According to data compiled in the *Third Industrial Census* in 1995, while traditional SOEs have about the same proportion of knowledge workers as nonstate firms, state-controlled shareholding enterprises – all converted from SOEs – are better endowed with quality human capital. (In the mid-1990s, many of the newly established SOEs were reorganized as shareholding corporations. The government still owns the majority of their shares. Traditional SOEs are those that were not converted. Unless noted otherwise, I refer to the unconverted SOEs as traditional SOEs and SOEs as both traditional SOEs and state-controlled shareholding enterprises.)

This is seen in Table 3.3. In terms of the engineer/employee ratio, the traditional SOEs, at 6.4 percent, rank number four in the table, and in terms of the manager/employee ratio, the traditional SOEs rank number three. The advantage of state firms is more apparent in the case of the state-controlled shareholding enterprises. State-controlled shareholding enterprises have roughly the same manager/employee ratio as foreign-funded FIEs and have more engineers on their staff than all other firms. Furthermore, employees at SOEs and state-controlled shareholding enterprises are more educated. The proportion of college graduates is 7.95 percent at SOEs and 9.18 percent at state-controlled shareholding enterprises, the second and highest ratios in the table, respectively.

As late as 1999, when SOEs were beset with massive financial difficulties, surveys of SOEs and nonstate firms still showed a human capital advantage for SOEs. According to a survey conducted in the fall of 2000 of 800 companies, SOEs on average had 6.8 engineers/technicians per firm, as compared with

Table 3.3 *Human and Physical Capital Measures in Chinese Industry Across Ownership Types, 1995*

	Human capital measures: entire industry (percentage of employees)			Physical capital measures: machinery industry only (physical units per firm)				Average assets per firm (RMB million), machinery industry
	Engineers	Managers	College graduates	Precision machine tools	Forging presses	Vehicles	Computers	
Traditional SOEs[a]	6.4	10.8	8.0	110.3	17.9	12.5	5.3	837.6
State-controlled SHEs[b]	7.9	11.2	9.2	191.4	31.4	24.0	16.0	2,308
Collective firms	5.3	10.2	1.9	35.9	9.9	4.2	1.3	179.1
Private firms	6.5	10.0	3.6	32.3	7.0	7.0	6.3	756.6
Township enterprises	5.9	9.6	1.1	–[c]	–	–	–	–
FIE (1): Foreign-funded	7.0	11.3	7.8	58.2	10.5	11.6	15.7	2,327
FIE (2): Overseas Chinese funded	5.8	10.5	5.3	41.1	9.8	7.8	5.8	619.3

[a] Traditional SOEs refer to those SOEs that retained the traditional corporate structure during the ownership reforms in the mid-1990s.
[b] SHEs refer to shareholding enterprises. Many of the state-controlled SHEs were converted from SOEs beginning in the mid-1990s.
[c] –: Data not available.

Sources: Office of Third Industrial Census (1997) and machinery industry database (see Chapter 6 for a detailed explanation).

6.47 engineers/technicians per firm in the non-SOEs. SOEs employed 9.47 college graduates per firm in 1999, compared with 4.24 in the non-SOEs.[43]

Advantage in Hard Assets. The quality of physical capital is harder to measure and data are more limited. One measure is the fixed asset turnover ratio, which is the ratio of sales to net fixed assets. This measure is the amount of sales generated per unit of net fixed assets. The lower the ratio, the more fixed assets are required to generate sales. By this measure, the SOEs use capital stock most heavily. Based on the 1995 *Third Industrial Census*, the fixed asset ratio was 1.22 for traditional SOEs and 2.45 for state-controlled shareholding enterprises. In contrast, the ratio for private and township firms was 4.13 and 3.38, respectively.

The fixed asset turnover ratio, however, is also a measure of the capital intensity of production, and one can argue that SOEs have a lower fixed asset ratio simply because they operate in more capital-intensive sectors. The fixed asset ratio is also a performance measure. A lower ratio implies, all else being equal, an inefficient use of capital. Thus, the fact that SOEs have the lowest fixed asset ratio may be evidence of their inefficiencies, not necessarily of their asset advantages.

One way to avoid confounding our results with intersectoral differences in capital intensity is to focus on only one industry. Differences in capital intensity are smaller across product lines within the same industry than across different industries. To cleanly separate the performance aspects of SOEs from their asset positions, we can assess the firms' capital stock in terms of physical units, that is, a count of major capital goods used in the production process. Table 3.3 provides details on a number of key equipment installations across different ownership types in the machinery industry.

As shown in the table, traditional SOEs and state-controlled shareholding enterprises hold a substantial asset advantage over nonstate firms and a modest advantage over FIEs. Traditional SOEs and state-controlled shareholding enterprises average 110.3 and 191.4 units of precision machine tools per firm. No other firms even come close to these numbers. Traditional SOEs and state-controlled shareholding enterprises also command a considerable lead in ownership of units of forging presses and vehicles. Traditional SOEs own fewer computers as compared with other firms, but state-controlled shareholding enterprises own more computers (16) compared with the enterprises with the second most computers, foreign-funded FIEs, with 15.7 units. The equipment advantage held by traditional SOEs and state-controlled shareholding firms is not due to the fact that they are large. As shown in Table 3.3, in terms of assets,

---

[43] Reported in Keister and Lu (2001).

traditional SOEs and private firms are comparable in size, while state-controlled shareholding firms and FIEs – funded by "foreign," that is, non-ECE, firms – are quite comparable in asset size.

Poor Performance and Incentive Problems

SOEs have enjoyed advantages in every conceivable way. They have had more hard and better assets; they have had privileged access to financing and market opportunities; and they have had quality personnel. But throughout the reform era, their financial performance has deteriorated almost continuously. There is also evidence, reviewed below, that SOEs know how to accumulate assets and but do not know how to operate them efficiently. This is an important characteristic that explains why many SOEs became attractive acquisition targets in the 1990s, a topic I touch on in Chapter 4 and analyze in greater detail in Chapter 5.

These performance problems raise a fundamental issue about the suitability of governmental ownership of firms. In this section, building on many of the studies on SOEs, I suggest that it is the governmental ownership itself that is the problem. This is not based on the idea that the government is inefficient or corrupt. Instead, the idea is that the government is a complex organization that pursues many objectives. In this context, it is difficult for the government to pursue one objective – such as profitability – at the expense of other equally worthy objectives.

Inefficient Utilization of Assets. The substantial asset advantages enjoyed by SOEs, however, fail to translate into operating and financial advantages. Jefferson, Rawski, and Zheng (1999) show that despite the technical edge of SOEs, they are less innovative. In their study, innovation is measured by the share of new product production in the gross value of industrial output. By this measure, new products accounted for 9.5 percent of the gross value of industrial output of SOEs between 1987 and 1989, compared with 11.5 percent for the collective firms and 20.1 percent for the TVEs. In their regression analysis, Jefferson, Rawski, and Zheng (1999) show that the marginal productivity of technicians in TVEs surpassed that of technicians in SOEs by a factor of 2.5. The marginal productivity of TVEs is even higher compared with that of SOEs – by a factor of four – when the expenditures on new product development are used to predict patterns of innovation activities.

Poor utilization of valuable and abundant resources by SOEs is widespread in China. The governments and firms import costly turnkey projects but do not utilize them efficiently. The emphasis on technical sophistication rather than on market needs led to an excess demand for technology, as well as to an under-utilization of existing technological and asset capacity. According to a study of fifty-three technology acquisition projects, only twenty-three met expected targets. The total cost of these projects amounted to RMB 300 million (State Council and State Planning Commission 1990). A survey of firms in Jiangsu province shows that most of the projects with imported technology failed to meet profit targets. Of the 1,890 turnkey importation projects, only 31 percent of the project managers reported meeting or exceeding expected profit targets; 69 percent reported not meeting expected profit targets or being unable to evaluate the results (He, Gu, and Yan 1996). A 1988 study by the Statistical Office of the Beijing Municipal Government reports very low utilization ratios, below 50 percent and some as low as 23 percent, for imported precision machine tools among SOEs in Beijing (State Statistical Bureau 1988, pp. 62–63).

Inefficient utilization of acquired technology is one piece of evidence; another piece of evidence is that SOEs overspend on technological acquisitions while they underfund those activities that matter the most to a firm's bottom line: integration of the imported technology into production processes. According to a Chinese study (Wu 1996), for every ten dollars of imported equipment, Chinese firms spend one dollar on technology assimilation. In contrast, Korean and Japanese firms spend one dollar on technology acquisition but ten dollars on integration. The primary objective of SOEs is to qualify for state allocation of foreign exchange to finance technology acquisition. Thus, they are interested in spending the money rather than in generating positive returns from improving their technological base. After all, if a firm acquires technology at a lower cost, the bureaucracy reclaims any foreign exchange savings. This leads to cost-maximizing rather than profit-maximizing behavior and poor acquisition decisions.

Governmental Ownership and Incentive Problems of SOEs. Reflecting both the magnitude and the persistence of the problems in the SOEs, the literature on SOEs is voluminous. Here I summarize some major themes and suggest that to the extent there is a consensus view it is that the SOE problem stems from governmental ownership. The implication for my analysis of FDI is direct: Throughout this volume, I have stressed that FDI is an ownership arrangement. A portion of the FDI inflows that financed acquisition of the assets of SOEs in the 1990s, in essence, was a solution to the problem associated with governmental ownership of firms. FDI as a privatization vehicle is neither new nor unique to China; but what may be unusual is the fact that at the same time FDI was encouraged, domestic private firms were restricted from bidding for the assets in the state sector.

A common view in the SOE literature is that SOEs face soft budget constraints. Soft budget constraints refer to a bureaucratic readiness to provide financial assistance and, ultimately, to prevent bankruptcy.[44] Soft budget constraints imply zero risks for the investment activities undertaken by SOEs and are an important reason why restraints on capital spending by SOEs are not self-enforcing. SOEs are not sufficiently motivated to economize on production factors, especially capital, and, by extension, SOEs are not motivated to maximize profits. The corporate organization of SOEs is another problem.[45] For example, Laffont argues that the problem with government-owned firms is rooted in poor selection and motivation of managers.[46] SOEs are hierarchical. In a large hierarchy with many layers, incentives are distorted and monitoring is costly. Performance becomes suboptimal as a result.[47]

Another approach is to stress the imposition of the wrong objectives on SOEs. Here, the analytical focus shifts from SOEs to government, the owner. Political interferences are inefficient and are designed to advance political rather than economic objectives. This way of analyzing SOEs is best illustrated by the failures of the SOE reforms in China. Managerial decentralization – delegating controls to SOE managers – creates an insider problem: Managers are able to siphon off profits or maximize employment. But taking away controls from managers creates an opposite set of problems: Bureaucrats then have an avenue to intervene in decision making and to impose noneconomic objectives on those firms under their charge. Yingyi Qian (1996) argues that China's reform approach – to delegate decision-making power to managers while preserving state ownership – has led to the following dilemma: "[E]ither the agency costs are high because managers lack accountability or the political costs are high because the government causes political interference."

The above accounts are not an exhaustive list, but many important explanatory elements are included. Almost all these explanations can be subsumed under a general framework that portrays the government as an inappropriate owner of firms. Scholars offer many perspectives on this issue. One is the idea that the state promotes social rather than economic welfare and uses SOEs as instruments. Thus, while SOEs can be economically inefficient, they serve larger social goals. A more critical view is that "politicians do not maximize social

---

[44] For a classic illustration of soft budget constraints, see Kornai (1980). Grosfeld (1989) comments, "[S]oftness of the budget means that there is no danger of a forced exit. Even if enterprises have to repay credits (which is not always necessary) insolvency is not a real threat; they can always rely on subsidies, price adjustment, tax facilities, and so on."

[45] A good summary of corporate governance issues is found in Aoki and Kim (1995).

[46] The study is cited in Shleifer and Vishny (1998).

[47] See Milgrom and Roberts (1990) and Qian (1994).

welfare and instead pursue their own selfish objectives." This is the "grabbing-hand view" of the state.[48]

One does not have to assume the state to be either benign or malicious to reach the conclusion that the state is an inappropriate owner. The only assumption needed is that the state is a complex organization. My analysis below adopts this perspective and is largely based on Wilson (1989). Two sources of complexities are especially relevant to an analysis of the SOE question. First, a government is not supposed to maximize profits to the exclusion of other goals. Indeed, a government would be considered a very bad one if it were to do so. Governments pursue multiple objectives: collecting taxes, controlling pollution, enhancing local education, as well as running SOEs efficiently. It would be extremely harmful to evaluate the performance of a government official only on a single dimension – such as the profitability of the firms under his management – when operating SOEs may very well involve trade-offs with other objectives. For example, a governor rewarded excessively for industrial production may enforce antipollution regulations less stringently. Holmstrom and Milgrom (1991) illustrate this issue by citing an example from the debate in American education about the wisdom to link teachers' pay with students' test scores. While proponents argue that the scheme will make teachers work harder to raise test scores, opponents point out that the scheme will discourage creative thinking and intellectual curiosity – qualities not easily captured by test scores.

Second, control and revenue rights are substantially more separate from each other in the case of SOEs compared with privately owned but publicly traded firms. There is a bureaucratic separation: The Ministry of Industry may possess control rights, but the Ministry of Finance may possess revenue rights. Another separation is more fundamental. Under state ownership, bureaucrats exercise control rights, but they possess none of the actual rights to cash flows. Whether or not they make the right managerial or operating decisions entails few consequences for their compensation. As Kornai (1992, pp. 74–75) remarks,

> Whatever state-owned firm one takes as an example, there is no individual, family, or small group of partners to whom one can point as owners. Since no one can pocket the profits and no one need pay out of his own pocket for the losses, property in this sense is not only depersonalized but eliminated. State property belongs to all and to none.

In this respect, SOEs are similar to nonprofit organizations in market economies. Nonprofit organizations are "owned" by a trust but the trust

---

[48] For these contrasting perspectives, see Vernon and Aharoni (1981) and Shleifer and Vishny (1998).

officers do not have cash flow rights from the owned assets; instead, the trust officers are supposed to execute their fiduciary responsibilities in the best interests of the donors and customers of the organizations. These trust officers execute their tasks well not because of monetary incentives but because of their sense of duty and high morality.[49]

The analogy to nonprofit organizations makes it easy to appreciate the practical difficulties of operating and managing SOEs. Essentially, one needs morally upright, socially conscientious, and altruistic bureaucrats to perform the ownership functions of the SOEs. While it is possible to find a few high-quality bureaucrats to manage a small number of SOEs (such as Singapore Airlines), it is an entirely different question when the number of SOEs gets very large, as noted by Perkins (2001).[50] Our analysis also sheds light on why TVEs – smaller SOEs controlled by the lowest levels of government in China – can be efficient. There are two reasons. One is that the incomes of township and village officials are tied to the performance of TVEs, which links control with revenue rights. The other is that at the lowest level of the political system, the objectives of the government are fewer and less in conflict with each other. This line of analysis also implies that continued governmental ownership will pose problems for TVEs that have grown large, as we see in the next chapter in the case of Kelon. (More details on why TVEs can be successful when they are small are contained in the appendix to this chapter.)

ECONOMIC FRAGMENTATION AND COMPETITIVENESS OF DOMESTIC FIRMS

The Chinese economy has been variously described as a "cellular" economy, federalism, Chinese-style, or de facto federalism.[51] However phrased, the basic idea is that China has a decentralized economic structure, under which each region is operationally and financially autonomous, as if it were a profit center in a firm. Such an arrangement provides some benefits, such as a hardening of budget constraints at the local level, but it also entails some substantial costs. The miniaturization of Chinese firms, as I have shown at the beginning of this chapter, is one such effect, but there are other and more subtle effects as well. One is that a large and competitive market often can serve as a training ground

---

[49] For a good discussion of nonprofit organizations, see Hansmann (1996).

[50] This is the contrast between Korea and Singapore, on the one hand, and China, on the other. The high performance of an SOE such as POSCO in Korea requires a high degree of management autonomy and consistent evaluation on the basis of profitability.

[51] These various concepts are drawn from Donnithorne (1981), Qian and Xu (1993), Huang (1996), and Qian (1999).

for firms to develop their capabilities. Economic fragmentation reduces such a benefit. For this reason it is possible that Chinese firms are less competitive than they might have been otherwise because they are forced to operate in smaller and more homogeneous local markets. I explore this and related issues in this section.

One Country, Thirty-One Economies?

Market segmentation means that goods, services, and factors of production, such as capital and labor, are not easily mobile across regions. There is extensive statistical and anecdotal evidence that shows that China's goods market is fragmented, although an intriguing paper by Barry Naughton presents a contrarian perspective.[52] Sure, some of China's market segments are quite large on their own, and a moderate degree of market segmentation is natural. What is unusual is not the low level of economic integration among Chinese provinces but the fact that China's market appears to have become more segmented over time. The most telling evidence concerns the physical distance over which a freight shipment travels. A longer distance implies a greater mobility of goods. The average distance traveled by a freight shipment fell from 395 kilometers in 1978 to 310 kilometers in 2000, despite a huge expansion of national highways, ports, and air cargo facilities during this period ("China's Local Trade Barriers: A Hard Nut to Crack" 2001).[53] The World Bank, in probably the most comprehensive study of this issue to date, presents data showing increasing price variations across Chinese provinces. Between 1986 and 1991, for seven broad categories of consumer goods, regional variations in prices increased. Cross-regional variations in returns on capital increased even while variations in profit rates across industrial sectors declined between 1985 and 1991. After controlling for differences in tax rates, the average coefficient of the variation value for twenty provinces was 0.193 in 1986 but 0.657 in 1990. The World Bank draws the following conclusion: "The overall finding is that there is no evidence to support a convergence of returns on

---

[52] See Naughton (1999). Specifically, Naughton shows that the degree of intraindustry trade – that is, final manufactured goods – is very high. However, as detailed in the text, most economists agree that China's capital market is segmented. This low capital mobility would seem at odds with the portrayal of China as having a highly integrated goods market. For works that purport to show a high degree of market fragmentation, see World Bank (1994) and Young (2000b). For a vivid account of the tactics and methods local governments use to protect their own industries, see Wedeman (forthcoming).

[53] This is an indication of an absolute decline in interregional trade, which is a better measure of market segmentation than the one that tracks a relative decline. I thank Professor Lou Wells for a clarification of this issue.

capital across different provinces. Other things being equal, this suggests that capital mobility has not increased noticeably since 1985" (World Bank 1994, p. 54).

In fact, there is evidence to suggest that capital mobility decreased, at least until the early 1990s. Two researchers, Shaoguang Wang and Angang Hu, show that net exports as ratios of provincial GDP declined uniformly across all Chinese provinces in the 1980s and 1990s (Wang and Hu 1999). Net exports are the differences between savings and investments in a province. When a province saves more than it invests, its net exports are positive, that is, it is exporting capital to other provinces (or to the central government). When a province invests more than it saves, it is importing capital in order to finance the portion of its capital requirements it cannot fund on its own. What these two researchers show is that provinces with an initially large positive net export position in the late 1970s (such as Beijing, Tianjin, and Shanghai) ended up with a significantly smaller positive net export position in the early 1990s. On the other hand, provinces that received a large amount of capital from other provinces in the late 1970s received far less by the early 1990s. Although this measure is imprecise, it can serve as a rough indicator of the extent of the barriers to interprovincial capital mobility.[54]

More direct and reliable indicators come from surveys. A survey of 800 firms in China administered in the fall of 2000 reveals that the investment activities of Chinese firms are overwhelmingly local in nature. According to this survey, although 48 percent of the firms have invested in other firms, 85.8 percent have invested in firms in the same city and 91.1 percent have invested in firms in the same province (Keister and Lu 2001). Basically, Chinese firms do not venture outside their respective localities. Nor do they finance their investments by borrowing capital from other provinces. As shown previously, much of the interprovincial bank lending appeared to finance the social obligations of SOEs rather than business expansions of private firms.

That the Chinese economy is fragmented or that it has become more fragmented over time is not a new revelation to students of the Chinese economy; what may be less familiar is the striking extent of this fragmentation. As shown in Chapter 1, some Chinese provinces depend more heavily on FDI than on investments from other provinces. China's economic fragmentation is also surprising

---

[54] Wang and Hu do not net out the portion of capital exported to the central government. This weakens their claim that there was substantial interprovincial capital movement before the reforms. There may have been substantial movement of capital across provinces before the reforms, but it was organized by the central planners.

considering how centralized its political system is. Political unification is often thought to facilitate economic unification as trade in goods, services, and assets is transacted under common, or at least similar, regulatory and legal frameworks and standards. Political integration is also supposed to reduce transaction costs of trade by creating a common currency area and allowing for freedom to travel across different regions. It is thus unusual for a country to have a high degree of political centralization coupled with a substantial degree of market segmentation. The aforementioned World Bank report makes the following comment, "In China today, there is an anomalous situation where major elements of economic union including a single currency and a common external tariff are combined with a lack of some basic features of a free trade area" (World Bank 1994, p. 7).

Economic Fragmentation and State Ownership

The Chinese economic system classifies enterprises according to their level of administrative supervision. An enterprise is categorized as a "central enterprise" (*zhongyang qiye*) if the control rights – managerial appointments, asset disposals, strategic directions – of the firms and some or all of the income rights reside with the central government in Beijing. A regional enterprise (*difang qiye*), as the name suggests, is one where the same control and income rights belong to a regional government. Regional enterprises can be further divided into provincial enterprises (*shengshu qiye*) or city or county enterprises (*shishu* or *xianshu qiye*). In 1995, according to the *Third Industrial Census*, there were 87,905 industrial SOEs, of which 83,167 were owned by regional governments. Regional SOEs accounted for 65 percent of total SOE assets and 64 percent of sales.[55] In addition to control and revenue rights, the Chinese system also divides the tax base between the central and local governments according to the administrative classifications of firms. Central firms pay income taxes to the central government while local firms' tax revenues go to the local coffers.

Local governments protect their firms through various measures, as noted in a report by Chinese economists from the Academy of Social Sciences (Institute of Industrial Economics 1996, p. 294):

Some local governments shut one eye when local firms produce low-quality products or products with false trademarks. They even extend

---

[55] Among the regionally owned SOEs, most are controlled by county-level governments. County governments controlled 50,123 SOEs out of the 83,167 regionally owned SOEs. The data are from the 1995 industrial census. See Office of Third Industrial Census (1997).

administrative protection to these firms. On the other hand, they harass firms from other regions on a number of dimensions, such as firm registration, health inspection, and technical standards, even if these firms produce superior products. Some local governments discriminate against outside firms in bank lending, even going so far as to forbid bank lending to the outside firms. The local courts, when handling economic disputes, favor local firms.

The dominant view in studies of the Chinese economy attributes the rise of local protectionism to the system of assigning administrative controls of firms to local governments. The idea is that since locally controlled firms constitute the main revenue and tax bases, the local governments have an incentive to restrict imports from and prevent capital exports to other provinces.[56] This view is incomplete. We have to ask why the Chinese state has chosen administrative decentralization to manage its firms in the first place.

The policy to divide the controls of firms between the central government and local governments has a long history in China. The broad principle of this enterprise administration was laid out in a March 1951 State Council circular entitled, "Decision to Establish a Tax Division System for 1951."[57] Despite the widely acknowledged fragmentation effect of this way of administering tax collection and assigning control and income rights of SOEs, the system enjoys remarkable resiliency. The reason is that administrative decentralization is one of the few policy instruments available to the government to improve the efficiency of firms *within a framework of state ownership.*

As mentioned, in 1995 there were almost 90,000 industrial SOEs in the country. The informational requirements to run this number of firms are simply beyond the capacity of a single bureaucracy.[58] As long as the Chinese state insists on retaining control rights over these firms, the enormous managerial and administrative complexities leave no choice but to partition control rights among different branches or levels of the bureaucracy. The decentralization of income rights and tax authority, for example, gives regional governments a financial stake in the operation of SOEs. This serves the purpose of alleviating the intrinsic complexities of running a socialist economy because it is an incentive device to ensure that local governments put their resources to create value since the system allows them to retain a portion of the value creation. The effect of

---

[56] Shaoguang Wang and Angang Hu advocate this view in a series of influential articles and books. Their views are summarized in Wang and Hu (1999). See also World Bank (1995b).

[57] For a detailed history of economic management, see Zhao (1989a).

[58] Perkins (2001) argues that the sheer number of firms in China would make it infeasible for the Chinese state to pursue an industrial policy fashioned after that in Korea.

this system is to ease the need for the central government to constantly monitor and supervise the actions of the local governments.[59]

From this perspective, economic fragmentation did not result from poor policy designs or mistakes; it is a costly by-product of a conscious decision by the state to preserve socialism while searching for a way to minimize the high informational costs of administering such an economic system. In this respect, our analysis goes to the very heart of the theme of this book: The political pecking order of firms is also the foundation of China's economic fragmentation. The solution to this problem is a shift away from administrative decentralization – that is, moving managerial responsibilities and financial resources from a higher-level bureaucracy to a lower-level bureaucracy – to *economic* decentralization. Economic decentralization moves the same responsibilities and resources from the government to private entities and entrepreneurs. Privatization is a form of economic decentralization, and when this option is not available, FDI becomes a de facto solution, a theme I return to in Chapters 5 and 6.

Fragmentation and Firm Competitiveness

One may argue that market fragmentation is not as harmful as commonly feared. One consideration is that market fragmentation may benefit some local firms because it allows them to sell to a captive market. This is true, for example, if the protected local market is sufficiently large.[60] This consideration requires some attention to the characteristics of the industries being selected for analysis. The industry should be characterized by scale economies, and the costs of market fragmentation should be obvious and substantial. Thus, in discussing the FDI-fragmentation connection in this book, I focus on the automotive industry. The motor vehicle market, while growing rapidly at the national level, is very small within individual provinces. A provincial market is insufficient to sustain the kind of geographic dispersion of production facilities one observes in this industry. Also, it is important to distinguish between a regional firm and a domestic firm. Local protectionism is a benefit to a regional firm in that protected market, but it restricts market access on the part of a domestic firm located in another province. Our analysis of the competitiveness effects of economic fragmentation focuses on domestic, not on regional, firms.

Another consideration concerns the role of the export market. During the reform era, as China's marketplace became more segmented, the country was

---

[59] Lyons (1986) explains China's economic fragmentation in terms of the characteristics of the planning system. My explanation complements his explanation but the main emphasis is on the state ownership, and less on the central planning approach.

[60] I thank Professor Pankaj Ghemawat for this observation.

more open to foreign trade. Chinese firms, while not able to compete with other Chinese firms located in other jurisdictions, may still be able to compete with foreign firms in the overseas markets. (Imports are still restricted.) This issue leads to a discussion of the importance of a home market. Home market characteristics, according to one prominent theme in economics, tend to play a more important role in shaping the competitiveness of firms compared with the role of foreign markets. Below, I borrow the framework developed by Michael Porter to illustrate the connections of the home market and its various characteristics with firm competitiveness.

Home Base of Firms. The home base of a firm plays a large role in creating and shaping competitiveness at the firm level. The home base consists of both production factors as well as demand-side factors. A firm is more likely to attain competitiveness, as measured against the best in the world, if it operates in an environment with the right home base conditions. The demand-side factors are especially important. Managers are more likely to pay attention to buyers' needs and characteristics nearby rather than to those far away. They also understand home buyers better. There is "an intuitive grasp of buyers' circumstances" that cannot be achieved for foreign buyers. Without cultural complications, communication is easier and free of misunderstandings between buyers and producers of the same country.[61] An export market, in contrast, is not able to supply the same functions as effectively, at least for some products.

The Size of a Home Market. There are many demand-side factors in this analytical framework. Of particular relevance to our analysis here are the size and quality of the home market demand. The effect associated with the size of the home market demand on firm competitiveness is not obvious. Countries often thought of as having a small home market, such as Switzerland, Sweden, and Korea, boast many of the most preeminent firms in the world. Indeed, precisely because of the small size of their home markets, firms in these countries were pressured to export and to excel on the global market. "Home market size proves to play a complex role in national advantage," as Porter (1990, pp. 92–93) remarks, "and other aspects of home demand are as or more important."

With these caveats in mind, it is still reasonable to argue that a large home market entails a number of advantages, especially in the Chinese context, where

---

[61] Apart from production factors and demand-side conditions, Porter also deals with the importance of related industries and firm strategy. These four aspects reinforce one another to constitute what he calls the "national diamond," a system that determines the competitiveness of nations. See Porter (1990).

a compression of home market demand does not readily translate into export pressures.[62] For one thing, a large market confers "static efficiency" on firms operating in industries characterized by economies of scale. In the case of China's automotive industry, the benefit of static efficiency is reduced due to the economic fragmentation. In this industry at least, when Chinese firms operate in artificially small market segments, the negative effect of economic fragmentation on competitiveness is unambiguous.

Competition. The quality of the home market demand, as much as or more than the quantity of the home market demand, has a strong bearing on national competitiveness. Sophisticated and demanding buyers prod firms to innovate and to invest in continuous product improvements. They also help firms identify the needs of the most advanced buyers. Among the most important factors affecting the quality of home market demand is the extent of competition. Vibrant domestic competition is among the most important factors that makes a nation competitive.[63] China fails this basic test, by a long shot. Artificially carving up a single market into several smaller segments lowers the quality of the home market demand. The effect of trade protectionism and capital controls at the regional level is that firms operate as near monopolies in highly regionalized markets and in pockets of high profits. The degree of rivalry is sharply reduced despite the presence of a large number of firms in the Chinese economy.

Deprived of choices, Chinese buyers are captive in those product segments targeted by regional governments. For example, it would be hard for taxi companies in Shanghai to staff their fleets with vehicles produced in other parts of the country. Similarly, a Shanghai auto firm will find it hard to source components outside Shanghai. (Specific illustrations of local protectionism are presented in Chapter 6.) These are not demanding market conditions that compel firms to be innovative and to make huge investments in product improvement.

Economic fragmentation also diminishes a natural and huge advantage China has over many other developing countries: the diverse demand conditions created by its vast geographic expanse. Diversity of demand conditions fosters competitive advantages. The commercial air-conditioning industry is advanced in the United States because the country encompasses practically all conceivable

---

[62] The lack of a compensating export outlet is important for our analysis. After all, the logic that a large home market does not matter rests not on the notion that large market size per se does not matter but on the notion that an export market often entails very exacting conditions on firms operating in that market.

[63] As Porter (1990) puts it, "Among the strongest empirical findings from our research is the association between vigorous domestic rivalry and the creation and persistence of competitive advantage in an industry."

climatic and industry conditions.[64] China is comparable to the United States in physical size and it encompasses extremely diverse geographic, climatic, social, and economic conditions. In addition, the rural/urban contrast is sharp. A firm that meets the heterogeneous market conditions and demands at home is better prepared to compete globally. Economic fragmentation decomposes a single market with many heterogeneous attributes into smaller and individually homogenous segments. Thus, the importance of a factor – its natural diversity – that ought to foster national competitiveness in China is greatly diminished as a result of its economic fragmentation.

CONCLUSION

This chapter goes into considerable detail to document many of the biases in the Chinese system that have operated against efficient private firms. This portrayal of the Chinese economy, while not necessarily directly contradicting the prevailing view in the economic literature on China, does emphasize one aspect of the Chinese reforms that has received relatively less attention. Throughout the 1980s and until 1997 or so, the main thrust of the strategy of the government was to reform SOEs, but a significant component of its strategy was also to strengthen the technical and production capacity of SOEs. To achieve this latter objective, the government designed policies, regulations, and a legal infrastructure to mobilize and then channel a massive amount of resources to the SOEs at the direct expense of domestic private firms.

There are many explanations for this way of allocating resources, some more charitable than others. Whether the strategy was politically wise or not, its economic imprint is very clear. In the early 1990s, China's corporate sector was uncompetitive. The SOEs were losing money, and truly efficient private firms were credit-constrained and legally disadvantaged. The goods and asset market segmentation only compounded the problem. An otherwise large internal market was reduced to many small segments, and the result was a huge diseconomy of scale on the part of Chinese firms. Chinese firms were both statically and dynamically inefficient. It was against this background the country chose to open its doors substantially to FDI in 1992, and it was in this large economic context in the 1990s that FDI played an important financing role in the Chinese economy. As I show in the following three chapters, many of the FDI patterns depicted in Chapter 1 can be understood only if we keep in mind the larger institutional and economic contexts of the 1990s. This is the premise of our institutional foundation argument.

---

[64] This section draws from Porter (1990).

Appendix to Chapter 3:
Why TVEs Can Be Successful
(as Long as They Are Small)

TVEs, as a number of economists have pointed out, have been enormously successful, but at their core, they are still SOEs, albeit owned by the lowest level of government.[65] The success of TVEs is in fact rooted in the reform of the government, not of firms. Township and village officials draw their income and bonuses only partially from a centrally determined budgetary process and they supplement their income from the profits of the firms under their control.[66] For township and village officials – the bureaucratic owners of TVEs – control and revenue rights are more integrated than in the case of traditional and large SOEs. Township and village governments preside over small localities and thus perform fewer tasks than governments above them. They are also less subject to time inconsistency problems compared with higher levels of the bureaucracy. In the Chinese system, bureaucratic changes are quite frequent.[67] This presents a problem: Today's bureaucrats make operating decisions, but tomorrow's bureaucrats may stand to reap the revenue benefits. The township and village governments are less afflicted with this problem. They are from local areas and tend to serve in their regions for life. They are not subject to rotations as officials at other levels of government.[68] And at the village level, there are rudimentary elections, which, by definition, guarantee the choice of local residents as leaders.

---

[65] For literature on TVEs, see Weitzman and Xu (1994), Li (1996), and Che and Qian (1998).

[66] For details of remuneration and evaluation mechanisms used in the township and village governments, see Whiting (2001).

[67] At the provincial level, the average tenure of governors was slightly more than three years in the 1980s.

[68] Rotations are a standard practice in the Chinese political system. It means the assignment of officials to other regions. Provincial government officials are subject to frequent rotations. See Huang (2002b).

In essence, the Chinese have rearranged ownership rights by conferring some residual claims on bureaucrats, rather than by privatizing the SOEs. This may be feasible only for very small firms. The reason is that for large firms, the asymmetry between ownership benefits and ownership costs will be extreme, that is, the bureaucratic quasiowners will reap only the positive cash flows, while the negative cash flows will go to the state. Excessive risk taking will result under this arrangement.

Another implication is that a full and explicit privatization program is the only solution to the owner's incentive problem in economies such as Russia and Poland, which are populated by very large firms. It is likely that over the long run, simply rearranging ownership rights is not even feasible when TVEs grow large and their business scope becomes multijurisdictional. The reason is that multijurisdictionality implies multiple tasks and the potential for trade-offs among different and conflictual tasks. Indeed, there are already indications that TVEs are not a stable ownership arrangement. Many have been converted into private corporations and some have failed as their scale of operations has grown. In Chapter 4, we encounter one of the most successful TVEs in China, Kelon, which had to be privatized in order to solve the problems associated with its TVE status.

4

Constraints on Nonstate Firms and Foreign Direct Investment

In a 1998 interview, in response to the question of why he decided to form a JV in 1991 with COSMOS Machinery International Co. Ltd., a trading firm based in Hong Kong, Bao Zhishu, the Suzhou entrepreneur we encountered in Chapter 3, had this to say:[1]

> We were a collective firm. The state did not invest in us at all. But our products were very advanced. An advanced firm needs a lot of capital. We needed an advanced working environment. Could we ask for funding from the state? Of course not. At that time, the state would not pay attention to whether you were a good or a bad firm. There was no money for you if you were a collective firm. Everything was by the book. The machine-tools industry was a priority industry for the state. There were seven or eight firms in the country producing products similar to ours. They were all SOEs. We were ranked the last.

To secure funding, Bao's firm, Sanguang, a precision machine-tools producer, formed a JV with COSMOS, which earlier had acted as an agent abroad for a state-owned machine-tools firm in Suzhou. COSMOS came into contact with Sanguang by chance when the manager of COSMOS visited his state-owned supplier. At the time, Sanguang was selling all its output on the domestic market. COSMOS contributed $800,000 in cash, an enormous amount of money considering that the entire book value of Sanguang's assets was only $112,000, and acquired a 25 percent equity stake in the JV. Bao's firm financed the rest of the equity capital by contributing its technology, property, and inventories. According to Mr. Bao, the negotiations were very easy.

---

[1] Interview with Bao Zhishu, September 28, 1998.

151

He remarked:

> They knew our products had a lot of potential. Our facilities and equipment were old and broken down, so they told us that they were teaming up with our "people." They trusted us and gave us complete management control. We also worked very hard and we were very conscientious. Their valuation of our assets was incredibly high. At the time, the book value of our assets was only RMB 420,000. They gave us a valuation of RMB 2.4 million. We really felt badly about it, but we have been doing very well in recent years and they recouped their investment costs a long time ago.

This JV deal is very revealing. In essence, COSMOS played the role of a venture capitalist, providing seed capital to a promising business whose economic value the Chinese financial system chose to ignore. But there are several differences from a normal venture capital deal. One is that the product was already developed and it had an existing market. The other is that the business did not face technological risks; rather, it faced a problem that was completely an artifact of the economic system.

Bao, a top engineer with a promising and technologically sophisticated product, could not secure financing from a Chinese bank, simply because his firm was ranked lower on China's political pecking order of firms. The overseas marketing channel controlled by COSMOS may have been attractive to Bao, but there was no reason why his firm could not sell its products contractually to COSMOS. (This was the nature of the relationship between COSMOS and the SOE supplier in Suzhou.) On purely technological grounds, Bao held all the bargaining power.[2] Indeed, the details of the deal prove this point. COSMOS was willing to pay what appeared to be a huge premium for establishing an equity stake in the firm because the market-oriented Hong Kong firm knew exactly where the value lay – with its high-quality human capital. COSMOS was perfectly content to let Bao manage the plant. Given its lack of technical expertise, it would not have been able to play a substantial managerial role anyway. ("COSMOS is a trading firm," Bao reported in an interview; "they had no technology or managerial expertise.") In 1994, Sanguang created another JV, this time with Sodick, a machine-tools firm in Japan.[3] With the initial capital from the Hong Kong firm and further capital and technology infusions from Sodick, Sanguang rapidly expanded its businesses in the 1990s.

---

[2] It is possible that this kind of dynamics may explain a finding reported in Young and Lan (1997) that a number of recipient firms hold a higher level of technology than FDI supplying firms.

[3] Sodick's corporate headquarters are based in Chicago. Its manufacturing headquarters are based in Yokohama, Japan. The Suzhou plant is managed from the Japanese division.

In comparative terms, Bao Zhishu did better than many other entrepreneurs in China. For one thing, he retained his business and was able to raise a huge amount of capital. He did not need to be completely dependent on the marketing channel controlled by COSMOS. His urban collective firm was ranked higher-tiered compared with purely private firms. In the 1980s, an openly private firm would not have been allowed to venture into the machine-tools business in the first place. Many of the private entrepreneurs, who were in the business of producing garments or shoes for export, were more credit-constrained than Mr. Bao was. They had similar financing needs to expand production, and they were more dependent on the marketing channels of foreign investing firms.

In this chapter, we first examine FDI that finances labor-intensive and export-oriented production in China. This is a sector in which private entrepreneurs face fewer entry barriers. While private entrepreneurs can establish a presence in this sector, they are still legally disadvantaged and credit-constrained. In this particular context, consistent with our political pecking order hypothesis, labor-intensive FDI alleviates both the credit and legal constraints on private firms. We use a case study on the garment industry to illustrate this argument.

In the second half of the chapter, we turn to a case study of China's largest refrigerator maker, Kelon. Unlike garments, the refrigerator market is internally oriented. Thus, the relevant issue is how the political pecking order of firms affected the relative advantages of foreign and domestic firms in capturing the fast-growing refrigerator market in the 1990s. In this, as well as in other industries, the allocation of financial resources and market opportunities has favored the least efficient SOEs. These allocation decisions have disadvantaged entrepreneurial firms such as Kelon, on the one hand, and have created large asset bases in the state sector, on the other. Both developments entail specific consequences for FDI.

The Kelon story is a double-edged one. It is about its success, but it is also about a possible failure of the firm to reach its full potential. It is not accidental that Kelon is located in Guangdong province, the province that embodies the kind of economic flexibility described in Chapter 3. Guangdong has adopted a *relatively* liberal policy both toward FDI and toward nonstate domestic firms; in some of its localities the political pecking order of firms is not enforced. While this kind of flexibility allowed Kelon to develop, it did have its limitations. In the early 1980s, when Kelon first started, Guangdong was still a rural province and industrial capabilities there were low. China's industrial centers were in Beijing, Shanghai, and Tianjin, where the political pecking order of firms was more stringently enforced. Thus, a more efficient economic policy was combined with an initially low level of industrial capabilities, while a less efficient economic policy was implemented in areas with a high level of industrial capabilities. It is possible that this matching problem may have hampered the competitiveness of domestic firms.

The chapter begins with the case study on garment production. I show that in this industry, an alternative to an FDI arrangement – contract production – is a feasible business practice. But, the political pecking order of firms, by restricting private entrepreneurs' access to bank loans and by political and legal discrimination, reduces the feasibility of contract production. Labor-intensive FDI rises as a result. Then we move on to a case study of Kelon. As a township and village enterprise (TVE), Kelon was ranked lower than the SOEs but was able to overcome many policy and regulatory obstacles and rose to the top of China's refrigerator industry by 1991. However, in an industry that typically confers advantages on local firms, in 2000 the market share held by the MNCs was high. While its achievements, especially relative to its humble origins, are impressive, Kelon is still a small firm by international comparisons despite operating in a large market. The chapter concludes by showing that an easing of the political pecking order since 1997 has already affected and "normalized" China's FDI patterns to some extent.

INDUSTRY CASE STUDY: GARMENT PRODUCTION

Based on the *Third Industrial Census*, FIEs accounted for 60.5 percent in the export of China's garments and footwear in 1995. Another source, based on customs data, gives a lower share, at 52.6 percent (Wang 1997, p. 353).[4] Either way, FIEs' dominance of China's export marketing is more substantial compared with that in Taiwan and Indonesia, as we see in Chapter 1. However, there is some evidence that the FIEs' share has declined in recent years. In the conclusion of this chapter I suggest that this is because the political pecking order of firms has been eased.

The garment industry is a good place to demonstrate how credit constraints on and regulatory discrimination against nonstate firms have affected China's FDI inflows. There are two reasons. First, contract production – export processing and subcontracting – is quite viable in this industry. The factors theorized by industrial organization economists to warrant FDI arrangements are absent. Or at least these factors are not so severe. While trademark issues and brand names are involved at the retailing end of the industry, garment manufacturers, especially small-scale manufacturers, employ simple and nonproprietary technology and production processes. The industrial organization rationale – transfer of proprietary and firm-specific know-how – thus is less relevant here.

---

[4] The data issues are discussed in the appendix to Chapter 1.

Furthermore, garment manufacturing is perfectly competitive, with many firms clustering close to one another and vying for purchasing orders. Those factors that theoretically give rise to hold-up problems and opportunism by and large are absent. Empirically, contract production in the garment industry is observed in other countries. But for some reason, FDI – an ownership arrangement – dominates the cross-border alliances in China's production of labor-intensive and export-oriented products. This requires an explanation.

Second, in the garment industry, private firms possess unrivaled advantages over SOEs. To succeed in this industry, an entrepreneur needs to work hard, be flexible, and be attentive to details, but even in this industry, private firms faced discrimination in the 1980s and 1990s in China. Legal discrimination and general credit constraints aside, access to foreign exchange was a special problem until the late 1990s. To export successfully, an entrepreneur needs unfettered access to foreign exchange. The matching problem – financial capital not being matched with quality human capital – is very pronounced.

In the following paragraphs, I first review issues related to contract production in the garment industry. I then describe the major problems confronting China's private firms. This is followed by a presentation of evidence that the discrimination against private firms has affected FDI patterns in the garment industry.

Contract Production

Contract production can be either closely coordinated between a buyer and a supplier or it can be arm's-length. In China, the more prevalent form of contract production is the closely coordinated kind in which a foreign buyer supplies, on credit, raw materials and other inputs and specifies product design and characteristics. An important attribute of this kind of contract production is that it does not require a local producer to have overseas marketing channels and design capabilities.

Advantages of Contracting. On some dimensions, subcontracting offers to a foreign firm and a local producer many of the same benefits as an FDI arrangement, such as access to overseas markets, transfer of simple technical and managerial know-how, and some financing. Probably, the greatest concern for a foreign firm is product quality at a subcontracting facility, but, as Ezra Vogel points out in his study of Guangdong province, a foreign partner can still supervise quality controls under a contractual arrangement. This is true elsewhere as well. In India, a merchant-exporter who specializes in exporting performs quality control at the fabrication sites. He generally works with ten to fifteen subcontractors and maintains a long-term relationship with them (Raman 1995). This is a rational arrangement, as the merchant-exporter is most informed of the quality demands and the tastes of the overseas customers. Such close supervision and reputational considerations can ensure satisfactory quality levels.

There are benefits to subcontracting. Under an equity arrangement, the investor is stuck with one group of managers and workers. This might be undesirable given the fast-changing nature of the business. Also, internal coordination within an equity arrangement is not costless, especially for those corporate structures with multiple shareholders. But the greatest benefit of contract production is its flexibility. Often a contractor encourages and plays off one subcontractor against another to get the best terms. Naujoks and Schmidt (1994) argue that contractual arrangements are "most useful in areas where the uncertainties are relatively apparent." Contractual arrangements are less risky because of the built-in flexibility.

The built-in flexibility associated with a contractual arrangement holds a special appeal in the garment industry, especially considering that many of the contracting firms in the business are fairly small. According to Kitty G. Dickerson, an expert on the garment industry, although contracting entails some loss of control as compared with direct manufacturing, in recent decades contracting has become more popular and has grown relative to the use of direct manufacturing (Dickerson 1999).

Mechanisms of Know-How Transfer in the Garment Industry. Hong Kong and Taiwanese firms are efficient, entrepreneurial, and dynamic. Through years of exporting, they command marketing know-how. Mainly based on these well-known characteristics of Hong Kong and Taiwanese firms, many analysts draw the conclusion that the know-how transfer through their export-oriented FIEs must be substantial. As representative of prevailing views on this matter, Richard Pomfret, when arguing for the benefits of low-tech FDI from Hong Kong and Taiwan, writes:

> What was missing in PRC, rather than capital, was the knowledge of how to make bags or teddy bears or wind-up pandas or cigarette lighters in attractive designs to reasonable quality standards and of how to market them overseas. (1991, p. 135)

Pomfret's observation is correct, but the issue is whether this explanation accords fully with the dramatic rise of FDI arrangements at the expense of subcontracting in China. It should be noted that subcontracting can also serve as a mechanism to transfer know-how. In fact, knowledge about products and processes is routinely passed from buyers to producers in the garment industry.

The following is a description of the kind of coordination between Marks and Spencer, the giant retail outlet based in the United Kingdom, and its suppliers:

> Not only does Marks and Spencer tell their suppliers how much they wish to buy from them, and thus promote a quantitative adjustment of supply to demand, they concern themselves equally with the specification and development of both processes and products. They decide, for example, the design of a garment, specify the cloth to be used and control the processes even to laying down the types of needles to be used in knitting and sewing. (Richardson 1972)

Notice in this account that knowledge about product designs and production processes is passed from the customer to the supplier even though their relationship is contractual. This calls into question whether this kind of know-how transfer is unique to an FDI arrangement. The evidence suggests that it is not. According to a survey by the World Bank, the most important source of product innovation, according to Korean exporting firms, was "foreign buyers of output."[5] Buyers of exports had a strong incentive to work intensively and closely with manufacturers to improve quality and to lower costs. In fact, the Korean experience suggests that the knowledge-transfer benefits from export-oriented FDI were quite limited. According to one observer, "neither the direct nor the indirect economic benefits of this [export-motivated] type of foreign investments are very great."[6]

Interestingly, despite the widely held belief that FIEs are an efficient mechanism to transfer know-how from foreign firms to Chinese facilities, available empirical evidence suggests that the degree of know-how transfer is limited. Sung, Liu, Wong, and Lau (1995), in their study of Guangdong province, do not find any evidence that managerial know-how transfer was superior in export-oriented FIEs compared with that in export-processing operations. In fact, they believe that export-processing operations were more efficient. A research team from MIT, which conducted work on Hong Kong's manufacturing industries, including manufacturing facilities run by Hong Kong firms in Guangdong, reports that there was a "very minimal training program in the Pearl River Delta plants"

---

[5] To be sure, Korean garment firms themselves invested abroad on a substantial scale, while they had developed in the 1960s and 1970s as contractees. This indeed is the central puzzle: Why is it that contract production was feasible in Korea but not in other countries in the same industry? This is a more productive way to think about this question as it brings up differences among host countries while controlling for industry characteristics.

[6] The World Bank analysis draws from a survey of 112 exporting Korean firms, the vast majority of which are 100 percent locally owned. All firms were asked to indicate the importance of their different sources of technologies. This is from Westphal, Rhee, and Pursell (1985).

administered by Hong Kong firms. The reason was the very high turnover ratio among employees (Berger and Lester 1997, pp. 154–55).

Another indicator comes from foreign employee presence in FIEs. A foreign employee presence can be thought of as a natural mechanism to transfer skills and know-how from a foreign location to a domestic location. In 1995, there were 5,695 FIEs in the garment industry, but the entire industry employed only 3,859 foreign employees. The same is found for leather and fur-related products as well as furniture manufacturing.[7] To be sure, there may be many explanations for this pattern, including the possibility that a single foreign firm operates many legally independent facilities. While this dynamic plausibly explains the foreign employee gap among large firms, it is less plausible for smaller labor-intensive operations in the garment industry.

There is also evidence that garment plants controlled by Chinese managers – and presumably owned by Chinese – also involve substantial managerial participation from Hong Kong firms, as reported in the aforementioned MIT study on Hong Kong's manufacturing industries. This observation reinforces the point made earlier in this chapter that contract production itself, in labor-intensive industries at least, does not preclude foreign managerial involvement. What seems to be a more important determinant of managerial involvement from foreign – that is, Hong Kong – firms in these circumstances is not ownership ties to Hong Kong firms but membership in the sales network constructed and maintained by Hong Kong buyer firms.

Industry Dynamics. In Chapter 1, I review a number of reasons why contract production in labor-intensive industries should not be a severely disadvantageous business practice as compared with an ownership arrangement. One reason is cultural. As Ezra Vogel uncovered, Hong Kong partners involved in about half of the export-processing operations in the Dongguan region of Guangdong had originally come from that region (Vogel 1989, p. 176). The trust level is high.

There are other reasons why contracting is viable as well. One is that there are natural constraints on hold-up problems and opportunism. A prominent characteristic of the garment industry is geographic clustering. Small producers tend to locate next to one another. This is true everywhere. In the United States, for example, in the 1970s, 46.7 percent of textile and garment plants were located in the southeast and another 32.4 percent were located in the mid-Atlantic states.[8]

---

[7] All the firms refer to those at or above the township level. Data are from Office of Third Industrial Census (1997). In fact this pattern is true for the entire population of industrial FIEs. In 1995, 49,559 industrial FIEs employed only 31,992 foreign employees.

[8] Exhibit 10 from Yoffie and Austin (1983).

Most of the Indian garment makers producing for export are located in a region called Tirupur.[9] In Guangdong province alone, in the early 1990s there were over 4,000 garment TVEs located only miles away from Hong Kong. Turkish garment production is similarly concentrated geographically. Geographic clustering entails a number of advantages. According to Pankaj Ghemawat and Murali Patibandla, the geographic clustering in India "improved the flow of information about export markets and how to serve them, reduced fears about buyer/supplier holdup that might prevail in smaller number situations, and facilitated organized cooperative efforts in areas such as lobbying the government for infrastructure" (Ghemawat and Patibandla 1999).

Labor-intensive industries typically lack a substantial degree of vertical integration. The footwear industry in Taiwan consists of independent firms subdivided along various production processes. Some specialize in the manufacturing of soles; others, in cutting materials for footwear uppers. Levy (1991) comments, "It is rare for a Taiwanese footwear firm to perform in-house more than at most two of the various subprocesses." In India, most of the garment makers, ranging from five to 500 workers, compete fiercely with one another. It is a situation as close as one can get to the textbook version of perfect competition. Skill requirements are low in this industry. Whereas garment design, especially high-fashion garment goods, involves quite sophisticated know-how and utilizes computer-aided devices, the manufacturing end is low-tech. It uses mature, standard, and general-type manufacturing technology and capital equipment. Barring government-imposed restrictions, labor substitution is easy and swift. These characteristics – geographic clustering, numerous firms, and the general nature of requisite physical and human capital – entail important implications for the nature of firm alliances in this industry. Switching suppliers is not costly and no single reneging garment maker can present much of a "holdup problem."

The organization of the industry is one mitigating factor against the theoretically derived "contract problems." Another factor is that contracting parties in this business have developed a set of long-standing practices to carefully manage relationships with suppliers and to minimize the effects of voluntary or involuntary contractual breaches. A buyer typically does not book 100 percent of the capacity of one supplier. Instead, he distributes the order among a number of suppliers. As such, if one supplier does not deliver, the supply disruption will be minimized. Furthermore, the suppliers whom the buyer relies on constitute a stable network that he uses on a long-term basis. Reputational effects and repeated interactions deter attempts to seek gains from engaging in

---

[9] See Ghemawat and Patibandla (1999).

short-term opportunism. Buyer/supplier practices in this business offer comfort not only to buyers but also to suppliers. Because fashions change quickly, and often unpredictably, to minimize risks to suppliers, a buyer offers a mixture of fashion goods – say 30 percent – and the rest of the order is in staple goods. In this way, if the fashion style changes suddenly, the financial costs to each individual supplier are less, as the costs are shared among a group of suppliers.[10]

For these reasons, garment retailers or their agents have no compelling reasons to shun contract production, to systematically prefer ownership production, or to vertically integrate backward.[11] The claim is not that the equity arrangements in garment production do not exist. They clearly do. Rather, one should not see a systematic and pervasive dominance of the equity approach over the contractual approach in this industry, and FDI arrangements should not prevail to the same extent as in an industry characterized by a high proprietary content, a heavy R&D focus, or a sophisticated and tacit organizational know-how requirement.

Contract Production in Other Economies

The theoretical viability of contract production is consistent with the empirical record of other economies. Firms in a number of economies relied successfully on subcontracting to develop their production and then, later on, their marketing capabilities. Many of the active investors in China today first started out doing subcontracting work for Japanese trading firms or Western retailers. Taiwanese footwear producers in the 1960s and 1970s performed contracting work for Mitsubishi, which controlled the marketing channels. Mitsubishi "identified and

---

[10] For a fascinating insight into how sourcing operations in the garment business work in practice, see an interview with Victor Fung in the *Harvard Business Review*. Fung is the CEO of Li & Fung, Hong Kong's largest export trading company. Fung describes the operation of a "virtual supply chain" across the globe to ensure timely delivery of quality products. For details, see Magretta (1998) and also St. George, Knoop, and Yoshino (1998).

[11] One may argue, for example, that Chinese suppliers desire equity arrangements with foreign firms precisely because fashions change quickly and unpredictably. An equity arrangement would thus give rise to the stability and assurances that the small Chinese suppliers value. (I owe this observation to Professor Christine Wong.) This is a reasonable hypothesis but its validity cannot be directly tested against data from the garment industry. In the appendix to this chapter, however, I show that the effect of the political pecking order of firms is independent of this industry characteristic. China's arts and crafts industry, producing such products as ivory and jade sculptures, enjoys considerable stability in terms of the nature and size of demand. Styles rarely change since an important source of the value of these products derives from their fidelity to tradition. Most of the findings generated from the garment industry are replicated in this industry as well.

encouraged reliable and ambitious individuals already employed in footwear factories to start-up production facilities of their own" (Levy 1991, pp. 155–56). The ownership of these facilities was Taiwanese.

Hong Kong firms pioneered and perfected contract production in the 1960s and 1970s and developed a thriving garment export business mainly on the strength of its own indigenous firms.[12] An example is Li & Fung Trading Co., a $3 billion global trading company in 2000. Li & Fung's key customers included the The Limited, Gymboree, American Eagle, Warner Brothers, Abercrombie and Fitch, Bed, Bath, and Beyond, Tesco, Avon Products, Levi-Strauss, and Reebok. During the 1960s and 1970s, Li & Fung was both a trading and a manufacturing concern. In addition to its core garment business, up until the 1960s it also produced inexpensive goods such as bamboo and rattan ware, jade, ivory, handicrafts, and fireworks. In the 1970s, the firm phased out its manufacturing operations. Today, it specializes in an agency role for Western clothing retailers, that is, sourcing and purchasing supplies for its customers. However, Li & Fung, similar to the role of Mitsubishi in sponsoring Taiwanese entrepreneurs in footwear production, goes beyond sourcing and purchasing services. For example, it helps the retailer with virtual design as well as helping the supplier secure raw materials and ensure quality control, according to Nancy Chen, assistant to William Fung, managing director of Li and Fung Trading Co.[13]

Contract production is not limited to Asian economies. Referring to cross-border contract production as outward processing (OP), two German economists, Petra Naujoks and Klaus-Dieter Schmidt, conclude that through OP in the garment industry "a subcontractor firm gets the opportunity to climb on a running tandem. The success story of labor-intensive industries in many developing countries cannot be written without OP" (Naujoks and Schmidt 1994). In the 1980s and 1990s, garment exports from Turkey grew rapidly, at an annual average rate of 31 percent between 1980 and 1993, compared with China's 21 percent during the same period. In 1995, Turkey dislodged China as the largest garment exporter to the European Union, accounting for an 11.7 percent share of the European Union's garment imports. Impressively, Turkey achieved this success before the European Union was due to lift its quotas on Turkey's garment exports.[14]

In 1997, as a Harvard Business School case study notes, "there were several tens of thousands of garment manufacturers in Turkey. Like most Turkish

---

[12] See Lall (1978) and Helleiner (1989).

[13] Interview with Nancy Chen, October 23, 2001.

[14] The information on the Turkish garment industry is based on Ghemawat and Baird (1998).

businesses, virtually all of them were family-owned and -managed" (Ghemawat and Baird 1998, p. 7). This is confirmed by the Economist Intelligence Unit (2001, p. 41), which notes, "The industry is made up of a large number of tiny, small and medium-sized firms displaying various degrees of specialization and achieving various levels of quality. Foreign investment in the sector is rare, and a large number of firms form the part of the hidden economy." In 2001, there were only 244 FIEs in Turkey.[15] Unable to do their own design work, local Turkish firms bid on designs on an extremely competitive basis. These designs are usually accompanied by detailed specifications and standards provided by the large retailers in Europe and the United States. Among this group of initially small firms, a few have become very large and are now able to do their own design work. They have invested heavily in automation and reduced the average age of their capital stock from twelve years in the early 1990s to five years in 1995. They are active participants in the major European trade shows. One firm, IPAS, directly contracts with Marks and Spencer and Tommy Hilfiger. These large Turkish garment firms have begun to outsource labor-intensive components of their production in Eastern Europe by entering into subcontracting arrangements with producers there (Ghemawat and Baird 1998).

Between the late 1980s and the mid-1990s, Indian garment exports grew at an annual average rate of 26 percent. Seventy percent of India's exports of cotton knitwear are accounted for by hundreds of firms, which range considerably in size. These firms are clustered geographically. The organization of production is mainly based on subcontracting. A typical exporter operates through a network of ten to twenty subcontractors, each with an average size varying from twenty to fifty machines. The advantages of this arrangement are the built-in flexibility to handle both large and small orders, low overhead costs, and the sharing of capital costs among numerous producers. In the 1990s, some of the large operations were set up either as JVs or as licensees with international branded firms such as Benetton and Lacoste. Unlike the small manufacturers, they are potentially capable of doing their own design work. However, most of these operations aim at domestic markets, not at export markets.[16]

The Political Pecking Order in China's Garment Industry

For analytical purposes, it is important to differentiate the garment industry from the textile industry. The textile industry is capital- and

---

[15] They are called foreign capital companies. This is from the web site of the Turkish government: http://www.treasury.gov.tr/english/ybs/ybsyeniing.htm, accessed in February 2002.

[16] A study of the Indian garment industry can be found in Ghemawat and Patibandla (1999).

technology-intensive, and scale is an important attribute. In contrast, the garment industry is labor-intensive and small-scale. Mom-and-pop sweatshop operations are quite common. Manufacturing operations often do not involve heavy capital spending or advanced technology. The important success factors in this industry are attention to details, flexibility in production organization and operations, and on-time deliveries so as to suit different fashion trends or seasonal needs. Because of such differences in the economic characteristics of these two industries, SOEs tend to dominate textile production, whereas nonstate firms, primarily TVEs and private firms, dominate the garment industry.

Regulatory and Policy Constraints on Nonstate Firms. In a paper explaining the role of officials/managers in the development of TVEs, two economists, Hongyi Chen and Scott Rozelle, distinguish between internal and external management functions. Internal management is defined as "activities needed to organize the daily in-house, production-oriented tasks of the firm." They give examples such as "on-floor labor management, scheduling, inventory management, monitoring of quality, shipping and receiving, etc." External management functions refer to those activities interfacing with other firms outside the jurisdiction of the firm. Chen and Rozelle note that internal management functions are particularly important for labor-intensive operations, which require intensive monitoring of workers (Chen and Rozelle 1999).

By this logic, private firms should hold an unrivaled advantage over SOEs in the garment industry, but even in this industry, the government favored SOEs. Although SOEs were better equipped, their performance was poorer. A government report in 1996, referring to SOE firms under the Ministry of Textile, notes the following (Development Research Center of the State Council 1996, p. 199):

> In 1995, garment firms in the Ministry encountered massive difficulties. These firms possess certain advantages in technology, equipment, product quality, and management. But because of the external constraints imposed by the system and internal operations that could not adjust to market developments, on top of their historical burdens, there is no way for them to compete with TVEs, private firms, and FIEs. According to information from various agencies, the number of firms that have terminated or suspended production has increased rapidly. By the end of 1995, these firms accounted for 68 percent of all firms [in the Ministry].

In the next chapter, I examine how the across-the-board failures of SOEs have increased China's FDI inflows; for now, my focus is on the other side of the same coin – how the unfavorable treatment of nonstate, especially private, firms has affected their demand for FDI. Aside from the legal and financial discrimination against all private firms, in the garment industry, the export licensing policies of the government had a particularly pernicious effect on nonstate firms. In the early 1990s, the export licensing policies discriminated against both TVEs and private firms, but over time the discrimination against TVEs eased but the situation did not change for private firms until 1998. In 1991, before the large-scale arrival of FIEs, TVEs accounted for 77.5 percent of garment exports, but in 1992, out of tens of thousands of TVE garment makers, only twenty were allowed to trade directly with foreign firms. In 1992, however, the export licensing policy was relaxed toward TVEs. In 1993, the number of TVEs in the industry that were granted export rights increased sharply to 156, but this was still far fewer than the number of SOEs with export licenses. In the early 1990s, some 300 SOEs were granted export licenses (Editorial Board 1993). Private firms fared much worse. It was not until 1998 that the government began to grant export licenses to private firms.

As a result of the export restrictions imposed on private firms, *direct* garment exports by private firms in the 1990s were a minuscule portion of China's garment exports, as noted in a report by the State Council (although the report does not reveal the share of exports by private firms).[17] The tiny export share by private firms does not mean that their output is not exported. Private firms still may have supplied a large quantity of garment exports through indirect trading channels. For example, they may have performed subcontracting work for SOEs or TVEs.[18] Or they may have sold their output to trading firms. In the early 1990s, according to an interview, private firms supplied only 1 to 2 percent of garment products to a garment foreign trading firm in Jiangsu. This share rose to 20 percent by the mid-1990s.[19]

But this arrangement is fraught with problems. The contact between seller and buyer is not direct, a problem Chinese garment producers persistently complain about, as noted by the Office of International Trade Administration of the U.S. Department of Commerce.[20] The lack of direct contact deprives private garment suppliers of critical access to market, fashion, and production process

---

[17] See the section on the garment industry in Development Research Center of the State Council (1999).

[18] Sonobe and Otsuka (2001) observed these types of practices in the garment industry in the Yangtze River region.

[19] Interview with Jimmy Chen, vice president of Import and Export Garment Corporation of Jiangsu province, October 2001.

[20] The report states, "Garment producers frequently complained that China's indirect trading system, which forces garment sales to pass through authorized trading companies, distanced producers from their buyers and their markets. While a number of structural reforms have expanded the number of trading corporations authorized to conduct the garment trade, this limitation continues to inhibit the rapid transmission of market information to China's producers." See International Trade Administration (1993).

information. Fashion and market conditions change quickly in this business and timely access to information is vital. Private firms, lacking this access, were rendered less competitive, as compared with FIEs.

Second, under an indirect trading mechanism, garment suppliers were paid in RMB, not in foreign exchange, and under the Chinese foreign exchange regulations in the early 1990s, a firm without an export license could not retain foreign exchange. Since during most of the reform era the government bureaucracy rationed foreign exchange to support import-substituting SOEs, private garment producers were not allocated foreign exchange quotas, even though many of their products, through subcontracting arrangements or sales to trading corporations, generated foreign exchange earnings. Although in 1994 China adopted currency convertibility for its current account transactions, this did not help private garment suppliers. Under China's foreign exchange regulations, the currency convertibility applied only to those entities authorized to conduct foreign trade, a condition that precluded most private firms.

The indirect trading system inflicted a financial penalty on private garment firms as well as impaired their competitiveness. During most of the 1980s and in the early 1990s, Chinese currency was overvalued. Thus, nonstate firms took a loss each time they had to convert their foreign exchange into RMB. Their export incentives were also dampened because TVEs and SOEs, even though less efficient in an operating sense, could use their policy advantage to extract benefits from private subcontractors. Timely and economical access to foreign exchange is a critical success factor in this business. Research on Taiwanese garment exports shows that imported inputs constitute 70 percent of production costs. As Scott (1979, p. 358) observes, "[a]ny appreciable taxes on these inputs or any premiums resulting from import controls (assuming the manufacturer must buy or can sell at premium-inclusive prices) are likely to make exporting unprofitable." For a firm to successfully engage in the production of garment exports, it needs to have access to foreign exchange to purchase at a low cost the exact types of fibers and cloth that will meet the design and textural specifications of the foreign buyer. The firm may also need to import machinery and equipment from abroad to fulfill an export contract.

The credit constraints and the restrictions on export opportunities faced by Chinese private garment producers appear to be considerably more severe than those faced by their Indian counterparts. India's banking system is similarly statist. In the mid-1990s, state-owned banks controlled 87 percent of total deposits, but Indian banks discriminate on the basis of the size of firms, as banks in many countries do, rather than on the basis of ownership. Indian banks require confirmation of an export order before it will issue a letter of credit. This requirement causes delays and is viewed as leading to inefficiency among Indian garment exporters.[21] Imagine the extent of inefficiencies in Chinese export production when even the largest private producers were not supposed to interact directly with foreign buyers and were denied access to bank credit.

Statistical Evidence on the Effect of the Political Pecking Order on FDI

One way to directly demonstrate our institutional foundation hypothesis is to treat credit constraints on, and legal discrimination against, private firms as parameters influencing choices between an FDI arrangement and a contractual arrangement. But data on subcontracting and export processing operations are simply unavailable, probably because economically they became unimportant compared with FIEs during the course of the 1990s. Data on FIEs are more easily available and are fairly detailed. Our approach, thus, is to examine private firms' choices of the different kinds of FIEs and their acceptance of foreign ownership controls as a reflection of the extent of the credit constraints imposed on them. A huge disadvantage with this approach is its inability to demonstrate the effect of legal discrimination. An FIE, regardless of its individual characteristics, entitles its owners to protection by the legal framework developed for FIEs. In the concluding section, I make some conjectures linking legal considerations with developments on China's FDI front.

Data for the analysis in this section come from a database on FIEs compiled by the All China Marketing Research Corporation, a consulting arm of the Chinese State Statistical Bureau. (Hereafter, I refer to this database as the "FIE database.") The FIE database contains firm-level information on foreign ownership, size of assets and employment, export value, and, most important, the administrative affiliation and ownership characteristics of the *Chinese* shareholding firms of these FIEs. This makes it possible to relate the patterns of foreign ownership to the administrative and ownership characteristics of the Chinese firms. The differences in the administrative and ownership characteristics of the Chinese firms are used as a proxy measure of the political pecking order; that is, a private firm is assumed to receive inferior treatment compared with other domestic firms.

The logic of the institutional foundation argument suggests that private firms should value foreign equity financing more than other domestic firms, in order to alleviate credit constraints. Thus, ceteris paribus, foreign control of FIEs with private firms as the Chinese shareholders should be greater than foreign control

---

[21] See the discussion on Indian banks and garment production in Raman (1995) and Ghemawat and Patibandla (1999).

of FIEs with shareholding ties to other types of Chinese firms. Our analysis requires the presence of a Chinese shareholder. For this reason, the analysis is limited to JVs that are owned jointly by foreign and domestic firms. Wholly foreign-owned enterprises are excluded from our analysis.[22]

Supply-Side Influences on Foreign Ownership. A critical step in our analysis is to separate the supply-side factors from factors on the demand side. Both affect the eventual foreign ownership stakes observed in the data, but my interest is to examine and demonstrate the preferences of Chinese firms for foreign equity financing. This is done by controlling for those factors that international business scholars have theorized and demonstrated as affecting foreign ownership controls.[23] These factors would include technological and organizational know-how, proprietary assets, and control of marketing channels. Here, the selection of the garment industry helps control for a number of these factors. Because the garment industry does not involve sophisticated technology and proprietary assets, any variance in foreign ownership controls is independent of these factors. Probably the most important factor that increases foreign bargaining power in the case of garment FDI is foreign controls of marketing. Fortunately, our database contains how much each firm exports. We can use the ratio of exports to sales revenue as a measure of foreign marketing power. One can also argue that organizational know-how may also bear on the extent of foreign ownership controls. We use two variables as proxies of foreign organizational know-how. One is FIE capital intensity and the other is the size of FIE employment. The underlying idea here is that when a JV is larger and more capital-intensive, and thus, presumably, more complex to manage, the foreign investing firm has a bargaining advantage.

The other factor that needs to be controlled for has to do with any differences in the production technologies of the firms. I deliberately choose a very narrow scope of the industry to ensure that both the human and physical capital

---

[22] The appendix to this chapter presents a regression analysis of data from both the garment industry and China's traditional arts and crafts industry, an industry in which Chinese indigenous firms should naturally excel. The findings are consistent with the findings from the garment industry.

[23] Equity ownership is often used as a measure of the bargaining dynamics between foreign and domestic firms. Scholars in international business studies have cautioned that it is an imperfect measure. The advantage of this variable is its relatively easy availability and uniformity across different firms. Ideally, one should collect information on all terms of arrangement, not just ownership splits. Fagre and Wells (1982), while recognizing potential problems with this measure, nevertheless used the measure to test the bargaining hypothesis. For a number of applications using foreign equity ownership to test the bargaining dynamics between foreign and domestic firms, see Krobin (1987) and Gomes-Casseres (1990).

deployed is as homogenous as possible. This is to control for the possible influences of different types of capital equipment and production processes on the equity structures of our firms. The data are disaggregated at a four-digit Chinese Industry Classification Standard level (1810) and are confined to garment makers using fiber and cotton-based materials. Leather, fur, and feather-based clothing are excluded, as are footwear and headgear products. The making of fiber and yarn is also excluded. This is a far more disaggregated treatment than many of the studies that use industry characteristics to estimate foreign bargaining power.

Additional controls can be imposed. All the FIEs included in the analysis are JVs. This is to ensure that the equity structure of these firms is a function of joint negotiations and decisions between foreign and domestic firms. To control for investor characteristics, I have limited the FIEs to those with investors from Hong Kong, Taiwan, and Macao, with the idea that ethnically Chinese investors may have similar equity preferences. (The results for most of the tests are not substantially different from results with non-ECE data.) Another factor that has been hypothesized to influence foreign ownership controls is the policy environment of the host country. A more liberal policy environment is associated with greater foreign ownership controls, while a more controlling environment is associated with fewer foreign ownership controls. To control for any effects arising from changes in China's FDI regulatory and policy environment, I have limited the FIEs to those established between 1992 and 1995. During this period, the policy environment was more liberal than in the 1980s; this has the additional benefit of ensuring that the outcome we observe is driven by firm-level dynamics, rather than by policy and regulatory constraints. (For the garment industry, FDI controls are not a binding constraint as compared with those in, say, the automobile industry because the garment industry has never been a priority sector for the central government.)

In Table 4.1 the FIEs are divided along three dimensions: employment size, fixed asset size per employee, and export propensity. The foreign equity ratios are ranked by these three categories. The hypothesis is that larger employment size, greater capital intensity, and greater export propensity tend to be associated with greater foreign ownership controls. Large firms and more capital-intensive firms may require more sophisticated managerial and organizational know-how, and foreign firms may be in a stronger bargaining position when such FIEs are involved. For example, large firms may be more vertically integrated and they may operate fabric weaving and finishing as well as garment fabrication operations. Smaller firms may be just "cut-and-sew" operations, which do not require sophisticated organizational management.

Table 4.1 *Foreign Equity Ratios, Employment Size, Capital Intensity, and Export Propensity in the Chinese Garment Industry*

Ranked by employment size			Ranked by fixed assets per employee			Ranked by export/sales ratio		
Unit: employee	Foreign equity ratio (%)	Number of firms	Unit: RMB 10,000	Foreign equity ratio (%)	Number of firms	Unit, %	Foreign equity ratio (%)	Number of firms
Less than or equal to 50	50.4	97	Less than 1.03	51.5	145	Less than 25	44.2	228
51 to 108	53.8	144	1.04 to 1.81	54.0	161	26 to 50	50.5	21
109 to 197	52.1	168	1.82 to 3.33	51.3	141	51 to 75	52.8	39
198 to 750	52.2	173	3.34 to 20.1	53.7	133	More than 75	58.8	299
More than 750	74.0	5	More than 20.1	34.5	7			

Note: All FIEs are JVs established between 1992 and 1995. Foreign investors are firms based in Hong Kong, Macao, and Taiwan. The Chinese investors are either TVEs or private firms.

Source: Based on data in All China Marketing Research Co. Ltd. (1999).

Empirical evidence does not bear out this hypothesis. Reading down the table, there is no positive correlation between the size of employment and capital intensity, on the one hand, and foreign equity shares, on the other. If anything, the correlation is slightly negative. The foreign equity share is lower if the average employment size of an FIE is between 109 and 197 persons than if the firm employs between 51 to 108 persons. Only when the firms are extremely large – those with more than 750 persons – does foreign ownership increase substantially, to 74 percent, as compared with 52.2 percent at the next lower level (between 198 and 750 employees). The lack of a clear correlation holds when the export propensity of the FIEs and when the regional effects – of being in Guangdong – are controlled for, either in a descriptive or statistical analysis of the data.[24]

Capital intensity is even a poorer predictor of foreign equity holdings. On average, FIEs that are more capital-intensive seem to exhibit fewer foreign equity controls, as indicated by the nearly monotonic decrease in the foreign ownership ratio as the fixed assets per employee increase in size. The highest foreign equity ratio is found among the less capital-intensive firms, whereas

[24] These results are reported elsewhere. See Huang (2001).

the smallest foreign equity ratio is found among the FIEs with the highest fixed assets per employee ratio. On export propensity, there is strong support for the standard bargaining perspective that foreign marketing controls increase foreign bargaining power. When the FIEs are divided into four categories – (1) those exporting less than 25 percent of their output, (2) those exporting between 26 to 50 percent, (3) those exporting between 51 to 75 percent, and (4) those exporting above 75 percent – the foreign equity holdings increase as the export/output ratio increases. When an FIE exports less than 25 percent of its output, average foreign ownership is about 44.2 percent, compared with 50.5 percent and 52.8 percent at the next two export levels, respectively. The high exporters, those exporting more than 75 percent, have an average foreign equity holding of 58.8 percent. Clearly, foreign marketing controls have a substantial and positive effect on foreign ownership controls.[25]

Demand-Side Influences on Foreign Ownership. Now let us turn to Chinese preferences for FDI. One measure of credit and regulatory constraints is the political hierarchy of Chinese investing firms in the FIEs. Almost all Chinese firms, regardless of ownership, are assigned to different levels of the government, from the central government down to the township governments, the lowest administrative level.[26] During the centrally planned era, the supervisory agencies had the power to allocate resources of value to firms, including production inputs. Now these agencies provide credit guarantees, regulatory relief, and legal and political protection. The government system consists of five administrative levels: central government, provincial government, prefecture, county, and township. (There is another layer of administration that provides some community services, but it is not a part of the governmental apparatus. It is called the neighborhood committee in the urban areas and the village committee in the countryside. These entities also operate their own firms.)

The FIE database classifies all firms as belonging to one of six categories in the political hierarchy: central government, provincial governments, prefectures, counties, neighborhood committees (in the urban areas), townships, and

---

[25] One can argue that this correlation is spurious. For example, it is possible that a greater export propensity and high foreign ownership merely reflect the fact that these firms are more internationally oriented. I am unable to resolve the causal ambiguity, but to illustrate the institutional foundation argument it is not necessary to resolve this issue definitively. All that is needed is to control for the export propensity of FIEs when one assesses the effect of the political pecking order so that one does not attribute an export effect to the ownership treatments of the firms.

[26] In the FIE database, the administrative levels refer to those of the FIEs and strictly speaking not to those of the Chinese partnering firms. But the classifications of the FIEs and of the Chinese FIE partners are consistent because the FIEs are classified according to the administrative levels of their Chinese partners.

villages (in the rural areas). The FIE database has a seventh category, which is denoted as "others." On the basis of the classification conventions used at the State Statistical Bureau, I was able to determine that these firms are private firms not formally affiliated with any government agencies or community entities. (This determination was confirmed by an official from the State Statistical Bureau.)[27] These are private firms in our analysis.

Not being affiliated with the bureaucracy entails both advantages and disadvantages. Such firms enjoy greater operating autonomy and fewer managerial interferences from the government, but, on the other hand, they miss out on the valuable functions that government agencies may provide. Chinese banks often demand credit guarantees or sizable collateral assets. Most important, a bureaucratic affiliation confers legitimacy on private firms that operate in a murky legal and political environment. The value of a bureaucratic affiliation is demonstrated by the fact that private entrepreneurs are often willing to pay a hefty price, in the form of ceding a substantial equity stake in their firms, to acquire such an affiliation.[28] It is safe to say that private firms without any bureaucratic affiliation are at the bottom of the political hierarchy of firms.

Column 1 of Table 4.2 presents foreign ownership ratios ranked by the political hierarchy of the firms. Firms at the top, such as those directly under the central government and provinces, are higher-tiered, while firms at the bottom, such as TVEs and private firms, are lower-tiered in terms of their political status. In general, top-tiered firms exhibit a lower foreign ownership ratio than bottom-tiered firms. For example, firms at or above prefectural level on average have a foreign ownership ratio of less than 50 percent; firms below this level exhibit a foreign ownership ratio greater than 50 percent. FIEs cofunded with private firms have the second highest foreign ownership ratio in the table.

Two issues need to be addressed before we conclude that the political pecking order seems to correlate roughly with the foreign ownership ratio in a direction postulated by our hypothesis. Because foreign marketing control strongly affects the foreign ownership ratio, we need to incorporate this variable to control for the bargaining power of foreign firms. Another important reason may be that since

---

[27] For example, the *Chinese Statistical Yearbook 1999* defines "enterprises of other types" as encompassing private enterprises, jointly owned private enterprises, shareholding cooperatives, and FIEs. (Shareholding cooperatives are employee-owned firms.) Thus, all the firms in this category are domestic private firms, except for the FIEs. Because all the firms in the FIE database are FIEs, this category would include all the firms in the category of "enterprises of other types" minus the FIEs. I thank Ms. Mei Jin, Director, Department of Economic Research, China Economic Monitoring and Analysis Center at the State Statistical Bureau, for a detailed explanation of firm categories in the Chinese statistical reporting system.

[28] The IFC study on the Chinese private sector documents many of the benefits to private enterprises provided through bureaucratic affiliation. See International Finance Corporation (2000).

Table 4.2 *Political Hierarchy of Firms and Equity Structures of FIEs in the Garment Industry, percentage (number of firms)*

	Foreign ownership ratio		
	(1)	(2)	(3)
Political hierarchy	All FIEs	High exporters[a]	Low exporters[b]
Central level	50.0 (4)	_[c]	50.0 (4)
Provincial level	42.5 (62)	41.3 (12)	41.8 (40)
Prefectural level	48.4 (218)	58.0 (63)	42.6 (133)
County level	52.5 (277)	62.3 (131)	43.8 (119)
Neighborhood level	66.5 (82)	73.1 (36)	60.7 (37)
Township and village level	51.6 (444)	55.9 (231)	45.2 (164)
Private firms	55 (143)	68.6 (68)	41.7 (64)

Note: Numbers in brackets refer to the number of FIEs in a given category. All the FIEs were established between 1992 and 1995. Foreign investors were from Hong Kong, Macao, and Taiwan.
[a] High exporters: FIEs with export/sales ratios of above 75 percent.
[b] Low exporters: FIEs with export/sales ratios of less than 25 percent.
[c] —: Data not available.
Source: Data are based on All China Marketing Research Co. Ltd. (1999).

private garment firms cannot export directly, it is possible that they especially value an FIE status and thus are more willing to "pay" for it by ceding greater equity shares. Thus, we need to distinguish between high and low exporters. Table 4.2 divides the FIEs into two categories, high exporters in column 2 and low exporters in column 3. High-exporting FIEs export more than 75 percent of their output, whereas low-exporting FIEs export less than 25 percent of their output.

By and large, the political pecking order hypothesis is confirmed. Except for firms at the neighborhood level, to which I return below, high-exporting FIEs at the bottom of the political hierarchy – those at or below the township and village levels – show the largest foreign ownership, whereas firms at the top of the political hierarchy are the least foreign-owned. Private firms exhibit a higher average foreign ownership ratio (55 percent) compared with TVEs (51.6 percent), firms one rung above the private firms on the political pecking order.

The rank ordering in Table 4.2 suggests that the political pecking order seems to matter only when high exporters are involved (i.e., firms exporting more than 75 percent of their output). Given the import-intensity of garment exports, this pattern suggests that compared with RMB loans, the foreign exchange constraint is more binding on private firms. This is probably because foreign exchange control is tighter and more centralized and because informal credit markets in many regions in China can supply small short-term RMB loans to private entrepreneurs. Notice that the political pecking order effect disappears when only low-exporting FIEs are included, as indicated in column 3.

The second issue is that the rank ordering is not strictly one-directional. High-exporting TVEs, on average, have a lower foreign ownership ratio (55.9 percent) compared with politically higher-tiered county FIEs (62.3 percent) and neighborhood FIEs (73.1 percent). In fact, FIEs cofunded with domestic firms at the neighborhood level exhibit the highest foreign ownership ratio among all the firms in the table. This is a reminder that our analysis is unable to control for a number of factors that may also affect the foreign ownership ratio. In particular, the performance and operating capabilities of the domestic shareholding firms of these FIEs are not controlled for. In the 1990s, small urban firms, many SOEs under county governments or collective firms affiliated with neighborhood committees, performed very poorly because they could not compete with the TVEs and private firms. Their higher foreign ownership ratio is a sign that they were being acquired by foreign firms. A telling sign is that the low-exporting FIEs at the neighborhood level also have a very high foreign ownership ratio, at 60.7 percent, an indication that foreign control is unrelated to overseas marketing channels for this group of firms.

Given that the operating capabilities of the firms are not controlled for in Table 4.2, the results reinforce the political pecking order idea even more powerfully. Private firms are the most efficient firms and are probably the most desirable JV partners from the point of view of foreign investors. Yet they seem to have ceded more substantial controls of their businesses (or future business opportunities) to foreign investors than all other firms in the table, except for neighborhood firms.

The effect of credit constraints on FDI arrangements can be demonstrated more directly and in greater detail by looking at the decisions of Chinese firms to enter into two types of JVs. These are equity (*hezi*) and cooperative (*hezuo*) JVs. Both are equity deals, but cooperative JVs (CJVs) are closer to contractual alliances than equity JVs (EJVs). In a CJV, the control rights of the FIE do not have to correlate perfectly with the revenue rights. The two sides negotiate to determine who has the control rights and the terms of the revenue rights. For example, a Chinese firm may have 100 percent control of such a firm, but the firm itself can be wholly owned by a foreign firm (or vice versa). While it is required by law that EJVs be established as separate legal entities from the investors, there is no similar requirement for CJVs. EJVs are structured as long-term deals, lasting fifteen years or more. The duration of CJVs is less fixed and depends on the specific arrangements negotiated between the foreign and domestic firms. The level of foreign managerial participation is less in a CJV. Sometimes, a foreign investor recovers her investments within a few years on an accelerated dividend payment schedule and then all the operating assets are turned over to the Chinese side. This is very close to a debt arrangement. In other situations, a foreign investor may decide not to recover her investments so quickly and instead to stay on as a long-term investor.

The latter feature brings up some critical differences between a cooperative JV and a pure debt arrangement. Under a CJV, a foreign firm has the legal right to the control of and the dividend income from the operation of the firm. This is quite different from a subcontracting arrangement such as an export-processing operation. The key feature of a CJV is its enormous flexibility. Negotiations can take place before the deal or during the operation of the firm. It is commonly perceived that a CJV favors the foreign side. For this reason, the Chinese government began to discourage this form of JVs in the early 1990s, and its share among the population of JVs began to decline thereafter.[29]

One notable indicator of the advantages accruing to the foreign side is the substantial equity stakes foreign firms have built up in CJVs. In the FIE database, the average foreign ownership of CJVs in the garment business was 71.1 percent, compared with 44.9 percent in EJVs. Out of 722 garment CJVs, 230 of them show a 100 percent foreign ownership even though they are legally recognized as JVs. (This is an important detail because as JVs, CJVs are subject to a set of regulations different from those that govern wholly owned foreign-invested enterprises, known as WFIEs.) The sizable foreign ownership constitutes a very valuable option to a foreign investor. A foreign investor may convert her investments into a short-term loan if she believes that the long-run prospects of the business are not promising. She can demand a dividend distribution in proportion to her large ownership stake. Or, if the current situation is unfavorable, she may decide to retain her investment stake.

The CJV dynamics allow us to demonstrate the powerful effects of China's political pecking order of firms. Because a private firm, which already excels in its internal management functions, is credit-constrained, it may have to resort to funding production or expansion by whatever means that are available. CJVs are a source of financing. Although it is extremely expensive because of the built-in flexibility enjoyed by the foreign investor, a credit-constrained private entrepreneur does not have the luxury of choosing from different financing instruments.

To a private entrepreneur, a CJV may entail an advantage over an EJV: It does not require the private entrepreneur to cede control rights over his business. If the private entrepreneur has full confidence in his ability to run a profitable

---

[29] For details, see Wu and Zhang (1995). For a more detailed illustration, see Chu and Dong (1993).

Table 4.3 *Foreign Ownership Ratios in Two Types of FIEs: Cooperative Joint Ventures (CJV) and Equity Joint Ventures (EJV), percentage (number of firms)*

	(1) Nationwide		(2) Guangdong province		(3) Foshan city, Guangdong province	
	(1a) CJV	(1b) EJV	(2a) CJV	(2b) EJV	(3a) CJV	(3b) EJV
Private Firms	89.3 (49)	46.9 (92)	89.5 (46)	46 (67)	71 (5)	64 (4)
TVEs	75.4 (116)	48.9 (238)	76.0 (100)	61.8 (106)	77.5 (65)	62.6 (92)

Note: Numbers in brackets refer to the number of FIEs. Foreign investors were from Hong Kong, Macao, and Taiwan. All the firms in the table are high exporters, that is, they exported more than 75 percent of their output.

Source: Data are based on All China Marketing Research Co. Ltd. (1999).

business, he may look for a foreign investor who has no long-term interest in operating a facility in China and who would be happy to capitalize her old equipment and machinery in a CJV as a way to exit the garment-manufacturing business altogether. One of the key features of a CJV is that after the foreign investor exits, the CJV remains as an FIE, thus entitling it to the legal framework developed for FIEs (Fu 2000, p. 104). This is an attractive way for a private entrepreneur to get some financing and superior legal treatment, but at the same time to have some possibility of retaining business controls.

We test these ideas in Table 4.3 in three ways. First, we compare the foreign ownership ratios in CJVs and EJVs along two ownership dimensions: private firms and TVEs. (These are the two types of firms whose ownership types are clearly identified in the FIE database.) They are among the most efficient firms in China, and, until the mid-1990s, TVEs dominated China's garment export production among domestic firms. We assume that the business capabilities of these two types of firms are roughly comparable, but their credit constraints differ. (This assumption about their business capabilities might be unrealistic, but I show later that a relaxation of this assumption will not affect the findings.) TVEs are higher-tiered firms than private firms on China's political pecking order.

Second, we compare foreign ownership patterns between CJVs and EJVs. Because control of EJVs is shared between a foreign and a Chinese investor on a long-term basis, a private entrepreneur would be more cautious than a TVE to enter into an EJV. Third, we compare these two aforementioned patterns under two different policy environments for domestic firms – one favorable to private sector development and one less favorable – but under identical policy treatments for FDI.

Column 1 of Table 4.3 shows the average foreign ownership ratios broken down between different types of FIEs – CJVs and EJVs – and between different types of domestic investing firms – private firms and TVEs. The foreign ownership in CJVs with shareholding ties to private firms is substantially larger than it is in CJVs with shareholding ties to TVEs: 89.3 percent versus 75.4 percent.[30] This is consistent with the idea that private entrepreneurs may have to pay more – in the form of forgone dividend revenue – than TVEs to secure this form of financing. It should be stressed that Table 4.3 controls for the export orientation of the FIEs as well as the foreign investor characteristics. All the FIEs in the table export more than 75 percent of their output and all the foreign investors are based in the ECEs.

Research by others has suggested that CJVs tend to be found in labor-intensive and lower value-added operations (Fu 2000, p. 103). Our finding here suggests a reason: Because private firms in general have been restricted to running businesses in lower value-added industries and because credit constraints on private firms leave them fewer financing options, CJVs are thus more prevalent in labor-intensive industries.

EJVs exhibit an entirely different pattern. Here, the foreign ownership ratio is in fact lower among EJVs with shareholding ties to private firms than it is among EJVs with shareholding ties to TVEs (46.9 percent compared with 48.9 percent). This confirms the idea that private entrepreneurs might be more wary than TVEs of giving up operating controls of their businesses. It is also possible that private firms that form EJVs are among the best firms in the business and thus they are desirable JV partners from the point of view of a foreign investor. As evidence, the average sales revenue of EJVs with shareholding ties to private firms (and with an export/sales ratio exceeding 75 percent) is larger than an average EJV as measured by sales revenues. In contrast, EJVs with shareholding ties to TVEs are smaller than an average EJV.[31]

---

[30] This foreign ownership differential between private firms and TVEs also holds for CJVs funded by investors from non-ECE economies, but the differential is smaller. This rules out round-trip FDI as the only factor driving up the difference in the foreign ownership between TVEs and private firms. The round-trip FDI dynamics should not affect the foreign ownership ratios. As long as a firm is classified as an FIE, it enjoys the legal and regulatory treatments accorded to FIEs. Whether this firm is 40 percent or 60 percent owned by a foreign investor is irrelevant.

[31] Sales revenue of an EJV with ties to a TVE is RMB 13.7 million, compared with RMB 15 million for an average EJV. An EJV with shareholding ties to a private firm averages RMB 18 million in sales. All these firms export more than 75 percent of their output.

Columns 2 and 3 compare foreign ownership patterns in Guangdong province as a whole with those in Foshan city of Guangdong. Located near Hong Kong and enjoying similar geographic characteristics to the rest of Guangdong, Foshan encouraged FDI. The difference with other parts of Guangdong is its policies toward domestic firms. Foshan pioneered the privatization drive in China. In 1992 and 1993, Shunde, at that time a county subordinate to Foshan, privatized all of its SOEs. (Shunde later became a separate administrative unit from Foshan.) As shown in columns 2a and 3a, while CJVs have a similar foreign ownership differential between private firms and TVEs in Guangdong province, in Foshan this differential reverses its direction: CJVs with shareholding ties to private firms have a lower average foreign ownership ratio, 71 percent, compared with that of CJVs with shareholding ties to TVEs (77.5 percent). Apparently, the more propitious business environment for private firms in the region has reduced the private firms' reliance on this extremely expensive form of equity financing.

This comparison between Foshan and the rest of Guangdong provides another analytical benefit: We can relax the assumption that private firms and TVEs are equally capable. For example, one might argue that a private firm is more efficient than a TVE and thus from the perspective of the foreign firm it is a more desirable JV partner. The greater efficiency of the private firm translates into a higher valuation of the contributions from the private entrepreneur (similar to the dynamics that influenced COSMOS's valuation of Mr. Bao's firm). If the valuation is high, as this reasoning goes, a private entrepreneur would be motivated to cede as many shares as possible to a foreign firm under a *CJV arrangement*. This is because under a CJV arrangement a private entrepreneur does not have to forgo operating controls of his business. Thus, at a given level of control, more share concessions will bring in more money. This dynamic is consistent with the findings in column 1a that show that foreign ownership is higher among FIEs cofunded with private firms than among those cofunded with TVEs.

The statistical analysis presented in the appendix shows that private firms, at a given level of foreign capital, still cede more controls to foreign firms compared with TVEs. (The foreign equity capital is expressed in two ways. One is the total amount of foreign equity capital in an FIE; the other is foreign equity capital divided by the percentage share of foreign to the total equity capital of an FIE.) The findings from Foshan also cast doubt on this hypothesis. Here, we find more efficient private firms ceding fewer shares than TVEs to foreign firms. In fact, we can extend this analysis to the rest of the country by examining the foreign ownership ratios of the smallest FIEs. The idea here is that small private firms and TVEs tend to form small FIEs, and the efficiency differences between the smallest private firms and the smallest TVEs are negligible. If the pattern established in column 1a still holds, we can rule out the influence of business capabilities.

We use the asset value of the FIEs as a measure of the size of the FIEs. The mean value of the assets of all FIEs in the database is RMB 11.7 million, whereas the median value is RMB 6 million, suggesting the presence of numerous small FIEs. We use the median value as the dividing line between big and small firms. For assets below the median value, the average foreign ownership ratio is 92.2 percent among FIEs cofunded with private firms. For those cofunded with TVEs, it is only 72.9 percent. The same results hold if we use the bottom quartile of the FIEs' asset value or the mean value of assets as the cutoff line between big and small firms. The higher foreign ownership ratio of the smallest FIEs cofunded with private firms than that found among median or mean FIEs is further confirmation of the lending bias against private firms. A small private firm is disadvantaged not only by its political status but also by its size.

COMPANY CASE STUDY: KELON

Kelon, whose full name is Guangdong Kelon Electrical Holdings Company Limited, is the top manufacturer of refrigerators in China today. In 2000, it accounted for 25 percent of the unit market share.[32] What makes this firm interesting is that its rise to the pinnacle of China's refrigerator industry was a surprise both to the economic bureaucrats in Beijing and to the executives of the MNCs such as Whirlpool and Maytag. Kelon was founded in a rural, obscure, and small township, Rongqi, in Guangdong province. Its two founders did not have any technical capabilities in refrigerator production. Both the Ministry of Light Industry and Guangdong province initially refused to grant the firm a production license. Rather, they supported the bigger and better-equipped SOEs.

The case richly illustrates all aspects – and the full complexities – of our political pecking order story. First, the failures of the refrigerator SOEs have little to do with technology, capital, and industrial capabilities. The SOEs had all of these but they still failed, because they lacked the innovativeness and entrepreneurship that characterize Kelon, a firm with far humbler origins. Second, the favorable treatments granted to SOEs, while failing to produce competitive firms, succeeded in creating attractive asset bases that the MNCs acquired on a large scale after China was opened to FDI in the mid-1990s.

---

[32] A better known firm, Haier, has greater penetration in the cities, but Kelon has a larger overall market share.

Third, the inefficient allocative decisions made by the state are not cost-free. One concrete cost is the fact that Kelon, while successful against SOE and MNC competitors, has not developed into a world-class home appliance firm, despite having the benefit of operating in one of the largest refrigerator markets in the world. It is still small-sized, and its market reach is limited. Also, the case illustrates both the flexibility of China's economic system during the reform era and the limitations of such flexibility. While the political pecking order was not uniformly enforced in the country, the parts of the country that had more liberal economic policies – such as the region of Guangdong where Kelon is located – were the least well-endowed with industrial and technical capabilities. In contrast, the parts of the country that enforced the political pecking order more stringently – Beijing, Shanghai, and Tianjin – had the country's highest level of industrial and technical capabilities. The experience of the refrigerator industry demonstrates this point most clearly.

Finally, in China's business environment in the 1990s, beyond a certain scale and size, a firm cannot develop further without political support. By the early 1990s, Kelon was recognized as a leader in the refrigerator industry and it had won political recognition. In 1992, Deng Xiaoping visited the firm, as did Jiang Zemin in 1994. In 1996, it was the first TVE to win the right to issue company shares on the Hong Kong Stock Exchange, and in 1997, another share placement raised $93.8 million for the firm.[33] The share issues raised a substantial amount of capital that enabled the firm to expand. It should be stressed that the political accolades received by Kelon, however, all occurred *after* the firm claimed top position in the industry in 1991. This is an important point for our analysis. Between 1984 and 1991, Kelon did not achieve market dominance because of its political status. During the growth phase of the firm, Kelon encountered many policy and regulatory obstacles.[34]

In the following paragraphs, I first go over some basic dynamics in the home appliance industry. The underlying idea here is that given the right conditions,

---

[33] According to its *Annual Report,* Hong Kong shareholders held 47.6 percent of the shares and the employees held another 10.5 percent. The rest was held by Guangdong Kelon (Rongsheng) Group. The data are reported in Guangdong Kelon Electrical Holdings Company Limited (1997). Because of the Hong Kong listing, Kelon is classified formally as an FIE, as the foreign share-holding exceeds the legal threshold of 25 percent. From the perspective of illustrating the political pecking order hypothesis, this is less relevant because the most interesting period is from 1984 to 1991 when it was 100 percent domestically owned. One huge difference between Kelon and other JVs set up in the home appliance industry is that Kelon is managed and controlled by local Chinese. From a control point of view, this firm, even after being listed, can be considered analytically to be a domestic Chinese firm.

[34] The Chinese leaders were sufficiently pragmatic to recognize its achievements after the fact, but obviously they were unable to recognize those private businesses that never got off the ground because of the adverse business environment.

local firms in this industry can hold some advantages over foreign firms. If one is to witness a competitive domestic firm, the home appliance industry is a likely venue. I then describe the history of Kelon. Last, I present an analysis of the key lessons from this case.

Home Appliances: A Multidomestic Industry

In a multidomestic industry, "[c]ompetition in each nation (or small group of nations) is essentially independent." According to Michael Porter, most of the firms competing in such an industry are owned locally, as foreign firms lack a competitive advantage. "Foreign ownership, to the extent it does occur," he remarks, "will tend to be largely passive and involve only modest control from central headquarters."[35] Home appliances are a multidomestic industry. Competition in this industry is heavily affected by country-by-country dynamics. One country-specific factor is culture. In an article that demonstrates the powerful influence of "distance" on international trade and investment, Pankaj Ghemawat (2001, p. 142) remarks:

> Most often, cultural attributes create distance by influencing the choices that consumers make between substitute products because of their preferences for specific features. . . . Consumer durables industries are particularly sensitive to differences in consumer taste at this level. The Japanese, for example, prefer automobiles and household appliances to be small, reflecting a social norm common in countries where space is highly valued.

The very term *home appliances* suggests the high relevance of culture in this industry. As John Quelch, a marketing professor at Harvard Business School, puts it, "The home is the most culture-bound part of one's life. Consumers in Paris do not care what kind of refrigerator they are using in New York."[36] Culture does not just differ among countries but also across regions within the same country. Gary Ng of Kelon noted in a 2000 interview that consumer preferences for refrigeration storage time and space vary enormously between northern and southern China.[37] (Until 2001, Gary Ng, a Hong Kong resident, was the executive corporate secretary for the then chief financial officer of Kelon,

---

[35] See Porter (1990), pp. 53–54. In contrast, in a global industry, rivals compete with one another on a global basis. Global industries include commercial aircraft, television sets, automobiles, etc. See Porter (1990).

[36] Quoted in Shukla (1999).

[37] Interview with Gary Ng, Hong Kong, September 6, 2000.

Don Lee.)[38] In the north, as Ng explained, people prefer larger refrigerators because they store more things and they store them for longer periods. In the south, consumers typically prefer fresher food and thus demand a shorter storage time. Agile adaptations to these nuanced regional and cultural differences may not be a compelling advantage for an average MNC.

Another factor is geographic distance. For bulky goods, such as refrigerators, dishwashers, and other large home appliances, transportation costs are high, and a cross-country integration of markets is hard to achieve. While the geographic distance may reduce international trade, it is not necessarily a deterrent to FDI. Here, the success of a foreign firm depends on the kind of strategies it pursues. This third factor, economic distance, is identified by Ghemawat as affecting the extent of market integration. He writes (2001, p. 147):

> More broadly, cross-country complexity and change place a premium on responsiveness and agility, making it hard for cross-border competitors, particularly replicators, to match the performance of locally focused ones because of the added operational complexity. In the home appliance business, for instance, companies like Maytag that concentrate on a limited number of geographies produce far better returns for investors than companies like Electrolux and Whirlpool, whose geographic spread has come at the expense of simplicity and profitability.

It should not be inferred from Ghemawat's analysis that local firms naturally dominate in the home appliance business. As his example of Maytag shows, the strategies of the MNCs critically determine their chances of success in a local market. It is conceivable that an MNC can pursue a local strategy – for example, servicing different local markets with different products – but this strategy may attenuate the economy-of-scale advantage that it holds.[39] All else being equal, consistent with Ghemawat's framework on distance, it is plausible to argue that a local firm has a better chance to succeed in the home appliance

---

[38] Don Lee joined Kelon in 1993, with a background in accounting, and rose to the positions of vice president for finance and company secretary. With an MBA from a British university, Lee had previously worked for a number of MNCs and listed companies.

[39] MNCs often do not pursue a multimarket strategy. In an interview with *Harvard Business Review*, David Whitman, CEO of Whirlpool, made this point explicit. He said, as quoted in Maruca (1994):

We looked at horizontal expansion and vertical expansion. And in the process, it became clear to us that the basics of managing our business and its process and product technologies were the same in Europe, North America, Asia, and Latin America. We were already very good at what we did. What we needed was to enter appliance markets in other parts of the world and learn how to satisfy different kinds of customers.

industry than in other industries competing against foreign firms (with the usual ceteris paribus caveat). In principle, the four distance factors – cultural, geographic, political, and economic – do seem to advantage local firms.

Empirical patterns of foreign/local market shares in home appliances do lend support to the notion that distance advantages local firms. In a number of countries, the top firms in home appliances tend to be local firms. For example, in the United States, the top three firms are all American. In 1990, Whirlpool, General Electric, and Maytag accounted for 74.4 percent of the unit market share; in 1997, their share increased, to 80.8 percent. In the refrigerator market, in the 1980s, the top three American firms accounted for 80 percent of sales and the top five accounted for 95 percent of sales. The European market is more fragmented, but the top firms are still European. In 1994, the two top European firms accounted for 39.9 percent of the unit market share.[40] The dominance of local firms is not only confined to developed countries. In Turkey, a local firm, Koc Holding, accounted for 54.6 percent of the refrigerator market (by unit) in 1995. Its competitor, Peg, accounted for another 38.2 percent in the same year.[41]

In China, the general pattern of the home appliance industry does not differ in that local firms dominate this market. There are, however, two issues that should be highlighted. One is that the dominance of local firms is achieved by the presence of a number of relatively small local firms rather than by the dominance of a few large firms. In 2000, Kelon accounted for 25 percent of the market. This is nowhere near Koc Holding's share of the Turkish market (54.6 percent in 1995). While China's market is much larger and therefore can accommodate more firms, Kelon's share is still considerably smaller than the market share held by the top firm in the United States. Whirlpool accounted for 35.8 percent of the refrigerator market in 1997. Even though Europe consists of different political entities and cultures, Electrolux accounted for 23.9 percent of the European market in 1994. (All ratios refer to unit market shares.) Second, the individual size of Kelon is not large at all, even compared with Koc Holding in Turkey. Third, the market share of the MNCs is still quite considerable. In 2000, MNCs accounted for 28 percent of the unit market share of refrigerators in China. Considering that China imposes substantial restrictions on the operations of MNCs, the MNC market share appears somewhat high. A detailed case study of Kelon will help us understand this phenomenon better.

---

[40] See Shukla (1999). Until the 1980s, local producers supplied to each of the European countries. In addition to the sources cited above, Professor Pankaj Ghemawat has generously provided me with data on the home appliance industry.

[41] Peg, however, was sold to Bosch-Siemens of Germany in 1995. Its pre-1995 sales are not available. See Root and Quelch (1997).

The Rise of Kelon (1984–2000)

The history of Kelon, in many ways, reflects China's unfolding economic reforms in the 1980s and 1990s. The following brief description begins with the origins of the firm, describes the critical support of the township government, and analyzes the sources of its dynamism.

Origins of the Firm. In the early 1980s, Wang Guoduan ran a small factory in rural Shunde county of southern Guangdong province, making cheap transistor radios for a Hong Kong company.[42] Fierce competition among the small Guangdong factories forced Wang to look for new business opportunities in the rapidly expanding local consumer market. In 1984, he secured RMB 90,000 (about $30,000 at the prevailing exchange rate) from Rongqi township and founded Kelon. Rongqi township assigned one of its officials, Pan Ning, as the general manager of the firm. The firm was named Guangdong Shunde Refrigerator Factory.[43]

Pan and Wang knew nothing about refrigerator production. They initially contemplated producing electric cookers, but they settled on refrigerators after seeing many Hong Kong people carry them to relatives in Guangdong. In the early 1980s, Chinese consumers hoped to acquire the *san da jian* ("three big items") – a refrigerator, a TV set, and a washing machine. Wang asked his Hong Kong relatives to bring him two refrigerators, which he disassembled to learn how they worked. Pan and Wang then recruited 4,000 workers from factories that made MSG, rice cookers, and car parts.

The beginning of the firm was very humble. "Our first refrigerators were made by hand," Pan recalled. "We didn't have the equipment to make the shells, so we hammered iron sheets into shape bit by bit." To test the units, workers stashed Coke inside. "The next morning, we discovered that all the bottles had burst. We were very excited. What a success!" Pan and Wang then built an assembly line out of timber stripped from an old factory. Workers wore raincoats and gas masks while spraying paint in the heat of a tarpaulin shed. Pan tried to hire university graduates to help run the township venture. "Some came, but went away after seeing how shabby we were," he said.

The Support of Rongqi Township. Kelon could not have started without the critical support of Rongqi township. As a township (the lowest level in China's

---

[42] Unless otherwise noted, the factual details on the history of Kelon are contained in Huang and Lane (2001).

[43] The name was changed to Guangdong Pearl River Refrigerator Factory in 1988 and then to Kelon Electrical Holdings in 1992.

political system), Rongqi was subordinate to Shunde county, which reported to Foshan city (population 345,000 in 1988). Rongqi itself had a population of only 55,000 in 1996. By Chinese standards, this was an extremely small town.

Rongqi provided seed capital and arranged for a loan of RMB 4 million. This arrangement made the township government the formal owner of the firm. However, as in similar arrangements elsewhere, an informal but effective arrangement often differed from the formal arrangement. According to some accounts, the RMB 90,000 provided by the township was a loan, not equity capital (Bruton, Lan, Lu, and Yu 2000). Formally, the firm was registered as a township and village enterprise.

The support from Rongqi township, however, went far beyond the initial seed capital. Above all, by standing behind Kelon, the township provided political cover for the firm. In the mid-1980s, private firms were simply not allowed to establish industrial facilities. By granting the firm operating autonomy while retaining an ownership tie, the township allowed the firm to be run as a private firm but to maintain political legitimacy as a collective firm. In the 1980s, almost all successful nonstate firms had such an arm's-length operating relationship combined with substantial ownership ties to the government, as research on a number of successful nonstate firms in China's high-tech industries shows.[44]

Rongqi township also lobbied on behalf of Kelon for a production license. To obtain such a license, both the provincial government and the central government had to review the application. Initially, Guangdong province was hesitant. It argued that the province already had a refrigerator maker, Wanbao, an SOE, and it did not need another one. Also, it felt that refrigerators used too much electricity. Both Rongqi township and Pan persisted, eventually winning provincial approval.

The founding of Kelon coincided with an effort by the central government to reduce the number of refrigerator producers. In 1978, only 28,000 refrigerator units were made. But attracted by the high demand, many local governments sponsored their own firms. In 1985, the number of refrigerator makers rose to 115, from twenty in 1978. The State Council decreed that the number of firms be cut from 115 to forty-one – all remaining firms were to be SOEs. To carry out the central government's policy, the Ministry of Light Industry rejected Kelon's application. This time, Guangdong province stepped in and helped persuade the ministry to grant Kelon a production license, as the forty-second and only

---

[44] Kelon's arrangement with Rongqi is quite similar to that between Sitong New Industry Development Corporation, an electric typewriter producer, and Evergreen Township in Beijing. Evergreen provided the seed capital and conferred a collective firm title on Sitong, but the firm itself was autonomous and financially independent (Lu 2000).

nonstate firm on the government's list. However, the designation did not entail any financial support from central or provincial authorities. On this list of forty-two firms, the Ministry of Light Industry designated five SOEs – in Beijing, Tianjin, Shanghai, Guangzhou, and Suzhou – as pillar enterprises targeted for support.

Support from the local government was critical. Although the production license did not entail any financial benefits, it did get Kelon into the door. In an interview, Xu Tiefeng, the Rongqi township official in charge of Kelon in the 1980s and its general manager between 2000 and 2001, reflected on this period in the following terms:

> For us the struggles in those days were indescribable. Back then China was still a planned economy and making refrigerators required government approval. Nationwide there was a total of forty-two approved manufacturing entities and we were ranked last, with a volume limit of 50,000. Fortunately we had support from our provincial, municipal, and county governments. They were behind us since they wanted to build blockbuster products.[45]

Kelon's Dynamism. From this humble beginning, Kelon grew rapidly in the 1980s. In 1991, Kelon was the largest refrigerator maker in China, accounting for 10.3 percent of the market by number of units sold. Its market share continuously increased in the 1990s. Its two brands together accounted for 13.5 percent of the market in 1995, 17 percent in 1996, 18 percent in 1997, 20 percent in 1998, 24 percent in 1999, and 25 percent in 2000.[46] Other achievements are equally impressive. It was the first firm in China to receive ISO 9001 certification. In 1996, it issued company shares on the Hong Kong Stock Exchange, generating 500 percent gains to its investors between 1996 and 1999. In the late 1990s, it garnered numerous international awards.[47] The firm also enjoyed healthy operating and financial performance. It increased its operating margin every year between 1993 and 1996, during a time when overall market conditions were adverse. Its posttax profits to sales ratio was 9.73 percent in 1993 and 16.2 percent in 1996.[48]

---

[45] Interview with Xu Tiefeng, Rongqi, Guangdong, China, April 23, 2001.

[46] From Guangdong Kelon Electrical Holdings Company Limited (various years).

[47] In 1999 it was voted in the top twenty of the world's 300 best small companies by *Forbes* magazine. In addition, Guangdong Kelon was voted the best managed company in the decade by *Asiamoney* (1999), best managed company in China and fourth ranked in Asia by *The Asset* (1999), runner-up for the best emerging market company investor relations award (1999), thirteenth in the top 100 best managed companies in the Asia-Pacific region by *Asiamoney* (1998), best strategy and best managed company in China by *Asiamoney* (1997, 1998, and 1999), and top performing economic growth company in East Asia by the World Economic Forum (1997).

[48] Reported in Guangdong Kelon Electrical Holdings Company Limited (1997).

A number of factors accounted for this success. But the most important one is that it was not an SOE. Compared with traditional SOEs, TVEs were more independent from the bureaucracy, more flexible, and more profit-oriented. The relationship between Kelon and the government differed from that of its SOE competitors. Even though Rongqi township was the formal owner, as already pointed out, the government chose not to exercise its control rights, remaining instead, more or less, a passive shareholder.[49]

But it is important to stress that the government retained formal ownership rights over firms such as Kelon. In strictly legalistic terms, there is no difference between an SOE and a TVE. Thus, the manner with which the government chose to exercise its ownership rights over the TVEs mattered enormously for the performance of the firm. In the case of Kelon, it was fortunate to have been located in a township under the most liberal county in Guangdong province – Shunde county. In 1992, Shunde implemented an across-the-board privatization program, and in 1993, it pioneered political reforms, reducing the size of the bureaucracy substantially. The government withdrew completely from enterprise management while it strengthened its social protection functions.[50]

In 1992, Rongqi township began to reduce its ownership stake in Kelon. Kelon was reorganized into a shareholding company and employees were given 20 percent of company shares. This was an unprecedented move for a company of this size in China at the time. Large-scale shareholding reforms did not occur in other parts of the country until 1998. In 1996, Kelon floated 52 percent of its shares on Hong Kong's stock exchange. As a part of the listing preparation, Rongqi township transferred all of its share ownership to Guangdong Kelon (Rongsheng) Group (GKG) in one of the earliest ownership reform experiments in China. Subsequent share listings on the Hong Kong and Shenzhen stock exchanges in 1996 and 1999 reduced GKG's ownership share and increased the ownership shares of arm's-length, private investors. As of 1999, GKG owned 34.1 percent of Kelon's shares, and the rest was split among company employees (8.5 percent), Hong Kong shareholders (46.3 percent), and Shenzhen shareholders (11.1 percent).[51]

A more meaningful indicator of the absence of pervasive interventions from the township is the long tenure of Pan and Wang, the two founders of the firm. Both started in 1984. Pan stepped down in 1999 and Wang stepped down in 2000. Such a long tenure is rare among Chinese firms. Because the government

---

[49] For a study on Kelon's less intrusive relationship with the township government, see Bruton, Lan, Lu, and Yu (2000).

[50] On the privatization program in Shunde, see International Finance Corporation (2000) and on the political experiments in the county, see Chen, Chen, and Zheng (1999).

[51] Company documents provided by Kelon.

views firms as training ground for civil servants, successful managers often change positions frequently. According to one economic study, the average tenure of SOE managers was only 5.5 years (Groves, Hong, McMillan, and Naughton 1995). Kelon's managers enjoyed autonomy in decisions on compensation, which they set on performance-based criteria. The five directors received RMB 8.8 million in bonus payments in 1996, roughly 2.5 times their salaries (Tanzer 1996). In an interview, Xu reflected on the compensation policies of the firm during the early period:

> [The founders] wanted to build the business, but they also wanted to improve their own financial situations by making the firm succeed. We chose to tie employee salaries to firm profitability. As a result, the whole team was strongly motivated and highly committed. They focused on quality, management, and technology, and they worked toward the standardization and professionalization of the organization.[52]

The superior incentive structures at the firm motivated managers and employees to be aggressive in identifying sales opportunities. Take its sales strategy as an example. SOEs typically relied on the existing distribution network for its sales, but, motivated by a desire to gather market information on its own, Kelon decided to create its own network of distribution centers and sales offices throughout China. Initially, Kelon salespeople crisscrossed the country, selling to department stores and city-supply bureaus. By 1997, Kelon had established 476 sales outlets in secondary cities and twenty-four in tertiary cities. It was one of the first Chinese companies to sponsor annual trade fairs. Remarkably for a small firm founded only in 1984, by 1991 some 60 percent of the annual sales revenue of RMB 720 million already came from outside Guangdong province.

The substantial operating autonomy granted to the firm gave Kelon another advantage. Compared with a traditional SOE, Kelon was freer to choose its investment and production sites in accordance with market demand rather than based on the political imperative of the local government to create jobs locally. Because Guangdong was far ahead of other provinces in the penetration levels of refrigerators, its refrigerator market was more saturated. Kelon was among the first firms in China to venture outside its own jurisdiction by investing in facilities in Liaoning and Sichuan provinces.

Although Kelon enjoyed a productive relationship with Rongqi township, the larger operating environment for this last-ranked and the only nonstate firm on the government's list was adverse. Because it was not designated as a "pillar" firm, Kelon found it difficult to obtain external funds for business

---

[52] Interview with Xu Tiefeng, Rongqi, Guangdong, China, April 23, 2001.

expansions. Banks were reluctant to make loans and suppliers insisted on being paid in cash. The hard budget constraints forced Kelon to be cost-conscious and market-oriented. Pan summarized Kelon's experiences as follows: [53]

> Other than the start-up money, we haven't received a single penny in subsidies from the government. We are like a plant that has grown up in the wild. That is why we always follow the law of the jungle. [SOEs] have been living in a greenhouse. As we compete in the wind and rain of a market environment, the state enterprises may face difficulties.

Another way was to differentiate itself from its competitors. Unlike its SOE competitors that typically produced existing models, Kelon actively designed products to suit customer preferences. The separation of the freezer from the refrigerator on Kelon's two-door model of 1986, copied from foreign models, for example, not only provided convenience but also had an esthetic appeal. Given the refrigerator's status as a big-ticket item, the Chinese often set them in their living rooms rather than in their cramped kitchens. The two-door refrigerator turned out to be hugely popular among Chinese consumers, who began to favor more sophisticated and better-designed products. Kelon's market leadership in 1991 was due in no small measure to the roll-out of the two-door refrigerator in 1986.[54]

The Political Pecking Order and FDI in the Refrigerator Industry

The Kelon case provides an angle on the institutional dynamics of FDI different from our case in the garment industry. Unlike the garment industry, this was a domestically oriented industry. In 1995, refrigerator exports accounted for 3.5 percent of output value, while the average annual growth of unit sales on the domestic market was around 33.5 percent between 1982 and 1998.[55] From an FDI angle, the relevant issue is the competitiveness of foreign and domestic firms in responding to the explosive market opportunities in the 1980s and 1990s created by China's rapid income growth.

FDI developments in this industry, as well as in the garment industry, in fact, are mirror images of each other. In the garment industry, private firms were credit-constrained, and they sought out foreign financing to expand their businesses. In the refrigerator business, as in other more capital-intensive industries,

---

[53] Quoted in Tong (1998).

[54] Interview with Gary Ng, September 6, 2000.

[55] The 1982 data are from Liu and Jiang (1997) and the 1998 data are from "Portrait of the Chinese Appliance Industry" (1999). Export data for 1995 are from Office of Third Industrial Census (1997).

the resources and market opportunities were allocated to the SOEs. During the critical growth phase of Kelon, between 1984 and 1991, the firm hardly registered on the radar screen of the central government. The introduction of the two-door refrigerator is a case in point. After its roll-out in 1986, the Ministry of Light Industry refused to believe that Kelon had done it. Recalled Pan, "The ministry said Cantonese were cunning – we must have bought the fridges from Hong Kong."

Three themes emerge from our analysis of the political pecking order in the refrigerator industry. First, heavy investments in machines and equipment do not create a competitive firm if the firm is not market-oriented. SOEs, in general, are not market-oriented. Market orientation can be changed only with a change in ownership, which changes the incentives of the firm. I use an acquisition of SOE assets by Kelon to illustrate this point.

Second, the allocative decisions favoring SOEs made in the 1980s entailed consequences for FDI inflows into this industry in the 1990s. The heavy investments in the asset bases of the inefficient SOEs made them attractive acquisition targets. The top-tiered SOEs imported expensive equipment and machinery from abroad, but their poor profitability incentives rendered them uncompetitive. In the late 1990s, Kelon acquired many operating assets of SOEs, often at a discount. The MNCs did the same in the mid-1990s. All five SOEs targeted for support by the government in the 1980s were acquired by MNCs through what I call a JV acquisition mechanism. (JV acquisitions are the main focus of Chapter 5.)

In China, a straightforward acquisition is not legally permissible. In a JV acquisition, a new firm is established by creating a JV between an acquiring and a target firm. The acquiring firm acquires the assets of the target firm, but not the firm itself. The target firm remains as a separate and, in many cases, ongoing entity. However, after the JV acquisition, the target firm no longer has any significant operating assets on its balance sheet; instead, it has equity claims as a minority shareholder.

Third, a firm that the central government discouraged in the 1980s – Kelon – turned out to be one of the few Chinese firms able to compete with the MNCs. The pullout of Whirlpool from China was attributed, in part, to the competitiveness of local firms such as Kelon. The Whirlpool episode illustrates the failure of China's political pecking order of firms rather dramatically.

Hard Assets but Wrong Incentives at SOEs. In Chapter 3, I argue that SOEs are motivated to build up their asset bases without due regard to profitability. This is in part a result of a reward system that evaluates performance on the basis of assets. It is also in part because of the political interventions that often prevent an SOE from pursuing a profitability objective on a consistent and long-term basis. An acquisition by Kelon of significant assets of an SOE in 1999 illustrates this point very well.

In November 1999, Kelon acquired most of the air conditioner production facilities and the brand name of Guangdong Huabao Air Conditioner Factory (Huabao) through a JV acquisition mechanism. The acquisition price was hugely discounted from the offer price: RMB 550 million from RMB 1 billion. Huabao was willing to accept the offer price due to its financial difficulties. The deal illustrates the profound incentive problems in the state sector. Huabao had all the advantages – state support and higher political status – that Kelon did not have. It also had all the advantages that Kelon did have, such as being located in a region that had a liberal and business-friendly regulatory and policy environment and was close to Hong Kong. (They were both located in Shunde.) Both had an equal opportunity to import marketing and financial expertise from Hong Kong.

Huabao was in an attractive product segment – air conditioner sales increased rapidly in the early 1990s. Guangdong province owned the firm and strongly supported its move into this emerging market segment. Huabao imported its fully automated and computerized production line from Italy. To Gary Ng of Kelon, the fundamental problem of the SOEs was that they had a manufacturing mentality, not a market mentality. SOEs were motivated to acquire fixed assets, and they equated competitiveness with having advanced equipment and technology. Market demand was an afterthought. Ng commented on the Huabao problems:

> They had a very advanced production line, imported from Italy. Their production system was completely computerized. They bought the most advanced system but they did not know how to operate and maintain it. Their products were often too advanced to be sellable and during a weak market their debt pressures were enormous because they had accumulated a lot of debt.[56]

The SOEs' Asset Base and FDI. One can tell a Huabao story about many other SOEs in the refrigerator industry. By 2000, of the forty-two firms on the Ministry of Light Industry's list, only fifteen were still around. As shown in Table 4.4, in 1982, the five priority SOEs dominated the industry, but they lost ground to the start-ups that entered the industry during the mid-1980s. For example, Beijing Refrigerator Factory occupied the top spot in 1982 but slipped to second place

---

[56] Interview with Gary Ng, Hong Kong, September 6, 2000.

Table 4.4 *China's Top Four Refrigerator Makers, 1982–1998*

	1982	1985	1994	1998
Top four firms, ranked by output	Beijing Refrigerator Factory	Guangzhou Wanbao[a]	Kelon	Kelon
	Guangzhou Refrigerator Factory	Beijing Refrigerator Factory	Hefei Meiling	Haier Group
	Shanghai Refrigerator Factory	Shanghai Refrigerator Factory	Haier Group	Henan Xinfei Appliance Co.
	Suzhou Refrigerator Factory	Suzhou Refrigerator Factory	Yangzi Group	Hefei Meiling
Output of top four firms (unit)	74,000	571,000	2,849,000	—[b]
Industry total output (unit)	100,000	1,448,000	7,645,000	10,140,000

[a] Formerly Guangzhou Refrigerator Factory.

[b] —: Data not available.

Sources: Liu and Jiang (1997) and "Portrait of the Chinese Appliance Industry" (1999).

in 1985. By 1994, none of the top four firms in 1982 and 1985 remained in the top ranks. Shanghai Refrigerator Factory, renamed Shanghai Refrigerator Compressor Co., Ltd., withdrew from refrigerator production altogether to focus on the upstream manufacture of air compressors. In 1994, only one of the top five, the Yangzi Group, was an SOE. Kelon was a TVE and the Haier Group – China's largest home appliance firm – was a collective enterprise, with close ties to the municipal government of Qingdao, in Shandong province.

The timeline established in Table 4.4 is highly significant for our story and deserves some emphasis. None of the top SOEs lost out to MNCs. Western MNCs did not begin to invest in China until 1994 or so. They all lost out to other more nimble and market-oriented Chinese firms in the second half of the 1980s. Recall a hypothesis proposed in Chapter 2 that the SOEs' troubles stemmed from the superior treatment accorded to FIEs. There is simply no evidence in support of this relative treatment hypothesis.

The poor financial performance of the top SOEs created one outcome that China's economic bureaucrats could never have anticipated: They became attractive acquisition targets once the country was opened to FDI. The first SOE to team up with a foreign firm was Guangzhou-based Wanbao. The firm, in the words of an advocate of Chinese industrial policy, was "[o]ne of the most striking successes."[57] In the mid-1980s, Wanbao was the largest refrigerator producer in China and by the early 1990s, the firm employed more than 10,000 people and was one of the world's eight largest manufacturers of refrigerators, with over 1 million units of output (Liu and Jiang 1997).

In the wake of the Tiananmen crackdown, the Chinese economy began to contract. Wanbao's after-tax profits plummeted 79 percent in 1990 from their 1988 level.[58] In 1993, it formed a JV with Matsushita, but unfortunately, the JV never turned in any profit. In 1998, it formed another JV, this time with Zanussi Electromechanic Co. of Italy, to produce refrigerator compressors. In both cases, Wanbao did not contribute cash but capitalized its equipment and machinery as equity stakes in the JVs.

As the largest refrigerator maker in the early 1980s, Beijing Refrigerator Factory created one of the best-known brand names in the country, Snowflake. Although profit data are unavailable, the firm's market position is an indication of its performance problems. Its industry position slipped from number one in the early 1980s to number fifteen on the eve of its acquisition by Whirlpool in 1994. Whirlpool contributed $17.7 million in cash and established a 60 percent stake in the newly created JV. The Beijing firm contributed all of its operating assets – machines and equipment – as well as its brand name. As a sign that Whirlpool believed that the brand name was quite valuable, it decided to retain the brand name and to continue to produce its refrigerators under the Snowflake name. In 1995, Suzhou Refrigerator Factory – another of China's five refrigerator SOEs – teamed up with Korea's Samsung, with Samsung controlling 80 percent of the JV. The same pattern was repeated for China's first refrigerator maker, the SOE in Tianjin. The Tianjin firm formed a JV with Korea's LG, which had 80 percent ownership in the enterprise.[59] Other MNCs that entered China during this period included Electrolux, Siemens, Sharp, National, and General Electric. They all formed alliances with SOEs on the list of the Ministry of Light Industry. A Chinese study on FDI in the home appliance industry described these JVs as a way to bring "a dying person back to life" (Wang 1997, pp. 226–27):

Through utilization of foreign capital, some of the Chinese home appliance firms quickly acquired the capacity to restructure and expand their operations. They got new product lines and gained overall strength. At the

---

[57] This is in the words of Nolan (1996).

[58] This section is based on "Mat-Sush-Ita's Chinese Burn" (1997) and State Statistical Bureau (1998b).

[59] The details of these refrigerator deals are given in Ministry of Foreign Trade and Economic Cooperation (1995) and Ministry of Foreign Trade and Economic Cooperation (1996).

same time, they imported foreign technology and management expertise. Some of the firms already losing due to market competition recovered, like "a dying person brought back to life by a doctor."

Kelon and the MNCs. While the SOEs were being acquired by the MNCs on a large scale, the firm that received the least support competed head-on with some of the world's strongest MNCs. By all indications, Kelon was winning the battle. In 1997, the American home appliance giant, Whirlpool, announced that it would exit from two of its JVs in China, one of which manufactured refrigerators. Under David Whitman, its CEO since 1988, Whirlpool has pursued an aggressive globalization strategy and one of its major targets had been China. Between 1994 and 1997, it invested over $300 million in four JVs in China, but it was not able to compete with the local competitors.[60] An article in *The Economist* reported on the causes of Whirlpool's troubles ("Infatuation's End" 1999):

When Whirlpool set up factories to make refrigerators, air conditioners, washing machines, and microwave ovens in China in 1994, it assumed that it was racing against other foreigners. Instead, its chief competitors turned out to be Chinese appliance makers such as Haier and Guangdong Kelon. Their technology was nearly as good as Whirlpool's, their prices were lower, and their styling and distribution were better suited to China. By 1997, having lost more than $100 million, Whirlpool had shut its refrigerator and air conditioner plants.

The twist of Whirlpool's misfortunes in China reflects the general predicament of MNCs in this industry. The MNCs did manage to beat many Chinese firms and to acquire the best-equipped and, during the 1980s, the most dominant firms. These were the SOEs the Chinese government had supported. The local firms that the MNCs lost out to all operated on the fringes of China's refrigerator industry in the 1980s. Haier, one of the biggest conglomerates and the second largest refrigerator maker in China today, started out as a small collective firm in Qingdao city, Shandong province. It got its start in the home appliance business when the Qingdao city government, concerned about rising unemployment, asked Zhang Ruimin, a government official at that time and a legendary manager in China today, to take over the struggling plant.[61] Haier was not targeted to be China's national champion by the central

---

[60] Information on Whirlpool in China is based on Clyde-Smith and Williamson (2001a, 2001b) and Williamson (2001).

[61] The early history of the Haier Group is described in Paine (2001).

government.[62] The MNCs did not see the rise of Kelon and Haier; nor did the central government.

For Kelon, the exit of Whirlpool was a sweet triumph. Kelon structured an original equipment manufacturing deal with Whirlpool's JV in Shanghai, producing washing machines under Kelon's brand. Traditionally, the MNCs had leveraged their brand names and mainly used local suppliers to economize on production costs. Thus, this arrangement was, as *The Economist* magazine put it, "a reversal of the usual hierarchy between Western and Chinese firms."

Another reason why the exit of Whirlpool is significant is that Whirlpool failed in China precisely for the same reasons the SOEs have failed in this industry. According to Gary Ng, Whirlpool ignored China's market demand and introduced a refrigerator that was much too big – between 300 to 400 liters. (Many of Kelon's refrigerators were in the range of 160 to 200 liters.) Beijing's Snowflake had lost its market share in the 1990s also because its refrigerators – all based on existing imported models – were too big. Another mistake was to continue using the Snowflake brand of the Beijing firm. Whirlpool paid a lot to acquire the Snowflake name because it was one of the best brands in China in the 1980s. But Ng believed that the value of this brand was high mainly because the Beijing firm had been given a privileged market position by the government, not because the product was good. After Whirlpool modernized the Beijing plant and introduced new products under the same brand, consumers merely thought that they were the same products as before, except at much higher prices.[63]

Kelon has also created JVs with foreign firms. In contrast to the SOEs, Kelon created these JVs as a way to acquire technology to move to new product areas, not as a vehicle to convert its own fixed assets into a more liquid form, such as equity shares in a better-managed firm. In the mid-1990s, it created two JVs, one with a Hong Kong company and one with Japan's Sanyo, to produce specialized components. In both JVs, Kelon held controlling stakes, 70 percent in the former and 54 percent in the latter. These JVs are similar to the strategic alliances in the business studies literature.

Kelon and China's Institutional Distortions

There is no question that the rise of Kelon is a remarkable story. It beat its SOE competitors and it withheld challenges from some of the world's strongest

---

[62] See Liu and Jiang (1997) for a detailed study of the history of the refrigerator industry. They argue that in the 1980s the Ministry of Light Industry consistently chose the wrong firms to support.
[63] Interview with Gary Ng, Hong Kong, September 6, 2000.

MNCs. Relative to its modest origins, this firm has gone further than probably its founders ever dared to imagine. However, our evaluation of its achievements has to start with a recognition that the overall institutional environment in which Kelon operated was difficult for innovative and dynamic firms. Kelon was successful against the inefficient SOEs and an MNC such as Whirlpool, which adopted a poorly thought-out strategy when it approached China, but Kelon today is far from a world-class home appliance firm. As I show, Kelon has gone through a tumultuous period in the last two years in part because of the problems created by its ownership ties to the township government. When Kelon was small, the ad hoc arrangement worked. Now that the firm is much larger, the relatively small shares held by the founders/managers have begun to create incentive problems. There is also some suggestive evidence that the political interventions have increased. It is a legitimate question whether China's adverse institutional environment has affected the healthy development of this firm.

In 2000, Kelon's market share was smaller than the collective market share of the MNCs in this industry (25 percent versus 28 percent), and it barely had any international presence. Because China's refrigerator market is extremely large, the more telling indicator is Kelon's absolute size. In 1998, Kelon reported sales revenue of $475 million. To put this number in perspective, Maytag, a smaller home appliance firm in the United States, generated sales revenue of more than $4 billion in the same year.

A more meaningful comparison is with a firm in a developing country. Koc Holding, the Turkish home appliance firm, generated sales revenue of $1.2 billion in 1996. But Koc Holding is a conglomerate, and thus the revenue of the entire group should not be benchmarked against the revenue of Kelon, which specializes in refrigerators. Koc's refrigerator sales generated $460 million in 1996.[64] This compares with Kelon's sales revenue of $332.7 million in the same year. The remarkable fact is that in 1996, China's refrigerator market was more than nine times the size of Turkey's market (9.9 million units compared with 1 million units), and yet Kelon was smaller than Koc Holding. To be sure, the price differential of refrigerators in the two markets is one reason, but another reason is Kelon's lack of scale.

In fact, if Koc Holding were located in China, it would have been the second largest home appliance firm in the country. (The largest home appliance firm, Chunlan, generated sales revenue of $1.5 billion in 1996 and Haier's sales revenue was $800 million in 1996 (Institute of Industrial Economics 1998, p. 253).) This combination of a large market and individually small firms may

---

[64] Information on Koc Holdings is based on Root and Quelch (1997).

suggest the presence of some constraints on the growth capacity of Chinese firms. The small individual sizes of Chinese home appliance firms provides further evidence of the miniaturization of Chinese firms as depicted in Chapter 3.

Below, let me offer two hypotheses, based on the political pecking order framework developed in this book, that may account for this observation. I also present some evidence that seems broadly consistent with our hypotheses. One is that Kelon suffered from two matching problems. First, economic efficiency is not matched with industrial and technical capabilities. Second, economic efficiency is not matched with financial resources. These two problems could have adversely affected the growth of the firm during a time when the market was growing extremely strongly and dynamically.

The second hypothesis is that China's institutional reforms have seriously lagged behind what is necessary to move Chinese firms from an entrepreneurial phase to a developmental phase. This is only speculative at this point, but emerging evidence seems to suggest that for a firm as large as Kelon, the ad hoc arrangement created with Rongqi township in 1984, in which the township granted operating autonomy to the firm but retained ownership control, has become problematic. It is no longer able to adequately align the incentives of the founders/managers with the overall objectives of the firm.

The other problem is that political interventions may have increased. As a large firm, many decisions made by Kelon now affect many parties. In the 1980s and the early 1990s, Kelon was grabbing more market shares but was doing so at a time when the overall market was growing extremely quickly. This was a fundamentally different situation from that in the late 1990s. As the acquisition of Huabao shows, Kelon's gains were achieved at a substantial expense to Huabao's shareholder, none other than the provincial government of Guangdong. This has created a different political dynamic than the situation in the 1980s and the early 1990s. Kelon's decision to remove all founders/managers in March 2000 may be a result of new political dynamics.

The Matching Problems. In the early to mid-1980s, when Kelon started to venture into the refrigerator business, these two matching problems occurred at both the governmental and the firm level. At the governmental level, regions that pursued efficient economic policies were least endowed with industrial and technical capabilities and, to a lesser extent, with capital resources. At the firm level, the most efficient firms were least endowed with industrial and technical capabilities, and they had fewer financial resources compared with the inefficient SOEs.

It is worth recalling that the two founders of Kelon started out without any expertise or capabilities in refrigerator manufacturing. This was not an accident.

While Guangdong is the home to many of the best industrial firms today, in the early 1980s it was primarily rural. Agriculture accounted for 45 percent of provincial output value in 1980. There is no information about Rongqi – the headquarters of Kelon – in the early 1980s. Let me use Shunde county and Foshan city to illustrate this point. (Rongqi was subordinate to Shunde, which was subordinate to Foshan.)

Shunde was largely agrarian at the beginning of the reform era. Ezra Vogel characterizes it as "overwhelmingly rural" in the early 1980s. Out of a population of 9.5 million, 7.3 million lived in the countryside. Unlike Shenzhen, one of China's first Special Economic Zones, Shunde did not receive any administrative and technical cadres from other parts of the country. In the early 1980s, the first industrial product Shunde ventured into was electric fans.[65]

Contrast this situation with the five refrigerator SOEs – in Beijing, Tianjin, Shanghai, Suzhou, and Guangzhou – that the central government designated as pillar firms in 1980. One of them, Tianjin Haihe Refrigeration Compressor Company, made China's first refrigerator in 1956, and the Shanghai firm, Shanghai Refrigerator Factory, was founded about the same time. In 1978, Shanghai, Beijing, and Tianjin accounted for 20.7 percent of China's industrial GDP compared with Guangdong's 4.7 percent. Although industry in Guangdong developed rapidly in the 1980s, in 1985, Shanghai's industry still produced 50 percent more by value than the entire province of Guangdong.[66]

The matching problem on the financial side was also severe. In 1988, Foshan, the city overseeing Shunde and Rongqi, had fiscal expenditures of RMB 654 million.[67] To put this account in perspective, the Tianjin refrigerator SOE spent RMB 200 million (about $87 million) on imported equipment. During the 1987–88 period, when Kelon just got started, the Tianjin firm already boasted production capacity of 1 million units, 200 technicians, and seventeen senior engineers. In 1980, during a time of extreme foreign exchange scarcity, Guangzhou Refrigerator Factory (Wanbao), the Guangzhou-based SOE, imported China's first production line (from Singapore), as did all the other SOEs. The Beijing Snowflake Electrical Appliances Corporation was able to spend RMB 4 million establishing a service station in Beijing.[68] This amount is the same as that of the bank loan Rongqi arranged for Kelon to launch its entire

---

[65] This account of Shunde is given in Vogel (1989) and Sung, Liu, Wong, and Lau (1995).

[66] Data here are provided in State Statistical Bureau (1996a).

[67] No information is available about Shunde and Rongqi. The budget data on Foshan are from Guangdong Statistical Bureau (1989).

[68] Information about firms in the early 1980s is extremely scarce. This is based on Ministry of Light Industry (1989) and Ministry of Machinery and Electronics Industry (1989).

production facility. Short of foreign exchange, Kelon relied entirely on domestic technology between 1984 and 1990.[69]

The bank financing was critical. In 1983, some 71 percent of fixed asset investments in refrigerator production was financed by bank loans (Liu and Jiang 1997, p. 197). In the 1980s, the ability of a government agency to arrange bank loans depended critically on the position of the agency in the political hierarchy. Rongqi was at the lowest level of government in China's political system, thus limiting its ability to mobilize resources compared with Beijing, Tianjin, and Shanghai, the three largest cities in China, with far superior political standing in the Chinese system. Remarkably, in 1995, even after Kelon won political recognition from the central government, its balance sheet showed only RMB 30 million in long-term loans ($3.6 million) against about RMB 2 billion in assets.[70]

Lagging Institutional Reforms. The ability of Kelon to invest outside Guangdong and the long tenure of its founders both indicate substantial operating autonomy granted to the firm by Rongqi township. However, the formal owner of the firm was still the township government, and it had full legal rights to exercise its revenue and control rights. Thus, the arrangement to separate control and revenue rights completely on an ad hoc basis was inherently unstable. Kelon's controlling shareholder, GKG, held 34.1 percent in Kelon, and GKG itself was 100 percent owned by the township government. Employees owned 8.5 percent of the firm, and the other owners were all arm's-length investors. The disproportionate share of equity interest held by the state during much of 1990s relative to that held by employees (including its founders) might have created an incentive problem more serious than when the firm was relatively small. Xu Tiefeng commented on this situation:[71]

> [W]ith the government still being the largest shareholder, the company had some bureaucratic weaknesses. For example, when Kelon was doing contractual work for other firms, if the customer was related to the managers, we would give them price discounts. This damaged the company's financial health as well as the credibility of the management team.

The second problem was more severe. While the ad hoc arrangement created during the founding of the firm might have worked for a smaller firm, it became

[69] Interview with Gary Ng, Hong Kong, September 6, 2000.

[70] According to various issues of Kelon's annual reports, beginning in 1997, long-term loans increased sharply: RMB 119 million in 1997 and RMB 188 million in 1998. See Guangdong Kelon Electrical Holdings Company Limited (1997, 1999).

[71] Interview with Mr. Xu Tiefeng, Rongqi, Guangdong, China, April 26, 2001.

increasingly less effective in achieving the goal it was originally designed for: to minimize political interventions. This was in part a function of the size of the firm and in part a function of the fact that decisions by Kelon could now affect the economic interests of powerful government agencies. Rongqi might still refrain from intervening in the firm, but at the lowest level in China's political system, it would be powerless if the higher-level authorities instructed it to intervene.

It is possible that this dynamic was behind the dramatic change in management in mid-2000. Four deputy presidents were replaced in March, and Wang Guoduan, one of the two founders, was replaced in June by Xu Tiefeng, who was a Rongqi township official.[72] This management reshuffling occurred four months after the controversial acquisition of Huabao. As pointed out before, Kelon agreed to pay only RMB 550 million for Huabao's assets. According to Ng, Kelon received pressure from the government to accept a higher price, but Kelon steadfastly declined, using its listed firm status and its accountability to shareholders as a defense.[73] In China's highly charged political environment, such a stance could have antagonized some government officials. After all, the shareholder of Huabao was none other than the Guangdong provincial government.

While the circumstances surrounding these management changes are not clear, it is clear that the new management team adopted a strategy that was substantially similar to the strategies of those SOEs that Kelon had defeated in the 1980s: heavy investments in modern technology and equipment and targeting urban consumers, moving away from economical models that had placed Kelon on the top of China's refrigerator industry. The results were disappointing. Kelon lost market shares and incurred massive financial losses in 2000 and 2001. It was revealed in 2001 that Kelon and GKG, Kelon's largest shareholder, had engaged in a series of inside transactions, many of which occurred during the reign of the new management. As of December 2001, the cumulative effect of these transactions was that GKG owed Kelon more than RMB 900 million. These inside transactions raised questions about the quality of corporate governance under the new management.

In November 2001, Rongqi township decided to privatize Kelon and sold its controlling interest to Greencool Enterprises Development, an industrial refrigeration firm listed on Hong Kong's Growth Enterprise Market Board. The new controlling shareholder immediately removed Xu Tiefeng and appointed its own management team. Kelon, now a privately controlled company, began yet another major milestone in its development.[74]

[72] The update on Guangdong Kelon is from press reports. See O'Neill (2000).

[73] Interview with Gary Ng, Hong Kong, September 6, 2000.

[74] See Wong (2001).

CONCLUSION

Recall the rationale offered by Chen and Rozelle that leader-run firms, such as TVEs, were successful. They were successful because their managers, that is, township officials, possessed external management skills (Chen and Rozelle 1999). This explanation, like many others in the economic literature on China, provides an efficiency-based analysis of major developments in the Chinese economy. At its core, such an explanation assumes that the underdevelopment of the market in China is exogenous and that government officials and managers choose the optimal course of action under the binding constraint of an immature market.

But the underdevelopment of the market in China is not wholly exogenous. For many years during the reform era, private entrepreneurs were systematically discriminated against. There is no compelling reason why private entrepreneurs could not have acquired external management skills on their own. The huge timing gap between the start of the economic reforms in 1978 and the emergence of a truly vibrant private sector in the late 1990s does not reflect a natural course of market maturation. It is because of a political decision to support the SOEs and those nonstate firms closely allied with the government. Whether this political decision is rational or not is one question; it is quite another to assert that this political decision is economically efficient.

An interesting observation is that the most competitive domestic firms in China today are located not in traditional industrial strongholds such as Beijing, Shanghai, or Tianjin but in Guangdong, a very rural province at the start of the re-forms. Kelon is one such firm, but there are others as well, such as Huawei in the telecommunications sector and Galanz Enterprise Corporation in home appliances. This is by no means accidental. Relative to other provinces, Guangdong has had a more liberal policy toward both domestic firms and FDI. The political pecking order of firms is there but it is less stringently enforced. Thus, flexibility within China's economic system is a major achievement of the reform era, and it is this flexibility that has led to China's remarkable economic growth.

If we move away from a macro perspective on aggregate GDP and export growth, and if we focus on micro issues such as the quality and depth of development of Chinese firms, the picture looks less favorable. Guangdong province had a relatively efficient economic regime but it was also more poorly endowed with technical and industrial capabilities. A small township such as Rongqi was more market-oriented but was poorer in financial resources compared with the SOE strongholds in Shanghai, Beijing, and Tianjin.

As I have shown, the matching problem created by this combination of efficient economic policies and an initially low endowment of industrial and technical capabilities may have entailed some costs. Of course, it is difficult to know what would have happened to China's refrigerator industry if China's financial resources and market opportunities had been allocated more efficiently. A counterfactual scenario can always be debated and challenged. But the hypothesis that Kelon was hampered in its development because of the various distortions identified in this chapter would be consistent with the fact that Kelon, one of China's most successful firms, is still a small firm by international standards. In an industry characterized by some degree of local advantages, the foreign share of the market appears to be somewhat high. This may be because a truly efficient firm such as Kelon is not as dominant as it could be, because it faced a steeper learning curve during the initial growth phase and its organizational deepening and development were hampered by the lag in China's institutional reforms. Another reason for the seemingly high MNC market share is that the massive investments in the asset bases of the SOEs could have provided a less expensive platform for MNCs to enter into China in the mid-1990s.

The FDI flows into labor-intensive and export-oriented industries, as the case study of the garment industry shows, were driven by a different dynamic altogether. Here, the main issue is not competition for market share; foreign firms control the overseas market. The relevant issue is the viability of Chinese firms to carry out contract production for foreign firms as independent business entities.

Severely restricted in their access to financing, private firms sought foreign capital to overcome their credit constraints. Foreign investors play the role of venture capitalists, although the industry in question is mature and free of any technological risks. The risks, instead, are political. Here, the insecurity of property rights is also relevant. Private entrepreneurs might have desired FDI arrangements as a way to protect their assets. Although data limitations do not allow us to directly demonstrate this motivation, analytical reasoning – that a contractual mechanism is feasible on business grounds – combined with some descriptive evidence suggests that this is a highly plausible hypothesis. For a Chinese firm to enjoy protection under the superior legal framework for FIEs, it needs to have at least a 25 percent foreign equity stake. The fact that it might sell 100 percent of its output to a foreign firm is irrelevant to its legal status. This consideration might have motivated private firms to convert their businesses into foreign-controlled operations.

The legal motivation is evidenced by the significant reduction in contractual alliances in 1989 – the year of the Tiananmen crackdown – to $380 million from $550 million in 1988. The Tiananmen crackdown resulted in a substantially higher level of property right insecurities for *domestic private entrepreneurs*, but not for foreign investors. In fact, FDI rose from \$3.2 billion in 1988 to \$3.4 billion in 1989. The total number of domestic private businesses fell in 1989 and 1990 in the wake of an assault on the private sector by the conservative post-Tiananmen leadership. In the FIE database, among 812 garment FIEs created between 1980 and 1990, some 521 of them were created in 1989 and 1990, two years known not for liberal FDI policies but for repressive internal political and economic policies.

In the context of an illiberal treatment of domestic private firms, labor-intensive FDI brought about substantial benefits to the Chinese economy. One huge benefit is that it provided equity financing to private entrepreneurs shunned by China's formal financial institutions. Thus, it offset the inefficient political pecking order of firms. China is extremely fortunate to have received FDI from the ECEs; otherwise, its private firms would have atrophied under the weight of China's inefficient financial and economic institutions. Our explanation complements that by Sachs and Woo (1994), who argue that China's nonstate sector grew rapidly because it was able to draw labor from agriculture. But the growth of the nonstate sector required both labor and capital, and labor-intensive FDI has supplied capital to many nonstate firms.

Even though labor-intensive FDI has benefited the Chinese economy, one cannot argue that this way of attracting FDI, by suppressing domestic entrepreneurship, is a first-best option. After more than twenty years of continuous economic and export growth, and even though Chinese-made garments are found in all corners of the world, China still does not have the likes of Li & Fung of Hong Kong, IPAS of Turkey, and Yuen Yuan of Taiwan, firms that engage in trading and design activities on an international scale. Much of the value-added in the garment business is in the design and branding. Although not based on the analysis developed in this book, the Chinese government reached a similar conclusion about its garment industry. A report in a publication of the State Council makes the following observation (Development Research Center of the State Council 1996, p. 199):

> From the very beginning, our country's garment export business has been on a purely manufacturing path. Our firms do not have our own brands or marketing channels. The high growth has been achieved on cost advantages, sheer quantity, and price competitiveness. Our market share is not stable and our development lacks depth. Garment exports face some tough challenges, which will adversely affect the sustainable development of this industry.

Chapter 3 describes a substantial alleviation of the political pecking order since 1997, as the central government embraced a limited privatization program, lifted the ban on lending to private firms imposed on the four state-owned commercial banks in 1998, and revised the Constitution in 1999 to protect private property rights. If our institutional foundation argument is correct, an attenuation of the political pecking order should lead to a departure from the prevailing FDI patterns as depicted in Chapter 1.

This, indeed, has occurred, in a rather dramatic fashion. As shown in Table 1.1 of Chapter 1, capital flows that financed contractual alliances increased from $410 million in 1996 to $1.47 billion in 1997 and $1.71 billion in 2000. Consistent with this development has been the rapid increase in subcontracting and export-processing operations undertaken by private firms. Exports by processing and assembly operations undertaken by private firms increased 82-fold from 1996 to 2000 (from $6.3 million to $526 million).[75] In Guangdong province, the share of exports by FIEs in 1999 declined slightly.[76]

There is also evidence, although scattered, that round-trip FDI has declined. For example, it is estimated that round-trip FDI accounted for 25 percent of China's FDI inflows in 1992, but only 7 percent in 1996. Another study uses China's declining outward investments since the mid-1990s as evidence that round-trip FDI has declined.[77] According to World Bank (2002a), the trend of round-trip FDI can correlate closely with the trend in the errors and omissions in China's balance of payments. After peaking at $22 billion in 1997, China's net errors and omissions declined to $18.9 billion in 1998, to $17.7 billion in 1999, and sharply to $11.8 billion in 2000 (International Monetary Fund 2001, p. 234).

In the garment industry, in 1998, after the government removed some export restrictions on private firms, direct exporting by private producers increased by 140 percent.[78] As a sign that private firms are able to carry out contract production, indirect exporting by private firms has also sharply increased. In the mid-1990s, the Import and Export Garment Corporation of Jiangsu province purchased about 20 percent of its garment supplies from private firms; in the late 1990s, this share increased to 65 percent.[79] Even the industry distribution of FDI has become more concentrated. In 1995, on an approval basis, the top

---

[75] The export-processing data are reported in General Administration of Customs of the People's Republic of China (1996, 2001).

[76] In 1999, FIEs in Guangdong province exported $39.4 billion, but the export share by FIEs declined slightly, from 51.8 percent in 1998 to 50.7 percent (Guangdong Statistical Bureau 2000).

[77] See Fu (2000) and a summary of some of the research findings on this topic in Tseng and Zebregs (2002).

[78] From Development Research Center of the State Council (1999).

[79] Interview with Jimmy Chen, vice president of Import and Export Garment Corporation of Jiangsu province, October 2001.

four industries with most of the FDI inflows accounted for 25.2 percent of the total manufacturing FDI; in 2001, for the months from January to June, the share went up to 41 percent.[80] The share of FDI in textiles declined from 7.8 percent to 4.5 percent.[81] This is entirely to be expected. Domestic firms have become more competitive in some industries; foreign firms decide either not to invest in or to contract with domestic firms in industries where domestic firms are perceived to be strong. In the late 1990s, China's FDI dependency ratio declined, especially as measured against domestic private investments, as shown in Chapter 1 – another development that is entirely consistent with our argument. This is a sign that the economy is getting healthier and the deep-seated institutional distortions are being eased.

[80] These are based on data on an approval basis and therefore may differ from data based on a paid-up basis. Data based on a paid-up basis, broken down by industries, are not yet available for 2001.

[81] Unfortunately, textile data are not further broken down between garments and textiles. The 1995 figure is calculated from data in State Statistical Bureau (1999a). FDI sectoral data for between January and June 2001 are available at http://www.moftec.gov.cn/moftec_cn/tjsj, accessed in January 2002.

Appendix to Chapter 4

I have presented descriptive data in the text to demonstrate the impact of China's political pecking order of firms on the appetite of private firms for FDI. Here, I present findings from a regression analysis on two industries: the garment industry and the traditional arts and crafts industry. The results are consistent with those from the descriptive analysis.

THE GARMENT INDUSTRY

For the regression analysis, I have limited FIEs to those funded either by TVEs or private firms on the Chinese side, as the FIE database provides clear owner-ship classifications for only these two types of firms.[82] To control for the FDI policies, only the FIEs established during the 1992–95 period are included in the analysis. Because of these controls, and after excluding those FIEs for which foreign equity data are unavailable, the maximum number of firms is reduced to 587 firms, compared with a total of 5,373 garment FIEs contained in the FIE database. For this group of firms, the average employment size is 166 persons, the export/sales ratio is 55.6 percent, and the foreign share is 52.4 percent.

Tables 4.5 and 4.6 report the results of a regression analysis of the garment data. Our measure of credit and regulatory constraints here is a categorical variable denoting the ownership classifications of Chinese investing firms in these garment JVs. The FIE database provides information about the owner-ship designation of two types of Chinese investing firms, TVEs and private firms. Although there is a greater variance in terms of financial and regulatory treatment between private firms and SOEs, TVEs are sufficiently favored over private firms to illustrate the effects of the political pecking order. In essence,

---

[82] Private firms here refer to those with no formal bureaucratic affiliations.

Table 4.5 *Tobit Analysis of the Effect of Private Ownership on the Foreign Equity Ratios*

Dependent variable: Foreign equity ratio	Garment industry				Arts and crafts industry
	Specification (1)	Specification (1a)	Specification (2)	Specification (3)	Specification (4)
Substantive variables:					
Private firm dummy	0.035**	0.041**	0.04		0.072**
	(0.02)	(0.029)	(0.035)		(0.047)
Foreign exchange use ratio and private firm dummy interaction term			0.05**	0.07*	
			(0.03)	(0.03)	
Foreign exchange use ratio				−0.00	
				(0.01)	
Control variable:					
Log foreign equity capital	0.16*		0.17*	0.17*	0.156*
	(0.01)		(0.01)	(0.01)	(0.13)
Log foreign equity capital per foreign share		0.038*			
		(0.01)			
Constant	−0.62*	0.419*	−0.66*	−0.66*	−0.54*
	(0.07)	(0.05)	(0.10)	(0.10)	(0.13)
Number of observations	573	573	384	384	153
Pseudo R-squared	0.53	0.02	0.42	0.42	0.52

Note: Standard errors in parentheses. Significance tests are one-tailed. The foreign exchange use ratio is the foreign exchange used for imports divided by export sales. The foreign equity ratio is the foreign equity capital divided by the total equity capital. Foreign equity capital per foreign share is the foreign equity capital divided by the percentage foreign equity ratio. All the FIEs were established between 1992 and 1995. Foreign investors were from Hong Kong, Macao, and Taiwan.

*: Significant at 5 percent.

**: Significant at 10 percent.

Table 4.6 *Tobit Analysis of the Effect of Private Ownership on the Foreign Equity Ratios in the Garment Industry*

Dependent variable: Foreign equity ratio	Specification (1)	Specification (2)	Specification (3)	Specification (4)	Specification (5)
Substantive variables:					
Private firm	0.06*	0.06*	0.06*	0.071**	
dummy	(0.03)	(0.03)	(0.03)	(0.04)	
Foreign exchange use ratio and private firm dummy interaction term				0.08* (0.04)	0.098* (0.04)
Foreign exchange use ratio					0.01 (0.01)
Control variable:					
Export/sales ratio	0.19*	0.19*	0.19*	0.17*	0.17*
	(0.03)	(0.03)	(0.03)	(0.06)	(0.06)
Log fixed asset		−0.01	−0.01	−0.01	−0.01
per employee		(0.01)	(0.02)	(0.02)	(0.02)
Log employment			0.00	−0.003	−0.01
			(0.02)	(0.02)	(0.02)
Constant	0.43*	0.44*	0.44*	0.48*	0.53*
	(0.02)	(0.05)	(0.10)	(0.15)	(0.15)
Number of observations	584	582	582	387	387
Pseudo R-squared	0.09	0.10	0.10	0.06	0.05

Note: Standard errors in parentheses. Significance tests are one-tailed. The foreign exchange use ratio is the foreign exchange used for imports divided by export sales. The foreign equity ratio is the foreign equity capital divided by the total equity capital.

*: Significant at 5 percent.
**: Significant at 10 percent.

TVEs are smaller SOEs belonging to the township governments. In the regression analysis, private firms are assigned a value of one, and our implicit comparator firms, TVEs, are assigned a value of zero. Thus, the private firm dummy variable should be positively correlated with foreign ownership controls.

Because our dependent variable is a ratio bound between zero and one, a Tobit regression technique is used. We offer two models conceptualizing how the foreign equity ratios are determined. Model One is very simple: It assumes that the foreign equity ratios are a function of the level of foreign equity capital that finances a JV. The larger the size of the foreign equity capital, the larger the foreign equity ratios. The idea behind this conceptualization is that the actual foreign equity ratios already incorporate all the theoretically relevant determinants of the foreign equity ratio. Since we have only partial or imprecise knowledge about what these determinants are, we can use a proxy variable that incorporates the combined effect of all the determinants.

The results from Model One are reported in Table 4.5. The foreign equity ratio is regressed on a private firm dummy variable and on the log value of foreign equity capital and the log value of foreign equity per foreign share. In the first specification of Model One, after controlling for the level of foreign equity capital, private ownership is found to be positively correlated with the foreign equity ratio at a statistically significant level. On average, a private firm cedes more equity controls to foreign investors as compared with a typical TVE with the same amount of foreign equity capital. This result does not change if we use foreign equity capital divided by the percentage share held by foreign firms rather than the total amount of foreign equity capital (specification 1a). These results suggest that shares held by private firms may be cheaper than shares held by TVEs: The same amount of foreign equity capital leads to a greater foreign ownership when private firms are JV partners.

In specification 4, this finding is replicated for data in the arts and crafts industry. Chinese indigenous firms should be competitive in this industry, and the know-how transfer from foreign firms should not be significant. But in this industry, too, the same amount of foreign equity capital is associated with a greater foreign ownership for private firms than for TVEs.

We suggest that a particularly stringent form of credit constraint imposed on private firms is the denial of access to foreign exchange. To test the effect of the foreign exchange constraint, we devised a variable called the foreign exchange use ratio, which is the foreign exchange used by a firm to finance its imports divided by its export revenue. The higher the ratio, the more demand a firm makes on the government to obtain foreign exchange. To illustrate the foreign exchange constraint unique to private firms, we created an interaction variable between the foreign exchange use ratio and the private firm dummy variable.

Specifications 2 and 3 of Model One test the effects of the foreign exchange constraint directly. Specification 2 suggests that the primary reason for equity concessions by private firms is their foreign exchange demand. When the status of a firm as a private firm is combined with a high foreign exchange use ratio, foreign ownership increases in the FIEs. In specification 2, the private firm dummy is no longer statistically significant, although it still carries a positive sign. Specification 3 suggests that the foreign exchange use ratio does not have a statistically significant effect on foreign ownership, but the interaction variable is positive and statistically significant. This implies that the positive effect on foreign ownership associated with the foreign exchange use ratio holds true only when a high foreign exchange demand occurs in conjunction with the status of a firm as a private firm. A high foreign exchange demand does not appear to affect the foreign ownership of FIEs.

Model Two explicitly spells out some of the theoretically relevant control variables and includes them in lieu of the level of the foreign equity capital in Model One. The findings are presented in Table 4.6. Our specification is guided in part by the literature on bargaining dynamics between foreign and domestic firms and in part by data availability. Three control variables are included: The export/sales ratio to denote the marketing controls by foreign firms, the log value of fixed asset per employee to denote the asset intensity of the production processes, and the log value of employment to denote the size of the operation. The regression results here are consistent with our descriptive analysis in that only foreign marketing control is found to be statistically significant, and it is found to be positively correlated with the foreign ownership of FIEs.

The results from Models One and Two are largely consistent with each other. All else being equal, the private firm dummy variable is consistently positive and statistically significant in all versions of the model when it is included in the regression. The foreign exchange constraint imposed on private firms is again found to be positively correlated with foreign ownership. In specification 4 of Model Two, both the private dummy variable and its interaction term with the foreign exchange use ratio are statistically significant and positive. This means that private JV partners normally cede more equity controls to foreign investors as compared with TVE JV partners. But private JV partners that invested in FIEs with a high foreign exchange demand on the government (i.e., relative to their foreign exchange earnings) can be expected to cede equity controls even more. A high foreign exchange demand by itself does not seem to affect foreign ownership, as in specification 5 of Model Two.

THE ARTS AND CRAFTS INDUSTRY

Let me turn to the political status and foreign ownership of FIEs in the Chinese arts and crafts industry. Examples of products in this industry include ivory and jade sculptures, carpets, personal ornaments, silk handicrafts, porcelain, and cloisonné. These are levels 4311 to 4319 in the Chinese Industry Classification Standard. This is an indigenous industry par excellence. Like apparels and garments, it is also highly export-oriented. In 1995, on average, FIEs in this industry sold 62 percent of their sales overseas. Unlike the garment industry, however, it is characterized by a high degree of stability. Fashions and styles do not change easily and a substantial premium is placed on fidelity to tradition. To the extent that rapid and unpredictable fashion changes might have induced

Table 4.7 *Political Status of Firms and Foreign Equity Ratios in FIEs in the Chinese Arts and Crafts Industry (%)*

Export status of FIEs/ Political status	Provincial level	County level	Township level	Private firms
Low exporters[a]	43.7	44.8	47.2	45.5
Low-medium exporters[b]	33.9	57.3	39.7	39.5
High-medium exporters[c]	47.9	49.9	55.7	64.3
High exporters[d]	48.8	48.8	58.1	63.0

Note: All FIEs are joint ventures classified as small firms in the Chinese industry classification.

[a] Low exporters: FIEs with an export/sales ratio of less than 25 percent.

[b] Low-medium exporters: FIEs with an export/sales ratio of between 25 and 50 percent.

[c] High-medium exporters: FIEs with an export/sales ratio of between 50 and 75 percent.

[d] High exporters: FIEs with an export/sales ratio of above 75 percent.

Source: Data are based on All China Marketing Research Co. Ltd. (1999).

Chinese suppliers to value a stable equity relationship with foreign firms, this calculus does not apply here.

Similar to or more than the garment industry, this industry is not characterized by any substantial proprietary know-how. Production is small-scale and labor-intensive. To be sure, it requires highly developed artisanship and specialized skills, but Chinese indigenous firms should command this kind of production and organizational know-how. As pointed out in Chapter 1, many foreign investors in this industry originated from the ECEs, but a sizable portion did not. The FIE database records some 1,504 FIEs operating in this industry as of 1995, of which 518 were funded by investors outside the ECEs. (The equity stake of non-ECE investors amounted to 63.5 percent, whereas the equity stake of ECE investors was 73.7 percent.) While one might conceive of scenarios in which ECE investors also excelled in traditional arts and crafts, it is difficult to extend these scenarios to non-ECE investors.

Table 4.7 presents the foreign equity shares of FIEs in this industry on two dimensions: the export orientation and the political status of the Chinese investing firms. International business research suggests that foreign equity shares should be positively correlated with the export orientation of the invested firms. Our own analysis of the garment industry shows a strong positive correlation between these two variables. The institutional foundation hypothesis postulates a negative correlation between the foreign equity share of an FIE and the political status of the Chinese coinvesting firm. Export orientation again matters, but not in a linear fashion as observed in the garment industry. FIEs that export less than 50 percent of their output by and large are less controlled by foreign firms than FIEs that export more than 50 percent of their output. But high exporters, that is, those exporting more than 75 percent, do not necessarily exhibit a higher foreign equity stake than high-medium exporters (those that export between 50 to 75 percent of their output). Our institutional foundation hypothesis is borne out by the data; although similar to the garment industry, the effect of credit constraints is the strongest with respect to export-oriented FIEs, that is, those that export more than 50 percent of output. FIEs cofunded with private firms, again, are most foreign-controlled. For example, in the case of high exporters, the foreign equity share was 63 percent for private firms, 58.1 percent for township firms, and 48.8 percent for county and provincial firms. A similar ranking holds in the case of high-medium exporters.

5

State-Owned Enterprises and Insolvency-Induced Foreign Direct Investment

Suzhou Peacock Electronics Group Co. Ltd. (Suzhou Peacock) is an SOE located in Suzhou city, Jiangsu province. Suzhou Peacock was one of the first and largest TV producers in the country. Today its main product is a remote-controlled lamp. The firm derives most of its income from investments in two of its major affiliates: one JV with Philips and another JV with Matsushita. Four years after its formation of the JV with Philips in 1994, Ni Suping, the general manager of Suzhou Peacock, reflected on what remained with Suzhou Peacock after the formation of the JV:

> All these desks and chairs that you see here were purchased after 1994. They [the JV] took everything away. After they were gone, the old manager of Suzhou Peacock [Ni's predecessor] used a cardboard box as a desk and sat on another cardboard box as a chair. This is how ruthless the market economy is.

Mr. Ni's account is a familiar tale in China's corporate scene in the 1990s. The firms that formed JVs with foreign firms in this manner – by capitalizing all of their major operating assets and brand names as equity stakes – had been among the best firms in China in the 1980s. Suzhou Peacock was founded in 1970 and was the first firm in the country to import a production assembly line and technology (from Sony) in 1979, at a time of great foreign exchange shortages.[1] In the 1980s, its Peacock televisions were one of the top three brands in a rapidly expanding market and were exported to more than forty countries abroad. Each year, the Ministry of Electronics Industry published a list of the largest firms in

---

[1] Suzhou Peacock was formerly known as Suzhou Television Factory. Information on Suzhou Peacock is from an interview with Ni Suping as well as Editorial Committee (1991) and Ministry of Electronics Industry (1993, 1994). The yearbooks contain data on Suzhou Peacock and other electronics firms that are cited in this chapter.

the electronics industry. In 1990, Suzhou Peacock was ranked fifteenth on the list. With strong technical capabilities, it boasted 600 technicians among its 2,100 employees.

Similar to the SOE refrigerator makers in Beijing and Tianjin, Suzhou Peacock had begun to experience difficulties in the late 1980s before the entry of MNCs. (Philips did not invest in China until 1994.) In 1990, Suzhou Peacock cut its output to only 50 percent of production capacity. Two developments contributed to its difficulties. One was a softening of the market demand brought about by the austerity policies of the central government to cool inflation. The other factor was more important. Like Kelon, a number of upstart Chinese firms emerged seemingly out of nowhere in the late 1980s to challenge the incumbent SOEs. There is another remarkable similarity with our story in the last chapter: Many of these upstart firms, such as TCL and Konka, were based in relatively rural Guangdong province.

A notable revelation about this JV deal is the low valuation of the assets and the brand name contributed by Suzhou Peacock. For a firm that once ranked among the top three TV producers in the country, all of its fixed assets – including office furniture, apparently – and its once valuable Peacock brand were valued at $9 million. In 1990, Suzhou Peacock had reported a book value of $11 million for its fixed assets. This is an indication of the amount of value that was destroyed by this SOE, considering China's large TV market and Suzhou Peacock's previously leading position in it.[2] Between 1986 and 1993, the market size roughly tripled.[3] In 1993, about 28 million televisions were sold in China. Total market sales amounted to about $5 billion.

To meet its RMB 200 million capital contributions to establish a 49 percent stake in the JV, Suzhou Peacock had to take out a loan of RMB 122.6 million ($14 million). This is equally remarkable. Recall Mr. Bao from the last chapter, who, located in the same city as Suzhou Peacock, was unable to open a credit line with a bank. Here, we have a generous infusion of credits extended to a practically insolvent SOE so that it could be acquired by a foreign firm at a price deemed acceptable to the government.[4] There is another revealing detail here.

---

[2] There is no suggestion that the assets of Suzhou Peacock were "undervalued." The valuation was the price that Suzhou Peacock accepted and by definition it was the market price. The main point here is that relative to the size of the overall TV market and relative to Suzhou Peacock's privileged market position, much of the value had been destroyed by the poor management of this firm.

[3] About half of the televisions were small black and white sets. The data are from Ministry of Electronics Industry (1994).

[4] Philips's equity contribution was RMB 208 million. If Suzhou Peacock had just capitalized its operating assets and brand name in the new JV, the total equity capital would have been

Even though Mr. Bao was shunned by China's banks, COSMOS was willing to pay a premium to establish a minority stake in a JV with Mr. Bao. Now we have an SOE, which had every conceivable advantage to succeed – first mover advantage, financial support from the state, a high-quality human capital base, an expanding market, and a well-known brand – being acquired at an apparent discount.

In this chapter, I show that what happened to Mr. Ni's firm was by no means an isolated event. One can find similar examples in every industry dominated by SOEs in the 1980s. The JV created by Suzhou Peacock, in essence, was a disguised acquisition. In the last chapter, I call such an acquisition a JV acquisition. In a JV acquisition, a foreign firm acquires the assets of an SOE but does not absorb the target firm itself. The specific arrangements differ regarding the actual operation of a JV created in this fashion. In all the cases I have looked at, the foreign firms are the controlling shareholders. The differences arise as to the extent of the continuous Chinese participation in the management. Some SOEs participate more; others participate less.

JV acquisitions expose a number of problems regarding three aspects of the conventional wisdom about China's FDI inflows during the 1990s. One is the idea that the surging FDI inflows beginning in 1992 were driven by China's alluring market prospects.[5] This idea itself, by definition, is not wrong, but it is seriously incomplete. Philips was obviously attracted to China's expanding market but so should have been Suzhou Peacock. The market allure argument would predict increased investments on the part of both Philips and Suzhou Peacock. But this is not what happened. Attracted by the prospect of selling televisions to increasingly affluent Chinese consumers, Philips invested in China, but Suzhou Peacock divested from TV production. The simultaneous foreign investments and Chinese divestments led to a rising FDI/capital formation ratio. This is what is presented in Chapter 1: FDI as a percentage share of total fixed asset investments surged from 4.2 percent in 1991 to 17.1 percent in 1994.

The Suzhou Peacock case is a concrete illustration of the distinction I make in Chapter 1 between an absolute level of FDI and a relative level of FDI. The

---

RMB 285.4 million (RMB 208 million + RMB 77.4 million). That would have given Suzhou Peacock an equity stake of 27 percent (RMB 77.4 million divided by RMB 285.4 million). It is particularly hard to understand the decision by the Chinese bank to help Suzhou Peacock increase its stake from 27 percent to 49 percent. In operating terms, the two arrangements are not significantly different. Either way, Suzhou Peacock was a minority shareholder in the firm.

[5] Rosen states, "Chinese authorities are keen to lure foreign investors into the Chinese marketplace, and foreigners drawn by China's growth have been eager to leap into that market. These overlapping interests have led to huge flows in FDI into China. . . ." See Rosen (1999a).

market allure argument applies if one wishes to explain the absolute level of FDI, but something else is driving changes in the relative level of FDI. One can argue that Suzhou Peacock divested because it rationally calculated that it did not stand a chance of competing with Philips, which previously had been restricted but now was allowed to enter China. If this were the case, we would expect to see the sale of its assets and brand name to Philips at a premium, not at a discount. The fact is that Suzhou Peacock was already in trouble long before the arrival of Philips.

The second view on China's FDI is that it financed "green-field investments." For example, Graham and Wada (2001, p. 1) comment that "China's FDI consists largely of green-field investment, while inward FDI in the United States by contrast has been generated more by takeover of existing enterprises than by new establishments." The evidence cited to support this view is that the main entry vehicle for MNCs in China is the formation of JVs. Under a standard JV format, an MNC and a Chinese firm jointly create, own, and sometimes operate the newly created business unit. Of the 233,353 approved FIE projects between 1993 and 1998, some 132,084 of them, or about 56.6 percent, were JVs.[6] The prevalence of JVs leads to the impression that much of the incoming FDI funded green-field projects. In the case of Suzhou Peacock, however, this is clearly not a JV in a conventional sense. On its balance sheet, Suzhou Peacock no longer had any operating assets; instead, it had financial claims on the JV with Philips. This was a privatization event.

The third view is related to the last. Researchers often date the acquisitions of Chinese firms by foreign firms to the passage of the 1994 Company Law. The 1994 Company Law and the subsequent legal and regulatory clarification regarding asset transactions by MNCs were viewed as steps toward a more explicit privatization stance and toward the sanctioning of foreign acquisitions of existing Chinese firms.[7] Yadong Luo (1998), a specialist on international business at the University of Hawaii, comments, "Many state enterprises have been re-structured into limited companies, allowing foreign investors to buy into these firms by purchasing company shares." This view is much too narrow and too legalistic. As I show below, foreign acquisitions of the assets of SOEs via a JV format began to occur as early as 1984.

This chapter focuses on acquisition activities by MNCs in the 1990s. Three claims are made. First, a portion of FDI materializing into China's capital-intensive industries in the 1990s financed the acquisition of existing assets rather than the creation of new assets. Second, many of the acquisition

---

[6] The FIE project data are provided in State Statistical Bureau (1997a, 1999a).

[7] For summaries of these views, see Howson (1997, 1998).

targets were SOEs, which, despite the fact that the state had invested heavily in their technology, equipment, and distribution networks, were incurring large and growing financial losses. SOEs thus were ideal acquisition targets because they had built up good asset bases while generating low or negative profits. Third, while the mismanagement of the state sector rendered SOEs into acquisition targets, the overwhelmingly *foreign* role in acquisitions was driven by something else. One should ask why domestic nonstate firms did not acquire SOE assets on a similar scale. The answer is that asset acquisitions by domestic nonstate firms would have amounted to privatization, a policy stance the Chinese government refused to embrace until 1997. Thus, FDI may have played a disproportionately large role in China's de facto privatization process than otherwise would have been the case, both because the state actively courted FDI and because it ruled out a domestic privatization policy.

This chapter presents evidence on insolvency-induced FDI through two case studies. These two studies show in greater detail how SOEs "sold" their assets using a mechanism commonly associated with green-field investments: JVs with foreign firms. Let me begin by delving more deeply into some of the issues related to JV acquisitions.

JV ACQUISITIONS

An important reason why JV acquisitions have been so popular is that they help maintain the façade that Chinese firms have not been "acquired." Some SOEs have remained as ongoing business entities. Ni Suping, in 1998, was actively thinking about how to reorient his firm toward a new line of business. His intention was to become a supplier to the JV affiliate with Philips. The continuous equity participation of the SOEs has allowed Chinese policy makers to view FIEs created in this manner not as a deliberate privatization move but as the creation of long-term, strategic alliances between domestic and foreign firms. The term "acquisition" is still considered sensitive, in cases of not just foreign acquisitions but also acquisitions by domestic nonstate firms. For example, Kelon's acquisition of Huabao's air conditioner production assets was announced as a merger.

In an economic sense, JV acquisitions are not strategic alliances, as I explain below. Because aggregate data are not available, I present some suggestive evidence to show the scale and scope of JV acquisitions in the Chinese economy. I use the SOEs in the machinery industry to show the effect of JV acquisitions on their balance sheets. This is followed by an illustration of the motivations of SOEs to be acquired in this way.

JV Acquisitions and Strategic Alliances

The Chinese term for a JV acquisition is *jiajie hezi*, literally translated as "grafted JV." The word "graft," as Gallagher (2001) explains, comes from horticulture: "the grafting of a new branch to the trunk of a sickly tree in order to revive it." This is a vivid and apt description of the insolvency crisis among SOEs in the 1990s. Gallagher (2001) writes, "The increase in grafted JVs is directly related to the declining fortunes of the SOE sector, a veritable forest of sickly trees."

To show the underlying dynamics behind such JV acquisitions, it helps to contrast them with the more standard forms of JVs, known as strategic JVs among business scholars. A standard rationale for strategic alliances in management literature is to pool knowledge and share risks among partnering firms when venturing into a new product line with considerable uncertainty about its success.[8] Business research suggests that a strategic alliance is a way for firms to acquire capabilities through "external networks" from outside the firm. Traditionally, these capabilities were accumulated in-house over many years. An alliance with another firm can accelerate the learning and acquiring of new capabilities. Another rationale for strategic alliances is to improve a firm's competitive position versus its rivals. This can be done in a number of ways. Costly duplication in R&D among firms can be avoided or entry can be deterred (Kogut 1988). The common theme in the literature is that a strategic alliance is the use of an offensive strategy to maximize profits, not a strategy dictated by an insolvency situation.

Clearly, Suzhou Peacock did not form a strategic alliance with Philips. It transferred its existing operating assets, including the desk of the general manager, and its brand to the JV. In this case, FDI financed the transfer of assets, not the creation of new assets. The only reason that these transactions took on a JV acquisition format rather than a straightforward acquisition format is that in many instances the government restricts entry of MNCs to a JV format.[9] This is not to suggest that there have not been strategic alliances formed between foreign and domestic firms or that there have not been green-field investments in the 1990s. The point here is to show that some of the JVs formed during the 1990s were of the acquisition kind.

---

[8] See Yoshino and Rangan (1995). The following vastly simplifies the discussion in this volume. Yoshino and Rangan (1995) in fact explicitly recognize that many JVs in developing countries are created because of host government pressures, and they specifically exclude JVs in developing countries in their definition of strategic alliances.

[9] MNCs may also have genuine business reasons to form JVs in China. JVs are a low-cost mechanism to gain local know-how and to share investment risks. But otherwise straightforward acquisitions may also take a JV form for regulatory reasons.

Estimates of Scale

It is difficult to quantify how much of the SOE-bound FDI during this period financed the acquisition of existing assets, because Chinese data do not break down JVs into green-field and acquisition categories. Also, the Chinese data do not disclose the amount of FDI bound for SOEs or the amount of FDI bound for other firms. We have only some indirect indicators. One partial and suggestive indication is the increasing portion of cash in the composition of the FDI inflows. In 1994, the value of equipment imports, used by both foreign and Chinese investors to finance their equity stakes in FIEs, accounted for 60 percent of the total FDI inflows. In 1998, the share declined to 31.8 percent. Unlike a green-field project in which each partner can contribute either cash or production equipment, the purchase of existing assets requires more cash or other financial instruments such as company shares. However, because the equipment import figure includes the capitalization value by both foreign and Chinese investors,[10] we do not know whether this decline was driven by changes in the investment behavior of foreign or of domestic investors.

The second piece of suggestive evidence comes from our Local Leadership Survey. The survey asked the respondents to list the three most negative effects of FDI. The respondents were given twelve choices, ranging from an increase in unemployment to economic control by foreigners. The negative effect that most concerned the respondents was surprising: "Chinese assets were under-valued during the FDI process, causing the loss of state assets." Some 36.1 percent of the respondents chose this item as the most negative effect of FDI, compared with 22.7 percent who chose "driving our firms to bankruptcy and causing unemployment."[11] This is an indirect indication of the substantial scale of JV acquisitions, since in JV acquisitions such issues regarding valuation

---

[10] It is unlikely that the domestic firms would be able to finance their equity stakes in this way due to their insolvency. In 1994, the total value of equipment imports used by FIEs as investments was $20.28 billion. In that year, the materialized FDI was $33.8 billion. The ratio of the two produces the 60 percent cited in the text. In 1998, equipment import investments fell to $14.5 billion, while materialized FDI reached $45.5 billion. The 1994 capitalized equipment import figure is from General Administration of Customs of the People's Republic of China (1995) and the 1998 figure is from General Administration of Customs of the People's Republic of China (1999).

[11] The survey question is: Do you think that FDI will have the following negative effects on our country? The choices are: (1) driving our firms to bankruptcies and causing unemployment, (2) exploiting workers, (3) Chinese assets were undervalued during the FDI process, causing the loss of state assets, (4) controlling the Chinese market, (5) dishonest behavior, (6) increasing SOE losses, (7) creating environmental problems, (8) cultural clashes, (9) foreign controls of pillar national economic sectors, (10) defeating our famous brands, (11) tax evasions and reduction of state revenue, and (12) no negative effects.

of Chinese assets arise more frequently.[12] The respondents were comparing the valuation with the book value of the SOE assets and implicitly assumed the book value to be the "right value." Many Chinese officials know the book value of the SOE assets but have very little understanding of an asset's market value. This ignorance presumably gave rise to the impression that these FDI deals caused "losses" to the state, when in fact it was the large operating losses of the SOEs that had led to a low valuation of their assets. What their response does suggest, as an empirical inference, is that the value of SOE assets during the FIE formation process – a proxy of the market value in the Chinese context – is lower than the book value of the same assets.

Some qualitative accounts also indicate that JV acquisitions have taken place on a substantial scale in the 1990s. As early as 1984, local governments in Fujian province began to sell SOE assets on a substantial scale to foreign firms in exchange for financial stakes in the newly created JVs. The government prepared a list of 499 SOEs and 711 projects for the purpose of attracting JV acquisitions (Study Group on SOEs Using Grafted FDI in Fujian Province 1994). By the early 1990s, 65 percent of the SOEs in Fuzhou (in Fujian province) had turned to foreign investors for restructuring. By 1993, out of 2,592 SOEs in Fujian province, about 37.3 percent (966 firms) were involved in JV acquisitions.[13]

JV acquisitions were not limited to this one southern province with a liberal FDI regime. The JVs formed with all the major SOE refrigerator makers in Beijing, Tianjin, Shanghai, and Suzhou, as reported in the last chapter, also resulted from JV acquisitions. Field research for this book project in Beijing and Suzhou reveals extensive use of JV acquisitions. Accounts from Shandong and Liaoning provinces in northern China suggest that JV acquisitions were quite common there as well. According to a Chinese report, by 1994, some 44 percent of all FDI projects involved JV acquisitions, accounting for 57 percent of the total materialized FDI inflows in Yantai city of Shandong province. In 1993 alone, 22 percent of all JVs in Qingdao city, also in Shandong, were JV acquisitions, accounting for 25.4 percent of the materialized FDI value. By the end of 1993, $1.3 billion of FDI in Dalian city, in Liaoning province, had gone to finance JV acquisitions, involving 906 SOEs, of which 11 percent were large or medium SOEs.[14] The geographic spread of the JV acquisition phenomenon, from China's northeastern provinces to its southern region, is an indicator of both its scale and its systemic nature.

---

[12] Of course, such a valuation issue would also arise during straightforward acquisitions, but these acquisitions have been relatively rare.

[13] This is reported in Study Group on SOEs Using Grafted FDI in Fujian Province (1994).

[14] These figures are reported in Gallagher (2001). Her paper is based on Chinese research papers and government reports.

Balance Sheet Consequences

A JV acquisition results in the following change on the balance sheet of an SOE partner: The SOE holds fewer operating assets, but its financial investments in other firms have increased. This asset substitution reflects the fact that SOEs exchange their machinery and equipment for financial claims on other firms. Over time, as SOEs invest more heavily in creating JVs, their balance sheets begin to resemble those of investment funds rather than manufacturing concerns.

The second consequence is that because of JV acquisitions, SOE shareholders increasingly rely on dividend payouts from their JV affiliates as their source of income. The reason is simple: They no longer have any operating income. This is one of the main areas in which MNCs clash with the SOE shareholders. The SOEs demand dividend payouts, while the MNCs insist on reinvesting the earnings. Below I present some evidence to document both dynamics.

Machinery Industry Example. Table 5.1 provides some balance sheet information on firms in the machinery industry. It shows long-term investments by SOEs and other firms[15] as a proportion of total assets, net fixed assets, and fixed assets used for production. It also shows how much income SOEs and other firms have derived from investing in other firms versus their income from directly engaging in production. Although the data are not broken down between ownership claims on JVs with foreign firms and ownership claims on JVs with domestic firms, at least in the case of SOEs it is likely that the majority of the long-term investments represents ownership claims on JVs with foreign firms. The reason is that domestic JVs are rare. For example, in the machinery industry, domestic JVs generated 0.6 percent of sales in 1997. In contrast, foreign JVs generated 20 percent of sales in the same year.

As firms ostensibly in the business of making machine tools, automobiles, tractors, and so on, SOEs in the machinery industry have accumulated sizable financial assets in the form of equity shares in other firms. On average, between 4 and 10 percent of the total assets of SOEs and collective firms – basically, subsidiaries of SOEs – are in the form of long-term investments. Their equity holdings constitute between 15 and 25 percent of net fixed assets and fixed assets

---

[15] Long-term investments refer to equities or bonds held by a firm that cannot be converted into cash within one year. Although theoretically some of these long-term investments may be equities or bonds that the firm purchased on the securities market, here most of them are equity claims in corporate affiliates of the firm, such as JVs with foreign or domestic firms. The reason is that the government severely restricts purchases of securities on stock markets by manufacturing firms.

Table 5.1 Investment and Production Roles of SOEs in the Chinese Machinery Industry, 1995 and 1997

	Long-term investments/total assets ratio (%)	Long-term investments/net fixed assets ratio (%)	Long-term investments/fixed assets for production (%)	Operating income (RMB 100 million)	Investment income (RMB 100 million)	Investment income/total income (%)
SOEs						
1995	3.85	17.0	11.5	−33.4	22.9	190.4
1997	10.8	19.1	16.9	−10.8	16.1	121.6
1998	6.86	23.2	20.3	—[a]	–	–
Collective firms						
1995	4.63	20.3	15.8	83.8	4.95	5.49
1997	11.4	26.0	21.6	8.36	1.59	15.5
1998	7.66	30.8	24.9	–	–	–
Private firms						
1995	0.42	1.5	1.3	–	–	–
1997	1.19	2.0	2.0	0.20	0.001	0.23
1998	2.56	7.7	8.0	–	–	–
Foreign-funded FIEs						
1995	1.48	9.18	6.39	–	–	–
1997	1.52	3.38	2.6	33.46	0.48	1.13
1998	0.70	2.34	1.75	–	–	–
Overseas–Chinese–funded FIEs						
1995	2.37	9.61	7.40	–	–	–
1997	4.46	8.21	6.79	8.98	0.15	1.39
1998	2.17	7.02	5.61	–	–	–

Note: Total income equals operating income plus investment income plus subsidies plus other net nonoperating income plus shareholder gains and losses from previous years. Long-term investments refer to equity and bond holdings by a firm that cannot be converted into cash within one year.
[a]: Data not available.

Sources: Data on 1995 operating, investment, and total income are from Office of Third Industrial Census (1997). Other data are from the machinery industry database.

used for production purposes, such as machinery and equipment. (SOEs also maintain housing and other non-production-related assets.) Another indicator is the fact that SOEs have become extremely reliant on their shareholding ties to JVs as a source of income. In both 1995 and 1997, SOEs as a whole in the machinery industry incurred large operating losses – RMB 3.3 billion and RMB 1.1 billion, respectively. But the operating losses were partially offset by the investment income they earned (RMB 2.3 billion and RMB 1.6 billion, respectively). The size of the investment income was in fact larger than the total income received by these SOEs in those two years. In 1995, the investment income was about twice the total income, and in 1997 it was about 1.2 times. (The total income is the sum of operating income, investment income, subsidies, other nonoperating income, and shareholder gains and losses from previous years. The total income is smaller than the investment income because the SOEs had accumulated shareholder losses from previous years.)

This is quite remarkable. For firms that are supposed to be manufacturing concerns, the financial benefits from simply owning a piece of the manufacturing operations in fact exceed the financial benefits of making these goods themselves. This is an indication that the SOEs increasingly are moving away from being manufacturing concerns to becoming shareholding concerns. It is also striking how different SOEs are from other types of firms in the industry. Table 5.1 shows the asset holdings and sources of income of other types of firms. SOEs are in a class by themselves in terms of their financial dependence on investment ties to JVs. For all other firms, the operating income is positive and the investment income constitutes only a small portion of their total income. For private firms, as an example, the investment income was about 0.23 percent of their total income in 1997, and for FIEs, the portion was slightly more than 1 percent. Another pattern is obvious as well in Table 5.1: The more a firm is state-controlled, the more important the investment income is to its overall financial performance. This is another piece of evidence that shows that state ownership directly contributes to ideal conditions for JV acquisitions. On the one hand, the SOEs are endowed with more "acquirable assets," and, on the other hand, their profits have been consistently poor. It is this combination that renders them attractive acquisition targets.

Joint Venture Conflicts. The composition of an SOE's balance sheet exerts enormous pressures on the SOE to demand and maximize dividend distributions. Dividend policy is one of the most frequent conflict areas between foreign and Chinese JV partners. A Chinese scholar on FIEs, Professor Wang Zhile, calls this phenomenon "a joint venture but not a joint effort" (*hezi bu hezuo*). In his study of thirty-three very large FIEs, seven had experienced such partnership conflicts. In more recent years, these conflicts have led the Chinese side to cede equity shares to the foreign side. Foreign JV partners often complain about the short-term horizon of their Chinese partners (Wang 1996, pp. 47–48). The complaints are correct, but there is a reason why the Chinese partners are short-term: The dividend income is their only source of income.

Another pressure on the Chinese firms comes from their high debt. Because of their easy access to banks, SOEs often borrow excessively, either to invest in new facilities or to invest in a new JV. As indicated earlier, Suzhou Peacock took out a loan of RMB 122.6 million, while its entire assets were valued at only RMB 77.4 million. Another SOE in Suzhou, Suzhou No. 1 Telecommunications Factory, also borrowed heavily. In 1988, the firm raised RMB 10 million in an RMB loan from three banks, and the Chinese government arranged a concessionary loan of $4.3 million (approximately RMB 17 million) from the Dutch government for the firm to import equipment and technology from Philips. The firm itself contributed only RMB 1 million toward this purchase. In the 1990s, like many Chinese firms, it began to form JVs as its operations faltered. Between 1992 and 1998, it formed three JVs. For the first two JVs, it capitalized its operating assets and borrowed to establish equity stakes at 40 percent and 50 percent, respectively. Neither of these two JVs turned in any profits, which led the firm to form a third JV, with Philips in 1998. This time, it had run out of operating assets to capitalize. So it borrowed to establish a 5 percent equity stake in the JV with Philips. The debt burden was enormous. Wang Fusheng, director of Suzhou No. 1 Telecommunications Factory, commented on the quandary of his firm:[16]

> They [the foreign partner, in this case, Philips] think differently from us. What they want is to expand and become big, but we have a different perspective. We have a lot of financial pressure. We took on debt to form this JV, and we have people to feed. We need the returns to support ourselves.

Motivations

In every interview with SOE managers, when asked why they wanted to form JVs with foreign firms, the first reason was always technology. This obsession with technology – understood as equipment and machinery with a high scientific content together with the necessary knowledge to operate them – is extremely puzzling. As pointed out in Chapter 3, SOEs are widely regarded as the most

---

[16] Interview with Wang Fusheng, director of Suzhou No. 1 Telecommunications Factory, September 28, 1998.

advanced firms in the Chinese economy, and in the machinery industry, SOEs have more computers and technicians than any other firms, including the best-performing FIEs.

The inordinate emphasis placed on tangible resources, hard science, and technology in fact reflects an enduring bureaucratic tendency to value certainty, routines, and procedures. When profits do not serve as a guiding criterion, it is infinitely easier for bureaucrats to evaluate firm performance in terms of the quality and quantity of tangible inputs. The SOE management philosophy often equates the quality and quantity of the machinery and equipment with the firm's competitiveness. Little emphasis is placed on the intangibles, such as incentives, business judgment, and more tacit types of know-how and capabilities. In essence, SOEs can be compared to warehouses that store valuable machinery and equipment. This view of a firm as an inanimate collection of machines and equipment contrasts sharply with a long-standing perspective among Western researchers that a firm is a living organism and a repository of knowledge, not just of tangible resources. Edith Penrose, in a book published in 1959, remarks, "it is never *resources* themselves that are the 'inputs' in the production processes, but only the *services* that resources can render."[17]

This fixation on technology and hard assets among government officials and SOE managers is terribly destructive, both to the economy and to the firms themselves. SOEs pile up hard assets and the government allocates resources not according to market demand for the product but according to the technological vintage of the plants and facilities. Government reports on firm performance often contain page after page of details on the size of fixed assets, the number and the technological make of major equipment installations, and production capacity.[18] Remarkably, nowhere in these reports can one find the information that probably matters the most: the capabilities and visions of the managers. (To appreciate this difference with a market economy, just imagine reports about GE without ever mentioning the name of Jack Welch.) In the same interviews, when they explained their motivation for FDI as being "to acquire the latest

[17] Quoted in Nonaka and Takeuchi (1995). Emphasis in the original.
[18] For example, in 1989 the State Council and the State Planning Commission published a comprehensive study on the status of Chinese industry. The study was based on data from the 1985 Second National Industrial Census, which collected balance sheet and performance data from all industrial firms in China. A major conclusion was that Chinese industry seriously lagged behind that in the developed economies in terms of technological development. An array of technical data was cited. The study broke down 1,200 major equipment installations among 19,000 SOEs by their levels of technology and found the following: 12.9 percent reached international standards of the 1980s; 21.8 percent were "state of art" by domestic standards; 47 percent met the average domestic standard; and 18.3 percent were considered backward. State Council and State Planning Commission (1990).

technology," none of the SOE managers viewed personnel training and human resource investments as a high managerial priority.

The result of this management philosophy is poor performance, high debt, and excess accumulation of assets. On the other hand, nonstate firms are starved of resources and are being crowded out, both because of their low political status and because the low-tech industries they are in are not considered high priority. The JV acquisitions are but one natural consequence of this way of allocating economic resources. It is not surprising that JV acquisitions began to occur on a large scale in the mid-1990s, coinciding with an unprecedented rate of bankruptcies in the state sector. The two developments are in fact mirror images of each other.[19]

Asset Surplus. As a result of many years of overinvestments, capacity utilization in many branches of Chinese industry is low. In 1995, capacity utilization was below 60 percent for more than 900 major industrial products. For some products, the rate was extraordinarily low. For example, for photographic film, the rate was 13.3 percent; air conditioners, between 30 and 40 percent; color televisions, 46.1 percent; and machines tools, less than 40 percent (Lardy 1998, p. 30). The overinvestments have equipped SOEs with many acquirable assets.

An example of a firm using surplus assets to finance a JV is the case of China Suzhou Instrument Factory, a state-owned manufacturer of electronic educational equipment. According to its deputy director, the firm imported advanced gold-plating equipment from Japan in 1986 and was incorporated into a large-scale technical renovation project financed and managed by the Ministry of Machinery Industry. The firm received targeted support from the state. But for years, its equipment and factory buildings were underutilized. In 1995, the firm was quite pleased when it formed a JV with Matsushita of Japan and was able to get a $500,000 valuation on two factory buildings that had been empty for years. Matsushita chose not to use its equipment but valued the technicians from the Chinese side. The deputy director commented that idle property and equipment were plentiful among the SOEs in the Suzhou area, and the situation was becoming worse in the late 1990s.[20]

Forming JVs thus became a way for SOEs to liquidate their assets and realize some cash benefits from owning these assets. JV acquisitions also improved the usage of these assets. According to Zhu Xun, the manager of the Foreign

---

[19] Another consequence is asset stripping. The Chinese sources put the drainage of assets from SOEs at RMB 50 billion (about $8.8 billion) per year. Quoted in Lardy (1998).

[20] Interview with Zhou Minzhi, deputy director, China Suzhou Instrument Factory, September 26, 1998.

Department of Beijing Automotive Industry Corporation (BAIC), 90 percent of the capital goods contributed by the Chinese firms were fully utilized at the FIEs, even though the FIEs often employed the same managers and workers who had earlier been employed at the SOEs.[21] More efficient management by foreign firms led to an improvement in the capacity utilization.

Insolvency. As pointed out in Chapter 3, the heavy investments in the asset base of SOEs were financed by bank borrowing. Thus, overinvestments had a cost: They increased the debt burdens on the SOEs and increased their production costs. As the example of Kelon shows, the hard budget constraints forced the firm to increase its margins by squeezing gains from operations. SOEs are not similarly motivated. It is no accident that Chinese SOEs, such as Wanbao in the last chapter, began to experience financial problems in 1990 when the market softened and when the central government drastically cut the money supply to cool inflation. The SOEs critically depend on bank loans to pay their workers and to extend generous credit to customers so as to "force" sales in order to book paper profits to qualify for a new round of lending (Steinfeld 1998).

The firm we began with in this chapter, Suzhou Peacock, fits this description exactly. Between 1988 and 1993, China's TV market size, in terms of units sold, expanded by 21 percent, but Suzhou Peacock's sales revenues contracted by 3 percent between 1990 and 1994. Its market position kept sliding as well. In 1993, it was ranked 19th; in 1993, 30th; and in 1994, 42nd. In 1993, it reported a posttax profit of RMB 18.1 million, and its ratio of posttax profits to sales revenue was only 2.4 percent. In a year when real GDP growth was 13 percent, this was a very low profit margin indeed. Many consumer electronics firms at that time were reporting margins in excess of 50 to 60 percent. The year before it formed a JV with Philips, Suzhou Peacock was in serious trouble.

It is not necessarily the case, however, that on the eve of forming JVs the SOEs were technically insolvent. Suzhou Peacock, for example, was making money, but its sliding market position was giving to a sense of pessimism about the future. In 1998, Ni Suping sighed with relief that his firm had decided to form the JV with Philips in 1994. The firms that had decided to wait fared much worse later on. Even with some positive earnings, the SOE managers were not confident that their situation was sustainable. The deputy director at Suzhou No. 1 Telecommunications Factory was explicit about this. He said that his factory "could still get by," but, as he said, "we anticipated that the market was going to change. Competition was going to increase, and support from

---

[21] Interview with Zhu Xun, manager of the Foreign Department, Beijing Automotive Industry Corporation, November 28, 1998.

the government, even though available, would not be sufficient. We calculated that forming the JV would bring a brighter future."[22] While foreign firms were attracted to China's market potentials, SOE managers were pessimistic about the future. JV acquisitions resulted from these two diametrically opposite views of the future.

An Alternative Hypothesis: Tax Motivations. An alternative hypothesis is that tax burdens, rather than insolvency, motivate SOEs to seek FDI.[23] The statutory income tax rate for FIEs ranges from 15 percent to 33 percent, with many exemptions and concessions. Until the 1994 Unified Tax Law, SOEs were taxed at the much higher rate of 55 percent.[24] Thus, as the reasoning goes, SOE managers are motivated to form FIEs in order to place their profits under a more hospitable tax regime.

A tax-centered explanation, however, contradicts the well-known fact that SOEs operate on the verge of insolvency. The central idea is that there are still profits to be taxed, when the reality is that many SOEs cannot service their debt and tax obligations at all. Thus, the reasoning is flawed, on several counts. High statutory tax rates do not mean high *effective* tax rates. SOEs operate under soft budget constraints, that is, SOEs face a reasonable, ex ante prospect of being bailed out by the government in times of financial distress. The bailout typically takes the form of debt and tax forgiveness and explicit subsidies. To this extent, the effective taxation on SOEs can be very low or even negative (as subsidies are a negative tax). Because FIEs in general face harder budget constraints, it is likely that their effective tax rates are closer to their statutory rates and are invariant with respect to their posttax profitability. China's tax code historically has also benefited SOEs. For many years, SOEs could deduct their payment of loan principals against their tax liabilities, while all other firms could deduct only the interest payment. Considering the indebtedness of the SOEs, there is a huge tax benefit to stay as an SOE.

Many of the SOEs formed JVs with foreign firms at a time of financial distress. Differences in statutory tax rates really mean very little for loss-making SOEs. The actual tax payment, not the statutory tax rate, is the more relevant motivating factor. One piece of evidence that tax arbitrage cannot be a preponderant factor is the large foreign equity stake in Chinese FIEs, around

---

[22] Interview with Wang Fusheng, director of Suzhou No. 1 Telecommunications Factory, September 28, 1998.

[23] For example, Fu (2000) argues that "disparate treatments between FIEs and domestic firms . . . give rise to what may be conceptualized as abnormally high demand for FDI. . . ." In the interest of full disclosure, I have also advocated this view of FDI motivation. See Huang (1998).

[24] The discussion on SOE taxation issues is drawn mainly from Wong, Heady, and Woo (1995).

55 percent in the manufacturing industries as of 1995. A strong tax motivation would result in a foreign equity stake closer to 25 percent, because that is the sufficient amount to qualify for the preferential tax treatments. A foreign equity stake substantially higher than 25 percent indicates that the Chinese are making equity concessions in exchange for something more than tax benefits.

There are also empirical difficulties with tax-centered explanations of China's FDI. If arbitraging tax rates were such a strong motivation, one would see this effect across firms of all ownership types, not just between SOEs and JVs. Prior to the 1994 Unified Tax Law, tax treatments of SOEs and TVEs differed drastically. TVEs were taxed at a 20 percent flat rate, whereas SOEs were taxed at 55 percent, but, as far as this author is aware, not a single case of conversion from an SOE to a TVE has been attributed to a tax-arbitraging motivation.[25]

A major impetus for FDI originates from local governments, not just from the firms themselves. This is a bit perplexing from a tax perspective. Local governments, as tax collectors and shareholders in most of the SOEs in the country, derive their financial flows from the taxes on and dividends from the SOEs. Converting SOEs into JVs would entail levying a lower tax rate on the assets previously owned by the SOEs and a smaller share of dividend income to the local governments. To be rational, local governments must believe that the financial flows – the sum of the tax and dividend flows from FIEs – are greater than the current financial flows from the SOEs. A logical inference is that local governments must reason that the pretax profits of FIEs will increase by a sufficient amount to more than offset any decreases from a lower tax rate *and* any dilution of their shares in the SOEs. Keep in mind that SOEs are 100 percent subsidiaries of local governments, while FIEs are only partially owned by them.

Ultimately, the decision by local governments to transfer assets from SOEs to FIEs has very little to do with tax considerations. The decision rests on a belief that SOEs are vastly inferior to FIEs as economic entities. The larger the equity concessions local governments are willing to make to foreign firms and the more substantial the tax benefits they grant to FIEs, the stronger that belief is. (In the appendix to this chapter I give a stylized example to illustrate this point.)

Financial flows may not be the sole determinant in a JV acquisition decision. Many other factors may also play a role. For example, local governments may be concerned about employment generation, technology transfer, and so on. But these considerations reinforce the notion that JV acquisition decisions are

---

[25] In fact, I am unaware of any instances whatsoever of conversion from an SOE to a TVE. It may be that such conversions took place but they must have been on a modest scale, as academic researchers have not noted them as a significant economic phenomenon.

a function of a belief in the relative competitiveness of foreign firms over SOEs. For a local government to decide to sell SOE assets in order to generate more employment, it must be true that it believes that an SOE is less efficient in generating employment opportunities compared with an FIE. Chinese FDI decisions depend on an ex ante belief that FIEs are more competitive firms than SOEs and that SOEs are insolvent or becoming insolvent. Agreeing to JV acquisitions, then, results from a combination of optimism about FIEs and pessimism about SOEs on the part of Chinese local governments. As pointed out before, there was plenty of information to lead local officials and SOE managers to be diffident about the future. Their margins were slim and their once supreme market positions were increasingly challenged by upstart firms from Guangdong province.

TWO CASE STUDIES

In this section, we take a close look at two cases of JV creation in China. One is Beijing-XYZ Gear, created in 1992 by XYZ Automotive and Beijing Gear Factory (BGF).[26] The other case is PPG-Nanchang Chemical Industrial Corporation (PPG-NCIC), located in the city of Nanchang in Jiangxi province. PPG, a Pittsburgh-based giant chemical firm, was the equity partner to the FIE established in 1993. We examine the creation of these two FIEs primarily through the prism of their Chinese shareholders in order to understand their rationale for forming JVs with MNCs and the impact of the resultant JVs on themselves. Both of the Chinese investors were SOEs that had undertaken significant capital spending to acquire and upgrade their operating assets prior to forming the alliances with the MNCs. The methods they relied on to finance their respective equity stakes were similar. They contributed their core equipment and machinery, main products, and customer bases, and capitalized these tangible and intangible assets as equity stakes in the newly formed FIEs. Both ended up in a similar situation. After transferring most or all of their operating assets and their most productive capabilities to the FIEs and capitalizing these transferred assets as equity stakes in the JVs, both firms became "holding firms" loaded with nonoperating capital stock, such as employee housing and social facilities, or auxiliary and supporting production facilities. In one case, although the Chinese shareholding firm retained majority control, it had agreed to managerial controls by the foreign firm in the JV contract and to majority ownership by the foreign

---

[26] Beijing-XYZ Gear and XYZ Automotive are disguised names. The American JV partner asked that its real name and that of the JV not be used. Beijing Gear Factory is the real name of the Chinese company.

firm at some point in the future. In the other case, the Chinese firm ceded operating control altogether.

These two cases are particularly well suited to illustrate insolvency-induced FDI in the state sector. Both SOEs produced capital-intensive products and both were heavily promoted by their local governments. In the 1980s, at a time when foreign exchange constraints in China were extremely stringent, both were allocated foreign exchange resources to import equipment from abroad and to arrange for technology licensing with foreign firms. Both experienced financial difficulties in the early 1990s, in part because of the tight monetary policy at the time and in part because of competitive market pressures. The most valuable assets of these two firms were acquired – through a JV format – by MNCs during a period of surging demand in the respective markets for their products. Both Chinese firms supplied inputs for automotive manufacturing. Between 1991 and 1995, the real compound annual growth rate of the industrial output value of the automotive sector was 25.6 percent.[27]

The asset transfers and equity concessions are all the more telling considering that China was viewed as one of the most attractive destinations for FDI between 1992 and 1996. There was a rush of FDI into China as the country was lauded as the next economic superpower. One might expect the Chinese firms to have been in a strong bargaining position with the foreign firms on the basis of the strength of China's macroeconomic conditions. In fact, the negotiation outcomes are more a reflection of the microeconomic conditions of the SOEs at the time. These two cases are well suited to illustrate the bargaining dynamics between foreign and domestic firms. In both cases of JV formation, the central government did not play a direct role in negotiating with the MNCs over the JV contracts. Thus, the terms of the JV agreements accurately reflect firm-level motivations of both the Chinese and foreign investing firms and illustrate JV acquisition dynamics at work. A greater role by the central government in negotiating with the MNCs might have resulted in an outcome more favorable to the Chinese side, but the outcome would not have been driven by the firm-level dynamics we are trying to analyze here.

Beijing-XYZ Gear

At the time of the creation of the JV, BGF held 61 percent and XYZ Automotive held 39 percent of the equity stake in Beijing-XYZ Gear.[28] From the

---

[27] Calculated from China Automotive Technology Research Center (1996).

[28] Three managers were interviewed for this project. One was the general manager of Beijing-XYZ Gear and another was the chief engineer of the firm, who had served as the chief engineer of the

very inception of the JV, the question of who controlled the firm was never in doubt. In the JV contract, XYZ Automotive had the right to increase its equity stake to 60 percent at some point in the future. The contract also gave effective managerial control of Beijing-XYZ Gear to the foreign side. The general manager was appointed by XYZ Automotive, not by BGF, despite the fact that BGF held a majority stake. The total capitalization value of the FDI project was $46.4 million and registered capital was $15.8 million.

History of BGF. Before partnering with XYZ Automotive, BGF had produced two main product lines. It was the industry leader in transmissions and transfer cases for light-duty vehicles, such as passenger sedans and jeeps. (Transfer cases are devices attached to transmissions to distribute the torque to facilitate the turning of the vehicle.) Its first transmissions, fitted for the BJ212, a popular jeep in China for many years, began production in 1965.[29] It commanded a huge first-mover advantage over industry competitors. Tangshan Gear, a competitor, did not begin production of comparable light-duty transmission systems until 1980, and not until 1985 did Shanghai Gear, another competitor, begin to offer similar product lines. BGF's products were known for their quality, reliability, and state-of-art technology. In the 1980s, BGF improved its technological capabilities by entering into a technology transfer agreement with the German firm, ZF Friedrichshafen AG, a specialist in transmission systems, and Isuzu, a Japanese firm. Its BC175 five-speed transmissions were the best in the country. Rare among Chinese SOEs in the 1980s, BGF ran its own R&D institute, employing 277 technicians, and the engineering capabilities of BGF were widely recognized. In 1985, its synchromesh gear change products received a "State Scientific and Technological Progress Award." In 1988, two of its transmission product lines, the Lingshan BC131 and the Lingshan BC17C, won the top quality prizes from the Ministry of Machinery Industry and from the Beijing municipal government. In 1990, BGF was ranked among the top 500 "most efficient" firms in the country. Its output volume at the time was 53,000 units in transmissions and 44,000 units in transfer cases. In contrast, the second-place

Chinese JV partner, BGF, before the formation of Beijing-XYZ Gear. Both of these managers requested anonymity. The third manager interviewed was Zhu Xun, the manager of the Foreign Department of Beijing Automotive Industry Corporation, the parent company of BGF. The interviews took place on November 23, 24, and 28, 1998. Supplemental sources of information and data are from the following publications: China International Engineering Company (1992), Ministry of Machinery and Electronics Industry (1993), Ministry of Machinery Industry (1993, 1996, 1997a, 1999), and State Bureau of Machinery Industry (1998).

[29] The model for the BJ212 was the Chrysler Jeep, used by the U.S. Army during the Second World War.

Table 5.2 *Beijing Gear Factory, Selected Output and Financial Results,*
1985–1996

Year	Output volume (market position)		Transfer cases	Sales revenue (RMB million)	Pretax profits (RMB million)	Gross profit margins (%)
	Transmissions	Transmissions for sedans				
1985	24,000		25,000	57.9	17.8	30.8
1986	29,000		29,000	67.9	20.5	30.2
1987	31,000		33,000	75.7	20.7	27.0
1988	42,000		40,000	113.7	27.0	24.0
1989	44,000		43,000	121.1	28.1	23.0
1990	53,000 (1st)		44,000 (1st)	155.3	20.9	13.0
1991	63,000		52,000	223.3	21.7	9.7
1992	51,065 (3rd)	11,000	43,760 (1st)	257.0	15.0	5.9
1993						
BGF	8,000 (24th)	2,000	0	199.9	0.0	0.0
BXG	85,000		39,000	146.6	−1.9	−1.3
1994						
BGF	35,000 (5th)		0	127.6	0.17	0.0
BXG	31,000		56,000	183.7	10.4	5.7
1995						
BGF	52,000 (5th)		0	193.7	3.3	1.7
BXG	24,000		80,000	279.7	−20.5	−7.3
1996						
BGF	42,000 (9th)		0	146.8	0.31	0.2
BXG	58,000		65,000	281.4	17.9	6.4

Note: Gross profit margins equal pretax profits divided by sales revenue. BGF stands for Beijing Gear Factory. BXG stands for Beijing-XYZ Gear.

Sources: Ministry of Machinery Industry (1996, 1997a).

manufacturer, Tangshan Gear, was considerably smaller, with an output volume of 33,219 and 2,545, respectively, in transmissions and transfer cases (Ministry of Machinery Industry 1991).

Eroding Profits. The profit performance reflects the leadership position of the firm, whether due to the underlying strengths of its products or due to its monopoly position. As Table 5.2 shows, between 1985 and 1990, BGF's profitability was substantial. The gross profit margins, that is, pretax profits divided by sales revenue, were consistently in the double digits (30.8 percent in 1985 and 23 percent in 1989). Furthermore, output volume increased steadily. Between 1985 and 1990, its output volume of transmissions and transfer cases roughly doubled. BGF supplied its products not only to firms in Beijing under

BAIC (its parent company), but also to automotive firms in Nanjing and firms in other provinces. Driven by strong industry growth during this period, between 1988 and 1992 sales revenue more than doubled, from RMB 114 million in 1988 to RMB 257 million in 1992. However, increasing sales and output production were accompanied by declining profit margins. The profit margins, at 27 percent in 1987, declined to 23 percent in 1989 and 13 percent in 1990, as shown in Table 5.2.

Also, BGF did not respond to the dramatically changing market dynamics wisely. It failed to increase its output quickly in response to a surging market demand and to more competitive market conditions. As the chief engineer of the firm explained in an interview, BGF did not increase its production capacity to reduce average unit costs so as to be able to compete on the basis of low costs. Instead, it turned to price reductions to defend its market shares. Unlike a typical SOE, which has to resort to credit-financed fixed asset investments to extricate from a loss-making situation, BGF had money. Its profit margins were very high, and yet it was investing less rather than more in the face of increasing competition and challenges to its market leadership position. Its capital expenditures, as measured by percentage shares of sales revenue, declined every year between 1985 and 1990. The low capital expenditures meant that the firm's aging equipment was not continuously updated. Indeed, between 1986 and 1992, the ratio of the value of net fixed assets to gross fixed assets – all measured in book value terms – declined, from 55.5 percent to 47.2 percent. The growing gap between net and gross fixed assets means that an increasingly large portion of the firm's capital stock was not upgraded.

The declining capital expenditures in response to market opportunities reflects a profound problem of political control of SOEs. BGF's high profits invited bureaucratic predation. For the municipal government, BGF was a huge cash cow to be milked rather than a source of long-term capital appreciation. As the chief engineer explained, the municipal government had a "whipping the fast cow" tax policy, that is, the most profitable firms were slapped with punitively high tax rates, which reduced their internal sources of funds for investment financing. Between 1985 and 1988, taxes amounted to 32 percent of BGF's pretax profits, and in 1990 they rose to 42 percent.[30] Furthermore, the municipal government insisted on large dividend distributions or profit remittances. Profit remittances to the municipal government during the 1980s routinely amounted to 40 percent of pretax profits. Thus, these two sources of government extraction ate away 70 percent of BGF's profits, leaving little for capacity expansions after meeting the financing needs of current operations. The chief engineer also

[30] Tax data are reported in Ministry of Machinery Industry (1996).

pointed out that bank loans were not allocated to BGF, despite its high margins, because the Beijing municipal government had its own industrial policy goals. BAIC and the Beijing municipal government regarded vehicle assembly as a high priority and therefore underfunded components production. In fact, BGF's healthy cash-flow situation reduced its attractiveness to the banks. The mentality was, "If you are doing so well, why do you need us?" The redistributive rather than the intermediary roles of the Chinese banking system dried up a critical source of financing that BGF could have used to rapidly expand its production and to defend its entrenched position. Also, like other SOEs, BGF had excess workers on its payroll whom it could not fire due to government restrictions.

The JV as a Solution. Although BGF maintained its leading market position until 1992, its margin was rapidly eroding as the growth of market opportunities in the auto industry enticed entry of other firms. By 1991, BGF accounted for 18 percent of the market in transmissions and 61 percent in transfer cases. At the same time, its gross profit margins and returns on assets deteriorated to their lowest points, at 9.7 percent and 14.7 percent, respectively. Something needed to be done quickly to raise the necessary capital either to expand BGF's existing capacity or to move to a new line of products.

XYZ Automotive presented just such a solution. XYZ Automotive is the world's premier producer of engine technology and automotive accessories. It is a specialist in transmission manufacturing and technology, which accounted for 38 percent of its 1997 sales. Its largest customers are Ford, General Motors, and DaimlerChrysler (formerly Chrysler). Its strong supplier relations with the Big Three motivated XYZ Automotive to expand into China. Chrysler was the JV partner in Beijing Jeep Corporation, the first auto JV in China, established in 1984. Beijing Jeep Corporation produced the sport-utility-vehicle model BJ2021, a four-wheel-drive vehicle based on Chrysler's Cherokee model. The BJ2021 series replaced the smaller BJ212 that the shareholding firm of Beijing Jeep Corporation, Beijing Automobile Industry Corporation, had produced since 1960 before it formed the JV with Chrysler. In 1990, Beijing Jeep Corporation produced 6,000 BJ2021 vehicles. In 1992, another customer of XYZ Automotive, General Motors, was actively pursuing an investment deal to assemble S-10 pick-up trucks with Jinbei Auto in Liaoning province. In the United States, XYZ Automotive supplied the transmission systems – known as T-4 and T-5 – to both the Cherokee and S-10 truck series. XYZ Automotive also intended to introduce the T-4 and T-5 to China.

For BGF, an alliance with XYZ Automotive was attractive on several fronts. First, BGF had supplied transmission systems to be fitted on the BJ212 for many years, but it would not be able to do so for the BJ2021, the new vehicle introduced by Beijing Jeep Corporation and Chrysler. The BJ2021 heavily utilized Chrysler's technology in suspension, braking, transmission, cooling, and steering systems, and so on. Its much larger engine, measured by emission displacement, was 2.4 liters, while the BJ212 had a 1.8-liter engine. BGF's transmission systems, while perfectly compatible with the smaller engine in the BJ212, could not meet the needs of the BJ2021. Before 1992, Beijing Jeep Corporation had imported its transmissions and transfer case systems from Japan because none of the Chinese producers were able to supply the required systems to the BJ2021.

The Chinese government considered import substitution an important criterion for approving the Beijing-XYZ Gear project. In the feasibility study prepared for the project, engineers from China International Engineering Consulting Company, a firm designated by the government to perform feasibility studies for FDI projects, pointed out that Beijing Jeep Corporation had not sourced from BGF for its Cherokee production and that Beijing-XYZ Gear would replace T-4 and T-5 imports. The study forecasted that the project would achieve an output volume of 90,000 units within a short period of time, of which 40,000 units would be supplied to Beijing Jeep Corporation and 50,000 units would be supplied to the Jinbei-GM JV (China International Engineering Company 1992).

The project was approved quickly, and Beijing-XYZ Gear formally launched operations in September 1992. The financing arrangements and BGF's deliberations in entering into the JV reveal the financial pressures on SOEs as early as 1992, even when the credit supply was expanding at a double-digit rate. For BGF, partnering with XYZ Automotive killed two birds with one stone. On the one hand, BGF believed that its shrinking profit margin meant that its current product segment was unattractive. According to its thinking, the problem stemmed from the fact that its transmission system was too low-end. Teaming up with a technological leader in the field would move BGF's production to a higher technological terrain. Second, BGF could also access the customer base of XYZ Automotive, such as that for the pending S-10 truck project, as well as its technological capabilities. In that way, BGF could move to a new market less crowded with competitors compared with that for its lower-end transmission products.

Financing Structure . But there were purely financial motivations as well. BGF was short of investment funds to expand its product lines. Unlike other SOEs that formed JVs in 1994 and 1995, BGF was not in deep financial trouble and was partially motivated to form the JV on strategic grounds. But it was clear that BGF was beginning to experience some financial strains that would

Table 5.3 *Financing Structure of Beijing-XYZ Gear (RMB million)*

Financing structure	Equity contribution	Components of the equity contribution			
		Equipment	Inventory	Cash	Technology
Equity	91.4				
Beijing Gear Factory (61%)	55.8	38.3	17.5	0	0
XYZ Automotive (39%)	35.6	2.81	0	27.6	5.2
Debt	155.7				
Total capitalization	247.1				

Sources: Interviews and Ministry of Machinery and Electronics Industry (1993).

engulf the entire state sector by the mid-1990s. The financial constraints played as strong a role as the strategic considerations in motivating BGF to form a JV with XYZ Automotive, substantially affecting the way BGF capitalized its equity stake in Beijing-XYZ Gear. BGF viewed the project as an opportunity to raise much-needed liquid capital – cash – and more liquid financial stakes in a better-managed operation and a more profitable product line.

Table 5.3 presents details of how the equity capital of Beijing-XYZ Gear was financed. The equity investments came to RMB 91.4 million and the total capitalization value of the project came to RMB 247.1 million. This means that Beijing-XYZ Gear had to borrow about RMB 155.7 million. BGF's initial equity share was 61 percent and its equity investment amounted to RMB 55.8 million. Because BGF was severely cash-constrained, it could contribute only its nonfinancial current and fixed assets, such as work in progress, raw materials, and equipment. Of the RMB 55.8 million in its equity contributions, about 69 percent, or RMB 38.3 million, consisted of BGF's fixed assets. The rest of its equity contribution came from the drawing down of its inventories, which amounted to RMB 17.5 million. Equity contributions from XYZ Automotive consisted primarily of cash (RMB 27.6 million), some equipment (RMB 2.81 million), and technology (RMB 5.2 million).

This is a very good illustration of a JV acquisition at work. The essence of the deal was that BGF exchanged its operating assets for – hopefully – more profitable financial assets, that is, equity shares in Beijing-XYZ Gear. There was some strategic consideration, but financial relief was an important motivation as well. In a direct strategic move, a firm normally launches a new product line on the basis of strengths in its main businesses and core product lines. BGF did exactly the opposite: It contributed its most profitable product line, transfer cases, and retained the low-margin transmission product line, which it itself had concluded was unpromising. In 1991, the entire value of BGF's net fixed assets was RMB 67.2 million; thus, a RMB 38.3 million fixed asset transfer reduced its total fixed assets by 57 percent. And the contributed fixed assets represented the best of what BGF had. China International Engineering Company (1992) points out that financing Beijing-XYZ Gear required BGF to relinquish "80 percent of its production capacity and market" to the JV.

BGF apparently also sold its inventories to XYZ Automotive for cash. In 1992, BGF contributed inventory worth RMB 17.5 million, but the value of its current assets in fact rose from RMB 80.8 million in 1991, to RMB 99.9 million in 1992 and RMB 151.2 million in 1993, all during a period when the profitability of BGF suffered enormously. This is possibly due to the fact that BGF was revaluing and selling its inventory holdings to XYZ Automotive to obtain cash. There was another source of cash as well. In 1991, BGF occupied a land area of around 110,000 square meters; in 1992 its property was reduced to 71,923 square meters. As a part of the JV agreement, BGF rented out its facilities to Beijing-XYZ Gear, and it received a steady flow of cash in the amount of RMB 8.5 million annually. The rental payment alone was about 40 percent of its pre–Beijing-XYZ Gear profits.

Effects on BGF. Because BGF transferred its most valuable assets to Beijing-XYZ Gear, its operating income suffered. The feasibility study prepared by the Chinese side fully predicted the dire impact of Beijing-XYZ Gear on BGF's operations. It forecasted that BGF would turn a gross profit of RMB 21 million in 1991 into a loss of RMB 14 million in 1992. The actual result was not as drastic, but still devastating. In 1992, BGF made a profit of RMB 15 million, down from 21.7 million the year before, but in 1993, its profit was zero and in 1994 it recovered only slightly, to RMB 17,000. Gross profit margins and returns on assets suffered enormously after 1991, and profitability never returned to the prevailing level before the creation of Beijing-XYZ Gear. The impact on the top line of BGF, its main business, was equally dramatic. In 1991, production of transmission systems and transfer cases numbered 63,000 units and 52,000 units, respectively, both ranking first in the country. But in 1993, BGF produced 8,000 units of transmission systems, dropping to twenty-fourth in the country, while it stopped manufacturing transfer cases altogether. BGF had contributed the entire transfer case production line and some of its transmission production capabilities to Beijing-XYZ Gear. Overnight, BGF turned itself from a market leader in this business to a virtual nonplayer.

The mirror image of BGF's plight was the rise of Beijing-XYZ Gear. Beijing-XYZ Gear quickly replaced BGF's production and market positions. Because the formation of Beijing-XYZ Gear mainly meant that it assumed control over existing fixed assets rather than constructing new assets or refitting previously separate assets, production disruptions were minimal. In 1993, the first full year of Beijing-XYZ Gear's operations, output of transmission systems reached 85,000 units and that of transfer cases reached 39,000 units.

The decimation of BGF's top and bottom lines does not imply that BGF was irrational, however. It did the best it could under the circumstances. BGF viewed Beijing-XYZ Gear as the optimal way to realize value on its assets. BGF succeeded in raising some cash, from a steady source of rental payments and from the conversion of illiquid inventory holdings. It received financial claims against future income streams that would come from both more efficient management of existing assets and an injection of new product lines. BGF could then use the newly raised cash to invest in those product lines it still retained. Indeed, after Beijing-XYZ Gear was created, BGF's capital spending began to increase. In 1992, its capital expenditure, as a ratio to sales, was 7.54 percent; it steadily rose in 1993, 1994, and 1995 to 14 percent. But BGF was struggling to retain its traditional market position as a supplier of transmission systems to low-end vehicle producers.

Poor Performance of the JV. In the end, BGF's strategy backfired. As BGF abdicated an operating role and took on a shareholding role (and an increasingly passive one, at that), the strategy would have worked only if Beijing-XYZ Gear had turned out to be a highly profitable proposition. This simply did not happen. For one thing, the government suspended Jinbei's deal with GM to produce S-10 pick-up trucks, which meant that the demand for 50,000 T-4 and T-5 transmissions simply evaporated. More devastating to Beijing-XYZ Gear, however, was the fact that demand from existing customers also collapsed. Beijing Jeep Corporation sharply cut back its production of the Cherokee series, the BJ2021, due to lack of market demand. The vehicle was priced too high and its bulky size made it an impractical choice for China's congested streets and tiny parking spaces. In addition, many other competing vehicles were rolled out during this period. Instead of producing 40,000 Cherokee-based BJ2021s, as forecasted in BGF's feasibility study, Beijing Jeep Corporation only produced 26,051 in 1996. (In 1998, production fell further, to only 8,344 units.) Beijing-XYZ Gear's profitability was uneven and anemic. In 1992, its losses amounted to RMB 187,000; in the next year it made a profit of RMB 10.4 million, but it lost RMB 20 million in 1995. The firm incurred substantial losses in both 1997 and 1998.

Failure to collect dividend payments hurt BGF badly. Financing Beijing-XYZ Gear via an asset injection directly reduced BGF's operating income and thus increased its dependence on nonoperating sources of income. Its pretax profits were zero in 1993, RMB 17,000 in 1994, RMB 332,000 in 1995, and RMB 31,000 in 1996. It lost money in 1998.

While its profits evaporated, BGF took on debt in part because of the financing need to form Beijing-XYZ Gear. In 1992, Beijing-XYZ Gear took on RMB 155.7 million in debt, which amounted to 63 percent of BGF's total assets and 170 percent of its equity. BGF, not XYZ Automotive, assumed the bulk of the obligation for this debt. According to Ministry of Machinery and Electronics Industry (1993), of the RMB 155.7 million in debt, RMB 65 million came from the technical renovation loan administered by the municipal government and RMB 41 million came from the Beijing branch of the Industrial and Commercial Bank. BGF directly assumed these two loans, which accounted for 68 percent of the total debt. Beijing-XYZ Gear itself assumed the rest, or about RMB 49.7 million. Thus, XYZ Automotive's debt exposure was relatively limited, and BGF's liability was much larger due to its direct borrowing and its equity share in Beijing-XYZ Gear. In 1997, BGF's debt-to-asset ratio was 60.5 percent, and in 1998 it rose to 68.8 percent.

The other source of unrelenting pressure on BGF was its social liabilities. In 1991, BGF employed 4,873 workers. One of the conditions in the JV contract was that Beijing-XYZ Gear would take over a number of workers from BGF. BGF's work force did decline, from 4,873 to 3,349, as 1,534 workers went to work for Beijing-XYZ Gear. Although this reduction alleviated some of the wage payables of BGF, it also presented problems. Most of the high-quality and skilled workers went to work for Beijing-XYZ Gear, which meant that BGF was saddled with a less productive work force. This kind of arrangement would have worked only if there had been continuous dividend payouts from its stakes in Beijing-XYZ Gear to finance the wage bills to its current work force. On top of its 3,000-strong work force, BGF was also paying pensions to 1,000 retired workers (China International Engineering Company 1992). Like other SOEs, BGF maintained housing, a cafeteria, and social service facilities for its employees, and it was still responsible for providing these facilities even for the part of the work force transferred to Beijing-XYZ Gear. A large portion of the fixed assets remaining on BGF's balance sheet after 1992 was not production-related, that is, it consisted of housing stock and amenities facilities. In 1993, its ratio of nonproduction assets to total fixed assets was 30 percent and rose to 54 percent in 1994, while it was zero for Beijing-XYZ Gear. Because there is no housing market in China, Beijing-XYZ Gear employees continued to live in BGF's housing complex and to receive the implicit subsidies embodied in this arrangement. (In China, this phenomenon is known as "one factory, two systems.") This is a concrete illustration that JV acquisitions have essentially converted SOEs from operating companies to providers of social services.

PPG-Nanchang Chemical Industry Corporation (PPG-NCIC)

Our second case study provides further details about the de facto privatization involved in JV acquisitions. PPG-NCIC is a JV formed by PPG–Feng Tai Co. and Nanchang Chemical Industrial Corporation (NCIC) in 1993. The main product line is silica.[31] Silica is a chemical ingredient applied to rubber to improve its physical strength, abrasion, and chemical resistance and to reduce the density of rubber products. Silica is also used for decorative purposes. Known as rubber filler, one of its many uses is in the manufacturing of vehicle tires to make them withstand more wear and tear on the road. PPG–Feng Tai Co. is registered in Hong Kong and is a 100 percent owned subsidiary of the Pittsburgh-based firm, Pittsburgh Plate and Glass Industries (PPG). PPG, founded in 1883, is the one of the leading chemical producers in the world and was rated as one of the most admired chemical firms among the *Fortune* 500. In 1998, according to its web site, PPG had net sales of $7.5 billion and employed 32,500 persons. PPG operates fifty production facilities in the United States and 110 worldwide. It is a major producer of glass products and specialty chemicals for manufacturing, construction, automotive, chemical processing, and numerous other industries.

NCIC. NCIC is an SOE located in the city of Nanchang in Jiangxi province with an annual production capacity of 10,000 tons. It was the largest silica producer in China until the formation of PPG-NCIC. In the 1980s, China's automobile industry began to grow rapidly, increasing the demand for tires. Silica was thus suddenly in high demand. In 1984, the plant was selected by the Jiangxi provincial government for a key technology-upgrading project, and the government spent RMB 100 million on the construction of a silica production facility, supporting facilities, and on land acquisition. During a period of great shortages of foreign exchange, the government allocated $4.43 million to NCIC to import technology and equipment. NCIC then purchased a technology license worth $1.75 million as well as machinery and equipment worth $2.68 million from PPG. Most likely, this was the first contact between the two firms. Like

---

[31] The primary sources for this section are Tang, Han, and Wang (1997) and Liu, Shao, and Pan (1997). The authors of these two studies examined all the original documents of the deal and interviewed all the major protagonists on the Chinese side. I have relied on Dr. Chunbin Zhang of Dow Chemical for a technical interpretation of the production processes involved in silica production. In researching this case, I invited Mr. Richard A. Beuke, the head of the Silica Unit of PPG Industries, Inc., to comment on the facts as depicted here. Mr. Beuke declined, citing the reason that he had not been involved in the project at the time. Mr. Beuke was also asked to suggest other managers at PPG who would be in a position to comment on the case. Mr. Beuke was not able to provide any names.

other SOEs, NCIC began to experience serious financial difficulties in the 1990s. It had a debt of RMB 90 million on its books, which translated into a multiple of 1.46 of its operating assets.[32]

The JV Deal and Outcome of the Negotiations. Negotiations for the JV began in early 1991, and the two firms reached final agreement about the terms of the deal in January 1993. In March 1993, PPG-NCIC received its business license and began operations as an FIE. The total capitalization of the project was $11.7 million, with an equity base of $5 million. The equity structure consisted of a 60 percent stake from PPG–Feng Tai ($3 million) and another 40 percent stake from the Chinese shareholder, NCIC.

PPG contributed $3 million in cash to the JV, while the contribution by NCIC consisted entirely of machinery and equipment. The first part of NCIC's equipment contributions went toward financing its 40 percent stake. The second part was a straightforward asset sale from NCIC to the JV. After the formation of PPG-NCIC, all silica production and related facilities were transferred from NCIC to PPG-NCIC. The remaining fixed assets of NCIC consisted of various types of nonessential auxiliary machinery and equipment that provided services for silica production.

How NCIC financed its equity contribution toward this JV is a concrete illustration of the phenomenon of large-scale JV acquisitions sweeping China in the 1990s. SOEs, unable to generate cash flows on their own, sought to convert their fixed assets into what were expected to be more profitable financial investments in JVs. During the process of forming their JV, PPG and NCIC negotiated intensively over two critical issues: First, which of the operating assets held by NCIC would be transferred to the JV? The second issue regarded the value of the transferred assets. On both issues, NCIC eventually agreed to the terms laid out by PPG.

On the first issue, NCIC wanted to inject its entire fixed assets – excluding property, which is not a part of fixed assets under Chinese accounting rules – toward its equity stake in the JV. NCIC's equipment and machinery consisted of a silica production facility, a water glass processing facility, an air compression station, a power station, a vapor generation facility, railway tracks, and some maintenance machinery. This constituted an integrated production chain. The silica production facility was the core facility of the plant, to which all other facilities supplied either inputs or services. For example, water glass was

---

[32] I have used the valuation by NCIC, which was RMB 61.6 million, to make this calculation. It should be pointed out that PPG was willing to pay only RMB 43.5 million. Using RMB 43.5 million would have yielded a much higher debt/operating asset ratio, at 2.07.

dissolved in water to produce sodium silicate, which became the raw material for silica production. The air compression station supplied high-pressure air to the silica facility, and the power station supplied electricity. Silica production also uses liquid vapor, supplied by the vapor generation facility.

NCIC's intention was very clear. Since it did not have any cash, it tried to increase its stake as much as it could by maximizing the size of its fixed asset contribution as well as the value of each individual fixed asset it contributed. PPG, on the other hand, wanted to minimize its cash exposure to the project. Agreeing to all of NCIC's demands would have forced PPG to increase its cash contribution in order to obtain a majority stake in the JV, a goal PPG had set out to achieve from the very beginning. Thus, it agreed to take only the core operating assets, the silica production line, water glass processing facility, and air compression station. This reduced the total size of the contribution from NCIC. But this is not the whole story. PPG further divided the contributed facilities into two parts. The first part counted toward NCIC's equity contribution and the other part was to be a straightforward asset sale from NCIC to PPG-NCIC. In value terms, the asset sale accounted for 75 percent of the contribution from NCIC, and the equity component accounted for only 25 percent. PPG-NCIC would purchase from NCIC the services of the equipment and machinery that remained with NCIC. PPG inserted a fair-pricing provision into the JV contract that these services were to be rendered at prices no higher than the prevailing prices received by other SOEs in the region.

NCIC did not like this arrangement at all. The equipment and machinery NCIC relinquished to the JV were its core operating assets, as silica was NCIC's only product. The assets it retained, such as the power station and the vapor generation facility, were specifically designed to support silica production activities, and without the silica production equipment NCIC was left with no choice but to be a captive service provider to PPG-NCIC. PPG's insistence to divide NCIC's asset contribution into an equity component and a sale component, rather than accepting the whole package as an equity contribution, reduced NCIC's equity shares in the JV. The asset sale (amounting to RMB 32.8 million) would be financed by a RMB loan to PPG-NCIC and arranged by NCIC itself. Because NCIC's stake in PPG-NCIC was 40 percent, NCIC essentially assumed 40 percent of the credit risk toward the purchase of its own equipment.

The second issue revolved around the equipment valuation. For each JV project that involves a contribution of state-owned assets, the government requires a certified accounting firm and the local Bureau of State Asset Management to assess the value of the contributed assets. NCIC hired a local accounting firm, which, based on the replacement cost method, assessed the value of the silica production line, water glass processing facilities, and air compression station to be at RMB 61.6 million. PPG came up with its own valuation of RMB 43.5 million, a difference of 28.6 percent. In the end, NCIC accepted the lower valuation by PPG.

The differences in valuation arose in four areas. First, PPG used a longer depreciation period than NCIC. NCIC dated operations beginning in May 1991, when NCIC passed the certification test of the Ministry of Chemical Industry. PPG argued that the starting date actually was much earlier, in August 1989, when NCIC went into trial production. The second disagreement was about the duration of the construction period. NCIC spent three years constructing the plant and thus incurred interest payment expenses for three years. It argued that the replacement cost ought to factor into the entire interest payment. PPG disagreed. Its position was that it had taken only one year to build its plants in Taiwan and Thailand, and thus only one year of interest payment should be incorporated into the replacement cost. The third disagreement had to do with choosing an appropriate exchange rate to convert the remaining value of the technology-licensing contract. In 1986 NCIC acquired a technology license from PPG at $1.75 million. At that time the exchange rate was RMB 4.19 per dollar, but in 1993, the yuan had depreciated to RMB 5.57 per dollar. NCIC wanted to use the current exchange rate, but PPG insisted on using the 1986 exchange rate. The fourth area involved the land charges. Because PPG-NCIC was to be set up on NCIC's property, NCIC wanted PPG to acquire land-use rights from NCIC for RMB 5.6 million. PPG refused, preferring instead to lease the land. In the end, NCIC agreed to all the terms as laid down by PPG. These four areas of disagreement are summarized in Table 5.4.

NCIC's Strong Preference for the Deal. The PPG-NCIC deal was controversial within the Chinese bureaucratic establishment. The provincial agencies, such as the Planning Commission and the Bureau of Chemical Industry, opposed the

Table 5.4 *PPG and NCIC Negotiations over Asset Valuation (RMB million)*

Asset items	A PPG valuation	B NCIC valuation	C Difference between PPG and NCIC valuation
Building and equipment	35.5	42.3	−6.8
Licensing contract	5.3	9.4	−4.1
Interest expense	2.6	4.2	−1.57
Land-use fee	0.0	5.6	−5.6
Total	43.3	61.4	−18.1

Source: Adapted from Tang, Han, and Wang (1997).

deal on the grounds that the terms were too generous to PPG. They had arranged for the initial funding for construction of the project and were angry that their investments had not yielded any payoffs before the assets were to be disposed of at what they viewed as a discount. The city of Nanchang, which owned NCIC, supported the deal, and NCIC acted very quickly to seal the agreement so that the provincial bureaucracy would find it difficult to intervene after the fact.

What the negotiation outcomes reveal is NCIC's strong preferences for a JV deal with PPG: NCIC complied with all the terms proposed by PPG. This cannot be explained by a lack of money per se. At the time that NCIC was negotiating with PPG, the Jiangxi provincial government stepped in and arranged for import credit in the amount of $1.6 million to be used at NCIC for a capacity expansion from 10,000 tons to 15,000 tons. NCIC refused the offer and pursued the JV option instead. This strong predilection for FDI is consistent with the notion that Chinese firms seek to realize not just the immediate financial benefits associated with a JV option, but also those benefits embodied in an FIE status. For example, PPG-NCIC would be taxed at a lower rate than a domestic firm. Lower taxes promised a greater posttax cash flow to NCIC than if NCIC were to produce silica completely on its own. Such calculations may have distorted NCIC's agenda when it negotiated with PPG.

Tax motivations, however, would be at odds with the strong enthusiasm of the Nanchang city government for the deal, as the city government stood to lose some revenue when converting the facility from a 100 percent owned subsidiary to a partially owned FIE and moving production from a high- to a low-tax regime. The more dominant factor in favor of this deal was a fundamental pessimism on the part of the city of Nanchang about continued Chinese management and, in essence, about the socialist system itself. Liu Lisheng, Shao Dongya, and Pan Jin (1997, p. 349), the authors of a detailed study on this deal, draw the following assessment:

> It would have been very difficult for NCIC to rely on its own capabilities to integrate and absorb the imported technology and to develop on its own. Such a strategy would have required not only technological capabilities and guaranteed sources of funding but also more importantly a different management system. Under the current system, managers and government agencies lacked incentives and risk-taking attitudes. On the other hand, through the "grafted JV" and by leaning on PPG as "a big tree," NCIC could acquire a competitive advantage from the technology, brand name, reputation, customer base, and management system of the foreign investor. This was an easier route. From this case, it is clear that avoiding risks and

market pressures were the most important motivations for the government and management to agree to the asset transfer.

One can assess JV acquisitions in a number of ways. One is to explain their incidence in terms of the motivations of the SOEs to be acquired in this way. I have already alluded to a number of reasons, such as asset surplus and insolvency. Here, let me provide a third and related factor: the pursuit of technology at the expense of market orientations. These transactions can also be assessed in terms of the specific terms of the deals. Many Chinese commentators are angered by the fact that the valuation of SOE assets is often lower than their book value. I show here that this complaint is unreasonable. It is far more productive not to focus on the terms of these individual transactions themselves but to look at the conditions under which these transactions occur. JV acquisitions take place in a specific context: Indigenous private firms have been restricted in their access to financing and market opportunities and have not been allowed to acquire SOEs on any significant scale until very recently. This policy has the detrimental effect of restraining competition over SOE assets. It is clear that the poor performance of SOEs has led to a low valuation of their assets, but such restraints on competition also were a contributing factor. I examine these issues next.

Technological Motivations versus Market Orientations

Through a JV vehicle, foreign firms mainly acquired those SOEs that were favored in the 1980s. All of the SOEs acquired through a JV method had imported technology and equipment in the 1980s. Thus, the first issue is why these SOEs were acquired. As pointed out earlier, SOEs are obsessed with technology. This has led them to produce products that are often ill-suited for the Chinese market and to increase their debt burdens to finance the expensive acquisition of technology and hard assets. Both these trends contribute to their poor performance and to the motivation to use JV acquisition to resolve their insolvency.

As Beijing-XYZ Gear shows, the pursuit of technology also led to the JV decision: BGF wanted to acquire the capability to produce the T-4s and T-5s and to supply to the BJ2021. In the end, the strategy did not work because the market for T-4s and T-5s collapsed. The question here is whether there was a market for low-end transfer case and transmission product lines in the 1990s. If there had been, then BGF could have avoided the costly JV deal and focused on the production of its low-end transfer cases and transmissions as a viable business strategy, an area in which the firm had accumulated capabilities since the 1960s. The answer to this question is yes, and BGF had every reason to know that such a market existed.

Throughout the 1980s and 1990s, the fastest-growing segment of the market was not vehicles produced by foreign-invested JVs but what were known as "agricultural utility vehicles." In 1980, some 10,000 such agricultural utility vehicles were estimated to be on the road; by 1995, the number had grown to 2.3 million, up from 1.6 million only one year earlier (Ministry of Machinery Industry 1996, p. 138).[33] These vehicles were stripped-down light trucks, devoid of the sophisticated technological and engineering features associated with modern vehicles. Yet their low prices, durability, and easy maneuverability appealed enormously to Chinese farmers, who needed practical vehicles to haul goods and people. In 1996, the largest firm specializing in agricultural utility vehicles, the Jinwa Group in Jiangsu province, already had an output volume of 260,421 units (Ministry of Machinery Industry 1997a, p. 100). This was three times the projected demand for the T-4 and T-5 transmission products. But the dramatic growth in the volume of agricultural utility vehicles eclipsed the attention of the SOEs, including BGF. They were completely oblivious to the fact that farmers, not urban residents, were the natural buyers of vehicles in China: Farmers operated over a greater geographic expanse than city residents and they did not have any alternative means of transportation.

BGF could have easily fit its low-end transmission product lines into these agricultural utility vehicles. A strategic focus on market demand rather than on technology would have propelled BGF into becoming a huge player in this business segment, and it could have avoided forming a costly alliance. By 1998, BGF finally realized that agricultural utility vehicles were a natural market for its products, and it wanted to shift its production to serve that market. But it was already too late. The general manager of Beijing-XYZ Gear, in an interview in 1998, made it clear that his next step was to focus on agricultural utility vehicles. Zhu Xun, the manager from BAIC, commented, "They are now cannibalizing each other." (In this interview, Mr. Zhu was extremely pessimistic about the future of the JV. He revealed that although the foreign firm demanded an increase in its equity stake, it still did not want to take control of the plant. Apparently, the firm did not want to disclose performance information about the plant in its annual report.)[34]

---

[33] Because these vehicles are low-tech and are not standardized, the Chinese government does not include them in its motor vehicle statistics in the standard statistical publications.

[34] Interview with Zhu Xun, manager of the Foreign Department of Beijing Automotive Industry Corporation, November 28, 1998.

In fact, BGF did not have to look far in the rapidly expanding market of rural utility vehicles to know that there was a huge market for lower-end vehicles. It had only to look at what its Chinese parent firm, BAIC, was producing. According to Zhu Xun, for years Beijing Jeep Corporation, the JV with Chrysler, was making money not from the BJ2021, but from the BJ212 and the improved model of the BJ212, the BJ2020. There was a good reason. The BJ2020 was smaller and cheaper and suited the Chinese income level and driving conditions far better than the bulky Cherokee-based BJ2021. In fact, the BJ2020 was so profitable that Beijing Jeep Corporation constantly complained about BAIC still producing them, even though by the JV agreement, BAIC was supposed to surrender the product line to the JV. In 1993, Beijing Jeep Corporation churned out 33,321 BJ2020 vehicles, compared with 13,809 BJ2021 vehicles. The BJ212, the predecessor to the BJ2020, also had a large market. After the Beijing firm shifted to the higher-end BJ2021, many firms in the country began to produce copycats of the BJ212. BGF, which had supplied transmissions to the BJ212 since 1965, easily could have dominated this market.

In the end, the technological content of the JV deal was not that significant after all. The value of the technology that XYZ Automotive brought to the deal was less than $1 million (RMB 5.2 million), representing 14.6 percent of the XYZ Automotive investment and 2.1 percent of the total capitalization value of the project. To be sure, the T-4 and T-5 did represent a technological improvement over BGF's existing product lines, but it was an incremental improvement. Mr. Zhu Xun commented, "The technology brought by XYZ Automotive was a little bit better than what we had, but not by much. Frankly speaking, we could not have used their most advanced technology anyway."[35] For this technological acquisition, BGF paid dearly by forgoing its own areas of strength and creating a competitor for itself in the process.

Asset Value Controversies

When examining foreign acquisitions of SOEs, a number of analysts are convinced that the prices paid are too low and the asset transactions are unfair. Tang Zongkun, Han Chaohua, and Wang Hongling (1997), economists at the Chinese Academy of Social Sciences and authors of a detailed study of the NCIC deal, suggest that NCIC's capitulation to PPG's demands is evidence that NCIC's managers shirked their responsibilities to maximize shareholder value and that asset stripping may have been involved. This view echoes the sentiment expressed in the Local Leadership Survey that FDI projects somehow

---

[35] Ibid.

cause losses to the state. The problem with this view is that the asset valuation process itself is deeply flawed. The valuation requirement is a quirk in the Chinese system, instituted because of the absence of a functioning asset market. In a market economy a guide to the value of a publicly listed firm is its valuation on the stock market, which represents the consensus view of investors about the worth of the firm. The value of an unlisted firm is assessed by analogy, that is, by making references to a similar but listed firm. Underlying this way of evaluating the worth of a firm is the idea that when capital is free to move from one firm to another, the opportunity costs of investing are a reliable indicator of the value of the firm. Asset valuation in China can be quite arbitrary, as appraisers lack a reliable benchmark to assess a firm's worth precisely because capital is not free to move from one firm to another.

In the case of PPG-NCIC, we do not really know whether the discrepancy between the appraisal value and the transaction value was the result of the transaction value being deliberately set too low or of the appraisal value being set at an unrealistically high level. The asset-stripping motive would depend on a view that the Chinese asset valuation was accurate, a questionable proposition given the fact that the local Bureau of State Asset Management had a heavy hand in the asset appraisal process and was hardly an impartial appraiser.

In fact, there may very well have been strong competitive reasons for NCIC to value ties to PPG very highly. NCIC faced some strong competitors. A silica producer in Qingdao had emerged to challenge NCIC's market position, and NCIC's profit margins had declined continuously since the late 1980s, despite a surging market demand. The valuation of assets and of a company, to a large extent, is a subjective affair, depending heavily on the relative bargaining power between the two parties. NCIC was in a weak bargaining position. Not only was NCIC operating at a loss; PPG had already started negotiating with the Qingdao producer about the possibility of forming a JV there. Revealing its weak hand, NCIC asked PPG to terminate its negotiations with the Qingdao firm. This stance essentially left NCIC very little choice but to accept whatever PPG had to offer. Because of these constraints, the offer by PPG was, a fortiori, the right price for NCIC's assets.

Competition Restraints

Are the Chinese better off with these JV acquisitions? Definitely. These JV acquisitions convert SOEs into partially foreign *and* privately owned firms. In this sense, allowing JV acquisitions is a de facto privatization policy. The relevant issue is not the specific dollar amount of the asset transactions involved. Nor is it whether these transactions are mutually beneficial. (Of course, they are, otherwise they would not be consummated.) Nor is it terribly relevant whether these assets eventually end up in foreign hands. The relevant issue is whether these asset transactions occur under sufficiently competitive conditions. Suppose two firms, A and B, both receive an offer that represents 100 percent of the book value of their assets.[36] Firm A gets its offer with no restrictions on the type or number of bidders, while the offer for firm B is generated when a specific class of bidders is excluded. Even if the two firms receive identical offers, one may still argue that the offer for firm A is priced correctly, whereas there is the possibility that the offer for firm B is priced incorrectly.

A Comparison with Russia. An illustration of the importance of conditions underlying these asset transactions is a comparison with Russia.[37] Studies on Russia show foreigners paid only a fraction of the presumptive book value of assets.[38] But it is important to note that foreigners bought Russian assets at a time of catastrophic economic decline, episodic macroeconomic and financial instability, and paralysis and even collapse of the state in some regions of the country, not to mention the pillaging and stripping of the most productive assets of the country by corrupt insiders. The JV acquisitions described in this chapter have occurred in China at a time of surging economic growth, widely acknowledged success at taming inflation in the mid-1990s, and a generally stable political environment. It is logical that the Chinese would get better deals on the basis of the strong macroeconomic fundamentals.

The microeconomic contrasts are as sharp as the macroeconomic contrasts between the two countries. The Russian government allowed foreigners to acquire Russian firms immediately after the abrupt end of seventy-three years of socialism. Indigenous and capable private entrepreneurs did not have the time or the opportunity to grow into a position to be able to seriously contend with foreign firms as acquirers. (The ones who were given the chance were bureaucratic insiders and turned out to be a hugely destructive force.) China is a different case altogether. By the mid-1990s, China had experienced fifteen years of uninterrupted economic growth and of incremental reforms. Because of financial and political biases, China's private sector was not as large as it could have been. Nevertheless, by the early 1990s, China already could claim a

---

[36] This exercise ignores many complications in book value valuation.

[37] I thank Professor Barry Naughton for suggesting such a comparison.

[38] One such study is Boycko, Shleifer, and Vishny (1995). Although the authors do not show specific values of foreign acquisitions of Russian firms, they show an incredible low valuation of all Russian firms. In 1993 and 1994, the implied aggregate value of the entire Russian industry was only $12 billion. This was less than the valuation of Kellogg or Anheuser-Busch at that time.

sizable group of genuinely capable entrepreneurs and managers. In the 1980s, many of the SOEs had been leased to managers who then accumulated valuable experience and know-how. Unlike Russia, China was not short of business entrepreneurship and basic managerial skills. What it lacked was an efficient combination of market orientation and entrepreneurship, on the one hand, and financial resources and productive assets, on the other.

The question is whether the Chinese could have gotten better deals than they actually did if the government had allowed and encouraged indigenous entrepreneurs to bid for SOE assets at the same time that it heavily courted foreign investors. A related question is whether under less restrictive conditions indigenous private firms could have also played a role in restructuring the SOEs. Here is a counterfactual hypothesis: If the government had encouraged and supported the growth of indigenous private firms as much as it did FDI, the restructuring functions of FDI would have been less important. In addition, because there would have been more bidders for the SOE assets (from both foreign and domestic firms), it is possible that the state might have obtained more favorable valuation offers than it did. Because this is a counterfactual claim, it is impossible to empirically evaluate it directly. But, fortunately, there are three pieces of suggestive evidence to show that indeed this is the case. The first comes from a comparison with Russia. Boycko, Shleifer, and Vishny (1995) show that Russian firms were able to obtain higher valuations when foreign investors participated in the asset auctions. For example, Unified Energy System obtained the highest valuation mainly because of foreign participation. For Russia, foreign participation bid up the asset value because of the dearth of private wealth in the country.

The Chinese Situation. The situation in China was just the opposite, which is the second piece of evidence. The level of private wealth in China is enormous. In 1998, urban and rural household bank deposits stood at RMB 5,341 billion, about 76 percent of GDP in 1998 (State Statistical Bureau 1999b).[39] China had been a net capital exporter since the early 1990s. Thus, the exclusion of Chinese participation must have led to a lower valuation of Chinese firms, similar to the effect of excluding foreign participation in Russia. There is direct evidence to support this point. There are two classes of shares listed on the Chinese stock markets, A shares and B shares. A shares are available to domestic investors, while B shares are available only to foreign investors. Neither type entails any control rights and thus their control premiums are identical. While in other

---

[39] Not all financial claims held by households are liquid because of the substantial NPLs in the banking system. I return to this issue in the concluding chapter.

countries foreigners pay a premium over what domestic investors pay, in China B shares are traded at a significant discount compared with A shares of identical companies. In one study, the discount was as much as 66.2 percent (Chen, Lee, and Rui 2001).[40] On the Shanghai Stock Exchange, the annual average price-to-earning ratios for B shares ranged between 6.0 and 14.0 from 1995 to 1998, whereas they ranged between 16.3 and 43.4 for A shares. Similar discrepancies are observed for A and B shares on the Shenzhen Stock Exchange (Ma 2000). The reason is the lack of demand in the B-share market. In February 2001, after the government opened the B-share market to domestic investors, the average price-to-earning ratios of B shares rose substantially, to 30 (Ma 2001).

The third piece of evidence comes from the regional variation in economic policy. Foshan in southern Guangdong province is known for its liberal FDI and pro-privatization policy. One of its cities, Shunde, undertook a large-scale privatization program beginning in 1992, far ahead of other regions in China. Various methods were tried, including employee shareholding, listing on stock exchanges, management leasing, and management buyouts. Competitive bidding was allowed, although incumbent management was given priority.[41]

Table 5.5 reports on the average foreign equity ratios (FERs) of those FIEs formed between 1992 and 1995 in the machinery industry across several regions in Guangdong province. The machinery industry traditionally has been dominated by SOEs, and thus the formation of JVs in this industry is likely to mirror the kind of JV acquisitions documented in this chapter. All of the selected regions – Foshan, Dongguan, Zhongshan, Huizhou, and Shenzhen – are clustered together. This is to ensure that their economic conditions and their geographic distance to Hong Kong are roughly comparable. Because the JVs in the machinery industry in Foshan were formed with ECE firms and were classified as small firms, our sample is limited to ECE firms and to JVs classified as small firms to ensure comparability of foreign investor and business profiles.

If a more vibrant private sector were to compete with foreign firms on either the asset market or product market, one would expect to see a smaller foreign presence in Foshan as compared with other regions (controlling for many of the factors listed above). This is indeed the case. For the period as a whole, between 1992 and 1995, the FER was the lowest in Foshan (at 48.4 percent), and Chinese firms retained majority controls of FIEs only in Foshan. In all other regions and in Guangdong as a whole, the FER exceeded 50 percent. Foshan also has a very liberal FDI policy, and thus its lower FER cannot be due to

---

[40] Studies of share prices for the Finnish, Thai, Swiss, and Mexican stock markets show that foreign investors all paid a premium. This research is summarized in Chen, Lee, and Rui (2001).

[41] For a description of the Shunde experiment, see International Finance Corporation (2000).

Table 5.5 *Average Foreign Equity Ratio (FER) in the Machinery Industry in Selected Cities in Guangdong Province, 1992–1995*

	Cities in Guangdong province					Guangdong province
	Foshan	Dongguan	Zhongshan	Huizhou	Shenzhen	
1992						
Foreign equity percentage ratio[a] (%)	60.4	67.8	69.5	—[b]	48.9	64.3
Number of FIEs established	5	6	3	0	2	41
1993						
Foreign equity percentage ratio (%)	46.7	56.3	55.9	70.3	59.2	55.7
Number of FIEs established	9	6	4	3	7	66
1994						
Foreign equity percentage ratio (%)	26.1	66.1	40.0	47.4	50.1	56.0
Number of FIEs established	2	5	1	2	3	37
1995						
Foreign equity percentage ratio (%)	48.1	46.9	65.5	87.8	82.8	66.7
Number of FIEs established	2	1	3	5	3	25
1992–95						
Foreign equity percentage ratio (%)	48.4	62.3	60.8	74.5	60.7	59.5
Number of FIEs established	18	18	11	10	15	169

[a] Foreign equity percentage ratio is the foreign equity capital divided by the total equity capital times 100.
[b] —: Data not available.

Source: All China Marketing Research Co. Ltd. (1999).

ownership restrictions on foreign investors. A more plausible explanation is its more liberal treatment of indigenous private entrepreneurs. The same dynamic is observed in Zhejiang province. FIEs in the machinery industry in Wenzhou, a city with a reputation for implementing pro-private-enterprise policies, have the lowest FER. In Wenzhou, the FER for the FIEs established between 1992 and 1995 is 27 percent, compared with 33 percent for Zhejiang province as a whole.[42]

Between 1991 and 1997, Chinese GDP grew on average 10.9 percent annually. Because of such rapid growth, one would assume that much of the FDI inflows during this period financed green-field projects and additions to Chinese capital capacity. A portion of the FDI capital did do this, especially the FDI capital that financed business expansions for nonstate firms that were chronically constrained by China's financial system. But some FDI going to the state sector served a vastly different purpose: It financed a transfer of ownership of existing assets from Chinese control to foreign control. This was a veritable privatization process.

In China, FDI has played a role in rescuing firms and businesses that have become fundamentally insolvent under poor management. To be sure, these SOEs still retain some good assets, if not in terms of physical assets, at least in terms of brand names, distribution networks, advantaged incumbent positions, and human capital. What the insolvency-induced FDI has done is essentially transform these SOEs into private but foreign-owned business units. Through JV acquisitions, SOEs have turned over their existing businesses and management controls to MNCs and have become, in many instances, passive shareholders. Their primary objective is to convert their poorly managed fixed assets into expectantly more profitable financial claims on better-managed operations. The shareholder SOEs have become corporate "shells," and their income comes from dividend payoffs proportionate to their ownership ties to the FIE rather than from actively operating and managing assets. Their managerial and operating roles are substantially reduced.

The privatization functions of insolvency-induced FDI also explain the prominence of the ownership dimension in this phenomenon. Many think of FDI as a transfer of assets or future profits from Chinese to foreign controls, but, first and foremost, FDI is about transferring controls from the state to private firms. That these firms are also foreign is partially incidental and partially driven by a conscious policy stance on the part of the Chinese state against an explicit privatization program. By definition, a contractual approach would not have worked if the truly needed change was an ownership change. Remember that the SOEs described in this chapter all had imported technology and equipment

---

[42] All the data in this section are drawn from the FIE database.

from foreign firms in the 1980s, and some had entered into technology-licensing contracts with foreign firms. The contractual approach was tried but it did not work. Advanced technology and fancy equipment imported from abroad do not instill a profit orientation, business acumen, or sensitivity to market signals. Nor do they prevent political interference in managerial decision making and poor resource allocations by the bureaucracy.

The JV acquisitions reflect the stark allocative inefficiencies in the Chinese economy. For example, within the city of Suzhou, some firms have abundant hard assets and yet cannot utilize them to create value; other firms are too credit-constrained to expand their businesses. FDI offers a solution to both types of firms. While JV acquisitions provide a face-saving way for SOEs to exit an active production role and in all likelihood improve efficiency, one has to recognize that the Chinese government did not explicitly sanction a partial privatization program until 1997, while it actively promoted FDI beginning in 1992. In transitional economies, FDI often plays a vital role in privatization and in supplying know-how and capital. For example, in the Central European countries, 70 percent of FDI is estimated to have financed the privatization of SOEs in the early 1990s (United Nations Conference on Trade and Development 1996). The unusual feature in China is that the government has encouraged FDI inflows while restricting privatization. This policy combination may have accentuated the privatization functions of FDI, thus leading to a larger inflow of FDI than if the encouragement of FDI had been combined with an active privatization stance.

Appendix to Chapter 5: SOE Insolvency and JV Acquisition

Through some simple illustrations, I show that for local government officials and SOE managers to agree to a JV acquisition, it must be the case that the SOE in question is not making money.

PROFIT EXPECTATIONS OF FIEs AND THE INSOLVENCY OF SOEs

Local governments derive their financial flows from two sources: taxes and dividends. Suppose an SOE that is 100 percent owned by a local government currently generates pretax profits of RMB 100. It would mean that this SOE generates RMB 100 in financial flows to the local government: It will pay RMB 55 in taxes and RMB 45 in dividends to the local government, assuming the income tax rate for SOEs is 55 percent. For a local government to agree to sell an SOE that is making RMB 100 at the time to a foreigner via a JV acquisition format and to take only a 49 percent stake in this FIE, it must believe that it will receive more than RMB 100. Suppose the local government aims at getting RMB 101 from this FIE, then it must believe that the resulting FIE will generate RMB 153.4 in pretax profits, assuming the income tax rate on FIEs to be 33 percent.[43] (This calculation is detailed in Eq. 6 below.)

The above example shows, rather dramatically, that even if the local government wants to receive only 1 percent more in total financial flows from the FIE, it must believe that the FIE is 53.4 percent more efficient than its SOE (RMB 153.4/RMB $100 - 1 = 0.534$). Such a high expectation of efficiency improvement is unrealistic, which suggests that the assumption that the SOE is making money at the time of forming the JV with a foreign firm is implausible.

---

[43] This exercise ignores complications arising from the time value of money by assuming that the JV will start making money immediately. The only payments the local governments receive are ownership stakes in the new JV. No cash is involved, which is the essence of a JV acquisition.

If the SOE is not making money at the time of forming the JV, the expectation of efficiency improvement would be lower and more realistic. This is confirmation of our insolvency hypothesis.

Now let us suppose that the actual tax rate on the FIE is not 33 percent but only 15 percent, which appears to be a common tax rate for FIEs.[44] In addition, further suppose that the equity share in the FIE is not 49 percent but 45 percent, which was the average Chinese equity share in manufacturing FIEs in 1995. In that case, the local government must expect the FIE to be able to generate pretax profits of RMB 189.7, which is 89.7 percent more efficient than the current SOE (RMB 189.7/RMB 100 − 1 = 0.897). (See Eq. 6a below.) This expectation is even more unrealistic.

If the current SOE is unprofitable and thus is generating zero financial flows to the local government, a JV acquisition would not require an unrealistic expectation of profitability improvement. (This is shown in Eq. 7 below.) This reasoning supports a plausible hypothesis that local governments are selling off only the loss-making and insolvent SOEs to foreigners, not the profit-making SOEs. Because the baseline scenario is zero tax and dividend benefits to the local governments from the SOEs, the expected required efficiency improvement would be less. This is, of course, the essence of a JV acquisition.

Of course, the above is a stylized and heuristic thought experiment and its purpose is only to highlight the importance of an ex ante belief about firm performance rather than to document the true belief of local officials. Many parameters need to be adjusted depending on what assumptions are used in the calculation. For example, not all income tax revenue accrues to the local government, and under the current tax-sharing arrangements between the central and local governments, a portion of the income tax will go to the central coffers. But this arrangement would increase the ex ante efficiency expectation of FIEs because more dividend income would be needed to offset the income tax revenue not going to the local government.

STYLIZED EXAMPLES

The financial flows (FF) to a local government consist of two sources: taxes (T) and dividends (D). Taxes depend on the tax rate (TR) and the size of the

---

[44] There is considerable evidence that local governments are trying to grant beneficial tax treatments to foreign firms. For example, the 15 percent income tax rate is supposed to apply only to high-tech manufacturing FIEs, but a JV is classified as high-tech because of the computer sales it generates, even though it does not have any high-tech in its manufacturing capabilities. Dunkin' Donuts in Beijing apparently is qualified as a "manufacturing" operation so that it can qualify for the lower tax rate (Rosen 1999a).

pretax profits (*PTP*) and dividends depend on the equity share (*ES*) of the local government in the firm and the size of the after-tax profits (*ATP*). The following formula calculates the *FF*:

$$FF = T + D = PTP \times TR + ATP \times ES \tag{1}$$

ATP, in turn, can be expressed as:

$$ATP = PTP - (PTP \times TR) = (1 - TR) \times PTP \tag{2}$$

Substituting (2) into (1), we get:

$$FF = PTP \times TR + [(1 - TR) \times PTP] \times ES \tag{3}$$

Through some simple manipulations, we get:

$$PTP = \frac{FF}{TR + ES - (TR \times ES)} \tag{4}$$

For an SOE, the local government in effect claims all the *PTP*, and thus the *FF* is identical to the *PTP*. The local government claims 55 percent of the *PTP* as *T* and 100 percent of the *ATP*, that is, 100 percent of Equation 2, as *D*. Suppose the *FF* is RMB 100, then the *PTP* would have to be RMB 100 as well. This can be derived from the following calculation:

$$PTP = \frac{FF}{0.55 + 1 - (0.55 \times 1)} = FF \tag{5}$$

$$\text{If the } FF \text{ is RMB } 100 : PTP = \frac{RMB\ 100}{0.55 + 1 - (0.55 \times 1)} = RMB\ 100 \tag{5a}$$

Now consider the case of a JV acquisition. In a JV acquisition, the local government does not receive any cash for its contribution of the SOE assets, but instead receives an equity stake in the newly created JV. The JV is taxed at 33 percent instead of 55 percent, which is the prevailing tax rate among SOEs. In most cases, the local government is the minority shareholder of the newly created JV and its *ES* is less than 50 percent. If the existing SOE is profitable, say, generating RMB 100 in *FF* to the local government, the local government must expect the *FF* from the JV to exceed RMB 100 in order for it to agree to a JV acquisition. Say the local government expects the *FF* from the newly created JV to be RMB 101, then the expected *PTP* from the newly created JV is given by the following equation:

$$PTP = \frac{RMB\ 101}{0.33 + 0.49 - 0.33 \times 0.49} = RMB\ 153.4 \tag{6}$$

The expected *PTP* is dramatically higher than the current *PTP* from the SOE. To be sure, Equation 6 is an example of an extreme JV acquisition, that is, it assumes that the current SOE has transferred all of its revenue-generating assets to the newly created JV. This is not far from being the case. As the example of Suzhou Peacock shows, even the office furniture was contributed to the newly created JV. There are other simplifying assumptions. For example, we ignore complications arising from the time value of money by assuming that the JV will start making money immediately. An important assumption is that the local governments receive no cash in the conversion from an SOE into a JV. This is the essence of a JV acquisition.

As a basic rule, the lower the *TR* is on a JV and the lower the equity stake held by the local government in the JV, the higher the expected *PTP* is from a newly created JV. Suppose the *TR* prevailing among JVs is 15 percent and the *ES* in a newly created JV is 45 percent. (In 1995, 45 percent was the average Chinese equity share in manufacturing FIEs, as shown in Table 1.4 in Chapter 1.) Under this set of conditions, if the expected *FF* is RMB 101, the expected *PTP* will be:

$$PTP = \frac{101}{0.15 + 0.45 - 0.15 \times 0.45} = \text{RMB } 189.7 \qquad (6a)$$

Equations 5a, 6, and 6a show, rather dramatically, the required improvement in operating efficiency for the JV acquisition to be worthwhile to the local government. If the current SOE generates RMB 100 to the local government, to receive a 1 percent increase in financial flows to the local government, the pretax profit has to increase by 53.4 percent or 89.7 percent (depending on the tax rate and equity shares). This is clearly an unrealistic expectation, and it in turn suggests that our assumption that the current SOE generates RMB 100 in financial flows is unrealistic. A more realistic assumption is that the current SOE generates no financial flows to the local government, that is, the SOE is insolvent. Assuming the SOE to be insolvent, then the size of the expected *PTP* will be much smaller. For example, suppose the current SOE generates zero *PTP* and the local government expects the *FF* from the JV to generate RMB 10. Then the expected *PTP* will be:

$$PTP = \frac{10}{0.33 + 0.49 - 0.33 \times 0.49} = \text{RMB } 15.2 \qquad (7)$$

This is clearly a more realistic profit expectation of the newly created JV. Two inferences can be drawn from our stylized examples. First, as indicated before, JV acquisitions occur only during an insolvency situation. It is not surprising that the large-scale JV acquisitions in the mid-1990s coincided with the rising bankruptcies in the state sector, and these two developments were closely related. Second, the claim that many JVs were created for technological motivations needs to be evaluated carefully. It is certain that in the case of JV acquisitions, technological motivations were less relevant. The purpose of this type of JV, first and foremost, was to transfer operating assets from inefficient management to efficient management. Foreigners could provide efficient management, but had they been allowed, indigenous private entrepreneurs could have done so as well.

6

Economic Fragmentation and Foreign Direct Investment

In 1993, Li Lanqing, then China's vice premier of the State Council, recounted a visit he paid to a truck factory in Chongqing, Sichuan province:[1]

> What is really interesting is my visit to a factory in Chongqing, producing a certain "Liberation" truck. ["Liberation" is a popular truck model in China.] But the name of the truck was not Liberation; it was, instead, "Forever Forward." I commented to the manager that you have a good name, indicating your willingness to march forward bravely. He [the manager] replied that in fact the name literally meant what it said. The truck did not have a reverse gear; it could only move forward.

This observation is a powerful statement about the state of the Chinese automotive industry in the 1990s. As pointed out in Chapter 3, in 1998, there were 115 motor vehicle assembly firms in China. The average output volume was only 14,165 units. While in other countries, automotive industries are clustered together geographically, China displays a highly dispersed pattern. In 1995, there were motor vehicle assembly plants in all but two provinces, Tibet and Qinghai, two extremely poor and rural high-altitude provinces. The Chinese government had long recognized this severe fragmentation and launched several major administrative initiatives to consolidate the industry, in the 1980s and 1990s. So far, the efforts have not been successful. One of the principal reasons is the fact that China has had historically high tariffs on automobile imports – in the range of 200 to 300 percent in the 1980s and 100 to 200 percent in the early to mid-1990s. The high profit margins induced local governments to invest heavily in local assembly facilities and to restrict trade with

---

[1] The speech was printed in Beijing Haitehua Machinery and Electric Technology Development Corporation (1994).

other provinces. Local governments derived substantial financial benefits from owning and taxing these local production facilities.[2]

The purpose of this chapter is not to delve into the details of the fragmentation of China's automotive industry but to suggest that China's FDI patterns, to some extent, both reflect and are influenced by China's economic fragmentation. A simplistic connection is that the geographic dispersion of FDI documented in Chapter 1 is a mirror image of the geographic dispersion of China's industrial facilities. There is some truth to this statement, but the connection goes beyond a mere geographic matching between the location of Chinese industrial facilities and the investment locations chosen by foreign firms. As I show below in the chapter, powerful local firms often demand that foreign firms invest within their jurisdictions as a condition to purchasing the products produced in a JV. Other linkages between economic fragmentation and FDI patterns are illustrated below as well.

I begin this chapter by describing a systematic and methodical effort by the largest automotive firm in China, Shanghai Automotive Industrial Corporation (SAIC), to create a supply base of automotive components in Shanghai. Its strategy was to build new facilities rather than to extend ownership controls over existing facilities located in other provinces. I then present the case of First Automotive Works (FAW), the oldest and the second largest automotive firm in the country, to illustrate the institutional barriers for a firm located in one province to acquire facilities in other provinces. The third section spells out a number of mechanisms whereby economic fragmentation has contributed to FDI patterns and presents some statistical evidence from the machinery industry to illustrate these linkages.

A CASE STUDY OF ECONOMIC FRAGMENTATION: SAIC

For many years in the 1980s and 1990s, local governments in China pursued a strong version of what can be called a "regional import substitution strategy." They protected their own industries by erecting high barriers against goods from other provinces, and they prevented firms they controlled from investing in other regions. The most immediate effect was the emergence of a "repetitive and duplicative" economic structure. As a result, regions do not specialize along the lines of their comparative advantages. Instead, they all push strongly into similar industries and product groups, resulting in a convergence of industrial production across different regions. Such convergence is most prominent

---

[2] I have dealt with this issue extensively elsewhere. See Huang (2002a).

in the manufacturing industries. Young (2000b) presents evidence that while provincial output shares in the manufacturing and construction industries varied between 34 percent and 77 percent in 1978, by 1995 the range of variation had declined to between 36 percent and 57 percent.

The effect of the regional import substitution strategies is probably most damaging in the automotive industry, an industry that is characterized by significant scale economies. Chapter 3 shows that this industry in China had one of the most fragmented structures in the world. Here, we take a look at an effort by one company, SAIC, to build up a local supply base and to replace existing component suppliers located in other provinces. We also look at the attempts by another company, FAW, to integrate its production across regions, as an illustration both of the extent of asset fragmentation and the institutional impediments to asset integration in China.

Rise of SAIC

Measured by sales, SAIC is the largest automotive producer in China.[3] In 1997, SAIC generated RMB 40.4 billion in revenue, while FAW, the second largest, generated RMB 34.1 billion. SAIC is smaller than FAW in terms of assets. SAIC had more than RMB 36 billion in assets, compared with RMB 59.8 billion at FAW. (In a partially reformed planned economy, sales figures are probably a better measure of the size of a firm than asset figures. The product market is more competitive than the asset market.) SAIC's star product, the Santana, accounted for half of the passenger cars sold in China during much of the 1990s. In 1998, SAIC launched a Buick manufacturing operation via a $1.5 billion JV with General Motors, which promised to put SAIC on the world's technological frontier in automotive manufacturing. For years, the Ministry of Foreign Trade and Economic Cooperation consistently ranked SAIC's flagship affiliate, Shanghai Volkswagen (SVW), as number one among the top 500 FIEs in China on the basis of annual sales (Sun 1996).

But as recently as 1990, SAIC was but one of several automotive firms trying to enter into China's fast-growing market for passenger cars. In the north, it faced competition from BAIC, whose flagship affiliate, Beijing Jeep Corporation, produced a sport utility vehicle, the Cherokee-based BJ2021. Beijing Jeep

---

[3] The sustained effort by SAIC to develop in-house capabilities in components production has been documented by a number of researchers. A thorough and careful study by Eric Thun shows a high level of political and policy commitment on the part of the Shanghai municipal government to transform the automotive industry into a pillar industry in the city. This section of the chapter draws from his work, as well as from other sources cited in the text. See Thun (1999).

Corporation was a JV between BAIC and Chrysler. In the south, SAIC faced competition from Guangzhou Peugeot, which manufactured a mid-sized sedan. SAIC was also behind in product quality. In a 1988 comprehensive quality inspection, its SH760A model received a passing score of only 84 (out of 100). The model was rated particularly low in its reliability category, scoring 14 out of 20 points. In comparison, Beijing Jeep Corporation received a score of 90, as did Guangzhou Automotive Works (the Chinese shareholder of Guangzhou Peugeot).[4] The quality of a vehicle can be directly measured by its failure rate. The standard measure used in the industry is the MTBF (miles traveled between failures). For the SH760A, the MTBF was 1,250 km; for Beijing Jeep Corporation models, it was 2,500 km.[5] By 1996, however, SAIC had surpassed its rivals. Its Santana subsidiary, Shanghai Volkswagen, generated sales revenue more than three times that of Beijing Jeep Corporation and Guangzhou Peugeot combined.

We focus on a Shanghai-Beijing comparison here. (By the late 1990s, Peugeot had decided to exit the Chinese market altogether.) Table 6.1 summarizes the sharply divergent developments at SAIC and BAIC during the course of the 1990s. As of 1990, the two firms were roughly comparable in size and performance. BAIC was larger in sales but a bit smaller in assets. (Assets here only refer to current assets and net fixed assets.) BAIC's gross margin was lower, at 7.1 percent, as compared with 9.6 percent for SAIC, but this difference is by no means large. In fact, BAIC seemed to possess some modest advantages in the composition of its work force. As measured by the proportion of technicians in the work force, the ratio for BAIC was 25.9 percent, whereas for SAIC, it was 14.7 percent. By 1997, the two firms had grown apart. SAIC was then dominant over BAIC in every conceivable dimension. In 1997, its sales revenue was 4.5 times that of BAIC, and its assets, 3.1 times. SAIC's share of technical personnel in the work force had grown, whereas the share for BAIC had shrunk. The profitability difference between the two firms also diverged significantly. SAIC was able to increase its gross margins further from its already healthy starting position in 1990 of 9.6 to 13.7 percent, while during the same period, BAIC went into the red.

---

[4] Guangzhou Automotive Works was later renamed Guangzhou Automotive Industry Corporation.
[5] The Guangzhou vehicle had the same MTBF as the SH760A, but it was considerably better in another quality dimension: the mileage traveled before the first failure. For the Guangzhou car, it was 1,469.5 km; for the Shanghai car, it was only 386.5 km. To illustrate how shoddy the Shanghai car was, 386.5 kilometers, or 242 miles, is roughly the distance between Boston and New York City. Thus, a brand new car manufactured by SAIC in 1988 would experience its first failure by making a one-way trip from Boston to New York. The data from the 1988 comprehensive quality inspection are given in Ministry of Machinery Industry (1991).

Table 6.1 *A Tale of Two Firms: SAIC and BAIC, 1990
and 1997*

	SAIC	BAIC
Size		
Sales revenue (RMB billion)		
1990	3.61	4.12
1997	40.4	8.87
Assets (RMB billion)[a]		
1990	2.05	1.43
1997	26.6	8.53
Financial performance		
Gross margins (%)[b]		
1990	9.6	7.1
1997	13.7	−2.2
Technological intensity		
Technicians as shares of work force (%)		
1990	14.7	25.9
1997	16.0	11.3

[a] Assets refer to net fixed assets plus current assets.
[b] Gross margins are given by pretax profits divided by sales revenues.
Sources: Ministry of Machinery Industry (1991, 1998).

Creating a Supply Base in Shanghai

Two developments accompanied the rise of SAIC to a leadership position in the industry. First, it relied heavily on the financing and technological capabilities of the MNCs. Second, since the late 1980s, it pursued an aggressive strategy of creating a components supply base in Shanghai by engaging in an expensive and systematic backward integration. The next section of this chapter links these two developments by arguing that the strategy of creating a supply base in Shanghai deepened SAIC's dependency on FDI. For now, let me describe the effort by SAIC to create a supply base in Shanghai.

SAIC's strategy to create a supply base, mainly to supply automotive components to its flagship affiliate, SVW, was extremely successful. (Success here is defined in terms of not costs but the existence of a supply base that previously did not exist.) In 1990, Shanghai was not a center of automotive components manufacturing. Its automotive output value was only 7 percent of the national total, as compared with 11 percent in Beijing and 9 percent in Sichuan (a traditional components manufacturing base because of the presence of many military plants). Measured in sales terms, Shanghai also lagged behind Beijing. It accounted for 8 percent of the sales revenue from automotive components, as compared with 12 percent in Beijing. Yet by 1996, their roles had reversed. Shanghai accounted for 20 percent of the output value in automotive components manufacturing, 14 percent of net fixed assets, and 22 percent of sales revenue. Beijing's shares declined to 4.3 percent in output value, 5.4 percent in net fixed assets, and 4.7 percent in sales revenue.

The rise in Shanghai's importance in components manufacturing resulted from SAIC's deliberate sourcing strategy. SAIC increasingly produced in-house or in Shanghai what it had previously sourced from outside. By value, in 1990, some 65 percent of the Santana components that were produced in China were sourced from outside Shanghai. By 1998, this share was to decline to 10 percent. By 1997, Santana's domestic content rate reached 92.7 percent,[6] and in 1998, 80 percent of Santana components were produced within SAIC. This means that basically the entire Santana was made in Shanghai. In 1997, the supply network for SVW consisted of 248 firms, of which forty were affiliate firms under SAIC and 158 were located in Shanghai. Although fewer in number, these forty SAIC affiliates supplied the majority of the components by value, suggesting that they were capturing the high-end spectrum of the components market (Thun 1999). This pattern of "regional sourcing" contrasts with other vehicle producers in China. Beijing Jeep Corporation, for example, sourced 30 percent of its components locally. For Guangzhou Peugeot, it was about 20 percent.

Replacing Imports from "Foreign" Provinces. SAIC's regionalization drive was methodical and well organized. For SAIC, regionalization entailed a simple objective: to replace imports not only from foreign countries but also from *foreign provinces* within China. Thus, a product from France was treated exactly the same as a product from Changchun in Jilin province, and the objective was to replace it with a similar product from Shanghai. Cost was not an issue; what mattered was the physical availability in Shanghai. In 1987, SAIC, with full backing of the Shanghai municipal government, began a concerted effort to create supply capabilities in the city.[7]

The extraordinarily high margins of the Santana sustained such an effort. In the late 1980s, the production cost was RMB 85,000 per unit, the factory gate price was RMB 104,000, and the retail price was RMB 174,000. All the gains from the huge retail markup went to SAIC, not Volkswagen. By the original JV contract, SAIC had exclusive marketing rights over the Santana.

---

[6] Interview with Tang Jianwei, vice director of Shanghai Clutch Factory and general manager of Shanghai TRW Automotive Safety Systems Co., Ltd., October 12, 1998.

[7] Much of this localization drive by the Shanghai government is described in Thun (1999).

The difference between the factory gate and retail prices was accounted for by a purchase fee, localization tax, and special consumption tax (Zheng 1994, p. 64). The "localization tax," imposed in 1988, amounted to 16 percent of Santana's retail price at the time. These massive funds were then plowed back as investments in Shanghai's supply sector. Between 1988 and 1994, Shanghai collected over RMB 5 billion through this tax. Apart from the provision of enormous financial resources, the Shanghai government also acted to boost the demand for the Santana. It forbade taxi companies in Shanghai from buying cars made elsewhere to staff their fleet.

This attempt at backward integration disrupted the existing supplier relationships that SAIC had developed since the mid-1980s. Because the components industry in Shanghai was not developed, initially SAIC had no choice but to turn to existing components producers located in other provinces in order to economize on precious foreign exchange expenditures. Supposedly, SAIC was to create a "China brand, not a Shanghai brand." To that end, in 1987 SAIC signed long-term contracts to source components from thirteen firms based in Guizhou province in southwest China. Guizhou province, although not an industrial powerhouse, had built up a large aeronautical industry in the 1960s and 1970s as part of Mao's "third front" program to move military-industrial production assets inland in order to shield them from a possible Soviet attack. Supplying components to SAIC provided an opportunity for Guizhou to convert its military production assets into civilian production assets.

In the 1990s, however, SAIC began to shift its components sourcing away from firms based in Guizhou province, severing its ties with supplier firms there. This is what happened to Guizhou Honghu Machinery in 1995. Guizhou Honghu had a contract to supply muffler systems to SAIC.[8] In 1992, Guizhou Honghu was the largest producer of muffler systems in China, with an annual output volume of 131,140 units. Guizhou Honghu solidified its market leadership over the next two years. By 1994, its output volume increased to 225,000 units. During this period the firm also added capacity. The number of employees increased modestly, from 2,870 to 2,890; fixed assets grew from RMB 47.7 million to RMB 65.6 million. In constant prices, output value grew by 68 percent during the 1992–94 period. But in 1995, output volume fell suddenly and precipitously, to 57,778 units, a reduction of almost 75 percent from the 1994 level.

What happened was that SAIC terminated its contract with Guizhou Honghu and turned to one of its own subsidiaries to source muffler systems. The

[8] All the statistics cited in this following section are reported in Ministry of Machinery Industry (1993, 1996, 1997b) and State Bureau of Machinery Industry (1998).

Shanghai muffler producer increased its output volume from 175,000 in 1995 to 280,000 in 1996. The financial impact was immediate and dramatic. In 1995, returns on assets were 2 percent for the Shanghai firm; in 1996, they increased to 16 percent. Guizhou Honghu's output value, in constant prices, plummeted by 28 percent in 1995 from the year before. The firm, an SOE, cut its work force drastically, from 2,890 to 1,276 employees. In 1996, the firm did somewhat better, as it apparently found other customers for its products. It won contracts to supply to FAW-Volkswagen and Nanjing-Iveco for their Jetta and Iveco series respectively. Its work force recovered to 2,829, but its financial performance continued to suffer. Output value increased by 23 percent in 1996, but it plunged in 1997, by 24 percent, reflecting the high volatility of this particular market segment without a stable source of demand for its products from the largest car manufacturer in China.

SAIC could not have replaced existing suppliers so systematically or on such a large scale without a high level of political support from the Shanghai municipal government. From the very beginning, the mayor's office set up a small "leading group" mandated specifically to coordinate and supervise SAIC's regionalization strategy. Shanghai's mayor, who was to become China's future president, Jiang Zemin, assured the small leading group of his full support. "When you have problems," he reportedly said, "come find me. We must maintain a hot line between us." The Shanghai municipal government and the management of SAIC had a close and revolving-door relationship. The career trajectory of a former president of SAIC, Chen Xianglin, is indicative. Chen headed SAIC from 1983 to 1986 and then became the director of the Shanghai Planning Commission, where he served until 1993. He thereafter moved on to be the vice party secretary of the Shanghai Communist Party Committee in 1993 and 1994. In 1995, Chen resumed the presidency of SAIC, while his predecessor, Lu Jian, took up a high-level position on the Shanghai Municipal Economic Commission.

Internalization Motivations. Economists explain the strong integration motivations of SOEs as a function of supply uncertainties in a centrally planned economy. Central planning often fails to allocate goods consistent with the firms' needs. Either the wrong goods are assigned or the required goods are simply not supplied. This supply uncertainty gives rise to a strong incentive to engage in backward integration, that is, investing in plants and facilities to produce inputs for final goods production.[9] But China was no longer a traditional centrally planned economy by the mid-1990s. In the case of SAIC, the calculus

[9] For works along this line, see Bauer (1978) and Harrison (1985).

was not about supply uncertainty, since SAIC bought directly from its suppliers and did not depend on poorly informed bureaucratic decisions. SAIC's officials often invoked the very stringent quality and technical standards imposed by Volkswagen as a rationale for integrating operations backward. Indeed, SAIC faced a daunting challenge to obtain quality components.[10] But, as the account of Guizhou Honghu makes clear, SAIC's regionalization drive in fact replaced existing suppliers that had already successfully met the high-quality standards of SVW. For a firm to become a supplier to SVW, it had to pass many stringent quality tests administered by engineers in Germany. In fact, German engineers participated in selecting the suppliers from Guizhou province, and they were reported to have had a very high opinion of the quality of the assets and the capabilities of the Chinese engineers working in the defense industry there (Liu 1999). Thus, product quality alone is not sufficient to explain SAIC's backward integration.

For the Shanghai government, localization of components production boosted employment locally. The objective here was explicitly political, and SAIC received pressure from the Shanghai government to switch suppliers, as confirmed in an interview with an SAIC manager.[11] But there may have been economic motivations as well. We offer three hypotheses to explain SAIC's strong backward integration drive. First, many regional governments were targeting the automotive industry for development, and provinces with a comparative advantage in components production were motivated to integrate forward into high-margin assembly operations. SAIC might have calculated very rationally that its dependency on suppliers located in other provinces could hurt its economic interests in the long run should supplier provinces divert components to their own assembly operations. This is precisely what was happening in Guizhou province. Throughout the 1990s, Guizhou province contemplated entering into production of a mini-car series, called the "Yunque." In 1994,

---

[10] Wang Rongjun, the managing director of SVW, described the challenge facing the firm in the mid-1980s:

> The technical standards of Chinese automobile component suppliers in 1986 were nearly 30 years behind component manufacturers of Europe, Japan, and the United States. For SVW, measures of technical excellence were in part defined by standards dictated by its European parent, Volkswagen AG. Furthermore, Chinese automotive suppliers in my time manufactured parts for trucks, not cars. We needed a fundamental shift, not only in parts design (as cars are a little different from trucks) but also in the technology. In the beginning there wasn't a single local parts supplier who could produce a part we could assemble into the Santana. (Upton and Long 1996)

[11] Interview with Tang Jianwei, vice director of Shanghai Clutch Factory and general manager of Shanghai TRW Automotive Safety Systems Co., Ltd., October 12, 1998.

some 1,600 Yunque cars were produced.[12] It may have been a rational decision for SAIC to move its supplier relationship away from Guizhou.

Second, in an industry dominated by inefficient SOEs, product quality was generally poor. Firms capable of producing high-quality products were highly valued and could exert an enormous leverage over their customers. For example, they could ask for a large price increase, knowing that the customers would have difficulties finding other suppliers. Thus, a quality components supplier could threaten its customers in the same way that General Motors could threaten Fisher Body after Fisher Body constructed a captive body plant in the vicinity of General Motors. The ability to produce quality products, in an economy notorious for scant attention to quality management and improvement, became a source of firm-specific advantage and bargaining power. Thus, in this case, SAIC might have cut its supplier ties with Guizhou Honghu not because Guizhou Honghu was bad in product quality but because it was good. It did not want to be held hostage to Guizhou Honghu.

Third, should components be diverted elsewhere, SAIC would have lost more than just prompt delivery of quality components. It would have lost those benefits associated with its investments in the quality of suppliers with whom SAIC maintained a long-term contractual relationship. The reason again has to do with the generalized low product quality in China's automotive industry. To cultivate Chinese supplier firms to meet technological and quality requirements acceptable to SVW – and ultimately to Volkswagen – required a massive transfer of money, time, and knowledge from SVW to its suppliers. SAIC organized many technical training programs taught by retired engineers from Germany. It provided technical assistance and introduced foreign firms to its suppliers in order to match the quality of the supplier firms to the more advanced manufacturing processes at SVW. To raise the quality of the locally produced components, Volkswagen transferred an entire testing lab from Germany to Shanghai, and Volkswagen engineers worked closely with supply firms to tackle quality problems.[13]

---

[12] Data for the 1994 production of the Yunque are from Ministry of Machinery Industry (1996). However, the Yunque, which means "skylark" in Chinese, never took off. In 1998, its output volume remained low, at 1,064 units, and the Guizhou firm was losing money. See Ministry of Machinery Industry (1999).

[13] These efforts paid off. Over time, the quality of Shanghai supply firms did rise as a result, as indicated by the growing number of products that were assigned high grades in SVW's internal quality audits. Within SAIC, supply firms are assigned grades from A to C, A being the top grade. In 1990, only one supplier was assigned an A; in 1997, twenty-seven firms were so designated. The number of B designees increased from 30 in 1990 to 203 in 1997. See Thun (1999).

All of these represent significant spillover benefits from SVW to its suppliers. Should Guizhou Honghu decide to supply to a different assembly firm, SAIC would have lost not just mufflers from Guizhou Honghu but all the intangible investments it had made there. It made perfect sense for SAIC to integrate backward to incorporate components production into assembly operations in order to capture the spillover benefits from assembly operations to components production.[14] Pervasive low product quality, due in part to the dominance of SOEs in this industry, created a strong motivation for integration.

A CASE STUDY OF AN ACQUISITION STRATEGY: FIRST AUTOMOTIVE WORKS

The potential for a hold-up problem involved in a supplier relationship across different political jurisdictions may have motivated SAIC to resort to backward integration. But why did SAIC have to build up a supply base from scratch to fully capture the benefits from its financial and nonfinancial investments in the supplier firms? Why, for example, could it not have simply acquired the supplier firms with which it had an existing contractual relationship? An acquisition might have been less costly considering the extent of overcapacity in this industry and considering the significant quality investments it already had made in its existing suppliers. An acquisition could also have allowed SAIC to recoup its nonfinancial investments in its suppliers.

During much of the 1990s, the Chinese economy suffered from a chronic overcapacity, especially in its manufacturing industries. According to a Chinese researcher who analyzed data from the 1995 *Third Industrial Census*, of ninety-four industrial products, thirty-five products, or 36 percent, had a capacity utilization rate at or below 50 percent (Zhao 1997). The automotive industry, the focus of the analysis in this chapter, had one of the most severe overcapacity problems in the country. The capacity utilization rate for truck production in 1995 was 36 percent; bus production, 29.8 percent; and passenger cars, 64.9 percent.[15] The insatiable investment appetite for new equipment and machinery and massive pile-up of excess capacity are an unusual combination. Some MNCs in the 1990s resorted to asset acquisitions – whether direct or via JVs – as an entry strategy. They were doing exactly the right thing, considering the extent of excess capacity in the Chinese economy. What is puzzling is why

[14] At SAIC, most of the technical training was performed in-house. It established the Automobile Industry Training Center, which trained supply managers and technicians from SAIC affiliates. It also rotated managers among different subsidiaries in order to diffuse knowledge and expertise throughout the SAIC system.

[15] Data are from Office of Third Industrial Census (1997).

Chinese firms favored building facilities from scratch when asset acquisitions might have been a cheaper option.

In the following paragraphs I first review those factors that impeded asset acquisitions in the Chinese economy. These factors are rooted in the state ownership of assets. All the successful acquisitions across provinces in the 1980s and during much of the 1990s were facilitated by interventions from the central government. This is one of the reasons why FAW, as a firm belonging to the central government, the subject matter in this section, was able to engage in an acquisition strategy to expand its production capacity.

Barriers to Acquisition in the Chinese Economy

Why the creation of a new facility is often favored over the acquisition of an existing facility requires an understanding of the institutional factors that hamper the viability of asset acquisitions across different jurisdictions. A remarkable fact about the Chinese economy is that assets change hands infrequently, even in situations where no genuine ownership changes are involved, as, for example, when an SOE is transferred from one bureaucratic agency to another. According to Shen Yifeng and He Yinqi (1998), the first merger and acquisition case took place in Baoding city of Hebei province in 1984. With direct intervention from the municipal government, a textile machinery factory took over a smaller, loss-making firm in the same city. In this instance, the acquiring firm took over the target firm in an administrative fashion, that is, the acquiring firm simply assumed ownership over all the assets, debt, and employees of the target firm at zero cost. Since the two firms belonged to the same government agency, no financial resources were needed to consummate this "transaction." In the 1980s, altogether 6,966 firms were taken over by outside firms, involving a transfer of assets in the amount of RMB 8.2 billion. However, most of these transactions involved firms located in the same jurisdiction. In reality, they were not real mergers and acquisitions since they did not entail a change of ownership. A better description is that they were an organizational process of consolidating different subsidiaries belonging to a single firm rather than a genuine asset transfer from one owner to another.

Again, as for much else in the Chinese economy, state ownership and control hamper asset transfers. The venue that would normally facilitate takeover activities across jurisdictions – China's two stock exchanges – is notably inefficient to serve such a purpose. The reason is the stringent requirement that the government and state-owned entities retain majority equity interests in listed firms and that their shares be nontradable. According to a detailed study of over 600 firms on the Shanghai Stock Exchange and the Shenzhen Stock Exchange in 1995, the three main groups of shareholders – the state, legal persons, and private individual investors – each controlled about 30 percent of outstanding shares. (Legal persons refer to institutional shareholders other than government agencies. They are typically SOEs themselves, although, in recent years, some are private institutional shareholders.) As long as the state and legal person shareholders together exercise controlling and nonalienable equity interests, the two stock exchanges cannot function as "markets for corporate control" (Xu and Wang 1997). The smaller "asset exchange centers" that emerged in the major cities in the 1990s in response to the rising losses of the SOEs have been more active. In 1993 alone, it was reported in the Chinese press that 2,900 firms were sold or merged at such venues, with a transaction value totaling some RMB 6 billion. Again, most of these transactions involved firms located within the same jurisdiction. Cross-jurisdictional mergers and acquisitions have been far fewer in number.

Other institutional factors also impede asset transfers. Political motivations, which led SAIC to create a supply base in Shanghai, could also cause some local governments to resist acquisition attempts by firms from outside. Regional SOEs often serve valuable noneconomic functions, which may attenuate the incentive to sell them, even in situations when financial considerations warrant a sale. For example, a regional firm may promote employment in the locale or it may be a power base for officials in the region regardless of whether or not it is making money. Bureaucrats pursue multiple objectives, and as long as retaining control over a firm serves one of their objectives, they may be reluctant to surrender control to an outsider. Negotiation costs are also high. Because SOEs are controlled by separate political entities, negotiating the sale of an SOE from one region to another is costly in terms of the necessary effort and amount of bureaucratic coordination required. For one thing, it is extremely difficult to negotiate an acquisition price. Theoretically, all SOEs have only one owner – the state – and because asset transfers are administrative affairs, there is no accounting framework that readily determines the financial basis of an acquisition. The benchmarks are simply not there to guide such transactions.

A more important reason for the high negotiation costs is that such deals require negotiations between two bureaucratic agencies. Direct communication between separate bureaucratic agencies is difficult because no ready channel to facilitate such communication exists. Information flows up and down through vertical channels, but not horizontally among equally ranked bureaucratic agencies. This is a hallmark of a politically centralized system designed to maximize the power and supervision of the central authority. In China, for example, agencies of equal rank are explicitly forbidden from issuing policy documents to one another. Provincial governments have the same rank and they cannot issue decrees to each other.[16] In part because of these formal restrictions on direct communications and in part because of other informal mechanisms, China specialists use phrases such as "fragmented authoritarianism" to describe the operations of the Chinese bureaucratic system.[17]

FAW as a Central Government Firm

Probably the best manifestation of institutional impediments to cross-jurisdictional acquisitions comes from a firm that has pursued an acquisition strategy most aggressively. This is First Automotive Works (FAW).[18] The way it has acquired numerous facilities currently under its organizational umbrella provides a fascinating account of both the process and the requirements of asset acquisitions in the Chinese economy. FAW came to be known as the "cradle of the automotive industry" in the post-1949 period.[19] It was founded in 1956 as one of the 156 large-scale industrial assistance projects by the Soviet Union in the 1950s. FAW relied completely on Soviet engineering expertise, design, and equipment. The first FAW product was the "Jiefang" (Liberation), a four-ton truck series designed by Soviet engineers. Of the entire production, 81 percent of the parts came from the Soviet Union. In 1958, FAW produced China's first passenger car, the "Red Flag," a luxury model based closely on the Daimler-Benz 200 sedan.[20] During the reform era, while SAIC was spending heavily to create a supplier base in Shanghai, FAW was acquiring facilities across the country, either as a market-entry strategy to venture into new product areas (such as light-duty trucks) or as a backward-integration strategy to acquire component-manufacturing capabilities (such as gears and engines).

What accounts for the ability of FAW to overcome the aforementioned institutional impediments to its acquisition strategy? The answer lies in the

---

[16] This aspect of bureaucratic operations in China is dealt with in Huang (2002b).

[17] See Lieberthal and Oksenberg (1988).

[18] Our analysis of FAW very much echoes an earlier study by William Byrd on another automotive firm in China, Dongfeng Motor. (I thank Professor Barry Naughton for kindly suggesting this reference.) The central government firm, Dongfeng Motor – also known as No. 2 Auto – was able to invest outside its home province of Hubei. Byrd describes its difficulties investing in and operating plants outside its own home province. See Byrd (1992).

[19] China's first automobile manufacturer, Minsheng Factory, was built as early as 1919, and its first cargo truck was assembled in 1931. In 1936, the Nationalist government established the China Automobile Production Company. The company received technical and production assistance from the German manufacturer Mercedes-Benz. But its volume remained low and the ensuing Sino-Japanese and civil wars disrupted the industry severely. The history of China's automotive industry is described in Harwit (1995).

[20] Shanghai Automotive Plant, the predecessor of SAIC, rolled out the second passenger car model, the "Phoenix," in the early 1960s.

institutional configuration of FAW itself. FAW is a central-government firm. The Ministry of Machinery Industry in Beijing appoints its management.[21] This means that Jilin province, where FAW is located, exerts relatively little influence over the operations of FAW. FAW's status as a centrally controlled firm also matters for its funding and tax base. Most of its funds come from the central government rather than from Jilin province. Conversely, most of its remittances go to the coffers of the central government rather than to those of the provincial government. In Chinese planning parlance, FAW is known as a separately listed firm in the central plan (*jihua danlie qiye*). The State Planning Commission of the central government directly allocates investment funds and some of its requisite inputs to the firm directly, as opposed to allocating them to the local governments first.[22] In other words, at least in principle, FAW is subject to the same planning authority and control of the central government as the Shanghai municipal government. Although during the reform era material allocations by the central government declined markedly, what turns out to be important for cross-jurisdictional acquisitions, however, is the organizational and coordination role of the central government.

In institutional terms, FAW and SAIC are two different types of firms, not in the nature of their ownership, as both are SOEs, but in the levels of government that exercise ownership rights. As pointed out previously, SAIC, as a municipal-level firm, is subject to the close supervisory authority of the Shanghai government. One indication of this difference between FAW and SAIC is the amount of state equity in the two firms. Traditionally, state equity is roughly proportional to the amount of equity interests held by the central government. In 1997, state equity interest amounted to 89 percent of FAW's equity capital, whereas it amounted to only 39 percent at SAIC.

This institutional difference means that an acquisition strategy is at least feasible for FAW (although still difficult, as shown below), but is inordinately costly for SAIC. When asked to comment on FAW's acquisition strategy, a manager at SAIC commented, "We are different from them. FAW is China's first auto plant and it is a national level firm. We are a regional army. We have different considerations."[23] FAW can rely on the central government to coordinate communications and negotiations with different regional governments. For SAIC, a "build" strategy is more feasible because all the coordination and organizational

---

[21] In 1998, the Ministry of Machinery Industry became the State Bureau of Machinery Industry.

[22] The State Planning Commission became the State Development and Planning Commission in 1998.

[23] Interview with Tang Jianwei, vice director of Shanghai Clutch Factory and general manager of Shanghai TRW Automotive Safety Systems Co., Ltd., October 12, 1998.

Table 6.2 *Comparison of FAW and SAIC, 1997*

	FAW (Subordinate to the Ministry of Machinery Industry)	SAIC (Subordinate to Shanghai city)
Assets (RMB billion)[a]	59.8	36.2
Sales (RMB billion)	34.1	40.4
Profits (RMB billion)	0.57	5.54
Employment (persons)	173,043	61,672
Vehicle output (units)	268,868	232,074
Number of affiliates[b]	20	38
Number of affiliates located outside home province	14	0

[a] Assets here include all the major items on a standard balance sheet, such as current assets, fixed assets, and ongoing construction projects. This is a broader definition of assets than the one given in Table 6.1.

[b] An affiliate is defined as a firm in which the parent company has a strong equity interest (usually above 50 percent).

Sources: Ministry of Machinery Industry (1998) and machinery industry database.

efforts associated with such a strategy take place within the municipal boundary of Shanghai. The difference in their strategies is indeed significant. This is apparent in the ratio of spending on new plant and equipment purchases to the capital stock of the two firms. Because FAW built up its fixed assets via acquisitions, it spent modestly on new plant and equipment purchases, as a percentage ratio to its fixed asset stock. In contrast, SAIC had a much higher ratio. Between 1990 and 1994, during a period in which both firms expanded rapidly, the ratio for FAW was 16 percent, whereas it was 39 percent for SAIC.[24]

Another indication is the geographic dispersion of the affiliates of the two firms. FAW is headquartered in Jilin province, but fourteen out of its twenty affiliates, that is, wholly owned subsidiaries or firms in which FAW has a significant equity stake, are located outside Jilin province. In contrast, even though SAIC had a greater number of affiliates – thirty-eight – not a single one was located outside Shanghai as of 1998. (SAIC apparently began to invest outside Shanghai in 1999.) To be sure, FAW is a larger firm in terms of assets, but the national scope of FAW's operations and the regional focus of SAIC are not solely a function of the size difference between the two firms. As shown in Table 6.2, FAW is larger in terms of assets and employment,

[24] The denominator used in these ratio calculations is the original book value of the fixed assets. To control for depreciation allowances, we can also use net fixed assets. The result is the same. New plants and equipment, as a share of net fixed asset stock, was 36 percent for FAW and 65 percent for SAIC. Data on SAIC and FAW are from Ministry of Machinery Industry (1996).

but it is considerably smaller than SAIC as measured by sales and profits. The two firms are comparable in terms of production volume. Another piece of corroborating evidence that size difference does not determine the geographic scope of the firms is the contrast between SAIC and China General Automotive Industry Corporation. The latter is a much smaller firm than SAIC. In 1997, it had RMB 9.5 billion in assets, or about one-fourth those of SAIC, and it generated sales revenue of RMB 6.5 billion, which was about one-sixth that of SAIC. Yet ten out of fourteen of China General Automotive Industry Corporation's affiliates were located outside the province where the headquarters of the firm was located.[25] The reason is that China General Automotive Industry Corporation, like FAW, is a central-government firm and thus it faces fewer constraints on investment activities outside its provincial headquarters.

FAW's Acquisitions of Light-Truck Facilities

As a central-government firm, the negotiation costs for FAW to acquire assets cross-jurisdictionally are more manageable because of the facilitating role of the central government. According to a survey, most of the "acquisition" deals by FAW were not financial transactions. Instead, the assets were simply administratively assigned to FAW at zero cost. In such deals, the coordinating role of the central government was critical. In one of its acquisition deals, a vice premier of the State Council personally intervened to make it happen. Still, more often than not, FAW had to rely on informal connections rather than mere interventions by the central government to facilitate its acquisition attempts. In two instances, former governors of Jilin province, who then were governors of the home provinces of the target firms at the time of the acquisitions, made the arrangements that facilitated the takeovers by FAW.[26]

China's administrative tax rules defined central-government firms as the tax base for the central government and local firms as the tax base for local governments. This tax system, which prevailed until 1994, created problems for FAW's acquisition efforts, as indicated by the acquisitions it made in light-truck production. Today, FAW is the second largest producer of light-duty trucks in China. Built as a predominantly medium-duty truck producer, FAW rose to the top in light-duty truck production mainly through a number of acquisitions it

---

[25] Data are reported in Ministry of Machinery Industry (1998).

[26] These two provinces were Yunnan and Hainan. The details of the acquisitions by FAW are provided in Unirule Economic Research Institute (1997) and Sheng (1999).

made since the mid-1980s. In 1986, FAW began its light-duty truck production not by a straightforward acquisition but by contractual alliances with two light-duty truck producers. These two alliances eventually evolved into full acquisitions by FAW in 1991.

This process is interesting in several aspects. First, both of the truck producers were so-called municipal enterprises, one under Jilin city – the namesake of the province in which the city is located – and the other under Changchun city. Because of the administrative tax rules, a full acquisition by FAW would have reduced the tax base of these two city governments. Thus, both cities opposed such a move. The contractual alliance was a compromise in order to preserve the original ownership ties between the city governments and the firms. Second, what is especially interesting about the institutional impediments in this instance is that FAW and the two truck producers were located in the same province, Jilin, and one even in the same city. Bureaucratic divisions are more powerful than the influence of geographic proximity.

Third, the contractual alliance was unwieldy and inefficient and was created purely to deal with an institutional artifact, in this case, the tax division rules, rather than being the result of rational business considerations. Because the assets of the two truck producers still belonged to their respective city governments, FAW could inject product lines, technicians, and managers into the firms but was unable to transfer production equipment and facilities from one firm to another. Thus, the larger gains from production integration and asset reorganization remained untapped, and production processes could not be optimized. FAW wanted the Jilin firm to assemble the one-ton trucks with chassis supplied by the Changchun firm, whereas the Changchun firm would produce two-ton trucks with the front body supplied by the Jilin firm. But FAW was prevented from integrating and transferring assets; instead, the two truck producers maintained their own duplicate facilities in chassis and front-body manufacturing equipment.

In the end, FAW took over these two truck producers in 1991 but under circumstances sharply different from those prevailing in 1986. Light-duty truck production had become congested and the two truck producers began to incur large losses. This changed the calculus of the two shareholding city governments. Selling off these two firms became a way to reduce their financial liabilities. Still, in one of the acquisitions FAW had to create a subsidiary in Jilin city that was designated as a municipal enterprise for the sole purpose of paying income taxes to the Jilin city government.[27]

---

[27] This account is given in Unirule Economic Research Institute (1997).

ECONOMIC FRAGMENTATION AND FDI

MNCs are not only multinational; in China they are first and foremost multiregional. Motorola, Schindler, Otis, Volkswagen, Ford, Nabisco, and others have all established operations across the country, and, increasingly, Western MNCs are creating holding company structures to coordinate their complex activities and interactions among subsidiaries or affiliates and to economize on shared overhead costs. These cross-regional investments or acquisitions are not limited to the *Fortune* 500 corporations. Much smaller MNCs have also actively acquired assets throughout the country. A prominent example is Hong Kong–based China Strategic Investment Ltd. (CSI).[28] Between 1992 and 1994, CSI, founded only in 1991 mainly in restaurant and real estate businesses and with sales revenue of $84 million in 1992, acquired 200 companies throughout China. Its JVs were located in more than nine provinces, and its China Tires Holdings, created by the acquisition of tire plants in five provinces, emerged to be the largest tire producer in China by1994. CSI was poised to become one of the largest industrial conglomerates in China until the central government intervened to put a brake on its acquisition bids in 1995.

Our question, as always, is, Why cannot Chinese companies do the same? We already provide one answer in Chapter 5: Because the government has refused to allow SOEs to be privatized, Chinese nonstate firms cannot acquire loss-making SOEs on a large scale, while MNCs can do so via a "JV acquisition" mechanism.[29] But this is not the whole answer because Chinese SOEs do not acquire other SOEs, either. SOE acquisitions by other SOEs clearly do not entail any ideological complications, and yet this type of acquisition has seldom occurred as well, especially acquisitions involving firms from different jurisdictions.

The answer to this question is already indicated in the two case studies presented in this chapter: The local political controls of assets create enormous difficulties for firms to venture outside their jurisdictions. A firm such as FAW could acquire assets, although with some difficulties, because of its ties to the central government. Most other firms cannot do so. Thus, a simple explanation for the CSI phenomenon is that Chinese domestic firms are politically and institutionally constrained from acquiring assets outside their jurisdictions. But, given the extent of substantial overcapacity in the Chinese economy, somebody has to do it, and that somebody, more often than not, turned out to be foreign firms.

---

[28] This account of CSI is based on Lee (1992), Lim (1994), and Liu, Shao, and Pan (1997).

[29] All of the acquisitions by CSI were JV acquisitions, that is, CSI contributed cash, while the target firms contributed themselves as equity stakes in the newly formed FIEs. The regional governments then owned these FIEs proportionate to the valuation of the contributed firms.

In this section, let me offer this and other hypotheses connecting economic fragmentation to FDI. All these hypotheses are based on the logic of the institutional foundation framework, which I have already applied to analyze a range of phenomena, including FDI in the garment industry and JV acquisitions. FDI induced by economic fragmentation is the third pillar of my framework.

Institutional Foundation Hypotheses

One straightforward effect of economic fragmentation is that Chinese firms, constrained to operating in smaller regional markets, are not competitive. In the automotive industry, although fragmentation clearly makes Chinese firms less efficient, as "Forever Forward" shows, there are multiple reasons why Chinese firms are not competitive. Even if China's automobile market were fully integrated, it was not clear whether the market size would be large enough to confer substantial "static efficiency" benefits on Chinese firms. With a fragmented market, Chinese firms are clearly not statically efficient. SOEs are another cause of the inefficiencies in this industry. The uncompetitiveness of Chinese firms, whatever the causes, would "induce" FDI when foreign firms believed that they could outcompete domestic competitors in a growing market. Although this hypothesis is fairly straightforward, we suggest it here as a plausible conjecture. It is difficult to directly test the hypothesis because of the multiple factors that can make Chinese firms uncompetitive and because of the lack of data. What is clear is that Chinese automotive firms perceive themselves as uncompetitive. In a study prepared by the Ministry of Machinery Industry, out of fifty-nine product groups, the ministry assigned forty-nine of them an infant industry status.[30]

The second hypothesis is that economic fragmentation requires more capital to develop China's automotive industry, and more capital requirements will confer advantages on foreign firms because they can bring in capital. There are two mechanisms whereby economic fragmentation is costly. One is that in an industry with high scale-economy requirements, fragmentation is costly. All else being equal, a fragmented industry structure incurs a higher average cost per unit of output as compared with a concentrated industry structure. Not only are production costs a falling function of production volume, investment costs also fall as the incremental output range grows.[31] Second, the kind of regional integration strategy that SAIC undertook basically means that China

---

[30] Based on Ministry of Machinery Industry (1994).

[31] A Chinese study shows that in the automotive industry investment costs for adding facilities fall as output capacity increases. For example, when output capacity is doubled from 100,000 units to 200,000 units, the investment costs increase not by 100 percent but by 40 percent. Wu Facheng (1997).

forgoes the economic gains from existing regional patterns of comparative advantages. Guizhou province had already developed a comparative advantage in automotive components, but SAIC intended to build up its own capacity by pursing a regional import substitution strategy. To reinvent the wheel in Shanghai required additional capital spending.

The third hypothesis is that economic fragmentation increases the bargaining power of foreign firms. Domestic firms are constrained in their investment and locational choices but foreign firms are not. This arrangement may benefit foreign firms. In theory, for any given fundable project, foreign firms are essentially competing with other foreign firms rather than competing with domestic firms as suppliers of capital. This dynamic plausibly explains why a small firm such as CSI was able to acquire and establish plants in multiple locations while SAIC was confined to operating in Shanghai. The final hypothesis is that an import substitution strategy at a regional level leads to a dispersion of industrial facilities, whether or not these facilities are built by Chinese or foreign firms. FDI dispersion, thus, can result from the kind of regional import substitution strategy SAIC engaged in.

Regional Import Substitution Strategy and FDI

Because it has engaged in a regional import substitution strategy most extensively, SAIC should have the strongest preference for FDI compared with firms that have not pursued such a decisive regional import substitution strategy. This is the second hypothesis linking fragmentation to FDI. Bargaining dynamics may also apply here. Because SAIC is not willing to cooperate with other Chinese automotive firms, its reliance on FDI will be higher. Indeed, compared with other regional automotive firms that are broadly similar to SAIC, the foreign ownership of FIEs within SAIC appears to be significantly high. I present some of the data here and consider a number of alternative hypotheses that might explain SAIC's heavy FDI dependency.

Added Resource Requirements and FDI. Strictly speaking, SAIC's strategy was designed not to create components supply capabilities under the umbrella of SAIC but to create a supply base *in Shanghai*. This is an important distinction. Theoretically, SAIC could have created components supply capabilities within the firm by acquiring other firms, but it did not do that. As of 1998, SAIC had not acquired a single facility outside of Shanghai.[32]

---

[32] Interview with Tang Jianwei, vice director of Shanghai Clutch Factory and general manager of Shanghai TRW Automotive Safety Systems Co., Ltd., October 12, 1998.

Let me take up the second hypothesis that more capital requirements associated with a regional import substitution strategy may lead to a greater FDI dependency. Regional integration implies forgoing a sourcing option based on existing patterns of comparative advantages of the Chinese provinces. This is quite costly, especially in an industry with scale economies. Building a completely new facility is more expensive than expanding an existing facility because a substantial portion of the new facility is "volume-invariant." One needs to complete an entire assembly line whether it assembles one vehicle or 10,000 vehicles per year. When SAIC decided to build a muffler production facility of its own despite the fact that Guizhou Honghu was already operating one on a substantial scale, more capital expenditures were required than if SAIC had continued to source from Guizhou Honghu and if SAIC had significantly increased the size of its orders. The added resource requirements had to be met.

For SAIC, one way was to mobilize domestic resources to invest aggressively in the development of a components sector. The costs were mainly borne by the Chinese consumers who were charged an exorbitant price for the Santana, a model that was already obsolete in Europe as of the late 1970s. As mentioned before, the Shanghai government levied a "localization tax" between 1988 and 1994 for the specific purpose of building the components sector in Shanghai, and SAIC, rather than Volkswagen, was the main beneficiary of the supernormal profits from the Santana. The ratio of retail to factory-gate prices for the Santana was 1.58, by far the highest among all the passenger vehicle producers in China.[33]

The other way to meet the added resource requirements was to actively solicit help from the MNCs. Herein is the connection between a regional import substitution strategy and FDI demand. A regional import substitution strategy creates a fund shortage that otherwise would not exist (or makes an existing fund shortage more severe than it otherwise would be). To make up for any shortfalls in funds, MNCs are courted and thus they become more valuable. An FDI demand of this sort is driven more by an institutional imperative and less by actual business needs to source price-competitive and quality components.

It is important to be specific about precisely why building a supply base in Shanghai would lead to a higher FDI demand. In our example about SAIC changing the sourcing of its muffler systems, neither Guizhou Honghu nor the replacement firm in Shanghai was an FIE, and thus no FDI was involved. However, our hypothesis does not require a direct linkage between replacing imports from foreign provinces and FDI. The reason is that money is both a fungible and finite resource. The amount of money that was spent to create a

---

[33] Price data are given in Ministry of Machinery Industry (1997a).

muffler firm in Shanghai could not be used to do other things. For example, the money could not be spent on investing in a project to produce a component that was not available anywhere else in China. For SAIC, it would be necessary to invest in production facilities to produce components for which there were no domestic substitutes because the central government required automotive firms to localize their component supplies. In essence, SAIC needed to replace imports from foreign provinces and from foreign countries at the same time. It thus had to raise additional capital. We can relate this reasoning to the measure we have been using as an indicator of FDI preferences, the foreign equity ratio of FIEs. The money SAIC spent on replacing its existing suppliers could not be used to finance SAIC's equity stakes in its JVs with MNCs. As a result, its equity stakes were smaller than if SAIC had not incurred the extra expenses to pursue a regional import substitution strategy.

Foreign Ownership Patterns of FIEs Within SAIC. We use foreign ownership of FIEs as a measure of China's FDI preference. The larger the foreign equity ratio is, the stronger Chinese FDI preferences are said to be. Although this measure is not perfect, short of alternative measures, it probably is the best proxy we can find. Here, we use the foreign equity ratio as an indicator of the extent of SAIC's demand for FDI. A logical inference from our analysis is that SAIC should exhibit a greater demand for FDI as compared with other automotive firms that pursue a less aggressive regional import substitution stance. Compared with those firms, SAIC should have ceded more corporate controls over its affiliates to MNCs. (Or to put it another way, SAIC might have ceded more future business opportunities to MNCs in those situations involving the establishment of new affiliates rather than the transfers of control over existing affiliates.)

Table 6.3 presents information on the various characteristics of FIE affiliates within four major automotive business groups: SAIC, BAIC, Tianjin Automotive Industry Corporation, and Guangzhou Automotive Industry Corporation. Until recently, these four groups were the dominant players in China's car production.[34] Tianjin Automotive Industry Corporation was a specialist in a mini car, the Charade (Xiali in Chinese), which was widely popular among households and smaller taxi companies. It also had a JV with Toyota for engine production, but the car assembly division was controlled by Tianjin Automotive Industry Corporation itself. Guangzhou Automotive Industry Corporation created a JV for car production in 1985, the same year SAIC created its JV. The JV,

---

[34] In the late 1990s, other car producers came on line, such as FAW's JV with Volkswagen to produce the Audi and Jetta series and a JV between Dongfeng Motor Corporation and Citröen to produce the Fukang series. All of the data cited in the text come from the sources for Table 6.3 as well as other sources as cited.

Table 6.3 *Four Automotive Business Groups Compared: Integration Strategy, Performance, and FIE Characteristics, Various Years*

Firms[a]	Automotive components[b] as shares of (%)			Various performance measures				Characteristics of the FIE affiliates within the four groups			
	Total output value		Investment in new fixed assets	Returns on assets[c] (%)		Localization ratios[d]	Output volume[e]	Number of FIEs established	Average size of equity capital per FIE ($ million)	Average foreign share of total equity capital (%)	
	1992	1997	1997	1992	1998	1996	1996	1983–97	1983–97	1983–97	1990s
SAIC	17.8	27.0	81.1	27.2	14.9	90.45	200,222	29	40.9	47.4	48.3
TAIC	14.3	30.5	63.7	29.8	1.43	93.29	88,000	25	20.6	53.3	53.1
BAIC	21.0	17.4	4.5	15.1	−2.99	77.38	26,051	17	23.9	44.8	46.2
GAIC	0.0[f]	5.6[f]	10.0[f]	10.4[f]	−3.64[f]	85.3	2,544	42	10.6	49.6 (47.1)[g]	49.2

[a] SAIC: Shanghai Automotive Industry Corporation; TAIC: Tianjin Automotive Industry Corporation; BAIC: Beijing Automotive Industry Corporation; GAIC: Guangzhou Automotive Industry Corporation.

[b] Components include engines, but not chassis.

[c] Returns on assets are given by pretax profits divided by the sum of net fixed assets and current assets. Pretax profits are used because tax rates often differ among firms.

[d] Localization ratios are measured in quantity rather than in value terms. The figures include passenger car vehicles only. The passenger cars being measured are: Santana (SAIC), Charade TJ7100 (TAIC), Cherokee BJ2021 (BAIC), and Peugeot (GAIC).

[e] Output volume refers to passenger cars only.

[f] Data on GAIC are not available. The data presented in the table refer to Guangzhou city.

[g] Figures in brackets do not include two wholly owned FIEs.

Sources: Information on FIEs is from Zhang (1998). Localization, output, and profitability data are from Ministry of Machinery Industry (1993, 1997a).

Guangzhou Peugeot Corporation, was with Peugeot of France, and at its height, in 1993, it churned out 16,765 mid-size cars. Plagued by a small volume and chronic losses, Peugeot withdrew from the JV in February 1997. (Honda took over the Peugeot facility in 1998 to assemble its Accord model.)

These four firms are comparable on a number of critical dimensions. All four were municipal SOEs under direct control of city governments. They were all primarily car and single-vehicle producers. Thus, comparing them, rather than multivehicle firms such as FAW and Dongfeng Motor Corporation, implicitly imposes a control on differences in technology, nature of market demand, and production processes. All four relied on MNCs for design, engineering expertise, and financial resources for their vehicle assembly operations (although, as shown later, the degree of their reliance differed). One important difference lies in the extent to which they pursued a regional import substitution strategy. SAIC carried out a methodical and systematic strategy to backward integrate into components production. Tianjin Automotive Industry Corporation adopted a similar strategy, albeit with less fanfare. In contrast, both BAIC and Guangzhou Automotive Industry Corporation did not actively promote components production.

The contrast in their integration strategies can be shown in a number of ways. Components production under SAIC and Tianjin Automotive Industry Corporation increased in importance between 1992 and 1997. As shown in Table 6.3, the share of components production doubled at Tianjin Automotive Industry Corporation, from 14.3 percent to 30.5 percent, whereas it increased more than 50 percent at SAIC (from 17.8 percent to 27 percent). The increase in components production was across the board, as measured by employment and net fixed assets (not shown in the table). By these measures, it is clear that BAIC and Guangzhou Automotive Industry Corporation did not stress the development of components production nearly as much as SAIC and Tianjin Automotive Industry Corporation. Components production in fact declined, from 21 percent in 1992 to 17.4 percent in 1997 at BAIC. At Guangzhou Automotive Industry Corporation, component production accounted for 5.6 percent of output value in 1997, up from 0 percent in 1992. Both SAIC and Tianjin Automotive Industry Corporation invested heavily in components production. In 1997, 81 percent of new fixed asset investments made by SAIC went to the components firms; at Tianjin Automotive Industry Corporation, the figure was 63.7 percent. In contrast, at BAIC, it was only 4.5 percent, and at Guangzhou Automotive Industry Corporation, 10 percent.

Table 6.3 gives the average foreign equity ratios in percentage terms. There is some, although not overwhelming, evidence that more substantial movement into components production is associated with greater foreign equity stakes. FIEs within Tianjin Automotive Industry Corporation by far have the highest foreign equity ratios, at 53.3 percent. FIEs at BAIC have the lowest ratio, at 44.8 percent. FIEs at Guangzhou Automotive Industry Corporation have the second highest ratio, at 49.6 percent, but this ratio is not substantially higher than that at SAIC, at 47.4 percent. In addition, the foreign equity ratio of Guangzhou Automotive Industry Corporation's FIEs is somewhat inflated by including two wholly owned FIEs. (Wholly owned FIEs are rare in this industry because of governmental restrictions. The fact that Guangzhou Automotive Industry Corporation had two of them must be attributed to the status of Guangdong province as a Special Economic Zone.) When these two wholly owned FIEs are dropped from the calculation, the foreign equity ratio is reduced to 47.1 percent. At this level, SAIC and Guangzhou Automotive Industry Corporation exhibit an identical extent of foreign ownership control.[35]

Alternative Considerations. Our institutional foundation hypothesis attributes the greater foreign controls to the more aggressive integration strategy pursued by SAIC and Tianjin Automotive Industry Corporation. Before we can firmly draw such a conclusion, alternative hypotheses must be considered. Neither of these alternative hypotheses, I argue, fully explains the foreign ownership patterns observed in the data. First, we must consider the role of the FDI regulatory environment in influencing the extent of foreign ownership controls among these four firms. Some regions are more liberal than others in their policies toward foreign equity controls. To the extent that FDI regulations play a role, it ought to reinforce our conclusion. By far, Guangdong is the most liberal province in terms of its FDI policies, and Shanghai is the most stringent. Yet, as shown above, the differences between these two provinces are not substantial. This is a startling result: Two provinces on the opposite end of the spectrum of FDI policy restrictions end up with roughly the same level of foreign equity holdings.

---

[35] The foreign equity data given in the text are not weighted by the size of the FIEs. It is possible, for example, that SAIC owned more of its larger FIEs than its smaller FIEs, while Beijing Automotive Industry Corporation had the opposite combination. If this were the case, then the simple arithmetic averages would be misleading. However, this was not the case. For 1998, we have paid-in capital data on a consolidated basis that show that Tianjin Automotive Industry Corporation and SAIC both had larger foreign equity holdings than Beijing Automotive Industry Corporation. (Data for Guangzhou Automotive Industry Corporation are not available.) For Tianjin Automotive Industry Corporation, the foreign equity holdings of its affiliates came to 39.8 percent; for SAIC, they amounted to 31.7 percent. But for Beijing Automotive Industry Corporation, the holdings were only 20.5 percent. Data are from State Bureau of Machinery Industry (1999).

MNCs seem to have been more active in Shanghai. Compared with Beijing, MNCs went to Shanghai earlier. Before 1990, only three JVs were established in Beijing, as compared with six in Shanghai. Even before the dramatic rise of FDI inflows into China, FIEs played a far more important role in Shanghai's automotive industry as sources of employment, output, and financing. In 1992, JVs accounted for 2.4 percent of industrial output value, 2.7 percent of employment, and 2.2 percent of net fixed assets in Beijing. But in Shanghai, the shares were much higher. FIEs accounted for 4.8 percent of industrial output value, 13.9 percent of employment, and 14.6 percent of net fixed assets.[36] The larger role of FDI in Shanghai's automotive sector was not the result of a greater receptivity to FDI during the 1980s. Foreign investors in Shanghai often complained about long delays in the approval process and complicated bureaucratic procedures, a perception, in the words of a study on this issue, that "resulted in an increasing distance between the speed of foreign capital utilization and the growth rate between Shanghai and its brother provinces" (Luo 1994). Nor was the larger role of FIEs in Shanghai's automotive industry a result of larger FDI inflows into Shanghai in the 1980s. In 1988, FDI inflows into Shanghai amounted to about 72 percent of FDI flows into Beijing. Shanghai was not a magnet for foreign investment until the central government granted the city Special Economic Zone status in 1990. By 1992, Shanghai quickly caught up with Beijing, and FDI inflows reached 226 percent of those to Beijing, a gap that grew to 256 percent by 1997.

The second hypothesis is that the foreign equity ratio is determined by the relative bargaining power between foreign and Chinese firms. Assuming that all Chinese firms face the same group of foreign firms, which thus controls for the bargaining power of the foreign firms, we can argue that the differences in foreign ownership are because of differences in the bargaining power *among the Chinese firms*. Chinese bargaining power can be a function of (1) the attractiveness of the Chinese firms as JV partners and (2) the profitability of the Chinese firms. On both counts, SAIC should command a huge advantage over the others, and yet the foreign ownership control of SAIC's FIEs is still substantial, possibly due to its greater need for FDI. SAIC was considered a far more desirable JV partner to MNCs than, for example, BAIC. The attractiveness of SAIC as a JV partner was confirmed by two Chinese managers within SAIC who were interviewed for this book. One manager revealed that SAIC always demanded that foreign firms be responsible for the placement of all the Chinese workers and that SAIC would walk away from the negotiation table if the number of workers the foreign firm asked to cut exceeded 10 percent of the labor

---

[36] Calculated from Ministry of Machinery Industry (1993).

force of the potential partner on the SAIC side.[37] Another manager, who headed Shanghai TRW, revealed that within SAIC most of the JVs' general managers were from the SAIC side, even though the equity split was typically 50–50.[38] Given this apparent hard edge, it is thus surprising that foreign ownership is still so high. The comment by the manager at Shanghai TRW is revealing. SAIC obviously viewed foreign managerial know-how as less important since it resisted foreign operating control. Instead, SAIC could have valued the capital contributions by MNCs very highly.

In contrast, BAIC was in a far weaker bargaining position versus the MNCs and over time it had to cede ownership controls to the MNCs. It initially held 69 percent of the equity stake in Beijing Jeep Corporation, but in 1990, it reduced its stake to 62 percent, and in 1994 to 58 percent. The same equity concessions occurred to the firm we encountered in Chapter 5. In 1997, when XYZ Automotive was negotiating to increase its equity stake, Zhu Xun, the manager of the Foreign Department of BAIC who had participated in the negotiations, commented that XYZ Automotive got whatever it wished. "We had no capability to increase investments," he said in an interview, "and if the foreign side wanted to increase their investments, the only thing we could do was to cede our shares."[39] Yet our data in Table 6.3, which incorporate these two equity adjustments, still show smaller foreign equity holdings among the FIEs within BAIC.[40]

Another test of the bargaining perspective is to assess the changes in the foreign equity ratio over time. As is well known, compared with the 1980s, China in the 1990s became far more attractive to the MNCs and the major automotive MNCs were knocking each other over in order to get into China. Therefore, Chinese firms in the 1990s should have been in a stronger position to negotiate with the MNCs simply because the supply of FDI was greater. This perspective, however, does not fit with the data on SAIC. For SAIC, the foreign equity ratios of FIEs established in the 1990s are larger than those of FIEs established in the 1980s. Instead of attributing this to a loss of bargaining power of SAIC compared with other Chinese firms, a more plausible hypothesis is that the demand by SAIC for the resources of MNCs grew over time.

---

[37] Interview with Zhang Xiao Yu, deputy director, Foreign Investment Department, SAIC, October 5, 1998.

[38] Interview with Tang Jianwei, vice director of Shanghai Clutch Factory and general manager of Shanghai TRW Automotive Safety Systems Co., Ltd., October 12, 1998.

[39] Interview with Zhu Xun, manager of the Foreign Department of Beijing Automotive Industry Corporation, November 28, 1998.

[40] If these equity adjustments had not been made to the data, Beijing Automotive Industry Corporation's foreign equity holdings would have decreased from 44.8 percent to 44.1 percent. SAIC's foreign equity holdings would have increased from 47.4 percent to 47.5 percent.

If bargaining power were a function of the profitability of the Chinese firms, then SAIC and Tianjin Automotive Industry Corporation should command more bargaining power than other Chinese firms. SAIC and Tianjin Automotive Industry Corporation were by far the more profitable firms as compared with BAIC and Guangzhou Automotive Industry Corporation. In 1992, returns on assets were 27.2 percent for SAIC and 29.8 percent for Tianjin Automotive Industry Corporation. The same measures for BAIC and Guangzhou Automotive Industry Corporation were only 15.1 percent and 10.4 percent, respectively. One would predict, all else being equal, SAIC and Tianjin Automotive Industry Corporation could have been more "choosy" and less willing to make equity concessions, precisely the opposite outcome from what we observe in the data.

The reason could be that despite being more profitable SAIC and Tianjin Automotive Industry Corporation had greater needs for capital because of their expensive investment strategies. They could court foreign investors by easing the terms for MNC entry or by allowing MNCs to claim a greater proportion of the revenue streams from future automotive industry growth in China. FDI rose because for a given unit of future business opportunity in China, the investment costs were lowered. This is one mechanism that might have increased China's FDI inflows, on the one hand, and raised the average foreign ownership of the FIEs, on the other.

Economic Fragmentation and FDI Fragmentation

An interesting aspect of China's FDI inflows is the fact that they are so dispersed geographically. Many factors may have contributed to this pattern, including the fact that domestic capital is somewhat immobile. CSI's acquisitions, for example, can be accounted for by this dynamic. But there is a more direct cause: A foreign firm may have no choice but to invest in different locations as a condition to supply to its customer. As the example from SAIC shows, the components supply facilities are set up both within the same automotive group and within the same jurisdiction as the vehicle firm.

A greater dispersion of investment projects is one consequence; the costliness of this dynamic is another. A foreign firm might have to invest in three facilities in order to supply to three vehicle producers, even in situations in which one facility might have been sufficient to supply to all three. If there are scale economies involved and if the assets are somewhat indivisible (i.e., the entire facility needs to be constructed regardless of whether 100 or 100,000 units are to be produced), the investment costs would be higher than they would be in the absence of economic fragmentation. The money that would have financed the operating budget and volume expansions ends up financing capacity creation instead. In the following paragraphs, let me present a number of examples to illustrate this dynamic.

Autoliv and ZF Friedrichshafen AG. In the following two cases, foreign firms established a greater number of and more geographically dispersed facilities than economically necessary or than foreign firms wished. One example concerns seat belts. Until 1997, SVW bought all of its seat belts from a supplier in the city of Nanjing, in Jiangsu province. The Nanjing supplier was a JV with Autoliv, Inc., of Sweden, which is one of the largest producers of seat belts and air bag systems in Europe. Volkswagen, SVW's German shareholder, is a large customer of Autoliv, and Autoliv often followed Volkswagen in its investments abroad. The Brazilian subsidiary of Autoliv, for example, supplies seat belts and air bag systems to Volkswagen. Its Chinese JV was formed in 1990 with the intention of supplying seat belts to SVW. The JV began with a total capitalization of $3.5 million. The Autoliv Group and its Chinese partner, a military firm that had previously produced parachute gear, each held 50 percent in the venture. For a while, the JV was doing very well. By 1996, it was the second largest producer of seat belts in the country, accounting for 22 percent of the market. The returns were good. In 1995, its gross profit margin was 23.7 percent, with an output volume of 430,000 units, and in 1996 it supplied all of SVW's seat belts.[41]

In January 1997, a subsidiary of SAIC, Shanghai Clutch Factory, formed a JV with TRW, Shanghai TRW Automotive Safety Systems Co., Ltd., to produce seat belts. As soon as the in-house production began, SVW immediately switched from the firm which it had purchased its seat belts, Nanjing-Autoliv, to Shanghai TRW. In 1997, Shanghai TRW churned out 239,800 seat belts (from zero in 1996), overtaking Nanjing-Autoliv as the second largest seat belt manufacturer in the country overnight. It accounted for 60 percent of the seat belts sourced by SVW in that year.[42] The effect on Nanjing-Autoliv was devastating. Its output volume plunged from 266,769 units to 132,356 units, creating great financial distress for the firm. By 1996, Nanjing-Autoliv had already built capacity sufficient for one million seat belts, and the effect of Shanghai TRW was that excessive capacity was accumulated in Nanjing. The switching of suppliers shifted profits from Nanjing to Shanghai. Pretax profits per employee at Shanghai TRW were RMB 3,283 in 1997, as compared with only RMB 911 for

---

[41] Interview with Tang Jianwei, vice director of Shanghai Clutch Factory and general manager of Shanghai TRW Automotive Safety Systems Co., Ltd., October 12, 1998.

[42] Interview with Tang Jianwei, vice director of Shanghai Clutch Factory and general manager of Shanghai TRW Automotive Safety Systems Co., Ltd., October 12, 1998.

Nanjing-Autoliv.[43] In an interview, a TRW manager explained that forming the JV with SAIC was the only way to win supply contracts from SVW. The hard edge of SAIC is illustrated by the fact that apparently Shanghai TRW is TRW's only JV in the world to which it has agreed to a less than majority-controlled arrangement.[44] It is doubtful that TRW would have been motivated to invest in Shanghai if it had not secured a guarantee from SAIC to source its seat belts.

ZF Friedrichshafen AG had a similar experience. ZF, the leading German parts supplier, maintained eight production sites in China. In 1994, ZF signed an agreement with FAW to produce hydraulic steering gears with the intention of supplying to the affiliates of Volkswagen in China. The operation apparently ran into difficulties because SAIC refused to source from a facility that was both outside of Shanghai and outside of SAIC. In 1996, ZF had no choice but to enter into an agreement directly with SAIC to establish a separate JV to produce steering systems for the Santana. SAIC held a 49 percent stake in this JV (Wagstyl 1996). Clearly, ZF invested more than it had wished because of the economic fragmentation.

Otis Elevator. Another example is from China's elevator industry, and it is even more revealing.[45] In 1984, Otis and Tianjin Elevator Company entered into an agreement to form a JV, China Tianjin Otis Elevator Company. As business expanded, Otis felt it was necessary to set up additional JVs in other parts of the country because of the market segmentation. However, this attempt was frustrated by the Tianjin government, which viewed such an attempt by Otis as exporting capital and fostering competition. In 1988, the Tianjin government rejected Otis's plan to set up a JV in Suzhou in Jiangsu province, despite the fact that China Tianjin Otis Elevator Company would have held a 50 percent stake in the new venture. (Tianjin Elevator Company itself had a controlling stake of 65 percent in China Tianjin Otis Elevator Company.) In another deal, Otis tried to set up a JV in Guangzhou to capture the booming market there. This time, the Guangzhou government rejected the proposal because the proposed project would have involved equity participation by Tianjin Elevator Company.

Both of these episodes illustrate the extent of local protectionism in China. Neither Tianjin nor Guangzhou was averse to Otis's participation, but each was wary of the other. The Guangzhou episode illustrates how strong this

---

[43] Firm performance data are from Ministry of Machinery Industry (1997b) and State Bureau of Machinery Industry (1998).

[44] Interview with Tang Jianwei, vice director of Shanghai Clutch Factory and general manager of Shanghai TRW Automotive Safety Systems Co., Ltd., October 12, 1998.

[45] This episode is from a Harvard Business School case on Otis in China. See Yoshino and Malnight (1997).

consideration is. The Guangzhou government was willing to accept a minority stake in the JV with Otis on the condition that Otis would drop participation by Tianjin Elevator Company. Tianjin's veto over Otis's plan to invest in Suzhou simply created an investment opportunity for another foreign firm. Schindler went there instead. The end result was greater foreign participation and a lower level of cross-regional domestic investments in China's elevator production than otherwise would have been the case. This episode is consistent with our hypothesis that an aversion to one another among Chinese provinces leads to a higher level of FDI inflows.

Statistical Evidence: FIEs in the Machinery Industry

We have shown that appetites for FDI differed among Chinese automotive firms in part because of the different extents to which they pursued integration strategies. SAIC embodied such a strategy. It systematically replaced components imports not only from foreign countries but also from *foreign provinces*. It seems to have relied more heavily on MNCs than other firms because it required more capital to build its own supply base than it would have needed to rely on established contractual relationships with existing suppliers in other provinces.

The descriptive findings reported in Table 6.3 are, at best, suggestive. The analysis is limited to four observation units, and there may be many other differences among them. Another problem has to do with how to demonstrate the effect of asset fragmentation on FDI. Our hypothesis rests heavily on a distinction between a "build" strategy and an acquisition strategy. Our premise is that a "build" strategy is more expensive than an acquisition strategy in the presence of huge idle capacity, and that SAIC and Tianjin Automotive Industry Corporation demanded more FDI in part because they could not acquire assets located in other provinces. The high level of FDI demand on the part of SAIC and Tianjin Automotive Industry Corporation was due directly to their integration strategies *in the context of asset fragmentation*.

But because all four of our firms are locally controlled firms and faced similar political constraints in investing outside their respective provinces, the linkage between asset fragmentation and FDI demand cannot be directly demonstrated. All we can do is demonstrate a linkage between pursuing an integration strategy and FDI demand, not a linkage between cross-regional acquisition constraints and FDI demand. A legitimate counterfactual hypothesis is that even if SAIC and Tianjin Automotive Industry Corporation had desired to integrate their production, it might not have been sufficient to trigger FDI demand. Suppose an acquisition option had been available. Then SAIC and Tianjin Automotive

Industry Corporation might have acquired their supplier-firms as a way to build up their supply capabilities. This could have been a less expensive alternative, since a substantial overcapacity had been built up in this industry.

In this section, I remedy this shortcoming by comparing the FDI preferences of two types of firms: central government firms and local government firms. Central government firms are freer to invest and to acquire assets cross-regionally because their operations are not constrained by regional authorities. Also, as our study of FAW shows, it is politically and administratively easier for the central government to negotiate with a province about asset transfers than it is for one province to negotiate with another province. Thus, central government firms are under less pressure to pursue a regional import substitution strategy and are more able to acquire assets across political jurisdictions than locally controlled firms. Because central government firms can acquire assets more easily, they have less need for FDI. This is the central hypothesis examined here.

The data are from the machinery industry, an industry that has been long dominated by SOEs. I have also analyzed the data for the automotive firms in the FIE database and the results are all consistent with what will be reported later on for the machinery industry. One huge drawback of the FIE database is that it does not contain any information about the characteristics of the Chinese investing firms other than their administrative designation (i.e., whether belonging to central or provincial governments).[46] The appendix to this chapter presents descriptive statistics showing that foreign ownership seems to be inversely related to the administrative ranks of the automotive firms in question. This is consistent with the notion that higher-ranked firms can acquire assets more easily across different jurisdictions and they may need FDI less. However, because of the aforementioned limitations of the FIE database, I have chosen to report findings on the machinery industry instead.

Machinery Industry Database. The data are compiled from various statistical sources on China's machinery industry, referred to as the machinery industry database in this book. The details are explained in the appendix to this chapter. The machinery industry is an extremely broad industrial branch that includes motor vehicles and automotive components.[47] The years for which data are available are 1997 and 1998. Unless otherwise noted, all the statistical results

---

[46] This is not a severe problem in a labor-intensive industry, since the size of the firms is small and production processes are simple. For capital-intensive industries, firms vary in many dimensions other than their administrative ranks.

[47] At the two-digit level, the machinery industry here refers to 35 (ordinary machinery), 36 (specialized machinery), 37 (transport equipment), 40 (electric machinery), and 42 (instruments).

Table 6.4 *Basic Characterstics of Central and Provincial Holding Firms in China's Machinery Industry, 1997*

	Number of holding firms	Average number of affiliates per holding firm	Average foreign equity ratio of affiliates per firm (%)	Average assets per affiliate (RMB million)	Average employment per affiliate (persons)
Central holding firms	13	38.5	9.08	1,530	7,721
Provincial holding firms	49	177	12.65	143.8	720

Source: Based on the machinery industry database.

are based on an analysis of 1997 data. The machinery industry database consists of sixty-two units of observations. Although the sample size is only moderately large, it still enables us to control for several firm-level characteristics that may bear on FDI preferences.

Our data are organized at the level of holding firms, all in the machinery industry. The provincial holding firms were previously regional bureaus of the machinery industry under the Ministry of Machinery Industry. During the reform era, the regional bureaus became more autonomous and independent from the Ministry of Machinery Industry in Beijing, reporting directly to the authorities in their respective regions.[48] Since the mid-1990s, as a part of the SOE ownership reform program, many of these regional bureaus have been converted into holding firms with enhanced power over internal management matters, such as rights over asset disposals and transfers within each holding firm. Often several independent business units were carved out from a monobureaucratic structure. For example, in 1997 in Tianjin, there were four separate holding firms in the machinery industry, while in the 1980s all the businesses had been under the jurisdiction of one machinery industry bureau in the city.

There are sixty-two holding firms in the machinery industry. Forty-nine holding firms are at the provincial level, that is, controlled by provincial governments, and thirteen are central holding firms, that is, controlled by the central government. SAIC, for instance, is a provincial holding firm and FAW is a central holding firm. Table 6.4 breaks down these sixty-two firms by their administrative status and presents their various characteristics. Measured by average

All the firms in this database were previously under the Ministry of Machinery Industry and its regional bureaus.

[48] In a few cases, some of the regional bureaus did not report to the Ministry of Machinery Industry but to other ministries that also produced lines of machinery products.

assets and employment, the central holding firms are about ten times the size of the provincial holding firms. On average, an affiliate of a central holding firm has about RMB 1.5 billion in assets and employs over 7,700 persons. In contrast, a regional affiliate has only RMB 143 million in assets and employs 720 persons.

There are numerous affiliates under these holding firms. Although the statistical source does not provide the definition of an affiliate, from the profiles of a number of affiliates of SAIC and BAIC, it can be ascertained that an affiliate is a firm that a holding firm either owns wholly or a firm in which a holding firm has a partial equity stake. Many of these affiliates previously had been factories under the charge of line bureaus of the machinery industry or directly under the Ministry of Machinery Industry itself. During the central planning era, they were simply administrative appendices to China's vast industrial bureaucracy. During the reform era, however, they became more independent, as they became locally independent entities from their supervisory agencies. They could, for example, negotiate FDI contracts with foreign firms (subject to supervision and approval from the holding firms) and enter into production and debt contracts with other firms. On average, each provincial holding firm operates some 177 affiliates, while a central holding firm has thirty-eight affiliates. Other descriptive data are presented in the appendix.

Hypotheses. Our analysis aims to determine whether FDI preferences systematically differ between central and provincial holding firms. Our hypothesis is that a central holding firm, all else being equal, has a lower FDI demand because it is able to acquire assets across different regions and has a lesser need to resort to a "build" strategy to integrate its production. As elsewhere in this book, we measure FDI preferences in terms of the foreign equity ratios of the FIE affiliates. Foreign equity ratios are the ratios of foreign equity capital to the total equity capital of a firm. In our database, foreign equity ratios represent the cumulative foreign equity claims in the FIE affiliates of the holding firms, not the foreign equity claims of the holding firms themselves. Holding firms themselves are not FIEs; they are either 100 percent owned by the state or majority-controlled by the state.

A Chinese investor in a JV can be an affiliate of a holding firm or can be the holding firm itself. A holding firm can negotiate directly with a foreign firm over an FDI deal or it can set the guidelines for the negotiation between its affiliates and the foreign firm. A holding firm must approve all the FDI agreements that its affiliates enter into. Thus, the characteristics of a holding firm have a direct bearing on all aspects of FDI deals, of which foreign equity share is the most important.

We operationalize asset fragmentation constraints by devising a dummy variable, central holding firm (CHF). CHF is assigned a value of one when it is a central holding firm and a value of zero when it is a provincial holding firm. Because central holding firms face fewer asset fragmentation constraints, they should demand less FDI. Therefore, CHF is expected to be negatively associated with foreign equity ratios in our statistical analysis. Apart from asset fragmentation constraints, many other factors may also bear upon the equity splits between Chinese and foreign investing firms. For example, foreign control of overseas marketing channels and marketing expertise is often said to lead to greater foreign equity controls. To ascertain the effect of FDI preference, it is necessary to control for the effect of other theoretically relevant determinants. In this book, these other determining factors, which mainly serve as controls, are called control variables. The purpose is to equalize statistically the variance along the control variables across different firms in order to isolate the effect of our substantive variable, that is, FDI preference.

Two Models. We offer two models conceptualizing how foreign equity ratios are determined. (The appendix to this chapter offers a more detailed explanation.) The first model is very simple: It assumes that foreign equity ratios are a function of the level of cumulative FDI inflows (FDI stock). The larger the cumulative FDI inflows are, the larger the foreign equity ratios are. The aim here is to see whether asset fragmentation constraints exert any additional influences on foreign equity ratios once the effect of the FDI levels is fully taken into account. The idea behind this conceptualization is that realized FDI flows already incorporate all the theoretically relevant determinants of the foreign equity ratio. Since we have only partial or imprecise knowledge about what these determinants are, we opt to use a proxy variable that incorporates the combined effect of all the determinants. Because our dependent variable refers to the foreign equity ratio at the level of affiliates, we use the average FDI per affiliate (FDIPA) in our analysis.[49]

Our other model explicitly spells out some of the theoretically relevant control variables and includes them in lieu of the FDI levels in the statistical analysis. Our specifications are guided in part by industrial organization conceptions of FDI determination. However, there are a number of differences with industrial organization theory that should be noted. One difference is that the standard approach typically examines factors influencing the distribution of FDI across different industries, whereas our study focuses on the distribution of equity shares across different firms within the same industry. But the machinery

---

[49] For methodological reasons, we use the log values of FDIPA in the statistical analysis.

industry encompasses products with different technological characteristics. The approach may make sense if, for example, firms specialize in particular industry segments. In addition, the industrial organization conceptualization has been extended to firm-level data by researchers who are interested in studying the bargaining dynamics between MNCs and host governments and firms. Such an extension has proven to be highly fruitful in illuminating pertinent issues in international business.[50]

The greater difference between my analysis and the standard approach concerns the analytical purpose of our inquiry. As I carefully set out at the beginning of this book, my interest is to study *Chinese demand for FDI*, not foreign supply of FDI. In the real world, obviously, demand factors intersect with supply factors to produce actual outcomes. Thus, to assess the effect of the demand factors accurately, it is necessary to control for the factors that affect the supply side. These industrial organization variables mainly serve this purpose in our analysis. It should be stressed that the industrial organization variables in our study serve as *control variables*. Unlike most studies in the industrial organization literature, these variables themselves are not the main subject of our inquiry. Our analytical interest is to understand how asset fragmentation constraints may or may not affect FDI preferences.

There are four control variables roughly based on the industrial organization perspective of FDI. They are: foreign marketing control (FMC), average asset size per affiliate (AAPA), R&D expenditures of holding firms (R&DE), and the proportion of the largest affiliates (PLA) of all the affiliates in the group. These variables are intended to capture the gist of the industrial organization perspective that FDI is a function of the market power and specialized know-how of the MNCs. However, our own specification differs from the standard approach. All our data are based on the industrial organization characteristics of Chinese firms, rather than the industrial organization characteristics of foreign investing firms. The standard approach is to use the industrial organization characteristics of foreign investing firms as those supply factors affecting FDI, but because of data limitations, this approach is not feasible. It is reasonable to expect that the industrial organization characteristics of the Chinese firms correlate strongly with the industrial organization characteristics of the foreign firms. Take industry concentration as an example. While institutional factors, as shown in this chapter, affect the extent of such industrial organization characteristics as industry concentration within an industry, they do not change the rank order of industry concentration across industries. China's automotive industry is less concentrated than in other countries but is still one of the most concentrated

---

[50] See, e.g., Krobin (1987) and Gomes-Casseres (1990).

industries in China. That said, all the findings on the industrial organization variables are not meant as an evaluation of the industrial organization theory of FDI and should be interpreted with caution.

FMC is operationalized by the share of exports in the total output of a holding firm. The more exports a firm produces, the more foreign marketing controls an MNC exercises. More FMC is one of the advantages held by MNCs and should lead to greater foreign equity controls. R&DE is measured as the ratio of R&D expenditures to sales in a holding firm. MNCs excel in R&D-intensive activities and thus they should enjoy advantages in technologically intensive areas when they negotiate with Chinese firms. R&DE should be associated positively with the foreign equity ratio. AAPA is the average asset size per affiliate within a holding firm. A large asset size is typically associated with market power and thus confers more advantages on the investing MNC. It should be positively correlated with the foreign equity ratio.[51] Finally, the presence of very large firms is used to measure the degree of entry barriers in a particular industry or industry segment. MNCs, according to industrial organization theory, enjoy advantages in industries with entry barriers.

The appendix to this chapter describes other renditions of the statistical methods and discusses results from alternative operationalizations of both the dependent and independent variables. The appendix also discusses problems that arise when the control variables themselves are caused by our dependent variable. Thus, the causal connection may go from foreign equity controls to some of our control variables, rather than the other way around. While this problem casts doubt on interpretations of some of the control variables, it is important to stress that there is no question as to the causal direction of our substantive variable, CHF. The purpose of including the control variables is to impose a ceteris paribus condition despite the fact that the underlying causal mechanism of these control variables may be misspecified.

Findings. Table 6.5 presents the results from our simple model in which the only control variable is the FDI level per affiliate (FDIPA). The dependent variable is the foreign equity ratio (FER), given by the percentage share of foreign equity to the total equity capital of all affiliates within a holding firm. Because our dependent variable is censored on both sides, we use a Tobit estimation technique. FER is regressed on a number of attributes of holding firms in the machinery industry. Four versions of Model One are run. In Version 1, only CHF and FDIPA are included; in the other versions, additional control variables are added one by one to the analysis. In all versions, the level of FDI,

---

[51] For methodological reasons, the logged version of AAPA is used in the regression analysis.

Table 6.5 *Tobit Analysis of the Foreign Equity Ratio in the Machinery Industry: Model One (dependent variable: foreign equity ratio of the FIE affiliates in the holding firms[a])*

	(1)[b]	(2)	(3)	(4)
Substantive variable				
Central holding firm	−12.5*	−11.8*	−11.67*	−11.67*
dummy (CHF)	(3.01)	(2.94)	(2.88)	(2.88)
Control variables				
FDI per affiliate	5.81*	5.6*	5.46*	5.46*
(FDIPA)	(0.61)	(0.61)	(0.67)	(0.67)
Coastal effect		5.21**	2.5	2.5
(COAST)		(2.86)	(3.14)	(3.14)
State equity ratio			−0.09**	−0.09**
(SER)			(0.06)	(0.05)
Social liability ratio				−0.024
(SLR)				(0.141)
Constant	−15.5*	−15.2*	−8.19*	−7.42
	(3.33)	(3.24)	(4.92)	(6.65)
Number of observations	62	62	62	62
Pseudo R-squared	0.195	0.20	0.21	0.21

Note: Standard errors in parentheses. Significance tests are one-tailed. For the variable definitions, see the appendix to this chapter. Data are for 1997.

[a] The foreign equity ratio is given by foreign equity capital divided by total equity capital times 100.

[b] See text for details on columns (1) to (4).

* : Significant at 5 percent.

** : Significant at 10 percent.

that is, FDIPA, is positively associated with FER at a statistically significant level, providing evidence for the unsurprising proposition that more cumulative FDI inflows do contribute to greater equity controls by MNCs. In Table 6.5 the dummy variable for central holding firms, CHF, is consistently negative and statistically significant. This means that a typical central holding firm has a smaller FER compared with a typical provincial holding firm after the levels of their cumulative FDI inflows are equalized. To put it another way, the same amount of FDI inflows generates a smaller degree of foreign ownership among central holding firms than among provincial holding firms. This is prima facie evidence that provincial holding firms may make larger equity concessions to MNCs than central holding firms.

To be sure, there may be other differences between central and provincial holding firms besides their FDI preferences that may lead to this outcome. For example, in the automotive industry, provincial holding firms such as SAIC and Guangzhou Automotive Industry Corporation are located in coastal provinces, whereas central holding firms such as Dongfeng Motor Corporation are located in interior provinces. FAW is located in Jilin province in the northeast of China, not a magnet for FDI. This locational difference may exert an effect on FER because FDI policies and regulations are more liberal in the coastal provinces than in the interior provinces. Another possibility is that the central government protects its own firms from foreign encroachment more than it protects regional firms. The central government has a greater equity stake in central holding firms than it does in provincial holding firms and it may restrict foreign ownership in order not to dilute its own equity shares.[52] While an aversion to equity dilution is germane to the FDI preference question, this leads to a smaller FER through a different mechanism than economic fragmentation and an inability to acquire assets across provinces. Thus, the aversion to equity dilution should be controlled for. Finally, SOEs carry a heavy load of social liabilities, such as pension payments to retired workers and provisions of social welfare. Social liabilities may deter FDI. Although this effect should be captured by the FDIPA variable, social liabilities may also weaken the bargaining position of the Chinese firms at a given level of FDIPA. To the extent that central holding firms may have a lower level of social liabilities than provincial holding firms, they may have greater bargaining power versus MNCs, but not necessarily because they face fewer asset fragmentation constraints.[53]

In Table 6.5, Versions 2 to 4 of Model One incorporate these three variables into the regression analysis. The coastal effect (COAST) is a dummy variable with a value of one for holding firms located in coastal provinces and a value of zero for holding firms in interior provinces. The state equity ratio (SER) is the ratio of the state equity stake to the Chinese portion of the total equity capital of the holding firm.[54] The social liability ratio (SLR) is calculated as the ratio of nonproduction fixed assets of a holding firm to its total fixed assets. Nonproduction fixed assets are assets that appear on a firm's balance sheet

---

[52] On average, the state equity share of the Chinese portion of the paid-in equity capital is 73.4 percent for central holding firms and 53 percent for provincial holding firms.

[53] Central holding firms hold a slightly lower social liability ratio as defined in this book, that is, the ratio of nonproduction fixed assets to total fixed assets. Their ratio is 23.1 percent, while that for provincial holding firms is 24.3 percent.

[54] It is necessary to exclude foreign equity from the calculation of this variable because otherwise the FER and SER would have the same denominator and their correlation would essentially be a mathematical relationship, that is, a greater value of SER would necessarily be associated with a lesser value of FER. There is also a substantive reason to use only the Chinese portion of the total paid-in equity capital in the calculation of the SER. Since the Chinese state has carefully excluded domestic private firms from the machinery industry, while actively courting FDI, it may be more accurate to say that the central government is more concerned about a dilution of its shares in the Chinese portion of the equity stake, rather than about a dilution of its shares in the entire equity stake of the firm.

but do not generate any cash flows. Examples of such assets include employee housing, communal bathing and dining establishments, schools, and health care facilities. If these variables better explain the seemingly lower FDI demand on the part of central holding firms, their inclusion in the regression analysis should either weaken or make the CHF effect disappear. This does not occur. Across Versions 2 to 4 in Table 6.5, CHF continues to be statistically significant and the sign remains negative even after all three other control variables are added. This is an indication that the FDI-suppressant effect of CHF is not explained by alternative theories of why central holding firms may enjoy a bargaining edge over provincial holding firms versus MNCs.

Table 6.6 presents an alternative model of determinants of the foreign equity ratio, using explicit measures of those factors that purportedly affect FDI flows. Thus, Model Two differs from Model One by substituting FDIPA by four variables that the industrial organization literature views as important influences on FDI flows and, as an extension of the industrial organization perspective to firm-level studies, as important influences on the bargaining power of MNCs. Our substantive variable, CHF, however, remains statistically significant and retains a negative sign across the four versions of Model Two. The size of the CHF coefficient ranges from −9.1 percent (Version 4) to −11.3 percent (Version 1). The findings from Model One and Model Two are consistent with each other. This is further proof that our conception of FDI preference is robust to the various specifications about the determinants of the foreign equity ratio.

CONCLUSION

Speaking in 1984, Deng Xiaoping declared, "Invigoration of the domestic economy also means opening the domestic economy. There are, in fact, two open policies: open to the outside world and open to the inside." Throughout the 1980s the central government issued instructions to local authorities to "unclog the channels of circulation" and to "smash blockades." In 1991, Hu Ping, then Minister of Commerce, reiterated the importance of the twin openings to the world and to internal markets.[55] But the reality has sharply diverged from the original policy intentions.

Economic fragmentation holds important implications for the roles and functions of FDI. Economic fragmentation costs capital, as regional governments in pursuit of an import substitution strategy need to import capital. Asset

---

[55] Deng's quote and Minister Hu's reiteration of the twin openings are recounted in Wedeman (forthcoming), p. 25.

Table 6.6 *Tobit Analysis of the Foreign Equity Ratio in the Machinery Industry: Model Two (dependent variable: foreign equity ratio of the FIE affiliates in the holding firms[a])*

	$(1)^b$	(2)	(3)	(4)
Substantive variable				
Central holding firm	−11.3**	−10.6**	−10.4**	−9.1**
dummy (CHF)	(6.06)	(5.81)	(5.45)	(5.27)
Control variables				
Foreign marketing	0.57*	0.51*	0.49*	0.40*
control (FMC)	(0.16)	(0.16)	(0.15)	(0.15)
R&D expenditure	0.33	0.21	0.379	0.155
(R&DE)	(0.67)	(0.65)	(0.63)	(0.60)
Average asset per	6.07*	5.35*	5.68*	4.48*
affiliate (AAPA)	(2.5)	(2.37)	(2.24)	(2.22)
Proportion of	−0.11	−0.08	−0.08	−0.07
largest firms (PLF)	(0.10)	(0.1)	(0.09)	(0.09)
Coastal effect		10.6*	3.37	3.09
(COAST)		(4.65)	(4.98)	(4.78)
State equity ratio			−0.23*	−0.19*
(SER)			(0.08)	(0.07)
Social liability				−0.42*
ratio (SLR)				(0.19)
Constant	−48.6*	−43.2*	−30.1	−9.98
	(22.4)	(21.5)	(20.7)	(21.7)
Number of observations	62	62	62	62
Pseudo R-squared	0.034	0.045	0.065	0.076

Note: Standard errors in parentheses. Significance tests are one-tailed. For the variable definitions, see the appendix to this chapter. Data are for 1997.

[a] The foreign equity ratio is given by foreign equity capital divided by total equity capital times 100.

[b] See text for details on columns (1) to (4).

* : Significant at 5 percent.

** : Significant at 10 percent.

fragmentation means that cross-regional capital mobility is low for domestic firms, but to the extent that asset fragmentation does not constrain foreign firms, FDI can rise to fulfill this unsatisfied demand for capital. This is the basic logic behind our hypothesis that economic fragmentation raises China's demand for FDI. Or to put it another way, the higher demand for FDI prompts regional governments to pay a higher price for it – by ceding more controls over either existing assets or future business opportunities than otherwise would be the case. This chapter provides some suggestive evidence documenting the effect of economic fragmentation on FDI demand by Chinese firms.

In the history of China's planned economy, administrative centralization was a sporadic response to what was viewed as excessive administrative decentralization. In other words, administrative decentralization has always been the reigning principle of China's economic organization, not administrative centralization. Administrative decentralization means that the central government has delegated many economic responsibilities, including the running, operating, and taxing of firms, to lower-level authorities. Such administrative decentralization should be distinguished from economic decentralization, defined here as moving economic responsibilities out of the governmental sphere and into private hands. Administrative decentralization thus is an efficiency-enhancing device *given* that true economic decentralization is precluded as a politically acceptable solution to the inefficiencies of the SOEs.

Throughout this book, we have argued that a high portion of the FDI inflows into China is induced by the way Chinese economic and financial institutions are organized. Economic fragmentation is an institutional creation. It is not only a function of configuring and reconfiguring resources and power between the central government and local governments but is fundamentally rooted in state ownership, as I argue in Chapter 3. For this reason, the two components of our institutional foundation argument of FDI are internally consistent: The root cause for China's FDI patterns is the paramount role – and the persistence of that role – of SOEs in the economy. During the reform era, the role of SOEs has shrunk relative to the role of nonstate firms, but it has not shrunk in absolute terms. This is an important dimension of China's reform strategy, to which we turn next.

Appendix to Chapter 6

The appendix reviews the findings generated by examining data in the FIE database, explains sources of the machinery industry database and variable definitions, and describes variable specifications.

RESULTS GENERATED FROM THE FIE DATABASE

Our FIE database contains information on FIEs in the machinery industry (as well as the automotive sector within the machinery industry), classifying all the FIEs according to their levels of administrative subordination. There are six main categories: central government, provincial governments, prefectures, counties, townships, and neighborhood committees and villages. (In addition, there is a category of unaffiliated firms.) This administrative classification allows us to test whether the foreign equity ratio (FER) varies between FIEs under the central government and those under local governments, controlling for other pertinent factors. (Local governments refer to government agencies below the central government.)

In the automotive industry, for FIEs affiliated with central-level firms, the average foreign equity ratio is 40.1 percent. For the FIEs affiliated with provincial-level firms, the average foreign ownership is 41.9 percent. For FIEs at the county level, it is 48.9 percent. The same rankings hold when the asset size of the FIEs is controlled for. For the machinery industry as a whole, the foreign equity ratio is lower, but the same ranking holds among FIEs affiliated with Chinese firms at different administrative levels. Using the Tobit regression technique, we find that FIEs subordinate to the central government have a lower FER than FIEs subordinate to local governments, that is, a dummy variable denoting central government FIEs is negatively correlated with the FER at statistically significant levels for both the machinery and automotive industries. This is true under alternative sets of controls as well, such as the level of foreign

303

equity capital, the asset and employment levels of FIEs, and export/sales ratios. The results hold when the central government FIEs are compared with FIEs under provinces, prefectures, and counties, excluding only TVEs and private firms. This is to ensure that approximate firm size is controlled for as most of the TVEs and private firms are very small. The results also hold whether we only include JVs or the entire population of FIEs (i.e., JVs plus wholly foreign-owned subsidiaries).

I have chosen not to report the results from the FIE database in detail because the results from the machinery industry database are more convincing. Other than the administrative affiliation, the FIE database does not contain any economic information about the Chinese FIE partners. Thus, we are not able to test whether a set of alternative variables, such as asset size, state equity ratios, and social liabilities, weaken the correlations between asset market fragmentation and the FER. However, the fact that the findings from the two separate databases are consistent with each other lends additional support to our hypothesis that asset market fragmentation increases Chinese firms' demand for FDI.

MACHINERY INDUSTRY DATABASE

The data used in the analysis are drawn from a machinery industry database. The database was compiled by the author from various issues of the *Machinery Industry Statistical Yearbook*, the *China Automotive Statistical Yearbook*, *China's Large and Medium Enterprise Yearbook*, and other sources. Most of the results reported in the text are based on an analysis of 1997 data, although data for 1998 are also available in the database.

DEFINITIONS OF VARIABLES

Our dependent variable is the percentage share of equity stakes held by foreign companies. It is calculated by taking the ratio of foreign equity to the total equity capital of a firm. The equity stakes refer to registered equity capital, that is, the amount of equity capital a firm reports when it registers with the State Bureau of Commerce and Industry. It is otherwise known as registered equity capital. The equity splits between Chinese and foreign firms are at the time of firm registration. Subsequently, a firm may elect to change its equity split, which requires approval from the Chinese government. The reason that we use the foreign equity ratio at the time of registration is that it best reflects the bargaining positions of Chinese and foreign firms at the time they negotiate the formation of the JV. Just to make sure, I have also run all the regression analyses in this chapter on the actual foreign equity ratio at the time the data were collected. The results are not different from those using the registered equity data.

Our substantive variable is a dummy variable with the value of one for central holding firms and the value of zero for provincial holding firms. It is abbreviated as CHF in the text. The control variable in Model One is FDI per affiliate (FDIPA), which is simply the cumulative amount of foreign equity capital in a holding firm divided by the number of its affiliates. In all the regression runs, FDIPA is transformed by taking its log values. This is done to remove the nonlinearity in this variable.

Four control variables appear in Model Two. Export, as a proportion of the industrial output value, is used to denote foreign marketing control (FMC). R&D expenditure (R&DE) is the ratio of R&D expenditure to sales of a holding firm. Average asset per affiliate (AAPA) refers to the assets of a holding firm divided by the number of affiliates within the holding firm. Like FDIPA, this variable is log transformed to remove the nonlinearity in it. The proportion of the largest firms (PLF) is the proportion of affiliates within the holding firm with production-related fixed assets in excess of RMB 50 million. The statistical sources give the number of affiliates for seven categories broken down by the size of the production-related fixed assets: (1) below RMB 1 million, (2) between RMB 1 million and RMB 5 million, (3) between RMB 5 million and RMB 10 million, (4) between RMB 10 million and RMB 30 million, (5) between RMB 30 million and RMB 50 million, (6) between RMB 50 million and RMB 100 million, and (7) above RMB 100 million.

Other control variables are COAST, state equity ratio (SER), and social liability ratio (SLR). COAST is a dummy variable with the value of one for the holding firms located in the coastal provinces and the value of zero for those located in the noncoastal provinces. SER is given by dividing the state equity by the Chinese portion of the equity capital of a holding firm. Subtracting the foreign equity capital from the total equity capital gives us the Chinese portion of the equity capital. SLR is given by dividing the nonproduction fixed assets of a holding firm by its total fixed assets. Both fixed asset figures are given as their original cost values. Table 6.7 presents descriptive statistics about the main variables used in the analysis.

MODEL SPECIFICATIONS

Model Two is guided by theoretical accounts in economics literature on FDI determinants. The dominant account of cross-industry FDI distribution is the industrial organization explanation. The literature is briefly reviewed in Chapter 2. The basic idea is that MNCs need to command firm-specific advantages to

Table 6.7 *Descriptive Statistics about the Main Variables, 1997*

	Number of observations	Mean	Standard deviation	Minimum value	Maximum value
Average foreign equity ratio of the FIE affiliates in the holding firms (FER) (%)	62	11.9	12.3	0	48.0
Logged value of FDI per affiliate (FDIPA)	62	4.54	2.67	0	9.15
Foreign marketing control (FMC) (%)	62	9.3	10.7	0	70.3
R&D expenditure (R&DE) (%)	62	2.22	2.68	0.26	19.5
Logged value of average asset per affiliate (AAPA)	62	9.66	1.31	7.5	13.1
Proportion of largest firms (PLF) (%)	62	30.7	28.3	0	100

Source: Based on machinery industry database.

overcome obstacles of investing abroad.[56] These advantages take the form of R&D capabilities, managerial know-how, organizational skills, marketing expertise, economies of scale, and so on. MNCs are hypothesized to be more prevalent in those industries that are characterized by a significant degree of product differentiation, high concentration ratios, scale economies, and deep R&D expenditures due to their superior market power over their domestic rivals. In general, industrial organization–motivated research on the interindustry distribution of FDI in more developed economies, such as Canada and the United Kingdom, has received more empirical validation than similar research on FDI in developing economies.[57]

As noted in the text, some of our control variables suffer from what is known as an "endogeneity problem"; that is, while our model assumes that the causal direction runs from these control variables to the FER, it may very well be the case that the FER is a cause of our control variables. For example, one may plausibly argue that higher values of the FER should lead to higher values of FDIPA, not the other way around. MNCs, for example, may demand controlling equity stakes before they invest. Otherwise they will refuse to invest. In this way, the FER really determines FDIPA, rather than being determined by FDIPA.

[56] For citation details, see Chapter 2.
[57] For a sample of such empirical work that provides support for the industrial organization postulates, see Caves (1974), Orr (1974), and Meredith (1984). In contrast, Aswicahyono and Hill (1995) find only mixed support for the industrial organization theory.

The nature of our inquiry makes it very difficult to completely eliminate the endogeneity problem. Our primary concern, however, is whether the statistical significance and the sign of our substantive variable, CHF, are affected by this endogeneity problem. On an a priori basis, there is no reason that the CHF designation should be affected one way or the other (and CHF itself, for sure, does not suffer from an endogeneity problem). Just to make sure, I have relied on alternative dependent variables, which may attenuate, although not remove, the endogeneity problem. One way is to lag the independent variables so that the values of the independent and dependent variables are not contemporaneous. I have regressed the FER for 1998 using the 1997 values of the same independent variables in Models One and Two. The results are not different. Of course, this does not really deal with the endogeneity problem, since the 1998 values of the independent variables are surely highly correlated with the 1997 values of the independent variables. I also use the ratio of the 1998 foreign equity capital to the 1997 foreign equity capital as the dependent variable. CHF is negative in both Models One and Two, but it is significant only in Model One. Thus, there is some evidence that CHF deterred FDI growth. This does not really get to the heart of our question, which is about foreign ownership control, while our dependent variable thus formulated is about the growth of FDI from 1997 to 1998.

There are eleven cases in the machinery industry database where FER values are zero, that is, there is no foreign ownership of the affiliates in these eleven holding firms. To minimize the chance that our finding on CHF is driven by these observations, I have run both Models One and Two omitting observations with zero FER values. (One way our finding may be affected is if many central holding firms have zero FER values. In fact, seven provincial holding firms have zero FER values, while only four central holding firms have zero FER values.) The results are not different. Throughout all versions of Models One and Two, CHF is consistently negative and statistically significant without those observations with a zero FER value.

7

Conclusion

In 1987, in a conversation with a visiting government delegation from Yugoslavia, Deng Xiaoping gave the following assessment on Chinese economic reforms:[1]

> In the rural reform our greatest success – and it is one we had by no means anticipated – has been the emergence of a large number of enterprises run by villages and townships. They were like a new force that just came into being spontaneously.... The Central Committee [of the Chinese Communist Party] takes no credit for this.

This is a powerful insight into both the success and the limitations of China's economic reform. The biggest success of the reform is to have allowed a substantial degree of flexibility in an otherwise rigid and statist economic system. This flexibility gave an opportunity to innovative and hard-working entrepreneurs to create and expand businesses, which over time would eclipse China's inefficient and wasteful state sector. Some of the specific economic policies and reform measures have also been important. These would include price liberalization, opening up the country to FDI and overseas export markets, creation of central banking and tax institutions essential to a functioning market economy, and a gradual emergence of rule-leaning, though not yet rule-based, governmental interventions in the economy and business-government relationships. These policy measures have led to macro stability, elimination of shortages, and abatement of anticompetitive barriers, all very impressive achievements during a short period of time.[2]

Despite these achievements, a fundamental institutional pillar of a capitalistic market economy is still missing in China: a strong commitment to private

---

[1] From Deng Xiaoping (1994), p. 236.
[2] For a review of China's reforms up to the early 1990s, see Perkins (1994).

ownership as the dominant way to organize the production of goods, provision of services, and allocation of economic and financial resources. Private ownership exists in the Chinese economy, but its size, especially in heavy industries and in certain service sectors, such as banking, insurance, and wholesaling, is minuscule. Operations of private firms are saddled with considerable regulatory, legal, and financial constraints. Although the privatization of SOEs has been accelerated since 1997, to this day the government has still not supported the privatization of large SOEs. During the reform era as a whole, compared with the pace of market liberalization and opening to the outside world, changes in the ownership structure of the state sector, as both a policy goal and an economic reality, have been modest. The size of the state sector, while having declined dramatically relative to nonstate firms, has not declined in absolute terms. The political pecking order of firms has been alleviated substantially since 1997, but it has persisted because it is rooted in many deep-seated social and political factors. Some of the government's policies and measures – such as investing heavily in SOEs – have counteracted the beneficial effects of the economic flexibility introduced by Deng's reform program.

In this chapter, we summarize the findings of and draw some implications from our analysis of the FDI phenomenon in China. We also move to a broader discussion of China's reform strategy and process. In many ways, the growth of FIEs mirrors larger developments in the economy. Fundamental economic factors, such as market expansions and low labor costs, are one part of China's FDI story; FDI liberalization is another. But a complete record of FDI should take into account the ability of the Chinese financial and economic systems to allocate capital and broader economic resources and opportunities efficiently. To tackle this question, we must inevitably assess the Chinese reforms. The aim here is to offer some broad conjectures; these conjectures, while based on the analysis in this book, have not been rigorously tested against empirical evidence. They are, thus, only suggestive in nature.

The chapter begins by summarizing the main empirical findings from our institutional foundation argument. I then propose some tentative ideas about its broader implications. Last, I offer an evaluation of China's reform strategy based on our analysis of the FDI phenomenon.

THE INSTITUTIONAL FOUNDATION ARGUMENT

Under identical macroeconomic conditions, whether a country gets more or less FDI relative to domestic investments depends on the competitiveness of its firms versus foreign firms. Conceptually, for FDI to occur, foreign investing firms need not be among the most technologically advanced and organizationally sophisticated MNCs in the world. All that is required is that they be more efficient than indigenous firms in the host economies. For this reason, the competitiveness of indigenous firms affects FDI incidence as much as the competitiveness of foreign investing firms.

Here, the quality of China's financial and economic institutions matters for FDI. At any given level of market size or labor costs, well-designed financial and economic institutions will make indigenous firms more competitive. It is unlikely that a massive amount of labor-intensive FDI would have been necessary if efficient local entrepreneurs had been able to access capital easily. Small foreign firms may have found it more profitable instead to engage in contract production. But poorly designed financial and economic institutions hamper local entrepreneurs from reaping the benefits of domestic and external market growth and may lead to greater investment opportunities for foreign firms. Thus, an extension of the institutional foundation argument is that FDI, conceptualized as fierce competition between domestic and foreign firms for scarce business opportunities, is also a reflection of the relative efficiency levels of foreign and domestic economic and financial institutions.

The bulk of this book has detailed the design and operations of China's financial and economic institutions. There is little information about the technological and economic attributes of the foreign investing firms. For a book billed as a study of FDI, this omission may strike some readers as strange. After all, FDI refers to investment activities undertaken by *foreign* firms; most studies on FDI focus on the financial, technological, and economic attributes of foreign firms. The basic contention of the institutional foundation argument is that the operation of China's financial and economic institutions also has a strong bearing on FDI.

Summary of Findings

Our book begins with noting a number of anomalous FDI patterns in China. These patterns include: (1) an inordinately high dependency on FDI relative to domestic investments and contractual alternatives, (2) a sharp rise in FDI inflows combined with a dramatic contraction of contractual alliances, (3) the dominance of FIEs in the production and exporting of labor-intensive industries, (4) a pervasive presence of FIEs and FDI across industries and regions, and (5) the presence of very small foreign investors. In this section, I use our institutional foundation argument to resolve these anomalies as a way to summarize both the conceptual framework of the book as well as the main empirical findings.

Relative Foreign Competitiveness. A basic insight of the industrial organization perspective on FDI is that FDI is a function of the *relative* competitiveness of foreign firms. The relative competitiveness of foreign firms is the ratio of the competitiveness of foreign firms to the competitiveness of domestic firms. In Chapter 2, I use a simple heuristic equation to illustrate this concept:

$$\text{Relative foreign competitiveness} = \frac{\text{Competitiveness of foreign firms}}{\text{Competitiveness of domestic firms}}$$

This shorthand equation forms the analytical basis of the institutional foundation argument, which differs from the standard industrial organization account in a critical way. My interest is to explain why domestic firms are uncompetitive, not why foreign firms are competitive. Furthermore, I do not take domestic uncompetitiveness as a given but as a phenomenon to be illustrated at length and to be carefully dissected. My claim is that the across-the-board uncompetitiveness of Chinese firms is caused primarily by inefficient Chinese economic and financial institutions, practices, and policies, rather than by factors inherent in a developing country. China is not short of entrepreneurial talent or inclinations; after all, many ethnically Chinese entrepreneurs do extremely well outside China and dominate the pool of foreign investors within China. It is also not short of expertise in the traditional arts and crafts industries in which the Chinese have excelled for hundreds of years. Nor is it lacking in the necessary organizational and execution skills in industries known for their detailed and specialized production subprocesses, such as garment making and footwear. It is prima facie unconvincing to argue that Chinese entrepreneurs and workers, compared with entrepreneurs and workers in Turkey, Hong Kong, Taiwan, and Korea, are less able to manage dedicated production subprocesses such as knitting a sweater, sewing a collar onto a shirt, attaching a button to a sleeve, stitching the uppers of shoes, or manufacturing soles. And there should not be a significant shortage of capital, as Chinese households each year save a large amount of their paychecks and deposit the money in Chinese banks.

But entrepreneurship itself does not equal firm competitiveness. Entrepreneurship has to be financed and has to have access to market and investment opportunities. The fruits of entrepreneurship have to be secure to motivate an entrepreneur to work hard and be innovative. Firm competitiveness is a function of a complementary relationship between capabilities and resources. The Chinese have a saying to depict how a complementary relationship works: "A clever woman cannot cook without ingredients." Now suppose an allocative system that does the following: It systematically assigns the choicest ingredients to a bad chef, while a superior chef is supplied with shoddy or no ingredients. Under this system, the culinary quality will be uniformly bad.

Now further suppose that there is an international tournament. The chefs from this system will lose out to chefs from other better-designed systems, *even if* their average cooking skills are higher. This is the gist of our institutional foundation argument.

Failures of SOEs. China's vast pool of financial resources has been allocated according to an economically inefficient political pecking order that favors SOEs at the expense of private firms. This allocative failure is particularly disturbing considering that China has so much going for it. It has an abundant supply of capital, a hard-working labor force, a high level of basic literacy, a potentially large home market, and basic social and political order and stability.

SOEs have failed to create value despite the advantages they hold, but they have accumulated a reserve of tangible and intangible assets, including the best human capital in China, through years of generous infusion of cheap bank credit, foreign exchange, and privileged access to the country's most profitable market opportunities. The value of assets is not determined by their purchase price but by the profits that can be generated by their utilization. SOEs sit on top of potentially valuable assets, brand names, and marketing networks, but they generate low or negative profits. This makes them perfect acquisition targets. This also explains why, during a period of surging economic growth between 1992 and 1995, MNCs acquired assets from SOEs via JV acquisitions, sometimes at a fraction of their replacement costs. Another factor contributed to the asset price depression during a period of strong economic growth: For ideological reasons, the government effectively precluded Chinese private firms from launching bids for SOE assets and prevented asset prices from being bid up. Foreign firms competed with one another but not with domestic private firms. The surging FDI during this period in part resulted from a combination of restricting privatization and actively courting FDI.

Marginalization of Domestic Private Firms. The SOEs acquired by MNCs were the incompetent chefs in our hypothetical illustration, but because they received resources, innately efficient private entrepreneurs were denied the necessary capital to expand their own businesses. Thus, private firms were rendered uncompetitive. This explains why FDI has gone to some industries in which the Chinese have excelled for centuries. Traditional handicrafts, furniture making, garments, and labor-intensive light-industry products are the strongholds of private entrepreneurs, but much of the country's financial resources, such as bank credits and foreign exchange, were not channeled to them. Three consequences ensued. One is that small foreign firms found weak competition in these industries and thus succeeded in establishing a production presence in these product segments despite the comparatively high fixed costs of investing and operating in China. Second, Chinese private entrepreneurs were left with no choice but to resort to the most expensive way of accessing capital: ceding equity controls over their own businesses to foreigners. Third, FDI allowed them to have some property rights security in a system in which they were politically and legally disadvantaged.

Labor-intensive and export-oriented FDI brings with it two things: a business opportunity, that is, an export contract, and broad benefits such as financing and a superior legal status. FDI rose in response to efficiency-improving opportunities to ease credit constraints artificially inflicted on innately capable Chinese firms. In essence, the poor allocative decisions of the Chinese state created some untapped profit opportunities. Only sizable returns that sufficiently offset the normally high transaction costs of doing business and investing in a country with a notoriously poor business environment can attract very small foreign firms to invest in China. The presence of these untapped current and future profit opportunities explains why FDI inflows – relative to domestic investments and contractual alternatives – are so large despite the high level of corruption, poor legal system, and low quality of general public governance, factors that have been found to deter FDI elsewhere (Wei 1996b). The business environment for foreign investors was poor in the 1990s, but it was poorer still for domestic private entrepreneurs in the 1980s and 1990s. The same dynamic also explains why contractual export production and exports by domestic private firms have sharply risen since 1997 when the government began to ease the inefficient political pecking order of firms.

Economic Fragmentation. Economic fragmentation is another factor contributing to high FDI inflows. Economic fragmentation drives up FDI demand by a number of channels. First, it prevents Chinese firms from being more competitive than they could be otherwise. It artificially carves up a large national market into many smaller segments and reduces both the size of the market as well as the quality of market demand. Second, economic fragmentation increases the bargaining power of foreign firms in the same way as a ban on privatization. It restrains competition. Domestic firms can invest only within their respective regions, while foreign firms, even some small foreign firms, can choose from projects throughout the country. Third, economic fragmentation increases the demand for capital and makes foreign firms more valuable than otherwise would be the case. The economic fragmentation hypothesis is consistent with the observation that FDI and FIEs are present in many regions of the country and that even very small foreign firms have established facilities in multiple locations.

SOME BROAD CONJECTURES

In this part of the book, I raise some broad conjectures that are plausible inferences drawn from our research findings. The first issue concerns implications
for foreign firms operating in China. So far, our analysis has had little to say
about the perspectives of foreign investors. Here, I use the institutional foundation argument to illuminate some managerial implications. The second issue
is whether the large FDI inflows, induced as they are by the allocative inefficiencies of the Chinese economy, are efficient in their effect. Here, one needs
to make a careful distinction between the causes of FDI and the effects of FDI.
The third issue concerns linkages between institutional distortions and FDI. We
offer some general observations about FDI patterns in economies beset with
large-scale institutional imperfections. Focusing on the unusual composition of
FDI flowing to China, our study also sheds additional light on an issue that has
long interested international business scholars: the rise of what are known as
"third-world" MNCs.

Managerial Implications

In Chapter 1, we show that China's FDI dependency is high even though its
FDI environment is not nearly as liberal as many other countries in the world.
I use our institutional foundation argument to place in perspective two issues
that managers of foreign firms often have to grapple with in China. One is the
quality of the operating environment and the other is the size and the growth of
China's market (as proxied by GDP growth).

Operating Environment. A growing frustration on the part of foreign investors
in China is that their operations are either unprofitable or not as profitable as
they expected. Several surveys suggest that only a fraction of the FIEs are in the
black and a growing number of foreign investors are finding the Chinese market
difficult to crack and the business environment overly bureaucratic.[3]

Our analytical framework illuminates this issue in several ways. One is that
the complaints about low profitability mainly seem to come from Western
MNCs. A cultural explanation – that Westerners do not know how to operate in
China – is unsatisfactory. Western MNCs can – and do – hire local or overseas
Chinese to help them navigate the Chinese environment. Cultural expertise can
be contracted. The deeper problem is that because Western MNCs operate in
capital- and technology-intensive industries, they tend to team up with SOEs

---

[3] Some of these issues are dealt with in Rosen (1999a).

when they invest in China, in contrast to firms from the ECEs that finance credit-constrained but efficient enterprises. Chinese economists, as quoted in Chapter 4, have compared an SOE in the home appliance business actively seeking out FDI in the mid-1990s to "a dying person." By the same token, a foreign firm is a doctor who has to incur significant restructuring costs. This is similar to a turnaround situation except for the fact that foreign firms do not really have complete operating controls because of the JV acquisition format.[4] The inability to exercise complete operating controls, coupled with a dire need to restructure operations, only compounds those problems inherent in a JV situation.[5] There may be another liability to teaming up with SOEs. SOEs, obsessed with technology, often demand foreign firms to transfer the latest technology. In some markets, such as mobile phone sets, introducing the latest technology may make sense. In many other markets, however, the prices would be too high for Chinese consumers to bear.

A related issue involves the rapid and somewhat unpredictable changes in China's marketplace. The failure of Whirlpool, described in Chapter 4, may have resulted from a fundamentally mistaken diagnosis of China's competitive landscape. Whirlpool might have identified its domestic competitors to be SOEs – such as the five top SOEs selected by the central government – and thus derived a false sense of confidence from witnessing the massive failures of these SOEs. It might have failed to see the rise of firms such as Kelon and Haier, both humble in origin and lower-tiered in China's hierarchy of firms, as a TVE and a collective firm, respectively. If Whirlpool did make such a mistake, it was in good company. As quoted at the beginning of this chapter, Deng Xiaoping himself did not see the coming of TVEs either.

The current operating difficulties of FIEs themselves may arise from many of the institutional imperfections analyzed in this book. To be sure, China's political pecking order disadvantages its most dynamic firms, but nothing in this line of inquiry suggests that it should be smooth sailing for the FIEs. The Chinese business environment is widely known to be one of the most difficult in the world, as shown in Table 1.2 in Chapter 1. The excessive government intervention, red

---

[4] There is a major difference between a straightforward acquisition and a JV acquisition. A JV acquisition enables a foreign firm to acquire the assets of an SOE, but at the end of the day it is still the Chinese firm that appoints some of the deputy managers and division heads. For example, at Beijing-XYZ Gear, the chief engineer was appointed by BGF, although the general manager was appointed by XYZ Automotive.

[5] The problems of JVs are treated in Stopford and Wells (1972). More recent empirical research shows that JVs tend to be unstable and suffer from a set of inherent problems in the corporate structure of this form of business organization. See Miller, Glen, Jaspersen, and Karmokolias (1996).

tape, corruption, and poor contractual enforcement are symptoms of incomplete economic reforms, a point that reinforces our institutional foundation argument.

The regulatory advantage on the part of FIEs is relative to that of indigenous private firms. This statement in and of itself does not imply that China's business environment is hospitable. While being treated better than private firms is good news, it is hardly a substantial source of comfort considering that private firms in China receive the worst treatment. As I show in Chapter 2, SOEs still command advantages in regulatory and tax treatments compared with both FIEs and private firms, and this constitutes a serious problem for those FIEs that have to compete with the SOEs.

Economic Performance. There is another way that the institutional imperfections directly bear upon the operating difficulties of the FIEs. Given the extent of the inefficiencies, perhaps Chinese economic performance has not been as stellar as widely believed, and maybe some of the expected market growth has not come to fruition. Assumptions about future economic growth would affect how the investing firm calculates the value of its offer to acquire Chinese assets. If the Chinese economy were assumed to grow at a very high rate, firms would be willing to pay more for the assets because of their high *expected* value. If economic growth were to falter, then the actual value of the acquired assets would fall. Thus, those foreign investors who held rosier outlooks than warranted, and who thought that they got good deals at the time of their investments, might regret them later on.

It is quite possible that one of the reasons why expectations were unrealistically high in the first place is because foreign investors did not take into sufficient account the growth-dampening effect of many of the institutional distortions described in this book. Domestic investors, more knowledgeable about these systemic problems, had lower expectations and thus rationally sold off the assets they controlled. Herein lies a major anomaly in our FDI story. Between 1992 and 1997, as foreign investors poured massive resources into China, Chinese were eager to sell their assets, some at apparent discounts. Surely, an economic system that creates such an extent of insolvency among SOEs at a microeconomic level must also affect macroeconomic performance in some ways.

Recent research by Alwyn Young, an economist at the University of Chicago, reveals the disturbing fact that Chinese economic growth may be inferior to what is indicated by the official statistics (Young 2000a). The official statistics exaggerate Chinese growth performance, not because of intentional lies or propaganda, but because of the built-in faults of the Chinese system in collecting and compiling data on price deflators. Unlike in countries that collect price data through sampling, in China the enterprises themselves are called on to report both nominal and constant values of output, which are then used by government statisticians to convert into price deflators. Some enterprises often assume equality between nominal and constant values of their output, which means that the value of the reported deflators systematically understates the true inflation and thus systematically overstates the real growth.

By calculating the Chinese growth rate using an alternative set of deflators, Young lowers the average annual GDP growth rate from 9.1 percent to 7.4 percent between 1978 and 1998. A growth rate at 7.4 percent a year is still extremely impressive, but it does mean that the real purchasing power of Chinese consumers was below what was commonly assumed. It is noteworthy that almost all of this statistical bias took place after 1986, because this is when China experienced several inflationary surges. In 1993 and 1994, when FDI reached its peak as a proportion of capital formation, the statistical bias was the most serious.

In recent years, the gap between official growth statistics and estimates by independent economists has grown. In a paper published in 2001, Thomas Rawski, a professor at the University of Pittsburgh, estimates the Chinese growth rate to be half of that reported by the government (i.e., 3 to 4 percent versus 7.3 percent). He bases his calculation on the trend in energy consumption and passenger traffic, all showing either a sharp decline or modest growth (Rawski 2001). While Rawski's estimate is controversial, some economists within China also believe that the official statistics overstate Chinese economic growth, but by a lower margin. *The Economist* magazine quotes Song Guoqing, a senior economist at the Stock Exchange Executive Council, as saying that the real growth rate in 2001 was around 5 to 6 percent ("How Cooked Are the Books?" 2002). While in the early to mid-1990s, the dampening effects of many of the institutional distortions may have been offset by the massive FDI inflows, sooner or later, China will pay a price for not having addressed many of those problems early on.

FDI Efficiency

My analysis portrays China's high FDI demand as a function of a number of institutional distortions. However, one should not infer from this analysis that the effects of FDI are inefficient. In fact, the opposite is true. As the FDI inflows were driven by opportunities created by the inefficiencies in the Chinese economy, the FDI effect was an increase in the overall efficiency of the Chinese economy. Potentially profitable but unfunded business ventures are now being funded by foreign entrepreneurs. As we saw in the case of Sanguang in Suzhou in

Chapter 4, FDI played a critical role in financing the firm's growth, which would not have been possible under China's inefficient political pecking order. CSI, depicted in Chapter 6, performed a similar function. The geographic dispersion of industrial facilities was inefficient. Because of the restrictions on the mobility of domestic capital, domestic firms were unable to integrate these dispersed assets. CSI, a small Hong Kong firm in the restaurant business and real estate, rose to the challenge. These examples powerfully illustrate both the inefficiencies in the Chinese economy and the ameliorating effects of China's FDI inflows. In assessing the efficiencies of FDI, the larger context in which the effect of FDI occurs needs to be explicitly recognized. In this section, I consider the efficiency and other possible effects of FDI.

Funding Private Entrepreneurs and Restructuring SOEs. The most efficient form of FDI is precisely the type of FDI Chinese economic officials most often deride: labor-intensive and export-oriented FDI originating from Taiwan, Hong Kong, and Macao. Here, I agree with the conclusion of Richard Pomfret about the positive effect of labor-intensive FDI but I disagree with his reasoning. The efficiency associated with this type of FDI has less to do with the transfer of marketing and management know-how and the provision of access to overseas markets. The more important effect is that this type of FDI counteracts the distortions and inefficiencies of China's economic policies and institutions.

This is a productive way to think about both the extent and the limitations of the efficiency effect of FDI. At its core, what labor-intensive FDI has done is to offset some of the inefficiencies in the Chinese system. By this logic, we must assess the contribution of labor-intensive FDI in more realistic terms. Its contribution to the Chinese economy is fundamentally ameliorative in nature. The econometric findings that FDI has promoted Chinese exports must be interpreted with a recognition that FDI's contributions to export growth occurred in a context of suppressing the potentials of indigenous private firms to make the same contributions.[6]

The same logic applies when assessing the efficiency contributions of FDI in the heavy industries and of foreign acquisitions of assets previously under the control of SOEs via JVs or more direct methods. In heavy and capital-intensive industries, SOEs mostly compete with other SOEs. Because all SOEs are subject to similarly soft budget constraints, such competition may not lead to the most efficient results. The ability of domestic private firms to compete with the SOEs in higher value-added industries is curtailed by regulatory restrictions, thus leaving the FIEs as one of the few sources of genuine competition with

---

[6] Wei (1996a) shows the positive contributions of FDI to China's export growth.

the SOEs. Again, by a deliberate policy of imposing market entry restrictions on indigenous private firms, by default, the FIEs' competitive effects on the Chinese economy are more substantial than they would have been if the entry policy had been more liberal toward the domestic private sector.

Foreign acquisitions of the assets of SOEs can be analyzed in the same way. All things considered, SOEs are better at providing social services than at providing commercial services and products. Asset acquisitions by foreign firms, in all likelihood, have the effect of introducing a market orientation, profit incentives, and quality focus. But restrictions on domestic private firms – in terms of their growth and ability to acquire the assets of the large SOEs – have the effect of easing the competition faced by FIEs. This is costly to the country. Remember that foreign firms are wooed to invest in China by tax breaks and the conferral of other benefits. To some extent, China desperately needs foreign capitalists to take over its insolvent SOEs precisely because it does not allow its own capitalists to do the same.

Value of Control. There are other types of FDI effects beyond the efficiency issue. The FDI phenomenon is a process of transferring controls over existing assets or over future profit opportunities from Chinese to foreign hands. Ceding economic controls can be a controversial proposition, and criticisms of FDI often are motivated on nationalistic grounds. In evaluating these criticisms, we should distinguish between two kinds of nationalism. One is economic nationalism, which focuses on how the economic pie is distributed between foreign and domestic citizens and views any distribution seemingly in favor of foreigners with alarm. Analytically, economic nationalism is flawed because what is important is not the distribution of the pie but the aggregate size of the pie. As long as foreign management is more efficient, the payoff is greater to the Chinese even if the Chinese control only a portion of the pie, compared with a situation in which the Chinese control the entire but smaller pie due to poor management.

The other kind of nationalism is psychological. Some people simply do not like foreign controls of national assets regardless of the economic payoffs. There may be historical reasons for such psychological aversions to foreign controls. For example, Koreans restricted access of Japanese firms to Korea's goods and asset markets because of deep resentment toward Japanese colonial rule. Two points are pertinent here. One is that if a society believes, for whatever reason, that there is a high psychological cost of losing economic control to foreigners, then it is perfectly appropriate for policy makers to take this preference into account in their economic policies. The psychological welfare of a country should be incorporated into policy discussions and formulation, just as the economic welfare should be included. Some may assign more weight to the psychological dimensions; others may assign less. Which way one comes down on this issue is very much a function of one's tastes and preferences. Although this author does not assign an overwhelming weight to the psychological dimension, there is nothing intrinsically wrong with others doing so. In the Chinese context, it is plausible to argue that the psychological cost of losing economic control may be high given the country's history of antagonistic relationships with the West. (The 100 years between the Opium Wars and the founding of the PRC are often called a "century of humiliation.") Suppressing domestic entrepreneurship, which increases FDI, entails this particular political cost, which could have been avoided.

The second point is more relevant to my analysis of FDI. The view that ceding control incurs only a political but not an economic cost is wrong. Control means decision-making power and as such entails benefits to those who own and control the assets.[7] The evidence here is that in a market economy, investors are willing to pay a premium to acquire assets when such an acquisition comes with control rights, compared with an acquisition without control rights. For example, the shares of publicly traded corporations with control rights are often traded at a premium compared with shares without such control rights. This is shown in two ways. One is that finance economists have documented that the block of shares with voting rights is traded at a premium in the range of 10 percent in Germany, 20 percent in the United States, and as high as 80 percent in Italy. Another way is to look at the control premium of the class of shares with voting rights compared with the class of shares without voting rights but with equal dividend rights. (This is known as dual class common stock.) The voting premium ranges from 5.4 percent in the United States to 6.5 percent in Sweden and 13.3 percent in Britain.[8]

There are, of course, offsetting benefits of ceding controls. One tangible benefit to Chinese private entrepreneurs is equity financing. But as any business owner knows, ceding equity is an expensive way to access managerial expertise, and usually one gives up equity only in the absence of alternative sources of financing. In venture capital projects, for example, debt financing is usually unavailable because banks value a stable source of revenue, while the entrepreneurial technology start-ups entail high risks (defined as a high variance in their revenues). Therefore, they have to rely on equity capital from venture capitalists who are seeking to reap the huge upside if the project succeeds.

---

[7] This is a positivistic observation only and does not imply that private benefits of control are either desirable or undesirable.

[8] Roe (2001) summarizes this line of research.

None of these conditions readily applies to Chinese firms in labor-intensive and mature industries actively seeking FDI. China's reliance on expensive equity financing, sooner or later, will create problems for the country. As a sign of things to come, the Chinese balance of payments recorded a sharp increase in the investment income debit in recent years, from $6.7 billion in 1994 to $27.2 billion in 2000.[9] The investment income debit reflects the dividend payments to foreign investors, and while it does not necessarily suggest a net outflow of capital (as a portion of it can be reinvested in China through the capital account), it does show the growing impact of FIE operations on the Chinese economy. In a few years, the investment income debit term may very well be large enough to offset the substantial surpluses on China's trade account, and China's current account will go into deficit as a result. If foreign firms reinvest less of their earnings, the current account deficit has to be financed by other means.

The expensive foreign equity financing of Chinese private firms raises some troubling welfare issues. Consider the following set of facts. Chinese banks, while steadfastly refusing to lend to private firms, supply generous credits to the SOEs. The SOEs misuse these funds and venture into economically wasteful projects. Their near insolvency forces them to liquidate their assets on the cheap, mainly to foreigners. The same funding mechanism causes Chinese private entrepreneurs to cede their business controls to foreigners in order to access the most expensive form of capital because of the severe credit constraints imposed on them. It is difficult to justify this system on rational economic grounds.

In recent years, many of the FIEs in China have been set up as wholly owned subsidiaries of foreign firms, and thus, one might argue, the Chinese did not cede control because they previously did not own these assets. This view is correct only in a static sense, and it is slightly misleading. Today's profits are tomorrow's productive assets. The relevant question is who owns today's profits, not just who owns today's productive fixed assets such as the machinery and equipment. A dynamic analysis should pay attention not only to the ownership of assets at the current time but also to how the assets will be owned in the future.

Suppose that there is a profitable business opportunity out there, which a Chinese entrepreneur has an a priori better capability of capturing. He may know more about the manufacturing processes, product designs, and so on in this industry. But the inefficient banking practices prevent him from obtaining

---

[9] The investment income debit was trending upward continuously. It was $22.2 billion in 1998, $22.8 billion in 1999, and $27.2 billion in 2000. In 1994, it was only $6.7 billion. See International Monetary Fund (2001).

the necessary financing. A better-financed foreign entrepreneur captures this opportunity instead, even though the foreign entrepreneur may not have the requisite know-how or skills. (She can always make up for this functional deficiency by hiring the Chinese entrepreneur who was turned away by the Chinese bank.) In this instance, the Chinese have lost some of the benefits from a business opportunity that should have been theirs in the first place. In an accounting sense, losing control over one form of assets – in this case, cash – is equivalent to losing control over machines and equipment, if not more costly (because the cash can also be used to buy machinery).

When Capital Crosses an Institutional Border

When small garment and furniture makers based in Hong Kong moved their operations into the Pearl River Delta region of Guangdong province, in terms of geography, this was a trivial event. One can cross Lo Wu Bridge from the New Territories of Hong Kong into Shenzhen of China in less than 30 minutes, including the time for all the paperwork. As an institutional event, however, these Hong Kong entrepreneurs crossed a deep gulf. They were moving from the world's most laissez-faire economy into one of the more state-owned and government-controlled economies in the world.

FDI from Hong Kong into China is essentially a process whereby efficient and market-savvy firms reap gains by arbitraging their ability to *finance* business entrepreneurship, not – at least not completely – to arbitrage business entrepreneurship itself. As the example of COSMOS shows, Mr. Bao at Sanguang was an extremely capable entrepreneur. He, not COSMOS, had the technological know-how. What China lacked was an efficient mechanism to fund his business ventures. In low-tech, export-oriented industries, there is a similar dynamic. Chinese entrepreneurs, like entrepreneurs in Turkey, Taiwan, and Hong Kong, have the requisite manufacturing capabilities, but they lack access to financing – or a secure legal status – to perform their manufacturing tasks as contractual suppliers.

This way of analyzing FDI entails analytical implications. Let me first distinguish between the traditional economic perspective on FDI and our institutional perspective. Both perspectives share a common premise: that FDI is a way of organizing economic activities under a common ownership roof by exploiting and reaping gains from imperfections associated with market and contractual transactions. But they differ in terms of the kind of "imperfections" emphasized in their frameworks. I first review the gist of these two perspectives and then draw some empirical inferences from them. The main empirical implication is that third-world MNCs – MNCs from more developed developing economies – are most likely to thrive in an institutionally imperfect context and that foreign firms may engage in capital arbitrage.

Market Imperfections Versus Institutional Imperfections. FDI theorists focus on imperfections of a particular kind, that is, those imperfections that accompany market transactions of a specific class of economically useful resources: business, organizational, or technological know-how. In contrast, the institutional foundation argument focuses on imperfections of a wider kind, called here institutional imperfections, which have to do with the poor functioning of the market to allocate *all* resources and *all* goods. In other words, market imperfections, as commonly understood in economics literature, refer to failures of the market to transact those products or resources endowed with some unique characteristics. The general presumption is that the market is otherwise efficient in allocating all other goods and resources. Institutional imperfections, however, involve failures or substantial deficiencies of the market as an economic system. *Simply put, they refer to failures of the market system to organize economic activities of all kinds.* These institutional imperfections are not a function of the specific attributes of the goods or resources being transacted but of deliberate choices made by governments.

This distinction between market and institutional imperfections cannot be emphasized enough because it explains why a similar underlying conceptualization of FDI – that it is driven by extant inefficiencies – can lead to quite different predictions about specific factors driving FDI flows. The focus on market imperfections is deeply and richly rooted in institutional economics. A fundamental question in institutional economics is, Why ownership at all? Coase (1937) posed this question in his seminal paper, "The Nature of the Firm": Why does the boundary of the firm lie where it does? What are the efficiency gains from having production and employment relations organized in a hierarchical and administrative manner as opposed to being organized on an arm's-length, spot-contract basis? The crux of the economic reasoning is that there are certain infirmities associated with market transactions that prevent efficient arm's-length exchanges, and these infirmities can be overcome only within a hierarchical organization. Although economists may disagree about what these market infirmities are, the general consensus within institutional economics is that a hierarchical organization arises to overcome these market infirmities and to create efficiency by reducing the transaction costs.[10]

---

[10] Coase stresses search costs as embodied in transactions intermediated through a price mechanism; firms reduce these costs by organizing transactions administratively. Alchian and Demsetz (1972), on the other hand, note the measurement problems and associated shirking behavior.

The idea that hierarchy is a product of market failures is extremely powerful. It has led to a proliferation of research in economics and other social science disciplines. The version of the economic perspective on FDI that I present in Chapter 2 is a natural extension of this idea. The economic paradigm equates FDI with a process undertaken by an MNC to internalize foreign production. The internalization thesis says, simply, that an investing firm will internalize its production in geographically dispersed locations when and if it is more efficient than a market transaction.[11] FDI theorists then supply a number of scenarios under which internalization is superior to market transactions, ranging from the "lumpiness" and the public-good nature of knowledge[12] to appropriability problems,[13] and so on. These problems are more common in know-how–driven industries, and thus FDI arrangements tend to prevail in these industries.[14]

But what if the market system itself is seriously deficient? Here, the market "fails" not because of the intrinsic economic characteristics of the transactions in question but because of a deliberate political and policy choice made by a government to alter, influence, or restrict market functions. To the extent that these policy interventions go beyond correcting familiar market failures, the imperfections necessarily encompass a far greater array of economic activities than those envisaged by institutional economists focusing on normally functioning markets. Take the example of property rights. In a market-imperfect economy, the appropriability problem can arise because of the intrinsic difficulties of

According to this logic, firms arise because they facilitate monitoring and supervision and thereby attenuate shirking behavior. Williamson (1975) argues that opportunistic behavior – gaming behavior and misrepresentation of information for strategic gains – combined with bounded rationality and small-number problems give rise to transaction costs. Bounded rationality refers to the fact that human beings are often quite limited in their computational and analytical skills and therefore they are generally not able to examine all available alternatives in an exhaustive fashion. This gives rise to "satisficing" behavior. See Simon (1982).

[11] There is a large body of economic literature on this topic. Two books are often closely associated with the internalization hypothesis. They are Buckley and Casson (1976) and Casson (1979).

[12] The dynamics work as follows. The value of information can be assessed only if its content is disclosed, but such a disclosure weakens any incentives to pay for it. This can be easily extended to an FDI situation. A foreign vendor might be wary of disclosing the design and technical specifications of a product to a domestic firm unless the product has already been paid for. The problem, however, is that the domestic firm cannot begin to evaluate the worth of the product unless the information is first disclosed. Just to complete the story, once the information is disclosed, the domestic firm will lose the incentive to pay for it. In the presence of the indivisibility inherent in technology and human know-how, the integration of plants and common ownership are created to economize on the utilization of these factors (Teece 1982).

[13] For an illustration of this problem in an FDI context, see Magee (1977). This type of dynamic applies not just to R&D-based technology but also to organizational and managerial types of know-how.

[14] These industries include vertically integrated processes, knowledge-intensive industries, and communications-intensive industries (Buckley 1988).

assigning revenue benefits to the rightful owners. But that there is a rightful owner is never in doubt. Contrast this situation with the one facing Mr. Bao in Chapter 3. There is no doubt that he built up the business, but it was still difficult for him to claim the business as his own.

These are the institutional imperfections examined in this book. They arise when the market transactions of those goods, assets, and services that are otherwise unencumbered by any conceivable market imperfections are also hampered. An important implication of this analysis is that an ownership mechanism, such as FDI, is not confined to playing a residual role in solving problems associated with a narrower category of imperfections created by transacting a group of resources with special characteristics. By extension, FDI, as an ownership arrangement, plays a far more important role in an economy beset with institutional imperfections.[15]

Third-World MNCs. The focus of economic literature on FDI concerns FDI going from one advanced market economy to another. Fundamentally, FDI is an economic activity among developed market economies. FDI from one advanced market economy to another is unencumbered by the kind of institutional imperfections that are analyzed here. Thus, a perspective focusing on market imperfections dominates the literature for a totally unsurprising reason.

Institutional imperfections are a fact of life in many less developed countries in general and in partially reformed socialist economies in particular. The implication is that the patterns and composition of FDI in institutionally imperfect economies should depart sharply from those predicted on the basis of a theory based on narrower market imperfections. The underlying reasoning need not change, that is, FDI is an ownership arrangement designed to overcome contractual imperfections, but two critical differences between institutionally imperfect and market-imperfect economies need to be noted. One is that there are more sources of contractual imperfections in an institutionally imperfect economy. The other is that the sources of contractual imperfections should be different in an institutionally imperfect economy.

The empirical implications are twofold. One is that FDI, as an ownership arrangement, supplies more functions in an institutionally imperfect economy and therefore plays a more encompassing role in such an economy as compared with an economy beset only by market imperfections (and identical in every other attribute that is relevant to FDI). The other is that the kind of

---

[15] I focus on FDI in this book, but the logic applies to any other ownership arrangement as well. As our example of SAIC shows, internalization of production facilities – owned and operated by domestic entities – can also be motivated by this consideration.

firm-specific advantages held by MNCs operating in such an economy can be different from the conventional advantages postulated by industrial organization economists. Both of these points bring us to the role of the so-called third-world MNCs.[16] Third-world MNCs, such as those based in the ECEs, although devoid of the financial and technological advantages held by first-world MNCs, nevertheless can play an active, and indeed a preponderant, role in the Chinese economy because they provide many solutions to institutional imperfections. Compared with domestic private firms, they have greater capabilities to finance entrepreneurship and a readier access to foreign exchange. Compared with the SOEs, they have greater freedom to impose quality controls, superior accounting and marketing skills, and more market orientations. None of these would constitute firm-specific advantages as envisaged by industrial organization theorists but they do in a setting in which the market allocation of many resources and products is problematic.

We have used this framework to account for the role of FDI from the ECEs in the Chinese economy, but its logic need not be limited to China. Let me offer a number of hypothetical cases in which third-world MNCs may conceivably play an important role. One scenario is a misallocation of foreign exchange. A tentative hypothesis is that third-world MNCs can be particularly active in those economies where allocations of foreign exchange are inefficient. For example, in the 1960s and 1970s many governments in developing countries adopted an import substitution strategy. Under such a regime, foreign exchange could be rationed by quota. In countries where the government allocated foreign exchange quotas to support large firms in capital-intensive industries, smaller firms were disadvantaged. Similar to the situation we examine in this book, this could have led to a high dependency on export-oriented FDI. (This assumes that the country was not short of basic manufacturing capabilities in labor-intensive industries.) In this respect one can cite Sri Lanka, which was "one of the most inward-oriented and regulated economies outside the communist bloc. . . ." Against this background, the country moved to an export-promotion path. Labor-intensive FDI dominated the country's export

---

[16] Third-world MNCs are, to some extent, a misnomer. Hong Kong is not a third-world economy, nor is Korea, but many researchers classify investing firms from these economies as third-world MNCs. In part, this is because researchers began to note FDI from these economies in the 1970s when they were still legitimately classified as third-world countries. Such MNCs have a different industrial focus and possess a lower level of technology compared to more conventional MNCs. For example, in the 1970s, FDI from Japan often differed from FDI from the United States and Europe in significant ways even though Japan was already a developed country. Thus, as used here, third-world MNCs should be understood as those MNCs that have different attributes from more conventional MNCs, rather than strictly as MNCs based in low-income developing economies. An entire volume is devoted to this topic. See Agmon and Kindleberger (1977).

production.[17] The opposite was true for Korea and Taiwan, two economies that relied mainly on contractual export production to develop their labor-intensive industries. As widely documented, in Taiwan and Korea an import substitution strategy was neutralized by a performance-based system of allocating foreign exchange and by a proexport policy stance.[18]

Another situation is a sudden mismatch of functional skills in the host economy. A simple illustration is a centrally planned economy in the process of shifting to a market economy system. Under central planning, managers built up a set of skills appropriate to the functioning of that type of economy. Marketing capabilities were unimportant under central planning; premium skills included the ability to formulate and defend one's input requests on sophisticated engineering grounds and political skills to negotiate favorable output targets with the bureaucracy. Accounting conventions, norms, and rules also differed dramatically under central planning.

A rapid transition to a market economy system, in essence, renders the know-how and skills cultivated during the central planning period obsolete *across the board*. By this logic, during the initial years of transition, foreign companies holding some basic functional skills required in a market economy can be very valuable. Some of these companies could be third-world MNCs whose know-how, such as accounting skills based on Western accounting standards, is high in demand. By definition, such opportunities are transitory in nature because the high returns on their accounting skills are based not on some permanent advantages held by the foreign firms but on a sudden mismatch between demand for and supply of market-economy skills.[19]

Another scenario may warrant an ownership arrangement even when the know-how involved is general and functional rather than proprietary or intangible and when contractual transactions are otherwise feasible on technical grounds. An example here is quality control. In developing countries, firms entering into an industry may need to obtain licenses from the government. For whatever reasons, some governments may systematically license those firms that are least quality-focused. In China, for example, for many years only the

---

[17] Reported in Athukorala and Rajapatirana (2000).

[18] The policy neutrality between the production of exportables and the production of importables in Korea and Taiwan is well known. See World Bank (1993) for an illustration.

[19] One example of this dynamic is the transfer of what would be normally regarded as a general skill in the West – competence in international accountancy – into Poland in the wake of its economic liberalization. Suddenly, as Robert Kennedy writes in a paper on the connections between policy reforms and FDI, "Western CPAs who spoke Polish were in high demand." Some of these accountants were granted expatriate packages at 300 to 500 percent of their standard billing rates. Reported in Kennedy (2000).

SOEs were allowed to enter into the automotive industry, but because SOEs were poor in quality management and controls, an SOE that had succeeded in establishing quality controls would acquire enormous bargaining power over its customers. For a buyer, switching suppliers while maintaining the same level of product quality is simply not an option. In this particular context, what is generally regarded as a general skill or know-how – quality control – becomes a specific skill or know-how and as such may very well create hold-up problems, which may motivate a buyer-firm to integrate backward.

A foreign firm may make the same calculation. For example, a Taiwanese firm has the theoretical alternative to contract with a Chinese SOE to produce automotive components. To ensure quality, it will incur costs to train its SOE supply managers about quality control and focus. Once trained, these managers will become extremely attractive to other Taiwanese buyers of automotive components in the overall context of a short supply of quality control among SOEs. Knowing this, our Taiwanese firm may be motivated to acquire control over the SOE to prevent hold-up complications. The institutional factors are relevant to this hypothetical example in two ways. First, the political pecking order of firms means that only SOEs are licensed for automotive production, and thus the total supply of quality control and focus is low because only the least quality-sensitive firms are licensed. Quality control becomes a firm-specific attribute as a result.

Second, good SOE managers are rotated frequently within the bureaucracy and among SOEs.[20] This makes sense to the bureaucrats, because they do not view a good SOE manager as someone promoting shareholder value on a long-term basis but as someone who solves problems. If an SOE manager proves to be capable, the natural inclination is to assign him to a troubled enterprise to solve the problems there. Thus, a rational approach is for our Taiwanese firm to acquire the SOE in the first place to prevent losing competent managers. This consideration may explain why firms based in the ECEs have sought to establish majority controls over their facilities in China even though they may be content with minority equity positions in other countries.[21]

Capital Arbitrage. A tentative theoretical contribution of our institutional foundation framework is a revival of the idea that MNCs may perform some

---

[20] There is empirical evidence that SOE managers are frequently changed. See Groves, Hong, McMillan, and Naughton (1995).

[21] For research on greater receptivity to minority equity positions of Singaporean and Hong Kong firms in the 1970s, see Giddy and Young (1982). For research that explicitly draws a distinction between FDI by Hong Kong firms in China and that in other countries, see Chen (1981).

important capital arbitrage functions.[22] The capital arbitrage hypothesis says that MNCs move capital from countries with low returns on capital to countries with high returns on capital. FDI scholars, on both theoretical and empirical grounds, however, have long discredited this idea. Theoretically, it is not clear why MNCs, as opposed to portfolio investors, are particularly suited to this task. Also the idea is inconsistent with the fact that FDI has moved in both directions; that is, some countries, such as the United States, have both exported and attracted direct equity capital at the same time. Empirical analysis has also failed to produce much evidence in support of this hypothesis.[23]

However, it is important to note that all the studies on this topic have focused on movement of FDI from one market economy to another, and it is possible that the negative findings on the capital arbitrage hypothesis are driven by the empirical foci of such analyses. If much of the FDI moves across economies that are institutionally indistinguishable from one another and that already operate at a high level of efficiency, it is only natural that there may not be persistent and sizable market inefficiencies left for MNCs to exploit. When capital moves across different economic systems and across countries with different levels of capital market development, capital arbitrage opportunities may arise, and MNCs may be uniquely capable of exploiting these opportunities.

EVALUATING CHINA'S REFORM STRATEGY

Because our analysis of FDI is firmly grounded in an analysis of the design and characteristics of China's financial and economic institutions, it is only natural that we end the book by reflecting on this broader issue and by moving beyond the FDI question. Our verdict is that these institutions have functioned rather poorly if economic efficiency is used as a criterion. Such a claim inevitably requires an assessment of China's reform strategy. Do these inefficiencies constitute overall failures or a transitional phase in the Chinese reforms? Is the political pecking order of firms likely to persist or to fade away? Does the Chinese reform strategy contain a self-enforcing logic that propels marketization and privatization on its own accord? These are complex issues, each deserving a dedicated treatment in one or even several volumes. The spirit of our assessment is not to offer a rigorous empirical analysis but to suggest a number of broad, tentative, and speculative perspectives.

In the following paragraphs, I first make the case that relative to its pace of external reforms, China's internal reforms have lagged. However, external and

---

[22] I owe this observation to Professor Pankaj Ghemawat.
[23] For a summary of these studies, see Lizondo (1995) and Caves (1996).

internal reforms are not wholly independent of each other. They may interact with each other in complicated ways. In the following paragraphs, I speculate on how external reforms, such as China's WTO accession, may reinforce internal reforms. I then evaluate China's gradualist reform strategy. This evaluation is necessarily multifaceted. While an overall assessment is positive, we still need to ask whether the strategy can be applied to other countries and whether there may be hidden costs associated with China's reform strategy that have not been fully accounted for.

Internal and External Reforms

In 1978, Deng Xiaoping formulated China's reform program to encompass two components: structural reforms of the economy and China's opening to the rest of the world (*gaige kaifang*). More than twenty years later, the Chinese economy is quite open, as judged by the foreign trade to GDP ratio and FDI dependency. Nothing suggests more powerfully China's commitment to open its economy further to foreign trade and investment than its acceptance of the obligations to the WTO. Under the WTO accession terms, China is obligated to eliminate all import quotas by 2006 and significantly scale down its tariff protection on industrial imports. Foreign firms will be allowed to own up to 50 percent of FIEs in the telecom and insurance industries. Foreign importers will be able to own domestic distribution networks, and foreign banks will be able to conduct local currency business with Chinese enterprises within two years of accession.[24] According to an analysis prepared by the Institute of International Economics, China's accession commitments exceed those of India, a member since 1947, and are comparable to those of Korea and Japan in a number of critical respects (Rosen 1999b).

As China has successfully attracted the lion's share of FDI among developing countries and has emerged as one of the world's export powerhouses, it is now bracing itself for the greater economic and business challenges of globalization. Many fear that Chinese firms are simply unprepared for these challenges. The reason is not hard to understand. While China has aggressively pushed forward its reforms on the external front, its internal reforms have lagged. This raises a number of questions, one of which is whether China's WTO accession can act as a catalyst to internal reforms. I take up this and related issues in this section.

Lagging Internal Reforms. A key measure of internal reforms is the development of a vibrant and vigorous private sector. By this measure, China has fallen

---

[24] These accession terms are summarized in International Finance Corporation (2000).

far short. In recent years, the Chinese government has encouraged the growth and development of private firms and has permitted a privatization program of small SOEs. During much of the reform era, however, China's private sector was viewed suspiciously in ideological terms and was afflicted with severe regulatory and financial discrimination. As a result, the most efficient firms in China, endowed with entrepreneurial drive and market orientation, are underdeveloped relative to their economic and business potentials. A telling indication is that although China has become an attractive manufacturing base for firms from all over the world, it has not produced many world-class and globally competitive firms. A few, such as Haier, Kelon, Legend Computer, and Huawei, have emerged in recent years on China's corporate scene, but it is important to note that these firms have succeeded despite, not because of, China's political pecking order. None of these firms received substantial support from the government in the 1980s. In contrast, those firms that did receive government support have all failed.

The lagging internal reforms are indicated by many of the investment barriers still confronting domestic investors, while those facing foreign investors came down substantially in the last twenty years (and will come down further when China implements its WTO commitments). As officials at all levels of the government eagerly court foreign investors, domestic private investors still face ideological and legal barriers and considerable financing constraints. Local protectionism, although greatly weakened in recent years, still hampers the mobility of domestic capital movement to a significant extent. Substantial efficiency improvements can be achieved if the policy makers begin to tackle these problems directly and more aggressively.

FDI is a means to economic growth, not an end in and of itself. Given China's size, a well-developed internal product and capital market is more important to its long-term growth trajectory than foreign capital supplies and foreign markets. An interesting comparison can be made with India. In many aspects, India still is not on par with China in economic terms, except, probably, in one area: India does not have the kind of ideological discrimination against its own indigenous private firms in the way China does. It is no coincidence that India today claims to be home to several world-class firms – owned and managed by Indians themselves – even though its economy is half the size of the Chinese economy and India began its reforms a full decade later than China. In software, Infosys and Wipro operate on a global scale to provide low-cost and high-quality products and services. In the pharmaceutical and biotechnology industries, firms such as Cipla, Ranbaxy Laboratories Ltd., and Biocon compete head to head and are beginning to win fierce competition with MNCs in certain product segments. The United States

Federal Drug Administration has approved twenty-five manufacturing plants in India.[25]

India's institutional developments have been quite substantial. According to a study by Credit Lyonnais on corporate governance in emerging markets, China ranks nineteenth out of twenty-five surveyed countries, far behind India (sixth).[26] While China's growth rate has declined since 1997, India's growth rate has remained steady. Between 1997 and 1999, its gross national product grew at an annual average rate of 5.9 percent, compared with China's 7.2 percent.[27] To be sure, India's growth rate was not as stellar as China's – and it was from a lower base as well – but India accomplished this growth against many exogenously given bad fundamentals, such as deep ethnic tensions and political divisions. Also impressively, while India's growth was about 80 percent of China's, India achieved this rate on the basis of about half of China's savings rate and less than 10 percent of China's FDI inflows. This is an indication that capital utilization in India may be more efficient. China's problem is not that it does not have enough FDI, but that its internal distortions are not being addressed adequately and its use of capital remains inefficient among the SOEs.

A potential warning sign from a high structural dependency on FDI is the economic performance of Singapore in recent years. In 2001, Singapore went into a deep recession after many years of rapid growth. One reason for this may be Singapore's inordinate dependency on the external sector, including FDI. To some extent, as a small city-state and an open economy, Singapore does not have the option to substantially insulate itself from the macroeconomic cycles of Western countries, but the issue is whether Singapore could have avoided such a high dependency on FDI. As shown in Table 1.2 of Chapter 1, China and Singapore are among the most FDI-dependent countries in Asia. Between 1992 and 1998, the FDI/capital formation ratio was 22.9 percent in Singapore and 13.1 percent in China. Another similarity is that both countries had a relatively large public sector. When the capital formation only includes private sector investments, Singapore's FDI dependency ratio rises to 30.3 percent and China's rises to 27.9 percent.

In fact the similarities between the two countries are more than skin-deep.[28] Similar to China, in the 1970s the Singaporean government systematically promoted SOEs (or government-linked companies) and FDI, while adopting

---

[25] See Jordan (1999), "India's Fermentation Queen" (2001), Pesta and Ramakrishnan (2001), and Huang and Hogan (2002).

[26] The study is cited in Mackenzie (2001).

[27] The GNP growth rate data are provided in World Bank (1999, 2002b).

[28] The following section is based on an enlightening discussion with Professor Linda Lim. All the information quoted in the text comes from Lim (2002).

policies that discriminated against local entrepreneurs. A disproportionate number of the People's Action Party leaders were English-speaking mandarins who benefited from the expansion of the civil service, the promotion of the SOEs, and the MNCs' high demand for professionals. Private entrepreneurs lacked political clout and a cultural fit. Nanyang University, which used Chinese-language instruction, was closed down in 1981. (Table 1.2 of Chapter 1 shows Malaysia to be one of the most FDI-dependent countries in the table. Malaysia, like Singapore and China, also heavily promoted SOEs and suppressed local – and mainly ethnically Chinese – entrepreneurship while liberalizing FDI controls in the 1970s and 1980s.)[29]

The legacy from this period is profound. According to Professor Linda Lim at the University of Michigan Business School, "Local business is disproportionately reliant on government and multinationals as customers (also privileged competitors)." Local private firms lack initiatives and innovativeness and follow the edicts of the government, often leading to failures. The preponderance of the public and foreign sectors has affected the composition of the economy – an extremely high share of manufacturing for Singapore's income level – as well as the allocation of talent and even the character of its people. Singaporeans are widely perceived, by outsiders and themselves, as "too careful, too rule-based." "[W]hen we have no rules," as Wim Wong Hoo, chairman of Singapore's Creative Technology, a private sector committee promoting high-tech entrepreneurship, puts it, "we are paralyzed." Lee Kuan Yew himself recognized the problem. "In Singapore," he said, "many of those who were most likely to succeed have been inducted into politics, the bureaucracy and the army, navy and air force. Hence too few are in business on their own and even fewer are entrepreneurs." China will do best to avoid being locked on this path.

External Reform as a Substitute for or as a Complement to Internal Reform?
At a deeper level, the issue is whether or not external reforms are a complement to rather than a substitute for necessary internal reforms. It is plausible to argue that in the early 1990s, external reforms acted as a substitute for internal reforms by providing temporary solutions, which may have obviated painful structural reforms. One can argue, for example, that had the massive FDI inflows not materialized in response to Deng Xiaoping's dramatic open-door policy initiatives in 1992, the SOE reforms would have been deeper and the political pecking order would have been alleviated earlier. The reason is that the solvency crisis in the state sector would have been more severe and China's financial strains on the private sector might have been more transparent. Instead, the massive

---

[29] See Lim and Fong (1991), esp. pp. 37–41.

FDI inflows, in conjunction with a loosening of the monetary policy, provided a temporary boost to the economy, probably contributing to a delay of the much-needed structural reforms to the late 1990s. Another effect associated with the inflows of labor-intensive FDI was the low institutional demands ECE investors placed on the Chinese system. Compared with Western firms, ECE firms are accustomed to using family and ad hoc solutions to solve their problems. The deep structural reforms were less important to attract this type of FDI. One can debate the legacy of this type of FDI: whether this type of FDI has delayed China's institutional reforms or whether it has merely filled an institutional gap that would have been difficult to fill under the best of circumstances.[30]

On balance, however, external reforms, such as China's WTO accession, are likely to complement internal reforms. The WTO accession is likely to promote internal reforms principally by weakening the force of the political pecking order of firms. It will do so in three ways. First, the Chinese leaders today are faced with a stark choice between socialism and nationalism. Socialism as an economic idea has failed all over the world, but in China it has failed in a particular fashion: It has created many profitable business opportunities for foreign firms. So far, the strategy has worked. In the early 1990s, when the economy was growing rapidly, there was less concern from the public about how the economic pie was divided between foreign and domestic firms. But as the economy begins to slow down, policy makers and the Chinese public will be more concerned about the distributive implications of such a strategy. It is likely that economic nationalism will be on the rise.

Many in China increasingly fear FIEs as formidable competitors in the marketplace and as threatening to drive indigenous firms out of business. It is likely that in the future the Chinese state may decide to support private firms out of a nationalistic imperative. It may conclude, as I do in this book, that the most efficient and the most competitive firms are private firms and that they constitute the only viable competitive force to the foreign firms. It is plausible that the increasingly encouraging stance of the government toward the private sector, including the statement by President Jiang Zemin on July 1, 2001, welcoming private entrepreneurs into the ranks of the Chinese Communist Party, was due to such a realization.

The second likely effect of WTO membership will come from the efficiency improvement in China's service sector. Reforms in China's service sector – banking, insurance, wholesale, retail, and telecommunications – have lagged behind reforms in the real sector. SOEs still dominate these service industries to a far greater extent than they dominate the manufacturing industries. But the

[30] For this observation, see Perkins (2001), pp. 250–51.

service sector is a particularly important component of an economy because service firms are in business for business and the inefficiencies of service firms have a significant dragging effect on the entire economy. The WTO accession will force China to open its doors to the most efficient foreign service providers. This will be beneficial to China's indigenous private firms. Inefficient service SOEs – the banks as just one example – have been a bottleneck for the growth, development, and maturation of China's indigenous private firms.

The third likely effect of WTO membership is that China will become more institutionally integrated into the global economy. So far, the open-door policy has increased China's *economic* integration, that is, an increasingly large share of its GDP is traded on the world market and a large portion of its capital formation comes from foreign sources. But China's economic, regulatory, and legal institutions remain quite insulated. WTO membership will change this. The Chinese government will have to rewrite many of its laws and regulations to conform to the requirements of WTO membership. The removal and streamlining of cumbersome business regulations will lower transaction costs for *all* firms, whether foreign or domestic, and will benefit efficient domestic firms operating in a local market niche or endowed with substantial local know-how.

Evaluating the Gradualist Strategy

The huge success of China's reforms is indisputable. Economic growth has been impressive, as a World Bank report comments: "[I]f China's thirty provinces were counted as individual economies, the twenty fastest-growing economies in the world between 1978 and 1995 would have been Chinese" (World Bank 1997a, p. 3). Poverty has fallen dramatically and the Chinese economy has been transformed from a shortage economy in the 1970s to one that today faces a chronic oversupply of many goods and services. (Of course, this is another type of inefficiency.) The Chinese people are enjoying economic and social freedoms unprecedented in the history of the People's Republic. Yes, an inefficient political pecking order of firms has persisted throughout the reform era and has led to a high dependency on FDI. But, in the grand scheme of things, this is not the worst possible outcome and many countries have done considerably worse.

One should also recognize the enormous challenges confronting Chinese policy makers over the last twenty years. The leadership has been managing two parallel developments, each fraught with a high degree of complexity and uncertainty. One is the transition from a planned to a market economy and the other is the transformation from a rural to an industrial economy. In the presence of massive uncertain contingencies about policy outcomes, as a number of economists stress, gradualism is a superior strategy (Dewatripont and Roland 1995). Our overall assessment of China's gradual reforms is strongly positive.

That said, it is still worth pondering three broad questions, all posed in the spirit of determining whether China could have done even better and whether its strategy is sustainable. The first question is whether China's reform strategy can apply to other transitional economies. So far, China's strategy has succeeded, but its success may depend on a number of China-specific conditions. One needs to recognize these specific circumstances before advocating this strategy for other countries. The second question is whether China's reform strategy – in particular, its steadfast refusal to privatize its SOEs – entails any costs. After recognizing these costs, one may still argue that the Chinese have done the right thing, but it would be wrong not to explicitly acknowledge the costs. The third question is whether China indeed pursued a gradualist strategy when it came to SOE reforms. The reason why I pose this question is that a gradualist strategy does not rule out privatization; it advocates sequencing privatization after certain reformist steps have been taken and certain conditions have been met. I argue that many of the conditions for undertaking a large-scale privatization already existed in the early and mid-1990s, but China did not choose a privatization path. Something else may have been at work.

China-Specific Factors. Our institutional foundation argument raises a question about whether or not China's reform experience can be readily replicated in other countries. An important reason why the Chinese economy was able to grow despite its institutional imperfections is, to some extent, a function of factors that have little to do with its reform strategy. China has a number of attractive macroeconomic fundamentals. It has a large internal market potential. (After all, the idea that if only every Chinese would buy one pair of shoes long preceded the economic reforms.) Its labor force is skilled, disciplined, and cheap. These conditions were fundamentally sound even before the economic reforms. Good macroeconomic fundamentals are necessary but not sufficient conditions for FDI. If indigenous firms fail to capitalize on the good macroeconomic fundamentals, foreign firms step in and fill the gap. This is not the best solution, but it is a second-best one. The question is whether this second-best solution is available to many other developing countries.

If the issue is why China gets FDI at all, as opposed to why FDI dependency is so high, China's location – in a geographic and cultural sense – is critical: It is situated close to Hong Kong and Taiwan, two sources of a ready supply of capital to the credit-constrained private firms. Absent these ties to the ethnic Chinese capital suppliers, the nonstate firms would have atrophied under the weight of the lending bias in the system, and economic growth would not have been as impressive. Countries without China's propitious conditions, but stocked with China's institutional inefficiencies, are unlikely to attract much FDI. The second-best solution is available to certain countries but not to all countries. Many countries may have no choice but to get their economic and financial institutions right.

China's impressive growth owes little to one component of the reform strategy that presumably matters most for transitional economies: reforms of the SOEs. An emerging consensus among China economists is that the SOE reforms failed to improve the productivity of the state sector.[31] The massive entry and growth of nonstate firms was more a function of China's developmental stage than of the reform strategy itself. Sachs and Woo (1994) show that the rapid growth of TVEs was due to a drawing down of the surplus labor in China's agricultural sector. Since the state sector in the late 1970s employed only some 18 percent of the entire labor force, the TVEs could draw labor from agriculture without directly competing with the SOEs. This is why an active privatization policy could have been avoided and why in China, but not in the more industrialized Russia, SOEs have been able to cohabit with a growing nonstate sector for a long period of time. Thus, this particular success – tempered by the recognition that a truly private sector still remains underdeveloped – is related to the status of the country as an agrarian economy rather than to the SOE reforms per se.

Implicit Costs of China's Reform Strategy. While the conventional wisdom in the general transitional literature espouses rapid market liberalization and mass privatization (the so-called big-bang approach or Washington Consensus),[32] the wisdom about the Chinese reforms is that a big-bang approach to transform from socialism to capitalism is neither necessary nor desirable.[33] In part, this view of China's reforms is driven by a focus on China's substantial economic successes, rather than on the costs of China's reforms. My hypothesis is that the costs of China's reform strategy have not been accounted for completely.

To the extent that a number of scholars have noted these costs, their conclusion is that they have been quite small. China did not experience the kind of "transitional recession" in the way that the Russian and Eastern European

---

[31] See Woo and Fan (1994) for an illustration.

[32] The big-bang approach usually refers to macroeconomic stabilization. Unless otherwise noted, here it refers to institutional transformation strategies rather than to macroeconomic stabilization policies.

[33] As Qian (1999) puts it, "the Chinese path of reform and its associated rapid growth seemed to defy the necessity part of the conventional wisdom: Although China has adopted many of the policies advocated by economists, such as being open to trade and foreign investment and macroeconomic stability, violations of the standard policy prescriptions are also striking."

economies did. The reforms have apparently improved the welfare of the population across the board, with no significant segment of the population suffering an absolute loss. According to a noted formulation, the Chinese reform has been "Pareto-optimal" in that it has created winners without creating losers (Lau, Qian, and Roland 2000).

It is worth noting that the provinces that have pursued more radical reforms (such as Guangdong and Zhejiang) have done the best, whereas provinces relying on an incremental approach, mainly in China's northeast, have stagnated. This is prima facie evidence that the economic collapse in Russia should not be attributed completely to its reform strategy. Under seventy-three years of central planning, Russia in the early 1990s was already poised for an economic collapse regardless of which reform strategy it adopted. (To be sure, the radical reform strategy and its distortionary implementation did not help.) Contrast this situation with China in the early 1990s. China was growing rapidly and continuously in the 1980s, and it is not at all clear that a faster pace of ownership reforms would have resulted in a catastrophic collapse of output.

The "Pareto-optimal" assessment of the Chinese reforms critically depends on limiting the analysis to "overt" losers, such as unemployed SOE workers. But there may be many "implicit" losers in the process. SOE employment has been maintained and expanded at the expense of the quality of the assets in the Chinese banking system. If this is a compensation policy, it is a very expensive one indeed. The cost of the massive nonperforming loans will have to be absorbed somehow. This burden will fall on bank depositors if the banks are allowed to go bankrupt. It will fall on current or future taxpayers if the Chinese government decides to recapitalize the banking system. Worse still, if the insolvency of the banking system triggers a financial crisis (such as that in East Asia in 1997) or if it is a catalyst to a prolonged recession (such as that in Japan in the 1990s), the entire population will be the losers. In any event, this compensation policy is no longer working. Unemployment in the state sector has been rising dramatically since 1995.

Another class of implicit losers is the private entrepreneurs who have forgone profitable growth opportunities and forsaken control over their own businesses, possibly at disadvantageous terms. Purely in financial terms, there is no reason why these forgone benefits should be less important than the actual losses incurred. China's failure to create competitive and globally operating firms, in the midst of a fast-growing market, a deep structural change in the economy, and unprecedented export opportunities, is a specific manifestation of this cost. In the medium to long run, the relative underdevelopment of an indigenous wealthy and entrepreneurial asset-owning class may act as a drag on the Chinese economy through a depression of domestic consumption and investment demand.

Should the Western economies, led by the United States, go into a prolonged recession, this effect will become more apparent.

So far, the explicit costs on the political side have been low. The rationale for sacrificing the interests of Chinese private entrepreneurs was political: Forgoing future benefits is more palatable politically than incurring actual losses because it is simply in human nature that people react more strongly to actual losses than to forgone benefits. There is another rationale as well why the regime has sacrificed the interests of private entrepreneurs: They are politically powerless. We need to keep in mind this distinction between economic and political costs. There have been economic costs – if of an uncertain form and magnitude – to China's reform strategy. The fact that gradualism may be the best political strategy is qualitatively different from stating that a gradualist strategy is actually a better *economic* strategy. There is now every indication that the political costs of sacrificing the interests of China's private entrepreneurs will rise. The political pecking order of firms has led to a high dependency on FDI and to a disproportionate share of future growth dividends accruing to foreigners. For a regime that prides itself on defending national interests, this is a serious political cost.

The Logic of Gradualist Reforms. The logic of a sequential reform strategy is very powerful and convincing. The basic argument is that reforms are fraught with uncertainties about eventual outcomes. Political support for reforms is best generated by bottom-up demand for deeper reforms as the public and government can take advantage of the successes of the initial and easy reforms to support further reforms. Apart from the political logic, the economic logic also dictates a sequential approach. Reform measures are complementary, and thus introducing one reform builds up the momentum for other reforms. China is often cited as one of the most successful examples of gradualist reforms.[34]

The argument here is that China has not pursued a gradualist reform strategy when it comes to SOE reforms. It is important to emphasize that the prediction of the gradualist interpretation is not that China will never undertake privatization, but that it is wise to undertake privatization in a sequential manner. McMillan and Naughton (1992) identify three reasons for delaying privatization: the entry of nonstate firms, the success of SOE reforms, and the SOEs as social safety providers. Once a number of prerequisites are met, for example, the emergence of a private sector and price liberalization, it may be both politically feasible

---

[34] There is a built-in virtuous cycle. The entry of nonstate firms reduces the SOEs' profitability, which forces the SOEs to reform. Naughton explains the feasibility of this self-enforcing reform mechanism in terms of the "interconnectedness" of the institutional features of centrally planned economies. Reforms are contagious because "unhooking a single key connection can cause the entire fabric to unravel" (Naughton 1996b).

and economically desirable to privatize Chinese SOEs. My contention here is that a number of critical prerequisites for privatization were already in place during the 1992–95 period (i.e., the period of rapid FDI liberalization), and, indeed, according to a prominent proponent of the gradualist reforms, Professor Gerard Roland, "it was only in 1993 and 1994 that political support could be found for the next stage of reforms, which included restructuring of SOEs with significant layoffs as well as privatization" (Roland 2000, p. 40). Yet to this day the Chinese government has not endorsed privatization of large SOEs, although it did support privatization of small SOEs in 1997. This contradicts the empirical prediction of the gradualist interpretation of the Chinese reforms.

There is an issue of semantics. Some economists have called the SOE reforms that were initiated in the mid-1990s "a privatization program" (Roland 2000). It is important to note that while the privatization of small SOEs was genuine, Chinese "privatization" of medium and large SOEs bears little resemblance to a standard privatization approach. The essence of privatization is to transfer controls of a firm from government to private hands. This is precisely the opposite of what the Chinese "ownership reforms" were designed to do. Most of the "ownership reforms" implemented in the mid-1990s focused on two issues. One was to ascertain who the original investors were among the government agencies and then to assign, or reassign, ownership rights among the different government agencies. This did not dilute state ownership. The other effort was to securitize the equity shares held by the state and to list some of the traditional SOEs on China's two stock markets. While a portion of the shares was privatized, the control rights were not. Xu and Wang (1997) report that on average individual shareholders controlled only 0.3 percent of the board seats of those firms listed on the Shanghai and Shenzhen stock exchanges, despite the fact that they owned 30 percent of the shares. In contrast, while state equity amounted to 30 percent, the state retained 50 percent of the board seats and state-owned institutions owned and controlled the rest.

Many of the so-called ownership reforms since the mid-1990s were motivated by the desire to *expand* rather than to reduce state controls of the economy. The following quote by Li Yining, a well-known economic adviser to the government, is revealing:[35]

The power of the public economy does not depend on the size of public capital but on the amount of resources public capital controls. For example,

---

[35] It is quite possible that Professor Li, known to be a strong supporter of privatization, is advocating partial privatization in politically acceptable language, and thus this statement may not accurately represent his true thinking. It is, however, a good indication of the thinking of the Chinese leadership and is evidence that the Chinese state has not embraced privatization as a reigning economic ideology. The quote is from Li (1999).

suppose the state has a fund of RMB 10 billion and it finances a big firm by contributing 100 percent of its capital. Because the state funds RMB 10 billion, it can only control RMB 10 billion. But suppose control can be established on the basis of 50 percent of equity, then the RMB 10 billion fund can be used to control RMB 20 billion. Suppose only one-third of equity is enough for control, then the state can control 30 billion, and so on. This is not a weakening of the public economy; it is in fact a strengthening of the public economy.

This reasoning is telling of the rationale behind the government's reform program: For the Chinese reformers, the dilemma has been how to leverage the state's limited and shrinking financial resources to achieve *greater* corporate control. The shareholding reform program was justified as a means to fortify the allocative functions and corporate control role of the state, not to weaken state control in the economy. It is difficult, if not impossible, to reconcile the official justification with the standard privatization rationale that seeks to reduce state interference in the economy and to introduce efficient management and supervision by private investors.[36] Another inconsistency with the prevailing privatization rationale has to do with the use of the privatization proceeds. Some of the privatization proceeds were used to finance investments and technology acquisition programs of the large and pillar SOEs.[37] Such a use of funds does not reduce the aggregate ownership role of the state in the economy; it only changes the composition of the state's role. It is far from clear how this manner of privatization provides an exit option to the state.

The government has also restricted privatization to those small loss-making SOEs. This policy directly violates an important principle in the gradualist approach. Roland argues that the best SOEs ought to be privatized first because they have the fewest employment redundancies. Their privatization will thus generate the fewest political repercussions and will maximize the probability of success (Roland 2000, p. 248). This restriction also turns the prevailing privatization rationale on its head. Other countries have used proceeds from privatization sales to finance retirement pension payments and unemployment benefits. The underlying idea is that while private investors and entrepreneurs

---

[36] The Fifteenth Party Congress sanctioned two policies that are somewhat contradictory. "Letting go of the small" is a genuine reformist move, but "grasping the big" has a strong industrial policy flavor to it. In his speech to the party congress, Jiang Zemin was emphatic about preserving the state economy in a controlling position "in the pillars of the national economy and other important sectors." See State Statistical Bureau (1998c).

[37] A number of researchers have documented instances in which local governments invested in SOEs, while at the same time divesting from smaller SOEs (Cao, Qian, and Weingast 1999).

are better at managing firms to create economic value, the state has a comparative advantage in managing social responsibilities. The prevailing privatization rationale would dictate that the state privatize profitable SOEs, but there may be good reasons to retain loss-making SOEs as the state's social responsibilities. This is precisely the opposite of what is happening in China. (In this regard, the JV acquisitions described in Chapter 5 are a genuine privatization program. Under JV acquisitions, the state retains social liabilities while private, but foreign, firms assume controls over economic assets.)

LARGE-SCALE PRIVATIZATION: THE NEXT STAGE OF REFORMS?

Only in 2001 were there some signs that the Chinese government was contemplating genuine ownership reforms of medium and large urban SOEs. In February 2001, the Ministry of Finance announced a program to reduce state shareholding in listed companies by 10 percent (via issuing hitherto nontradable state shares), and the IPO proceeds were to go into a National Social Security Fund (Ma 2001). This is an important departure from previous practices in two respects. One is that the government has traditionally regarded the listed SOEs as strategic firms over which it has been reluctant to relinquish controls. If this share tranche is the first of many to come, it could mark the beginning of a genuine privatization program. The second departure is that in the past, the government divested from and invested in SOEs at the same time (Cao, Qian, and Weingast 1999). Selling some SOEs while investing in other SOEs does not dilute aggregate state ownership in the economy. But using IPO proceeds to fund social welfare provisions from a 10 percent reduction of state shareholding, although far from sufficient to reduce state control of listed SOEs, is still a significant development.

In another development, in 2001 the Shanghai municipal government began to sell shares of a number of firms in the financial sector, such as Shanghai Bank, the Pudong Development Bank, the Bank of Communications, and Guotai Junan Securities (Murphy 2001). What is not clear is whether the government is willing to cede operating controls of these firms to the buyers or, as traditionally has been the case, is willing only to sell minority stakes. Also the apparent intention to use the sale proceeds to invest in Shanghai's high-tech industrial base would not reduce the aggregate role of the state in the economy.

During the reform era, the Chinese state has moved from a hostile stance toward the private sector to one of tolerance and then to one of encouragement since 1997. By any benchmark, the transformation has been remarkable. The transfer of stocks of assets from the state to private controls is still a sensitive policy issue, and ideological opposition is still substantial. The ideological constraints, probably more than pragmatic considerations, explain the Chinese aversion to embracing a large-scale privatization. In the following paragraphs, I first show that large-scale privatization in China is unlikely to lead to the kind of dislocations observed in Russia. I then review two pragmatic arguments against privatization to show that they are not as convincing as often assumed when explaining why the Chinese state has not endorsed an explicit large-scale privatization policy.

A Comparison With Russia

Could China have adopted a genuine privatization program earlier in the 1990s with a manageable level of economic and political disruptions? Many may answer in the negative, drawing on the disastrous experience of the Russian privatization program and arguing that China has done the right thing by not privatizing its SOEs. Joseph Stiglitz, for example, has noted that Russian GNP was about twice the size of Chinese GNP at the beginning of the 1990s, but by the end of the decade it was one-third smaller. Stiglitz also points out a number of problems with Russia's privatization program, such as asset stripping by insiders, the blocking of further reforms by vested interests, and capital flight (Stiglitz 1999). The implicit notion here is that China and Russia in the early 1990s were comparable in many aspects but differed only in their reform strategies. As Stiglitz himself is surely well aware, it was not the privatization per se that created problems in Russia, but the fact that privatization occurred under extremely adverse conditions. The relevant question here is whether China also suffered from these adverse conditions in the early 1990s.

The answer is no. China possessed many positive conditions that Russia did not have, which implies a far greater likelihood of success if a privatization program had been adopted. Economists generally agree that insider privatization is inefficient but may be necessary as a second-best policy under certain conditions. In Russia, one reason why insider privatization was adopted was because the country not only did not have its own indigenous private sector, but also was very wary of large-scale foreign control of its assets. There was not a similar level of wariness toward foreign asset controls in China, and by the early 1990s, the incremental reforms had created a large number of entrepreneurial managers in China. In the 1980s many SOEs were leased to genuinely competent entrepreneurs. Compared with Russia in the early 1990s, China had a substantial number of capable managers who already had some ten years of management experience. (The founders/managers of Kelon fit the description here.)

Insider privatization would have been unnecessary in China: The level of private wealth was enormous in the 1990s.[38] The savings rate was high and China had been a net capital exporter in that decade. A direct manifestation of the level of China's private wealth was the substantial oversubscription of minority shares in the initial public offerings of several SOEs at that time. (In fact, riots broke out in Shenzhen when potential investors failed to obtain the necessary share acquisition forms.)[39] A related point is that delaying privatization has made the window of opportunity for financing future privatization smaller rather than larger. By 1998, household bank deposits had grown to RMB 5,341 billion, from RMB 1,155 billion in 1992. But a significant portion of China's private wealth had become illiquid because of the huge nonperforming loans (NPLs) accumulated within the banking system. The NPL ratio was probably lower in the early 1990s than it was in the late 1990s. This means that it is now more difficult for Chinese households to convert their financial claims on bank deposits to equity claims on Chinese companies.

One of the key lessons from the Russian privatization program is that it matters who the owners are. A correct privatization strategy does not just transfer assets from governmental control to private control, but transfers them to the *right* private hands. Almost all the assets in Russia went to former SOE managers. These politically connected managers used their political power to rig the auctioning process to acquire the assets at fire-sale prices, and they then proceeded to strip the acquired assets.[40] Furthermore, because Russia began a massive privatization program without implementing any partial reforms beforehand, the managers-owners never acquired experience in operating in a market-economy environment. The situation in China could not be more different in the early 1990s. In the 1980s, the Chinese government had already contracted out many

---

[38] In Russia, as Boycko, Shleifer, and Vishny (1995) point out, the valuation of Russian companies rose from 1993 to 1994 largely because the savings rate and foreign portfolio investments rose. They argue that this is evidence that capital shortages played some – although not an overwhelming – role in contributing to the low valuation of Russian companies when they were privatized.

[39] In 1992, the government approved a listing quota of RMB 11.7 billion. In the same year, household bank deposits amounted to RMB 1,155 billion (State Statistical Bureau 1993a). In July 2001, price to earning ratios of the listed companies – widely acknowledged to be of poor quality – were as high as 50 times, approaching the NASDAQ level during the height of the Internet bubble (McCallum 2001). This suggests a possible mismatch between demand for and supply of tradable shares in the listed SOEs and substantial room for a deeper and broader privatization program.

[40] For a first-hand and revealing account of the Russian privatization process, see Black, Kraakman, and Tarassova (2000). All three authors participated in designing the Russian privatization policies.

SOEs to managers; a management buyout program thus would have been a logical extension of this practice. (Instead, the government chose to terminate many of the management contracts in the 1990s in the name of clarifying ownership rights.) In Jiangsu and Guangdong provinces, many of the nominal SOEs were "red-hat" firms in the first place; that is, private entrepreneurs had registered them as state or collective firms in the 1980s to seek political and legal cover. Again, it would have been a straightforward administrative task to privatize these firms. But large-scale privatization of nominal SOEs or collective firms did not occur until the late 1990s, and only in several provinces such as Jiangsu and Zhejiang.

Preserving or Dismantling Socialism?

Why has the Chinese state steadfastly refused to undertake a privatization program under conditions that proponents of the gradualist strategy might deem as favorable? Most observers take the economic benefits of a privatization program as given, but they note the significant noneconomic costs that impede such a policy course. When explaining why the Chinese state has refused to embark upon a privatization strategy, economists offer two kinds of arguments. The first is a normative argument, which stresses the high social costs of privatization. The second is a positive argument, which seeks to explain not only the absence of a privatization program but also the continuous policy preferences accorded to SOEs. Both arguments share one element in common: They portray the policy choices within an optimization framework; that is, the policy choices are viewed as grounded in rational and pragmatic calculations.

This book poses a fundamentally different, yet simpler, hypothesis: Chinese policy makers have not endorsed a large-scale privatization strategy because they want to preserve socialism. The Chinese government has stated this position repeatedly and consistently over the years. Rather than contriving to devise alternative motivations, I take the official position seriously and at its face value. The reforms in China have differed from those in the Central and Eastern European countries and Russia not merely in their pace and sequences but in their very goals. In China, the goal has been to preserve socialism, not to dismantle it, while in other transitional economies the goal has been to institute capitalism. Ideology, more than other more pragmatic considerations, may provide the single best explanation as to why China has not chosen a privatization path.

The effect of ideology, however, is easy to assert but hard to demonstrate rigorously. One can argue that the ideological rhetoric by Chinese policy makers is mere lip service and that the true underlying rationale is pragmatic in nature. If this is the case, an analyst is mistaken to take the ideological statements at their face value. The approach here is not to cite ideological statements as evidence for our hypothesis, but to show that the commonly invoked pragmatic rationales appear to be inconsistent with some of the well-known facts about the Chinese reforms.

Normative Argument: The Social Costs of Privatization. A normative argument against a full-blown privatization program is that it entails high social costs. Privatization may undermine political and social stability because it will lead to massive layoffs in the Chinese economy. The underdevelopment of a social safety net will call for caution and care in designing a privatization policy. These are entirely legitimate considerations. The issue is whether the underdevelopment of a social safety net itself is endogenous of policy choices. The Chinese state put the reform of the social safety system on the agenda as early as 1984, but for some reason progress has not been as rapid as reforms in the real sector of the economy.

Political prudence was a powerful rationale during the early stage of reforms in the 1980s. Since the early 1990s, judged on its own terms, the strategy is not working. SOEs have been very effective in destroying jobs. Between 1990 and 1999, the SOEs shed 17.7 million jobs and urban collective firms – mostly wholly owned subsidiaries of SOEs – shed another 18.4 million jobs. During the same period, China's private sector created 59.9 million jobs. Despite claiming a fraction of the financial resources that went to the SOEs, employment in the private sector in 1998 was about the same as in the SOEs (82.6 million versus 85.7 million in the state sector).[41] In the rural areas, private firms employed more people than did the TVEs. (In 1995, private firms employed 68 million people, compared with 60 million employed by TVEs.) Yet private firms accounted for only 14.6 percent of rural bank credits in 1995, compared with 85.5 percent for the TVEs.[42] If political prudence were the reason, one would expect to see support for private firms and an accelerated privatization program.

The normative argument against privatization also understates the high economic and social costs of supporting SOEs. It is important to stress that the state has not only ruled out a mass privatization strategy, but it has also expended precious resources supporting the SOEs. Social stability concerns do

---

[41] All the figures refer to the net number of jobs destroyed or created. The private sector here is defined as the sum of both urban and rural privately operated and individual businesses. The definition excludes FIEs and TVEs. The figures are from State Statistical Bureau (2000).

[42] Calculated from Table 3 in Oi (1999).

not explain the support and protection granted to the SOEs, because the private sector has been far more efficient in creating employment opportunities and because the SOEs, not the private firms, have been impairing the political and financial stability of the country, a fact the Chinese government itself is well aware of.[43] The poorly defined property rights result in massive asset stripping and corruption. Operating inefficiencies lead to the accumulation of huge nonperforming loans and hidden liabilities. Any social costs from a privatization strategy have to be weighed against those costs of continuing with the status quo.

Positive Argument: Political Constraints and Political Threats. The gist of the positive argument is that the state is constrained from undertaking a privatization strategy because of existing institutional arrangements or because of political opposition. For example, Qian (1999) puts forward a social contract theory. Historically, the state has been committed to protecting the welfare of SOE workers, but not that of nonstate workers. Thus, it bails out the SOEs in exchange for their support. Another consideration is a revenue concern: The government can observe the transactions of the SOEs since they are carried out in state-owned banks, and thus it is able to tax these transactions more effectively. Contrast this situation with private firms, which resort to cash transactions to elude the state's taxing power.[44]

The positive argument does not assume that the Chinese state necessarily maximizes social welfare – a more reasonable premise than what is implicitly assumed in the normative argument. It also explicitly recognizes the support granted to SOEs, not just the absence of a privatization program – a considerable advance over the normative argument. But there are still some anomalies. The political constraints implicitly assumed in the social contract theory appear to be excessive. China is not a democracy and its government still retains a substantial amount of operating autonomy. One example is its apparent successful effort to sever the business ties of the Chinese military in 1998, an indication of the substantial power of the Communist Party to take on its strongest power

---

[43] In a 1998 report, the State Development and Planning Commission provides the following gloomy analysis (State Development and Planning Commission 1998):

> On the one hand, about 50 percent of the SOEs often only utilize about 60 percent of their capacity. On the other hand, their operating difficulties have brought about a shortage of jobs, causing many workers to leave their jobs or to be unemployed. This is seriously affecting the lives of many workers and furthermore affecting the stability of the social, political, and economic order.

[44] For a sophisticated version of this argument, see Bai, Li, Qian, and Wang (1999).

base. Furthermore, the Chinese state has been extricating itself from its social contract for years. During the reform era, many SOE workers were hired on fixed terms, and by the mid-1990s the iron rice bowl appeared to be broken. The absence of mass privatization and the substantial financial relief granted to the SOEs in the late 1990s appear puzzling from a social contract perspective.

The claim that the state supports SOEs because of revenue concerns is based on the notion that the state maximizes *gross rather than net revenue*. A more reasonable assumption is that the state maximizes net revenue. In the public choice literature, bureaucrats are assumed to maximize budget but also to minimize effort. In the theoretical model developed by Niskanen (1971), a bureaucrat maximizes budget to increase his salary, perquisites, power, and prestige. But a critical element in this model is that bureaucratic expenditure – both effort and output – does not increase proportionately along with the size of the budget. This is an important assumption because it allows Niskanen to argue that social welfare is not served by increasing bureaucratic size.

Now consider the SOEs. It takes an enormous, and growing, amount of financial resources to support the SOEs. Thus, even if the assumption that the state maximizes revenue is correct, it is not a priori clear why the state should support the SOEs. According to a report by the Ministry of Finance, between 1981 and 1992 the state provided various tax relief measures to SOEs that amounted to RMB 458 billion, about 35.9 percent of the average annual value of GDP during this period. As such, it was a huge tax concession to the SOEs.[45] Because the nonstate firms are more efficient and operate under hard budget constraints, support for the nonstate firms may very well generate more revenue benefits to the state, even if the tax instruments on the nonstate firms are less developed.[46] In arriving at this conclusion, we do not have to assume that the Chinese state maximizes social welfare. Suppose that the state is predatory; it should still desire to see the growth of a private sector because then the predation base will be larger. Indeed, the revenue-maximizing motive has been invoked by a number of analysts as a reason why local governments have been keen to develop nonstate firms, such as TVEs.[47] Supporting private firms and privatization are perfectly consistent with a revenue-maximization motive.

[45] Figures are from Lou (2000), p. 4.

[46] Evidence from rural industry suggests that private firms in rural areas generate more tax revenues on a fraction of the resources received from the state. In 1995, private firms accounted for 36.8 percent of the tax revenues generated by rural industrial firms, compared with 32.6 percent by township firms and 30.6 percent by village firms. In the same year, loans going to private firms accounted for 14.6 percent of loans to all rural firms. See Oi (1999), Table 3.

[47] This is the idea of local corporatism developed by Oi (1999).

Private firms resort to cash transactions and to evasions of the reach of the state for a very good reason. As illustrated in Chapter 3, their property rights are insecure; they are often the targets of predation and political discrimination by government officials. The solution to this problem is not to further strengthen SOEs but to create a fair, politically neutral, and transparent regulatory and business environment. The current inability to tax private firms is due not simply to a technicality – the underdevelopment of tax instruments – but to a deep-seated political bias that forces private firms to go underground.

A final explanation for why privatization has not occurred is that private entrepreneurs and capitalists pose a threat to the socialist state. Thus, the state has rationally designed a reform strategy to curb their growth and power. Endowed with economic power and wealth today, some Communist officials might reason, private entrepreneurs will gain political power tomorrow. Of all the commonly invoked arguments, this one is the most empirically accurate description of the true political calculation of the state. This is also an analytically strong argument because it explains why the Chinese state is not similarly concerned about the rise of a foreign entrepreneurial class. Foreigners, after all, do not participate in domestic politics in the way that domestic entrepreneurs do.[48]

At its very core this hypothesis is based on an ideological conception of the world. To illustrate this point, consider the following thought experiment. It is commonly alleged that the Chinese state has reached an implicit bargain with the Chinese population. Under the terms of this bargain, the population will support the regime as long as the regime is successful in improving the living standards of the people. Let us extend the logic of this argument to the treatment of private entrepreneurs. It would be irrational for an ideologically neutral state to fear the rise and economic power of private entrepreneurs and private owners of capital. Probusiness policies and a faster pace of privatization presumably would earn the political support of a grateful private entrepreneurial and propertied class in China. Capitalists worldwide support governments that are probusiness and successful in preserving stability and promoting growth. They do not support only those governments that share ideological convictions with them. For instance, today ardent supporters of Communist Party rule are found among the wealthy business tycoons in Hong Kong. Further, the rural reforms in the early 1980s dramatically improved the welfare of the Chinese peasants, creating enormous goodwill toward the regime. On purely pragmatic grounds, the Chinese state does not have to view private entrepreneurs and private owners of capital as threats to its power.

---

[48] I benefited from a discussion with Professor Julio Rotemberg on this point.

A Political Perspective: Ideological Constraints. What may complicate this calculation is ideology. A fundamental tenet of socialist ideology is its commitment to state ownership, often not just for its instrumental value but also for its intrinsic value.[49] This commitment has been considerably weakened during the reform era, as competing ideas have come to be held by the top echelons of the Communist Party. But a doctrinal commitment to state ownership remains a first among equal governing principles in today's China.[50] The primacy of state ownership can be circumvented and even shortchanged but cannot be openly and explicitly challenged. Herein may be the reason why the first instinct on the part of the Communist Party is to view the rise of a private entrepreneurial class as a political liability rather than as a political asset. The Party Constitution states clearly that the dominance of private ownership is fundamentally incompatible with a socialist system. Some prominent Communist officials still choose to view private owners of capital as potential foes on purely doctrinal grounds, even though one can make a plausible case that a strong private sector may in fact promote stability and prolong the ruling status of the Communist Party in its current form.

The Chinese state is pragmatic, but up to a point. The famous aphorism by Deng Xiaoping – "it does not matter whether the cat is white or black, as long as it catches mice" – has not yet been applied to privatization of large SOEs. The color of the cat apparently matters, and matters a great deal. This has to be among the most sobering implications of our analysis. China has enormous economic potentials, but to fully realize these potentials, China will need to carry out substantial institutional reforms. This task not only will require a strong political will, but also it will necessitate an ideological commitment to private property rights. One can only hope that ideology will no longer be a stumbling block among the next generation of Chinese leaders.

---

[49] Kornai (1992) remarks:

> Socialism differs first and foremost from capitalism in having replaced private ownership with public ownership; so the elimination of private ownership and the establishment and stabilization of public ownership is an intrinsic value as well. Of course, instrumental values are expected as well from the creation of socialist ownership: it must ensure higher productivity than capitalist ownership provides. But it already has a vast intrinsic, internal value in that the capitalists are no longer exploiting the workers, the workers are no longer subordinate to the capitalists, and the capitalist class vanishes from the stage of history.

[50] For a comprehensive review of political developments in China, see Saich (2001).

Bibliography

Agmon, Tamir, and Charles P. Kindleberger, eds. (1977). *Multinationals from Small Countries*. Cambridge: MIT Press.

Alchian, Armen A., and Harold Demsetz (1972). "Production, Information Costs, and Economic Organization." *American Economic Review* 62 (December): 777–95.

All China Marketing Research Co. Ltd. (1999). *Quanguo sanzi gongye qiye shuju ku* (National Database of Industrial Foreign-Invested Enterprises). Beijing: All China Marketing Research Co. Ltd.

"Amendments to the Constitution of the People's Republic of China" (1999). *Beijing Review* 42, no. 18 (May 3–9): 14–15.

Aoki, Masahiko, and Hyung-Ki Kim (1995). *Corporate Governance in Transitional Economies*. Washington, D.C.: World Bank.

Asian Development Bank (1995). *Key Indicators of Developing Asian and Pacific Countries*. Manila: Oxford University Press.

Aswicahyono, H. H., and Hal Hill (1995). "Determinants of Foreign Ownership in LDC Manufacturing: An Indonesian Case Study." *Journal of International Business Studies* 26, no. 1: 139–58.

Athukorala, Prema-Chandra, and Sarath Rajapatirana (2000). "Liberalization and Industrial Transformation: Lessons from the Sri Lankan Experience." *Economic Development and Cultural Change* 48, no. 3 (April): 543–72.

Bai, Chongen, David D. Li, Yingyi Qian, and Yijiang Wang (1999). "Anonymous Banking and Financial Repression: How Does China's Reform Limit Government Predation without Reducing Its Revenue?" Unpublished paper, Department of Economics, University of Michigan, Ann Arbor.

Bai, Chongen, David D. Li, and Yijiang Wang (1996). "Can Productivity Analysis Be Misleading in Gauging Progress of State Enterprise Reforms?" Unpublished paper, Department of Economics, University of Michigan, Ann Arbor.

Baranson, Jack (1969). *Automotive Industries in Developing Countries*. Washington, D.C.: International Bank for Reconstruction and Development.

Bauer, T. (1978). "Investment Cycles in Planned Economies." *Acta Oeconomica* 21, no. 3: 243–60.

Beamish, Paul W., and Hui Wang (1989). "Investing in China Via Joint Ventures." *Management International Review* 29, no. 1: 57–64.

Beijing Haitehua Machinery and Electric Technology Development Corporation (1994). *Guojia qiche gongye zhengce xinbian* (New Selections of Documents on State Automobile Industry Policy). Beijing: Beijing Haitehua Machinery and Electric Technology Development Corporation.

Berger, Suzanne, and Richard K. Lester, eds. (1997). *Made by Hong Kong*. Hong Kong: Oxford University Press.

Black, Bernard, Reinier Kraakman, and Anna Tarassova (2000). "Russian Privatization and Corporate Governance: Why They Went Wrong." *Stanford Law Review* 52, no. 61: 1731–1808.

Boycko, Maxim, Andrei Shleifer, and Robert W. Vishny (1995). *Privatizing Russia*. Cambridge: MIT Press.

Bruton, Garry D., Hailin Lan, Yuan Lu, and Zhihong Yu (2000). "China's Township and Village Enterprises: Kelon's Competitive Edge." *Academy of Management Executive* 14, no. 1 (February): 19–29.

Buckley, Peter J. (1988). "The Limits of Explanation: Testing the Internalization Theory of the Multinational Enterprise." *Journal of International Business Studies* 19, no. 2 (Summer): 181–93.

Buckley, Peter J., and Mark Casson (1976). *The Future of the Multinational Enterprise*. London: Macmillan Press.

"Business Environment Scores and Ranks" (2001). *Transition Newsletter* 12, no. 3 (July-August-September): 48.

Byrd, William A. (1992). "The Second Motor Vehicle Manufacturing Plant." In *Chinese Industrial Firms under Reform*, ed. William A. Byrd. New York: Oxford University Press. Pp. 371–426.

Byrd, William A., and Gene Tidrick (1992). "The Chongqing Clock and Watch Company." In *Chinese Industrial Firms under Reform*, ed. William A. Byrd. New York: Oxford University Press. Pp. 58–119.

Cao, Yuanzheng, Yingyi Qian, and Barry R. Weingast (1999). "From Federalism, Chinese Style, to Privatization, Chinese Style." *Economics of Transition* 7, no. 1: 103–31.

Casson, Mark C. (1979). *Alternatives to the Multinational Enterprise*. London: Macmillan Press.

Caves, Richard E. (1974). "Causes of Direct Investment: Foreign Firms' Shares in Canadian and United Kingdom Manufacturing Industries." *Review of Economics and Statistics* 56, no. 3 (August): 279–93.

Caves, Richard E. (1996). *Multinational Enterprise and Economic Analysis*. Cambridge: Cambridge University Press.

Caves, Richard E. (1998). "Research on International Business: Problems and Prospects." *Journal of International Business Studies* 29, no. 1 (First Quarter): 5–19.

Che, Jiahua, and Yingyi Qian (1998). "Institutional Environment, Community Government, and Corporate Governance: Understanding China's Township-Village Enterprises." *Journal of Law, Economics, and Organization* 14, no. 1: 1–23.

Chen, Edward K. Y. (1981). "Hong Kong Multinationals in Asia: Characteristics and Objectives." In *Multinationals from Developing Countries*, ed. K. Kumar and M. G. McLeod. Lexington, Mass.: Lexington Books.

Chen, Edward K. Y. (1983). "Multinationals from Hong Kong." In *The New Multinationals: The Spread of Third World Enterprises*, ed. Sanjaya Lall and Associates. Chichester, U.K.: Wiley. Pp. 88–136.

Chen, G. M., Bong-Soo Lee, and Oliver Rui (2001). "Foreign Ownership Restrictions and Market Segmentation in China's Stock Markets." *Journal of Financial Research* 24, no. 1 (Spring): 133–55.

Chen, Hongyi, and Scott Rozelle (1999). "Leaders, Managers, and the Organization of Township and Village Enterprises in China." *Journal of Development Economics* 60, no. 2: 529–57.

Chen, Kuan, Hongchang Wang, Yuxin Zheng, Gary H. Jefferson, and Thomas G. Rawski (1988). "Productivity Change in Chinese Industry: 1953–1985." *Journal of Comparative Economics* 12, no. 4: 570–91.

Chen Zuhuang, Chen Wenxue, and Zheng Xianzao (1999). *Guoqi gaige: Zhuangui yu chuanxin* (Reform of SOEs: Transformation and Innovation). Guangzhou: Zhongshan daxue chubanshe.

Cheng, L. K., and Y. K. Kwan (2000). "What Are the Determinants of the Location of Foreign Direct Investment? The Chinese Experience." *Journal of International Economics* 51, no. 2: 379–400.

China Automotive Technology Research Center (1996). *Shijie qiche gongye tongji ziliao* (Statistical Sources on the World Automotive Industry). Tianjin: Zhongguo qiche jishu yanjiu zhongxin.

China Automotive Technology Research Center (1999). *Zhongguo qiche gongye nianjian 1999* (China Automotive Industry Yearbook 1999). Tianjin: Zhongguo qiche jishu yanjiu zhongxin.

China Finance Association (1997). *Zhongguo jinrong nianjian 1997* (Chinese Financial Yearbook 1997). Beijing: Zhongguo jinrong nianjian bianjibu.

China International Engineering Company (1992). *Guanyu Beijing XYZ kexingxing yanjiu* (Feasibility Study of Beijing XYZ Project). Beijing: China International Engineering Consulting Company.

China Managerial Survey System (1996). "Qiyejia dui hongguan jingji xingshi he qiye gaige de panduan yu jianyi" (Managerial Attitudes on the Macroeconomic Situation and Enterprise Reform). In *Zhongguo jingji nianjian 1996* (Almanac of China's Economy 1996), ed. Development Research Center of the State Council. Beijing: Zhongguo jingji nianjianshe. Pp. 943–60.

"China's Local Trade Barriers: A Hard Nut to Crack" (2001). *Transition Newsletter* 12, no. 3 (July-August-September): 11.

Chow, Clement Kong-Wing, and Michael Ka-Yiu Fung (1997a). "Profitability and Technical Efficiency." *In Advances in Chinese Industrial Studies* 5, ed. Nigel Campbell. Greenwich, Conn.: JAI Press. Pp. 249–67.

Chow, Clement Kong-Wing, and Michael Ka-Yiu Fung (1997b). "Measuring the Technological Leadership of International Joint Ventures in a Transforming Economy." *Journal of Business Research* 39, no. 2: 147–57.

Chu Baotai, and Dong Weiyuan (1993). *Zhongwai hezuo jingying qiye* (Sino-Foreign Cooperative Enterprises). Beijing: Zhongxin chubanshe.

Chu, Wan-wen (1997). "Causes of Growth: A Study of Taiwan's Bicycle Industry." *Cambridge Journal of Economics* 21, no. 1 (January): 55–72.

Clyde-Smith, Deborah, and Peter J. Williamson (2001a). *Whirlpool China* (*A*). Singapore: INSEAD Euro-Asia Centre. No. 301-170-1.

Clyde-Smith, Deborah, and Peter J. Williamson (2001b). *Whirlpool China* (*B*). Singapore: INSEAD Euro-Asia Centre. No. 301-171-1.

Coase, Ronald H. (1937). "The Nature of the Firm." *Economica* 4, no. 16 (November): 386–405.

Constitution of the People's Republic of China (1994). Beijing: Foreign Languages Press.

De Mello, Luiz R., Jr. (1997). "Foreign Direct Investment in Developing Countries and Growth: A Selective Survey." *Journal of Development Studies* 34, no. 1 (October): 1–34.

Demurger, Sylvie (2000). *Economic Opening and Growth in China.* Paris: OECD.

Deng, Xiaoping (1994). "We Shall Speed up Reform." In *Selected Works of Deng Xiaoping*, ed. Editorial Committee for Party Literature of the Central Committee of the Chinese Communist Party. Beijing: Foreign Languages Press.

Development Research Center of the State Council (1996). *Zhongguo jingji nianjian 1996* (Almanac of China's Economy 1996). Beijing: Zhongguo jingji nianjianshe.

Development Research Center of the State Council (1999). *Zhongguo jingji nianjian 1999* (Almanac of China's Economy 1999). Beijing: Zhongguo jingji nianjianshe.

Dewatripont, Mathias, and Gerard Roland (1995). "The Design of Reform Packages under Uncertainty." *American Economic Review* 85, no. 5 (December): 1207–23.

Dickerson, Kitty G. (1999). *Textiles and Apparel in the Global Economy.* Upper Saddle River, N.J.: Merrill.

Donnithorne, Audrey (1981). *China's Economic System.* London: Hurst.

Dunning, John H. (1977). "Trade, Location of Economic Activity and the MNE: A Search for an Eclectic Approach." In *International Allocation of Economic Activity*, ed. Bertil Ohlin, P. O. Hesselborn, and P. M. Wijkman. London: Macmillan.

Dunning, John H. (1988). "The Eclectic Paradigm of International Production: A Restatement and Some Possible Extensions." *Journal of International Business Studies* 19, no. 1: 1–31.

Dunning, John H. (1996). "Explaining Foreign Direct Investment in Japan: Some Theoretical Insights." In *Foreign Direct Investment in Japan*, ed. Masaru Yoshitomi and Edward M. Graham. Cheltenham, U.K.: Edward Elgar. Pp. 8–63.

Economist Intelligence Unit (1995). *Investment, Trading and Licensing Conditions Abroad: Taiwan 1995.* London: EIU.

Economist Intelligence Unit (2001). *Country Profile 2001: Turkey.* London: EIU.

Editorial Board (1993). *Zhongguo fangzhi gongye nianjian 1992* (Almanac of China's Textile Industry). Beijing: Fangzhi gongye chubanshe.

Editorial Committee (1991). *Zhongguo jijie dianzi gongye nianjian 1991* (*dianzi juan*) (Chinese Machinery and Electronics Industry Almanac 1991 (Electronics Volume)) Beijing: Jijie gongye chubanshe.

Encarnation, Dennis J., and Mark Mason (1990). "Neither MITI nor America: The Political Economy of Capital Liberalization in Japan." *International Organization* 44, no. 1: 25–54.

Fagre, Nathan, and Louis T. Wells Jr. (1982). "Bargaining Power of Multinationals and Host Governments." *Journal of International Business Studies* 13, no. 2 (Fall): 9–23.

Federation of Hong Kong Industries (1995). *Investment in China: 1994 Survey of Members of Federation of Hong Kong Industries*. Hong Kong: Federation of Hong Kong Industries.

Fu, Jun (2000). *Institutions and Investments: Foreign Direct Investment in China during an Era of Reforms*. Ann Arbor: University of Michigan Press.

Fujian Commission of Foreign Economy and Trade, and Fujian Statistical Bureau (1994). *Fujian duiwai jingji shiwunian* (Fifteen Years of Fujian's External Economy). Beijing: Zhongguo tongji chubanshe.

Fujian Statistical Bureau (1994). *Fujian tongji nianjian 1994* (Fujian Statistical Yearbook 1994). Beijing: Zhongguo tongji chubanshe.

Fukushima, Kiyohiko, and C. H. Kwan (1995). "Foreign Direct Investment and Regional Industrial Restructuring in Asia." In *The New Wave of Foreign Direct Investment in Asia*, ed. Nomura Research Institute and Institute of Southeast Asian Studies. Singapore: Institute of Southeast Asian Studies.

Gallagher, Mary (2001). "Grafted Capitalism: Ownership Change and Labor Relations in the PRC." Paper prepared for the conference "Uneven Transition in China: Reform and Inequality," Ann Arbor, April 7.

Gao, Shangquan, and Fulin Chi (1996). *The Development of China's Nongovernmentally and Privately Operated Economy*. Beijing: Foreign Languages Press.

General Administration of Customs of the People's Republic of China (1995). *China Monthly Exports and Imports*. Beijing: General Administration of Customs.

General Administration of Customs of the People's Republic of China (1996). *China Monthly Exports and Imports*. Beijing: General Administration of Customs.

General Administration of Customs of the People's Republic of China (1999). *China Customs Statistics Yearbook 1998*. Beijing: General Administration of Customs.

General Administration of Customs of the People's Republic of China (2001). *China Customs Statistics Yearbook 2001*. Beijing: General Administration of Customs.

Ghemawat, Pankaj (2001). "Distance Still Matters: The Hard Reality of Global Expansion." *Harvard Business Review* 79, no. 8 (September): 137–47.

Ghemawat, Pankaj, and Bret J. Baird (1998). *International Competition: Turkey and Its Garment Industry*. Boston: Harvard Business School Publishing. Case Study No. 799-033.

Ghemawat, Pankaj, and Murali Patibandla (1999). "India's Exports since the Reforms: Three Analytic Industry Studies." In *India in the Era of Economic Reforms*, ed. Jeffrey D. Sachs, Ashutosh Varshney, and Nirupam Bajpai. New Delhi: Oxford University Press.

Giddy, Ian H., and Stephen Young (1982). "Conventional Theory and Unconventional Multinationals: Do New Forms of Multinational Enterprise Require New Theories?" In *New Theories of the Multinational Enterprise*, ed. Alan M. Rugman. London: CroomHelm.

Gipouloux, François (2000). "Declining Trend and Uneven Spatial Distribution of FDI in China." In *China Review 2000*, ed. Chung-ming Lau and Jianfa Shen. Hong Kong: Chinese University Press. Pp. 285–305.

Girardin, Eric (1997). *Banking Sector Reform and Credit Control in China*. Paris: OECD.

Gomes-Casseres, Benjamin (1990). "Firm Ownership Preferences and Host Government Restrictions: An Integrated Approach." *Journal of International Business Studies* 21, no. 1 (First Quarter): 1–22.

Gomes-Casseres, Benjamin (1996). *The Alliance Revolution*. Cambridge: Harvard University Press.

Graham, Edward M., and Paul R. Krugman (1994). *Foreign Direct Investment in the United States*. Washington, D.C.: Institute for International Economics.

Graham, Edward M., and Erika Wada (2001). "Foreign Direct Investment in China: Effects on Growth and Economic Performance." Postconference draft paper, Australia National University, Canberra, September 6–7.

Grosfeld, Irena (1989). "Disequilibrium Models of Investment." In *Models of Disequilibrium and Shortage in Centrally Planned Economies*, ed. Christopher Davis and Charemza Wojciech. New York: Chapman and Hall. Pp. 361–74.

Groves, Theodore, Yongmiao Hong, John McMillan, and Barry Naughton (1994). "Autonomy and Incentives in Chinese State Enterprises." *Quarterly Journal of Economics* 109, no. 1: 183–209.

Groves, Theodore, Yongmiao Hong, John McMillan, and Barry Naughton (1995). "China's Evolving Managerial Labor Market." *Journal of Political Economy* 103, no. 4: 873–92.

Guangdong Kelon Electrical Holdings Company Limited (1997). *1996 Annual Report*. Rongqi, Shunde City: Guangdong Kelon Electrical Holdings Company Limited.

Guangdong Kelon Electrical Holdings Company Limited (1999). *1998 Annual Report*. Rongqi, Shunde City: Guangdong Kelon Electrical Holdings Company Limited.

Guangdong Statistical Bureau (1989). *Guangdong tongji nianjian 1989* (Guangdong Statistical Yearbook 1989). Beijing: Zhongguo tongji chubanshe.

Guangdong Statistical Bureau (2000). *Guangdong tongji nianjian 2000* (Guangdong Statistical Yearbook 2000). Beijing: Zhongguo tongji chubanshe.

Guiso, Luigi, Paola Sapienza, and Luigi Zingales (2001). "The Role of Social Capital in Financial Development." Unpublished paper, Graduate School of Business, University of Chicago.

Haggard, Stephan (1990). *Pathways from the Periphery*. Ithaca: Cornell University Press.

Hansmann, Henry (1996). *The Ownership of Enterprise*. Cambridge: Belknap Press of Harvard University Press.

Harrison, Mark (1985). "Investment Mobilization and Capacity Completion in the Chinese and Soviet Economies." *Economics of Planning* 19, no. 2: 56–75.

Harwit, Eric (1995). *China's Automobile Industry*. Armonk, N.Y.: M. E. Sharpe.

He Baoshan, Gu Jirui, and Yan Yinglu (1996). *Zhongguo jishu zhuanyi he jishu jinbu* (Technology Transfer and Progress in China). Beijing: Jingji guanli chubanshe.

Helleiner, Gerald K. (1989). "Transnational Corporations and Direct Foreign Investment." In *Handbook of Development Economics*, ed. Hollis Chenery and T. N. Srinivasan. Amsterdam: North-Holland. Pp. 1142–80.

Holmstrom, Bengt, and Paul Milgrom (1991). "Multitask Principal-Agent Analysis: Incentive Contracts, Asset Ownership, and Job Design." *Journal of Law, Economics, and Organization* 7 (Spring): 24–52.

"How Cooked Are the Books?" (2002). *The Economist* 362, no. 8264 (March 16): 45–46.

Howson, Nicholas C. (1997). "China's Company Law: One Step Forward, Two Steps Back" A Modest Complaint." *Columbia Journal of Asian Law* 11, no. 1: 127–73.

Howson, Nicholas C. (1998). "Buying a Business in the PRC." *Asia Law and Practice* (August): 37–54.

Huang, Yasheng (1996). *Inflation and Investment Controls in China: The Political Economy of Central-Local Relations during the Reform Era*. New York: Cambridge University Press.

Huang, Yasheng (1998). *FDI in China: An Asian Perspective*. Singapore: Institute of Southeast Asian Studies.

Huang, Yasheng (2001). "Why More May Be Actually Less: Some New Interpretations of China's Labor-Intensive FDI." Unpublished paper, Harvard Business School.

Huang, Yasheng (2002a). "Between Two Coordination Failures: The Automotive Industrial Policy in China with a Comparison to Korea." *Review of International Political Economy* 9, no. 3 (September).

Huang, Yasheng (2002b). "Managing Chinese Bureaucrats: An Institutional Economics Approach." *Political Studies* 50, no. 1 (March): 61–79.

Huang, Yasheng, and Harold F. Hogan (2002). *India's Intellectual Property Rights Regime and the Pharmaceutical Industry*. Boston: Harvard Business School Publishing. Case Study No. 702-039 (March 22).

Huang, Yasheng, and David Lane (2001). *Kelon: China's Corporate Dragon*. Boston: Harvard Business School Publishing. Case Study No. 701-053 (March 21).

Huang, Yasheng, and Kirsten J. O'Neil-Massaro (2002). *Korea First Bank (a)*. Boston: Harvard Business School Publishing. Case Study No. 701-022 (Rev. January 15).

Hymer, Stephen (1970). "The Efficiency (Contradictions) of Multinational Corporations." *American Economic Review* 60, no. 2: 441–48.

Hymer, Stephen H. (1976). *The International Operations of National Firms*. Cambridge: MIT Press.

"India's Fermentation Queen" (2001). *The Economist* 360, no. 8237 (September 1): 58.

"Infatuation's End" (1999). *The Economist* 352, no. 8138 (September 25): 71.

Institute of Industrial Economics (1996). *Zhongguo gongye fazhan baogao 1996* (Chinese Industrial Development Report 1996). Beijing: Jingji guanli chubanshe.

Institute of Industrial Economics (1998). *Zhongguo gongye fazhan baogao 1998* (Chinese Industrial Development Report 1998). Beijing: Jingji guanli chubanshe.

Institute of Industrial Economics (2000). *Zhongguo gongye fazhan baogao 2000* (Chinese Industrial Development Report 2000). Beijing: Jingji guanli chubanshe.

International Finance Corporation (2000). *China's Emerging Private Enterprises: Prospects for the New Century*. Washington, D.C.: International Finance Corporation.

International Institute for Management Development (1996). *The World Competitiveness Report 1996*. Lausanne: IMD.

International Monetary Fund (2001). *International Financial Statistics, September 2001*. Washington, D.C.: International Monetary Fund.

International Trade Administration (1993). *China: Industry Sector Analysis*. Washington, D.C.: International Trade Administration.

Investment Commission of Ministry of Economic Affairs (1995). *Statistics on Overseas Chinese and Foreign Investment, Technical Cooperation, Outward Investment, Outward Technical Cooperation, Indirect Mainland Investment*. Taipei: Ministry of Economic Affairs.

Jefferson, Gary H., and Thomas G. Rawski (1994). "Enterprise Reform in Chinese Industry." *Journal of Economic Perspectives* 8, no. 2 (Spring): 47–70.

Jefferson, Gary H., Thomas G. Rawski, and Yuxin Zheng (1992). "Growth, Efficiency and Convergence in China's State and Collective Industry." *Economic Development and Cultural Change* 40, no. 2. (January): 239–66.

Jefferson, Gary H., Thomas G. Rawski, and Yuxin Zheng (1996). "Chinese Industrial Productivity: Trends, Issues and Recent Developments." *Journal of Comparative Economics* 23, no. 2: 146–80.

Jefferson, Gary H., Thomas G. Rawski, and Yuxin Zheng (1999). "Innovation and Reform in China's Industrial Enterprises." In *Enterprise Reform in China: Ownership, Transition, and Performance*, ed. Gary H. Jefferson and Inderjit Singh. New York: Oxford University Press. Pp. 89–106.

Jilin Bureau of External Economic Cooperation and Jilin Statistical Bureau (1994). *Jilinsheng waishang touzi qiye quanlu* (Complete Collection of the Foreign-invested Enterprises in Jilin Province). Beijing: Zhongguo tongji chubanshe.

Jordan, Miriam (1999). "For Many Generic Antibiotics, the Supply Line Starts in New Delhi–Little Known Ranbaxy Makes a Splash in Look-Alike Drugs." *Wall Street Journal* (December 28): B1.

Kamath, Shyam J. (1990). "Foreign Direct Investment in a Centrally Planned Developing Country." *Economic Development and Cultural Change* 39, no. 1 (October): 107–30.

Keister, Lisa A., and Jin Lu (2001). "The Transformation Continues: The Status of Chinese State-Owned Enterprises at the Start of the Millennium." *NBR Analysis* 12, no. 3: 5–31.

Kennedy, Robert E. (2000). "Policy Reform, Globalization, and New Opportunities in Emerging Markets." Unpublished paper, Harvard Business School.

Khanna, Tarun, and Krishna Palepu (2000). "Is Group Affiliation Profitable in Emerging Markets? An Analysis of Diversified Indian Business Groups." *Journal of Finance* 55, no. 2 (April): 867–91.

Khanna, Tarun, Krishna Palepu, and Danielle Melito Wu (1998). *House of Tata, 1995: The Next Generation (a)*. Boston: Harvard Business School Publishing. Case Study No. 9-798-037 (April 28).

Klein, Benjamin, Robert G. Crawford, and Armen A. Alchian (1978). "Vertical Integration, Appropriable Rents, and the Competitive Contracting Process." *Journal of Law and Economics* 21, no. 2 (October): 297–326.

Kogut, Bruce (1988). "Joint Ventures: Theoretical and Empirical Perspectives." *Strategic Management Journal* 9, no. 4: 319–32.

Kogut, Bruce (1996). "Direct Investment, Experimentation, and Corporate Governance in Transitional Economies." In *Corporate Governance in Central Europe and Russia*, ed. Roman Frydman, Cheryl W. Gray, and Andrzej Rapaczynski. Budapest: Central European Press.

Kojima, Kiyoshi (1978). *Direct Foreign Investment: A Japanese Model of Multinational Business Operations*. New York: Praeger Publishers.

Kornai, Janos (1980). *The Economics of Shortage*. Amsterdam: North-Holland.

Kornai, Janos (1992). *The Socialist System*. Princeton: Princeton University Press.

Kraar, Louis (1994). "The New Power in Asia." *Fortune* 130, no. 9 (October 31): 80–82.

Krobin, Stephen J. (1987). "Testing the Bargaining Hypothesis in the Manufacturing Sector in Developing Countries." *International Organization* 41, no. 4 (Autumn): 609–38.

Krugman, Paul (1999). "Discussion Summary." In *International Capital Flows*, ed. Martin Feldstein. Chicago: University of Chicago Press. Pp. 186–89.

Kueh, Y. Y. (1992). "Foreign Investment and Economic Change in China." *The China Quarterly*, no. 131 (September): 637–90.

Lall, Rajiv (1986). "Third World Multinationals: The Characteristics of Indian Firms Investing Abroad." *Journal of Development Economics* 20, no. 2 (March): 381–97.

Lall, Sanjaya (1978). "Transnationals, Domestic Enterprises, and Industrial Structure in Host LDCs: A Survey." *Oxford Economic Papers* 30, no. 2: 217–48.

Lardy, Nicholas R. (1992). *Foreign Trade and Economic Reform in China, 1978–1990*. New York: Cambridge University Press.

Lardy, Nicholas R. (1994). *China in the World Economy*. Washington, D.C.: Institute for International Economics.

Lardy, Nicholas R. (1996). "Economic Engine? Foreign Trade and Investment in China." *Brookings Review* 14, no. 1 (Winter): 10.

Lardy, Nicholas R. (1998). *China's Unfinished Economic Revolution*. Washington, D.C.: Brookings Institution.

Lardy, Nicholas R. (2002). *Integrating China into the Global Economy*. Washington, D.C.: Brookings Institution.

Lau, Lawrence J., Yingyi Qian, and Gerard Roland (2000). "Reform without Losers: An Interpretation of China's Dual-Track Approach to Transition." *Journal of Political Economy* 108, no. 1: 120–43.

Lawrence, Robert Z. (1993). "Japan's Low Levels of Inward Investment: The Role of Inhibitions on Acquisitions." In *Foreign Direct Investment*, ed. Kenneth A. Froot. Chicago: University of Chicago Press. Pp. 85–112.

Lecraw, David (1977). "Direct Investment by Firms from Less Developed Countries." *Oxford Economic Papers* 29, no. 3: 442–57.

Lee, Han Shih (1992). "Oei Hong Leong Making Waves in Hong Kong." *Business Times* (June 16): 5.

Lemoine, Françoise (2000). *FDI and Opening Up the Chinese Economy*. Paris: Centre d'Etudes Prospectives et d'Informations Internationale. CEPII Working Paper No. 2000–11.

Levy, Brian (1991). "Transaction Costs, the Size of Firms and Industrial Policy." *Journal of Development Economics* 34, no. 1/2: 151–78.

Li, David (1996). "Ambiguous Property Rights in Transition Economies." *Journal of Comparative Economics* 23, no. 1 (August): 1–19.

Li, Shuhe, and Peng Lian (1999). "Governance and Investment: Why Can China Attract Large-Scale FDI Despite Its Widespread Corruption?" Unpublished paper, City University of Hong Kong and Chinese University of Hong Kong.

Li Yining (1999). "Gongyouzhi de shixian xingshi he guoyou qiye gaige" (Forms of the Public Economy and SOE Reforms). In *Zhongguo feiguoyou jingji nianjian 1998* (Almanac of the Chinese Nonstate Economy 1998), ed. Luo Hanxian. Beijing: Qunyan chubanshe.

Lieberthal, Kenneth, and Michel Oksenberg (1988). *Policy Making in China: Leaders, Structures and Processes*. Princeton: Princeton University Press.

Lim, Linda Y. C. (2002). "Shrimps among Whales: Local Business, Multinationals and the State in Singapore." Presentation at the MIT-Singapore Program, Cambridge, Mass., February 28.

Lim, Linda Y. C., and Pan Eng Fong (1991). *Foreign Direct Investment and Industrialisation in Malaysia, Singapore, Taiwan and Thailand.* Paris: OECD.

Lim, Soon Neo (1994). "China Strategic's Profit Surges to 138 Pc to HK$ 153 M." *Business Times* (May 17): 19.

Lin, Cyril (2000). "Corporate Governance of State-Owned Enterprises in China." Unpublished paper, University of Oxford.

Lin, Justin Yifu, Fang Cai, and Zhou Li (1996). *The China Miracle.* Hong Kong: Chinese University Press.

Lindblom, Charles E. (1977). *Politics and Markets.* New York: Basic Books.

Liu Lisheng, Shao Dongya, and Pan Jin (1997). *Waizi binggou guoyou qiye* (Acquisitions of SOEs by Foreign Capital). Beijing: Zhongguo jingji chubanshe.

Liu Shijin, and Jiang Xiaojuan (1997). "Jingzheng tuidong de chanye jingbu: Zhongguo bingxiang hangye shengchan kuozhang yu jizhong guocheng de shizheng yanjiu" (Industrial Policy and Growth: A Study of the Refrigerator Industry in China). In *Zhongguo zhi dubian qian di anli yanjiu* (Case Studies in China's Institutional Change), ed. Zhang Shugang. Shanghai: Shanghai renmin chubanshe.

Liu, Yia-Ling (1992). "Reform from Below: The Private Economy and Local Politics in the Rural Industrialization of Wenzhou." *The China Quarterly,* no. 130 (June): 293–316.

Liu Yun (1999). *Zhongguo zhizao* (Made in China). Chengdu: Xi'nan caijing daxue chubanshe.

Lizondo, J. Saul (1995). "Foreign Direct Investment." In *Readings in International Business: A Decision Approach,* ed. Robert Z. Aliber and Reid W. Click. Cambridge: MIT Press. Pp. 85–112.

Lou Jiwei (2000). *Xin Zhongguo 50 nian caizheng tongji* (Fifty Years of New China's Government Finance Statistics). Beijing: Jingji kexue chubanshe.

Lu, Qiwen (2000). *China's Leap into the Information Age.* Oxford: Oxford University Press.

Luo Gengmo (1994). *Shige zhuanti diaocha yanjiu* (Investigative Research into Ten Issue Areas). Dalian: Dongbei caijing daxue chubanshe.

Luo, Yadong (1995). "Business Strategy, Market Structure, and Performance of International Joint Ventures: The Case of Joint Ventures in China." *Management International Review* 35, no. 3: 241–46.

Luo, Yadong (1997). "Performance Implications of International Strategy: An Empirical Study of Foreign-Invested Enterprises in China." *Group and Organization Management* 22, no. 1 (March): 87–116.

Luo, Yadong (1998). *International Investment Strategies in the People's Republic of China.* Brookfield, Vt.: Ashgate.

Luo, Yadong, and Min Chen (1995). "Financial Performance Comparison between International Joint Ventures and Wholly Foreign-Owned Enterprises in China." *The International Executive* 37, no. 6 (November/December): 599–613.

Lyons, Thomas P. (1986). "Explaining Economic Fragmentation in China: A Systems Approach." *Journal of Comparative Economics* 10, no. 2: 209–36.

Ma, Jun (2001). "Financial Liberalization: Slow and Steady." *China Business Review* 28, no. 3 (May/June): 12–16.

Ma, Shiguang (2000). "China's Stock Market: Emergence, Development and Perspective." In *China's Trade and Investment after the Asia Crisis*, ed. Tran Van Hoa. Northampton, Mass.: Edward Elgar. Pp. 56–89.

Ma, Shu-Yun (1995). "Shareholding System Reform: The Chinese Way of Privatization." *Communist Economies and Economic Transformation* 7, no. 2 (June): 159–74.

Mackenzie, Davin A. (2001). "A Healthy Financial Sector Requires Enterprises That Deserve Financing." Paper prepared for the conference "Financial Sector Reform in China," Kennedy School of Government, Harvard University, Cambridge, Mass., September 11–13.

Magee, Stephen P. (1977). "Information and the Multinational Corporation: An Appropriability Theory of Direct Foreign Investment." In *The New International Economic Order*, ed. J. N. Bhagwati. Cambridge: MIT Press. Pp. 317–40.

Magretta, Joan (1998). "Fast, Global, and Entrepreneurial: Supply Chain Management, Hong Kong Style: An Interview with Victor Fung." *Harvard Business Review* 76, no. 5 (September): 102.

Maruca, Regina Fazio (1994). "The Right Way to Go Global." *Harvard Business Review* 72, no. 2 (March–April): 134–45.

"Mat-Sush-Ita's Chinese Burn" (1997). *The Economist* 344, no. 8035 (September 20): 75–76.

McCallum, Kenneth (2001). "China Stock Rally Looks Like History, at Least for Now." *Dow Jones International News* (July 27).

McDaniel, C.A. (1999). "Inventing Around and Impacts on Modes of Entry of Equity in Japan: A Cross-Country Analysis of U.S. Affiliate Sales and Licensing." Working Paper, Research Division, Office of Economics, U.S. International Trade Commission, Washington, D.C.

McKinnon, Ronald (1992). "Spontaneous Order on the Road Back from Socialism: An Asian Perspective." *American Economic Review: Papers and Proceedings* 82, no. 2 (May): 31–36.

McMillan, John, and Barry Naughton (1972). "How to Reform a Planned Economy: Lessons from China." *Oxford Review of Economic Policy* 8, no. 1:130–43.

Meredith, Lindsay (1984). "U.S. Multinational Investments in Canadian Manufacturing Industries." *Review of Economics and Statistics* 66, no. 1 (February): 111–19.

Milgrom, Paul, and John Roberts (1990). "Bargaining Costs, Influence Costs, and the Organization of Economic Activity." In *Perspectives on Positive Political Economy*, ed. James E. Alt and Kenneth A. Shepsle. Cambridge: Cambridge University Press. Pp. 57–89.

Miller, Robert R., Jack D. Glen, Frederick Z. Jaspersen, and Yannis Karmokolias (1996). *International Joint Ventures in Developing Countries*. Washington, D.C.: International Finance Corporation.

Ministry of Electronics Industry (1993). *Zhongguo dianzi gongye nianjian 1993* (Chinese Electronics Industry Almanac 1993). Beijing: Dianzi gongye chubanshe.

Ministry of Electronics Industry (1994). *Zhongguo dianzi gongye nianjian 1994* (Chinese Electronics Industry Almanac 1994). Beijing: Dianzi gongye chubanshe.

Ministry of Foreign Trade and Economic Cooperation (1995). *Zhongguo duiwai jingji maoyi nianjian 1995/1996* (Almanac on China's Foreign Economic Relations and Trade 1995/1996). Beijing: Zhongguo jingji chubanshe.

Ministry of Foreign Trade and Economic Cooperation (1996). *Zhongguo duiwai jingji maoyi nianjian 1996/1997* (Almanac on China's Foreign Economic Relations and Trade 1996/1997). Beijing: Zhongguo jingji chubanshe.

Ministry of Light Industry (1989). *Zhongguo qing gongye nianjian 1989* (China's Light Industry Almanac 1989). Beijing: Zhongguo qing gongye chubanshe.

Ministry of Machinery and Electronics Industry (1989). *Zhongguo jidian qiye daquan* (Directory of China's Machinery and Electronics Firms). Beijing: Zhongguo zhanwang chubanshe.

Ministry of Machinery and Electronics Industry (1993). *Beijing XYZ chilun hezi qiye xiangmu chubu sheji* (Preliminary Project Design of Beijing XYZ Gear). Beijing: Ministry of Machinery and Electronics Industry.

Ministry of Machinery Industry (1991). *Zhongguo qiche gongye nianjian 1991* (Chinese Automotive Industry Yearbook 1991). Beijing: Zhongguo qiche gongye zong gongsi.

Ministry of Machinery Industry (1993). *Zhongguo qiche gongye nianjian 1993* (Chinese Automotive Industry Yearbook 1993). Beijing: Zhongguo qiche gongye zong gongsi.

Ministry of Machinery Industry (1994). *Qiche gongye fuguan duice yanjiu keti baogaoji* (Collection of Research Reports on the Automotive Industry and GATT Membership). Beijing: Zhongguo qiche jishu yanjiu zhongxin.

Ministry of Machinery Industry (1996). *Qiche gongye guihua cankao ziliao 1996* (Reference Materials for Automotive Industry Planning 1996). Beijing: Zhongguo qiche jishu yanjiu zhongxin.

Ministry of Machinery Industry (1997a). *Qiche gongye guihua cankao ziliao 1997* (Reference Materials for Automotive Industry Planning 1997). Beijing: Zhongguo qiche jishu yanjiu zhongxin.

Ministry of Machinery Industry (1997b). *Zhongguo qiche gongye nianjian 1997* (Chinese Automotive Industry Yearbook 1997). Beijing: Zhongguo qiche jishu yanjiu zhongxin.

Ministry of Machinery Industry (1998). *Zhongguo qiche gongye nianjian 1998* (Chinese Automotive Industry Yearbook 1998). Beijing: Zhongguo qiche jishu yanjiu zhongxin.

Ministry of Machinery Industry (1999). *Zhongguo qiche gongye nianjian 1999* (China Automotive Industry Yearbook 1999). Beijing: Zhongguo qiche jishu yanjiu zhongxin.

Moran, Theodore H. (1998). *Foreign Direct Investment and Development.* Washington, D.C.: Institute for International Economics.

Morck, Randall, Bernard Yeung, and Wayne Yu (2000). "The Information Content of Stock Markets: Why Do Emerging Markets Have Synchronous Stock Price Movements?" *Journal of Financial Economics* 58, no. 1 (October).

Motor Vehicle Manufacturers Association (various years). *World Motor Vehicle Data.* Detroit: Motor Vehicle Manufacturers Association.

Murphy, David (2001). "Shanghai's Great Leap." *Far Eastern Economic Review* 164, no. 31 (August 9): 40–41.

Naughton, Barry (1996a). "China's Emergence and Prospects as a Trading Nation." *Brookings Papers on Economic Activity*, no. 2: 273–337.

Naughton, Barry (1996b). *Growing out of the Plan: Chinese Economic Reform, 1978–93.* New York: Cambridge University Press.

Naughton, Barry (1999). "How Much Can Regional Integration Do to Unify China's Markets?" Unpublished paper, Graduate School of International Relations and Pacific Studies, University of California, San Diego.

Naujoks, Petra, and Klaus-Dieter Schmidt (1994). "Outward Processing in Central and East European Transition Countries: Issues and Results from German Statistics." Kiel Working Paper No. 631, Kiel Institute of World Economics.

Naya, Seiji, and Eric D. Ramstetter (1988). "Policy Interactions and Direct Foreign Investment in East and Southeast Asia." *Journal of World Trade* 22, no. 2: 57–71.

Niskanen, William A. (1971). *Bureaucracy and Representative Government*. Chicago: Aldine.

Nolan, Peter (1996). "Large Firms and Industrial Reform in Former Planned Economies: The Case of China." *Cambridge Journal of Economics* 20, no. 1: 1–29.

Nonaka, Ikujiro, and Hiro Takeuchi (1995). *The Knowledge-Creating Company*. New York: Oxford University Press.

Office of Third Industrial Census (1997). *Zhonghua renmin gongheguo 1995 nian disanci quanguo gongye pucha ziliao huibian* (Data from the Third National Industrial Census of the People's Republic of China in 1995). Beijing: Zhongguo tongji chubanshe.

Oi, Jean C. (1999). *Rural China Takes Off*. Berkeley: University of California Press.

Oi, Jean C., and Andrew G. Walder (1999). "Property Rights in the Chinese Economy: Contours of the Process of Change." In *Property Rights and Economic Reform in China*, ed. Jean C. Oi and Andrew G. Walder. Stanford: Stanford University Press. Pp. 1–24.

O'Neill, Mark (2000). "Kelon Invests in Research Center." *South China Morning Post* (March 29): 4.

Organisation for Economic Co-operation and Development (2000). *International Direct Investment Statistics Yearbook 1999*. Paris: OECD.

Orr, Dale (1974). "The Determinants of Entry: A Study of the Canadian Manufacturing Industries." *Review of Economics and Statistics* 56, no. 1 (February): 58–66.

Oxley, Joanne Elizabeth (1997). "Appropriability Hazards and Governance in Strategic Alliances: A Transaction Cost Approach." *Journal of Law, Economics, and Organization* 13, no. 2: 387–409.

Paine, Lynn Sharp (2001). *The Haier Group* (*a*). Boston: Harvard Business School Publishing. Case Study No. 9-398-101 (Rev. July 27).

Pan, Yigang (1996a). "Influences on Foreign Equity Ownership Level in Joint Ventures in China." *Journal of International Business Studies* 27, no. 1: 1–26.

Pan, Yigang (1996b). "Cooperative Strategies between Foreign Firms in an Overseas Country." *Journal of International Business Studies* 27, no. 5: 929–46.

Park, Albert, and Minggao Shen (2000). "Joint Liability Lending and the Rise and Fall of China's Township and Village Enterprises." Unpublished paper, Department of Economics, University of Michigan, Ann Arbor.

Parker, Elliott (1997). "The Effect of Scale on the Response to Reform by Chinese State-Owned Construction Units." *Journal of Development Economics* 52, no. 2 (April): 331–53.

Pearson, Margaret M. (1991). *Joint Ventures in the People's Republic of China*. Princeton: Princeton University Press.

Perkins, Dwight (1994). "Completing China's Move to the Market." *Journal of Economic Perspectives* 8, no. 2 (Spring): 23–46.

Perkins, Dwight (2001). "Industrial and Financial Policy in China and Vietnam: A New Model or a Replay of the East Asian Experience?" In *Rethinking the East Asia*

Miracle, ed. Joseph E. Stiglitz and Shahid Yusuf. Oxford: Oxford University Press. Pp. 247–94.

Pesta, Jesse, and V. Ramakrishnan (2001). "Indian Software Firm Wipro Wins Praise for Reducing Its Reliance on Sales to GE." *Wall Street Journal* (January 4): A15.

Polanyi, Karl (1944). *The Great Transformation*. New York: Rinehart and Co.

Pomfret, Richard (1991). *Investing in China*. New York: Harvester Wheatsheaf.

Porter, Michael E. (1990). *The Competitive Advantage of Nations*. New York: Free Press.

"Portrait of the Chinese Appliance Industry" (1999). *Appliance* (October).

Pratten, C. F. (1971). *Economies of Scale in Manufacturing Industry*. Cambridge: University Press.

Pryor, F. (1972). "An International Comparison of Concentration Ratios." *Review of Economics and Statistics* 54, no. 1: 130–40.

Qian, Yingyi (1994). "Incentives and Loss of Control in an Optimal Hierarchy." *Review of Economic Studies* 6, no. 208: 527–44.

Qian, Yingyi (1996). "Enterprise Reform in China: Agency Problems and Political Control." *Economics of Transition* 4, no. 2 (October): 427–47.

Qian, Yingyi (1999). "The Institutional Foundations of China's Market Transition." Paper prepared for the Annual Conference on Development Economics, World Bank, Washington, D.C.

Qian, Yingyi, and Chenggang Xu (1993). "The M-Form Hierarchy and China's Economic Reform." *European Economic Review* 37, nos. 2/3: 541–48.

Raman, Ananth (1995). *Apparel Exports and the Indian Economy*. Boston: Harvard Business School Publishing. Case Study No. 9-696-065.

Ranis, Gustav, and Chi Schive (1985). "Direct Foreign Investment in Taiwan's Development." In *Foreign Trade and Investment*, ed. Walter Galenson. Madison: University of Wisconsin Press. Pp. 85–137.

Rawski, Thomas G. (2001). "What Is Happening to China's GDP Statistics?" *China Economic Review* 12, no. 5: 347–54.

Rhys, D. G. (1972). *The Motor Industry: An Economic Survey*. London: Butterworths.

Richardson, G. B. (1972). "The Organisation of Industry." *The Economic Journal* 82, no. 327 (September): 883–96.

Roe, Mark J. (2001). "The Quality of Corporate Law Argument and Its Limits." Working Paper No. 186, Center for Law and Economic Studies, New York.

Roehrig, Michael Franz (1994). *Foreign Joint Ventures in Contemporary China*. New York: St. Martin's Press.

Roland, Gerard (2000). *Transition and Economics: Politics, Markets, and Firms*. Cambridge: MIT Press.

Root, Robin, and John Quelch (1997). *Koc Holding: Arcelik White Goods*. Boston: Harvard Business School Publishing. Case Study No. 9-598-033 (September 29).

Rosen, Daniel H. (1999a). *Behind the Open Door: Foreign Enterprises in the Chinese Marketplace*. Washington, D.C.: Institute for International Economics.

Rosen, Daniel H. (1999b). "China and the World Trade Organization: An Economic Balance Sheet." *International Economic Policy Briefs*, no. 99–6 (June).

Rosenthal, Elisabeth (1998). "Funny, I Moved to Beijing and Wound up in Pleasantville." *New York Times* (November 15): 7.

Sachs, Jeffrey, and Wing Thye Woo (1994). "Structural Factors in the Economic Reforms of China, Eastern Europe, and the Former Soviet Union." *Economic Policy*, no. 18 (April): 102–45.

Saich, Tony (2001). *Governance and Politics in China*. New York: Palgrave.

St. George, Anthony, Carin-Isabel Knoop, and Michael Y. Yoshino (1998). *Li and Fung: Beyond "Filling in the Mosaic," 1995–1998*. Boston: Harvard Business School Publishing. Case Study No. 398-092 (Rev. June 23).

Scott, Maurice (1979). "Foreign Trade." *In Economic Growth and Structural Change in Taiwan*, ed. Walter Galenson. Ithaca: Cornell University Press. Pp. 308–83.

Sehrt, Kaja (1998). "Banks vs. Budgets: Credit Allocation in the People's Republic of China, 1984–1997." Department of Political Science, University of Michigan, Ann Arbor.

Shen Yifeng, and He Yinqi (1998). *Qiye binggou fenxi* (Analysis of Enterprise Mergers and Acquisitions). Beijing: Zhongguo duiwai jingji maoyi chubanshe.

Sheng Hong (1999). *Zuixin Zhongguo qiye binggou jingdian anli* (The Latest M&A Cases in China). Beijing: Zhongguo qing gongye chubanshe.

Shleifer, Andrei, and Robert W. Vishny (1998). *The Grabbing Hand*. Cambridge: Harvard University Press.

Shukla, Rajiv (1999). *The Major Home Appliance Industry: A Global Perspective*. Boston: Harvard Business School Publishing. No. N9-700-048.

Simon, Denis F. (1991). "China's Acquisition and Assimilation of Foreign Technology: Beijing's Search for Excellence." In *China's Economic Dilemmas in the 1990s: The Problems of the Reforms, Modernization, and Interdependence*, ed. Joint Economic Committee, U.S. Congress. Washington, D.C.: U.S. Government Printing Office. Pp. 565–98.

Simon, Herbert A. (1982). *Models of Bounded Rationality*. Cambridge: MIT Press.

Singapore Department of Statistics (1998). *Singapore's Direct Investment Abroad, 1996*. Occasional Paper on Financial Statistics, Singapore Department of Statistics.

Singh, Inderjit (1991). "Is There Schizophrenia about Socialist Reform Theory?" *Transition Newsletter* 2, no. 7 (July–August): 1–4.

Smith, Craig S. (1998). "Chinese Capital Helps Keep US Rates Low." *Wall Street Journal* (March 30).

So, Bennis Wai-yip (2000). "China's Private Enterprises at the Close of the 1990s: Their Growth and Legal Protection." In *China Review 2000*, ed. Chung-ming Lau and Jianfa Shen. Hong Kong: Chinese University Press. Pp. 307–30.

Sonobe, Tetsushi, and Keijiro Otsuka (2001). "Productivity Effects of TVE Privatization: The Case Study of Garment and Metal Casting Enterprises in the Greater Yangtze River Region." Paper prepared for the Twelfth Annual East Asian Seminar on Economics, Hong Kong, June 28–30.

State Bureau of Machinery Industry (1998). *Zhongguo qiche gongye nianjian 1998* (China Automotive Industry Yearbook 1998). Beijing: Zhongguo qiche jishu yanjiu zhongxin.

State Bureau of Machinery Industry (1999). *1998 nian jijie gongye zonghe nianbao* (Annual Report on the Machinery Industry 1998). Beijing: Guojia jixie gongye ju.

State Council and State Planning Commission (1990). *Zhongguo gongye xianzhuang* (The Current State of Chinese Industry). Beijing: Renmin chubanshe.

State Development and Planning Commission (1998). *Zhongguo chanye fazhan baogao 1998* (Report on Chinese Industrial Development 1998). Beijing: Zhongguo jingji chubanshe.

State Statistical Bureau (1988). *Gongye tongji fenxi baogao xuanbian* (Selection of Industrial Statistics Analytical Reports). Beijing: Zhongguo tongji chubanshe.

State Statistical Bureau (1993a). *Zhongguo fazhan baogao 1993* (China Development Report 1993). Beijing: Zhongguo tongji chubanshe.

State Statistical Bureau (1993b). *Zhongguo tongji nianjian 1993* (China Statistical Year-book 1993). Beijing: Zhongguo tongji chubanshe.

State Statistical Bureau (1994a). *Zhongguo duiwai jingji tongji nianjian 1994* (China Foreign Economic Statistical Yearbook 1994). Beijing: Zhongguo tongji chubanshe.

State Statistical Bureau (1994b). *Zhongguo tongji nianjian 1994* (China Statistical Year-book 1994). Beijing: Zhongguo tongji chubanshe.

State Statistical Bureau (1995). *Zhongguo tongji nianjian 1995* (China Statistical Year-book 1995). Beijing: Zhongguo tongji chubanshe.

State Statistical Bureau (1996a). *Gaige kaifang shiqi nian de Zhongguo diqu jingji* (China Regional Economy: A Profile of 17 Years of Reform and Opening Up). Beijing: Zhongguo tongji chubanshe.

State Statistical Bureau (various years). *Zhongguo dazhong xing qiye nianjian* (Statis-tical Yearbook of China's Large and Medium-size Firms). Beijing: Zhongguo tongji chubanshe.

State Statistical Bureau (1996b). *Zhongguo tongji nianjian 1996* (China Statistical Year-book 1996). Beijing: Zhongguo tongji chubanshe.

State Statistical Bureau (1997a). *Zhongguo duiwai jingji tongji nianjian 1996* (China Foreign Economic Statistical Yearbook 1996). Beijing: Zhongguo tongji chubanshe.

State Statistical Bureau (1997b). *Zhongguo tongji nianjian 1997* (China Statistical Year-book 1997). Beijing: Zhongguo tongji chubanshe.

State Statistical Bureau (1998a). *A Statistical Survey of China 1998*. Beijing: Zhongguo tongji chubanshe.

State Statistical Bureau (1998b). *Zhongguo duiwai jingji tongji nianjian 1997* (China Foreign Economic Statistical Yearbook 1997). Beijing: Zhongguo tongji chubanshe.

State Statistical Bureau (1998c). *Zhongguo fazhan baogao 1998* (China Development Report 1998). Beijing: Zhongguo tongji chubanshe.

State Statistical Bureau (1998d). *Zhongguo tongji nianjian 1998* (China Statistical Yearbook 1998). Beijing: Zhongguo tongji chubanshe.

State Statistical Bureau (1999a). *Zhongguo duiwai jingji tongji nianjian 1999* (China Foreign Economic Statistical Yearbook 1999). Beijing: Zhongguo tongji chubanshe.

State Statistical Bureau (1999b). *Zhongguo tongji nianjian 1999* (China Statistical Yearbook 1999). Beijing: Zhongguo tongji chubanshe.

State Statistical Bureau (2000). *Zhongguo tongji zhaiyao 2000* (China Statistical Abstract 2000). Beijing: Zhongguo tongji chubanshe.

State Statistical Bureau (2001). *Zhongguo tongji nianjian 2001* (China Statistical Yearbook 2001). Beijing: Zhongguo tongji chubanshe.

Steinfeld, Edward S. (1998). *Forging Reform in China: The Fate of State-Owned Industry*. New York: Cambridge University Press.

Bibliography

Steinfeld, Edward S. (2002). "Chinese Enterprise Development and the Challenge of Global Integration." Unpublished paper, Department of Political Science, MIT, Cambridge, Mass.

Stiglitz, Joseph E. (1999). "Whither Reform? Ten Years of Transition." Paper presented at the Annual Conference on Development Economics, World Bank, Washington, D.C.

Stopford, John M., and Louis T. Wells, Jr. (1972). *Managing the Multinational Enterprise: Organization of the Firm and Ownership of the Subsidiaries*. New York: Basic Books.

Study Group on SOEs Using Grafted FDI in Fujian Province (1994). "Guanyu Fujiansheng guoyu qiye jiajie waizi ruogan wenti de diaocha yanjiu" (An Investigation into Several Problems of SOEs with Grafted FDI in Fujian Province). *Jingjixue dongtai* (Developments in Economics), no. 10: 26–30.

Summers, Lawrence (1992). "The Rise of China." *International Economic Insights* (May/June).

Sun, Hong (1996). "Shanghai Volkswagen: Number 1 of Overseas Funded." *China Daily* (November 2).

Sung, Qun-Wing, Pak-Wai Liu, Yue-chim Richard Wong, and Pui-King Lau (1995). *The Fifth Dragon: The Emergence of the Pearl River Delta*. Singapore: Addison Wesley.

"Survey Report on CMA Members' Investments in the Mainland" (1998). *Hong Kong Entrepreneur* (April): 34–43.

Tang Zongkun, Han Chaohua, and Wang Hongling (1997). *Guoyou qiye chanquan jiaoyi xingwei fenxi* (Analysis of Property Rights Transactions of SOEs). Beijing: Jingji kexue chubanshe.

Tanzer, Andrew (1996). "Small Is Beautiful." *Forbes* 158, no. 7 (September 23): 90.

Taylor, Charles R., and Witold J. Henisz (1994). *U.S Manufacturers in the Global Marketplace*. New York: Conference Board. No. 1058-94-RR.

Teece, David J. (1982). "Towards an Economic Theory of the Multiproduct Firm." *Journal of Economic Behavior and Organization* 3, no. 1 (March): 39–63.

Thun, Eric (1999). "Changing Lanes in China: Industrial Development in a Transitional Economy." Ph.D. diss., Department of Government, Harvard University.

Tong, Amy (1998). "Kelon Looks Abroad as China Market Cools." *The Nikkei Weekly* (December 21): 28.

Tseng, Wanda, and Harm Zebregs (2002). "Foreign Direct Investment in China: Some Lessons for Other Countries." *IMF Policy Discussion Paper* (February).

Unirule Economic Research Institute (1997). *Zhongguo binggou jingdian* (Cases on Mergers and Acquisitions in China). Shanghai: Xuelin chubanshe.

United Nations Conference on Trade and Development (1996). *World Investment Report 1996*. New York: United Nations.

United Nations Conference on Trade and Development (1998). *World Investment Report 1998*. New York: United Nations.

United Nations Conference on Trade and Development (1999). *World Investment Report 1999*. New York: United Nations.

United Nations Conference on Trade and Development (2000). *World Investment Report 2000*. New York: United Nations.

United Nations Conference on Trade and Development (2001). *World Investment Report 2001*. New York: United Nations.

United States Department of Commerce (1995). *National Trade Data Bank: Country Commercial Guides–Taiwan*. Washington, D.C.: Dept. of Commerce.

Upton, David, and Diane Long (1996). *Shanghai Volkswagen*. Boston: Harvard Business School Publishing. Case Study No. 9-696-092 (April 23).

Urata, Shujiro (2001). "Emergence of an FDI-Trade Nexus and Economic Growth in East Asia." In *Rethinking the East Asia Miracle*, ed. Joseph E. Stiglitz and Shahid Yusuf. Oxford: Oxford University Press. Pp. 409–60.

Vernon, Raymond (1977). *Storm over the Multinationals*. Cambridge: Harvard University Press.

Vernon, Raymond, and Yair Aharoni (1981). *State-Owned Enterprises in the Western Economies*. London: Croom Helm.

Vogel, Ezra F. (1989). *One Step Ahead in China: Guangdong under Reform*. Cambridge: Harvard University Press .

Wade, Robert (1990). *Governing the Market: Economic Theory and the Role of Government in East Asian Industrialization*. Princeton: Princeton University Press.

Wagstyl, Stefan (1996). "ZF Investment in China to Rise." *Financial Times* (November 4): 27.

Wang Luolin (1997). *Zhongguo waishang touzi baogao* (Report on Foreign Direct Investment in China). Beijing: Jingji guanli chubanshe.

Wang, Shaoguang, and Angang Hu (1999). *The Political Economy of Uneven Development: The Case of China*. Armonk, N.Y.: M. E. Sharpe.

Wang, Zhenquan, and Nigel J. Swain (1995). "The Determinants of Foreign Direct Investment in Transforming Economies: Empirical Evidence from Hungary and China." *Weltwirtshaftliches Archiv* 131: 359–82.

Wang Zhile (1996). *Zhuming kuaguo gongsi zai Zhongguo de touzi* (Investment in China of Famous Transnational Corporations). Beijing: Zhongguo jingji chubanshe.

Wedeman, Andrew (forthcoming). *From Mao to Market: Local Protectionism, Rent-Seeking, and the Marketization of China, 1984–1992*. New York: Cambridge University Press.

Wei, Shang-jin (1995). "Attracting Foreign Direct Investment: Has China Reached Its Potential?" *China Economic Review* 6, no. 2: 187–99.

Wei, Shang-jin (1996a). "Foreign Direct Investment in China: Sources and Consequences." In *Financial Deregulation and Integration in East Asia*, ed. Takatoshi Ito and Anne Krueger. Chicago: University of Chicago Press. Pp. 77–101.

Wei, Shang-jin (1996b). "How Taxing Is Corruption on International Investors?" NBER Working Paper No. W6030, Cambridge, Mass.

Weinstein, David (1996). "Structural Impediments to Investment in Japan: What Have We Learned over the Last 450 Years?" In *Foreign Direct Investment in Japan*, ed. Masaru Yoshitomi and Edward M. Graham. Cheltenham, U.K.: Edward Elgar. Pp. 136–72.

Weitzman, Martin, and Chenggang Xu (1994). "Chinese Township-Village Enterprises as Vaguely Defined Cooperatives." *Journal of Comparative Economics* 18, no 2: 121–45.

Wells, Louis T., Jr. (1978). "Foreign Investment from the Third World: The Experience of Chinese Firms from Hong Kong." *Journal of World Business* 13, no. 1 (Spring): 39–49.

Wells, Louis T., Jr. (1993). "Mobile Exporters: New Foreign Investors in East Asia." In *Foreign Direct Investment*, ed. Kenneth A. Froot. Chicago: University of Chicago Press. Pp. 173–96.

Westphal, Larry E., Yung W. Rhee, and Garry Pursell (1985). *Korean Industrial Competence: Where It Came From*. Washington, D.C.: World Bank Staff Working Paper No. 469.

White, Lawrence J. (1971). *The Automobile Industry since 1945*. Cambridge: Harvard University Press.

Whiting, Susan (2001). *Power and Wealth in Rural China: The Political Economy of Institutional Change*. Cambridge: Cambridge University Press.

Whitla, Paul, and Howard Davies (1998). "Europe's Role in Technology Transfer to China." In *Trade and Investment in China*, ed. Roger Strange, Jim Slater, and Limin Wang. London: Routledge. Pp. 98–114.

Williamson, Oliver E. (1975). *Markets and Hierarchies*. New York: Free Press.

Williamson, Peter J. (2001). *Whirlpool China (C)*. Singapore: INSEAD Euro-Asia Centre. No. 301-172-1.

Wilson, James Q. (1989). *Bureaucracy: What Government Agencies Do and Why They Do It*. New York: Basic Books.

Wong, Christine P. W., Christopher Heady, and Wing T. Woo (1995). *Fiscal Management and Economic Reform in the People's Republic of China*. Hong Kong: Oxford University Press.

Wong, Victor (2001). "Guangdong Kelon Electrical Holdings." *Deutsche Bank Asia-Pacific Equity Research* (November 7).

Woo, Wing Thye, and Gang Fan (1994). "How Successful Has Chinese Enterprise Reform Been? Pitfalls in Opposite Biases and Focus." *Journal of Comparative Economics* 18, no. 3 (June): 410–37.

World Bank (1990). *China: Financial Sector Policies and Institutional Development*. Washington, D.C.: World Bank.

World Bank (1993). *The East Asian Miracle*. New York: Oxford University Press.

World Bank (1994). *China: Internal Market Development and Regulation*. Washington, D.C.: World Bank.

World Bank (1995a). *Bureaucrats in Business*. Washington, D.C.: World Bank.

World Bank (1995b). *China: Macroeconomic Stability in a Decentralized Economy*. Washington, D.C.: World Bank.

World Bank (1996). *Managing Capital Flows in East Asia*. Washington, D.C.: World Bank.

World Bank (1997a). *China 2020: Development Challenges in the New Century*. Washington, D.C.: World Bank.

World Bank (1997b). *China Engaged: Integration with the Global Economy*. Washington, D.C.: World Bank.

World Bank (1999). *World Development Report 1998/1999*. Washington, D.C.: World Bank.

World Bank (2000). *World Development Indicators 2000*. Washington, D.C.: World Bank.

World Bank (2002a). *Global Development Finance*. Washington, D.C.: World Bank.

World Bank (2002b). *World Development Report 2002*. New York: Oxford University Press.

Wu Facheng (1997). *Tansuo qiche gongye zhenxin zhilu* (Exploring Roads of Prosperity for the Auto Industry). Ji'nan: Shandong kexue jishu chubanshe.

Wu Jinglian and Zhang Zhuoyuan (1995). *Shangwu jingji zixun daquan* (Economic Compendium). Hong Kong: Commercial Press.

Wu Qiang (1996). "Ri, Han jishu yinjin zhengce ji Zhongguo de fazhan zhanlue" (Technology Import Policies of Korea and Japan and China's Development Strategy). *Jingji guanli* (Economic Management), no. 9 (September): 12–15.

Wu, Renhong (1997). "Capital Inflow, Investment and Current Account: The Case of China." Paper presented for the conference on "Financial Market Reforms in China," University of Southern California, Los Angeles, July 15.

Wurgler, Jeffrey (2000). "Financial Markets and the Allocation of Capital." *Journal of Financial Economics* 58, no. 1-2: 187–214.

Xu, Xiaonian, and Yan Wang (1997). *Ownership Structure, Corporate Governance, and Corporate Performance*. Washington, D.C.: World Bank Policy Research Working Paper No. 1794.

Yang, Dali L. (2001). "Governance and Regulation of the Securities Markets in China." Paper prepared for the conference, "Financial Sector Reform in China," Kennedy School of Government, Harvard University, Cambridge, Mass., September 11–13.

Yang, Jiawen (1997). "The Emerging Patterns of Taiwanese Investment in Mainland China." *Multinational Business Review* 5, no. 1: 92–99.

Yeung, Henry Wai-chung (1998). *Transnational Corporations and Business Networks: Hong Kong Firms in the ASEAN Region*. London: Routledge.

Yoffie, David B., and Jane K. Austin (1983). *Textiles and the Multi-Fiber Arrangement*. Boston: Harvard Business School Publishing. Case Study No. 9-383-164.

Yoshino, Michael Y., and Thomas W. Malnight (1997). *Otis Elevator Company (a): China Strategy*. Boston: Harvard Business School Publishing. Case Study No. 9-396-098.

Yoshino, Michael Y., and U. Srinivasa Rangan (1995). *Strategic Alliances: An Entrepreneurial Approach to Globalization*. Boston: Harvard Business School Press.

Young, Alwyn (2000a). "Gold into Base Metals: Productivity Growth in the People's Republic of China during the Reform Period." Graduate School of Business, University of Chicago.

Young, Alwyn (2000b). "The Razor's Edge: Distortions and Incremental Reform in the People's Republic of China." *Quarterly Journal of Economics* 115, no. 4: 1091–135.

Young, Stephen, and Ping Lan (1997). "Technology Transfer to China through Foreign Direct Investment." *Regional Studies* 31, no. 7: 669–79.

Zhang Houyi and Ming Lizhi (1999). *Zhongguo siying qiye fazhan baogao* (1978–1998) (Report on Development of China's Private Enterprises (1978–1998)). Beijing: Shehui kexue wenxian chubanshe.

Zhang, Shengman (1999). "Capital Flows to East Asia." In *International Capital Flows*, ed. Martin Feldstein. Chicago: University of Chicago Press. Pp. 177–81.

Zhang Xiaoyu (1998). *Zhongguo qiche gongye waishang touzi qiye huibian ji touzi zhinan* (Foreign-Invested Enterprises in the Chinese Automotive Industry and Investment Guide). Beijing: Ministry of Machinery Industry.

Zhang, Xun-Hai (1992). *Enterprise Reforms in a Centrally Planned Economy*. New York: St. Martin's Press.

Zhao Dexing (1989a). *Zhonghua renmin gongheguo jingjishi (1949–1966)* (An Economic History of the People's Republic of China (1949–1966)). Zhengzhou: Henan renmin chubanshe.

Zhao Dexing (1989b). *Zhonghua renmin gongheguo jingjishi (1967–1984)* (An Economic History of the People's Republic of China (1967–1984)). Zhengzhou: Henan renmin chubanshe.

Zhao Mingshan (1997). "Woguo moxie gongye chanpin shengchan nengli xiangdui guosheng yuanyin fenxi" (Analysis of the Reasons for the Relative Overcapacity of Production in Certain Industrial Products). *Jingji guanli* (Economic Management), no. 4 (April): 12–15.

Zheng Lixin (1994). *Zhongguo zhizhu chanye zhenxin fanglie* (Strategies of Developing China's Pillar Industries). Beijing: Zhongguo jihua chubanshe.

373